Spartacus

Spartacus
Film and History

Edited by
Martin M. Winkler

Blackwell
Publishing

© 2007 by Blackwell Publishing Ltd

BLACKWELL PUBLISHING
350 Main Street, Malden, MA 02148-5020, USA
9600 Garsington Road, Oxford OX4 2DQ, UK
550 Swanston Street, Carlton, Victoria 3053, Australia

The right of Martin M. Winkler to be identified as the Author of the Editorial Material in
this Work has been asserted in accordance with the UK Copyright, Designs, and Patents
Act 1988.

First published 2007 by Blackwell Publishing Ltd

1   2007

Library of Congress Cataloging-in-Publication Data

Spartacus: film and history / edited by Martin M. Winkler.
    p. cm.
  Includes bibliographical references and index.
  ISBN-13: 978-1-4051-3180-3 (hardcover : alk. paper)
  ISBN-10: 1-4051-3180-2 (hardcover : alk. paper)
  ISBN-13: 978-1-4051-3181-0 (pbk. : alk. paper)
  ISBN-10: 1-4051-3181-0 (pbk. : alk. paper)   1. Spartacus (Motion picture : 1960)
2. Spartacus, d. 71 B.C.   3. Rome–History–Servile Wars, 135-71 B.C.   I. Winkler,
Martin M.

  PN1997.S6425S63 2006
  791.43'72–dc22

                                                            2006022473

A catalogue record for this title is available from the British Library.

Set in 10 on 12.5 pt Photina
by SNP Best-set Typesetter Ltd, Hong Kong

FSC
Mixed Sources
Product group from well-managed
forests and other controlled sources
Cert no. SGS-COC-2953
www.fsc.org
© 1996 Forest Stewardship Council

For further information on
Blackwell Publishing, visit our website:
www.blackwellpublishing.com

Contents

List of Plates

Notes on Contributors

FREDERICK AHL is Professor of Classics and Comparative Literature and Stephen H. Weiss Presidential Fellow at Cornell University. He is the author of *Lucan: An Introduction, Metaformations: Soundplay and Wordplay in Ovid and Other Classical Poets, Sophocles' Oedipus: Evidence and Self-Conviction, The Odyssey Re-Formed* (with Hanna M. Roisman), and of articles on Greek music, Homeric narrative, ancient rhetoric, and Roman imperial poetry. He has also translated Seneca's tragedies and Virgil's *Aeneid*.

DUNCAN L. COOPER is an independent scholar and an authority on the production and censorship history of Stanley Kubrick's *Spartacus*. His researches on the film, first published in the journal *Cinéaste*, appear here substantially revised and updated.

MICHAEL PARENTI is the author of nineteen books and over 250 articles. His writings have been translated into several languages. Among his recent books is *The Assassination of Julius Caesar: A People's History of Ancient Rome*.

The late C. A. ROBINSON, JR. was David Benedict Professor of Classics at Brown University and the author of numerous books and articles. Among the former are *Ancient History from Prehistoric Times to the Death of Justinian, The Spring of Civilization, Athens in the Age of Pericles*, and

Alexander the Great: Conqueror and Creator of a New World, the last of his Alexander studies.

W. JEFFREY TATUM is Olivia Nelson Dorman Professor of Classics at Florida State University. He is the author of *The Patrician Tribune: Publius Clodius Pulcher* and of numerous articles on Roman history and Latin literature.

FRANCISCO JAVIER TOVAR PAZ is Professor of Classics at the University of Extremadura (Spain). His main research interests are Christian Latinity, Visigothic Spain, and the classical tradition, especially in Spanish literature and in the cinema. He has published articles on directors Billy Wilder, Ingmar Bergman, Arturo Ripstein, and Stanley Kubrick, among others.

ALLEN M. WARD is Professor Emeritus of History at the University of Connecticut – Storrs. He is the author of *Marcus Crassus and the Late Roman Republic* and several articles on that period of Roman history. After taking over from the late Fritz M. Heichelheim and the late Cedric A. Yeo, he is also the principal author of *A History of the Roman People*, now in its fourth edition.

MARTIN M. WINKLER is Professor of Classics at George Mason University. His books are *The Persona in Three Satires of Juvenal*, *Der lateinische Eulenspiegel des Ioannes Nemius*, and the anthology *Juvenal in English*. He is the editor of *Classical Myth and Culture in the Cinema*, a revised edition of *Classics and Cinema*, the first collection of scholarly essays on the subject of antiquity and film. More recently he has edited the essay collections *Gladiator: Film and History* and *Troy: From Homer's Iliad to Hollywood Epic*. He has also published articles on Roman literature, on the classical tradition, and on classical and medieval culture and mythology in the cinema.

Introduction

Martin M. Winkler

CRASSUS: There, boy, is Rome! The might, the majesty, the terror of Rome. There is the power that bestrides the known world like a colossus. No man can withstand Rome.

SPARTACUS: When just one man says "No, I won't," Rome begins to fear. And we were tens of thousands who said no. That was the wonder of it.

Among Hollywood's epic films set in ancient Rome, *Spartacus* (1960) stands out for a number of reasons. It had been a pet project for its producer and star, Kirk Douglas. It dealt with a topic that was politically suspicious to many when it was released. It was based on a novel by left-wing author Howard Fast, who had been imprisoned for his political views. Its principal screenwriter was Dalton Trumbo, who had been blacklisted for many years. It had a troubled production history that involved clashes between and among various parties concerning the script and the presentation of the film's hero. It was off to a shaky start when Douglas fired its original director, Anthony Mann, who had supervised preproduction and actually begun filming, and continued to have problems between Douglas and Mann's replacement, a young Stanley Kubrick. It ran into censorship troubles, was re-edited, and was exhibited for decades in truncated versions before being restored in 1991 to a form approximating but not identical to its original version. It was also one of the most expensive films made up to that time. (Its cost of $12,000,000 exceeded by three quarters of a million the price for which the entire studio was sold while the film was in production.) In subsequent years, *Spartacus* acquired a large following for its exceptional status among the works of a director who had become a cult figure and one of the most influential as well as idiosyncratic filmmakers only a few years later. And *Spartacus* dealt with a short but important episode in Roman history about which ancient sources are comparatively scarce but which, in part as a result of this circumstance, led to the birth of a legend that proved to be highly potent in Europe and America from the seventeenth century on. So the place of *Spartacus* as an unusual film set in antiquity is secure, and not only among aficionados of epic cinema or cultural historians. Its theme, summarized in the two quotations above, is of timeless appeal. So are the film and the period in Roman history on which it is based.

It is not necessary here to trace the literary, artistic, or political ramifications of the legend of Spartacus. Kubrick's film became the legend's most popular restatement in the second half of the twentieth century. Its modern development is, on the whole, well documented.[1] In the twenti-

1   See in particular the following works, all with additional references: Richard G. Lillard, "Through the Disciplines with Spartacus: The Uses of a Hero in History and the Media," *American Studies*, 16 no. 2 (1975), 15–28; Antonio Guarino, *Spartaco: Analisi di un mito* (Naples: Liguori, 1979); Wolfgang Zeev Rubinsohn, *Spartacus' Uprising and Soviet Historical Writing*, tr. John G. Griffith (Oxford: Oxbow Books, 1983); Roberto Orena, *Rivolta e rivoluzione: Il* Bellum *di Spartaco nella crisi della repubblica e la riflessione storiografica moderna* (Milan: Giuffrè, 1984); Wolfgang Schuller, "Spartacus heute," in *Antike in der Moderne*, ed. Wolfgang Schuller (Konstanz: Universitätsverlag Konstanz, 1985), 289–305; Anton J. van Hooff, *Spartacus: De vonk van Spartacus: Het voortleven van een antieke rebel* (Nijmegen: SUN, 1992); *Spartacus and the Slave Wars: A Brief History with Documents*, ed. Brent D. Shaw (Boston and New York: Bedford / St. Martin's, 2001), 1–29 (editor's introduction); and Theresa Urbainczyk, *Spartacus* (London: Bristol Classical Press, 2004), 106–117 and 132–133 (notes; chapter entitled "Spartacus in the Modern Imagination"). I quote, *exempli gratia*, the verdict on Spartacus by Karl Marx in a letter of February 27, 1861, to Friedrich Engels: "Spartacus erscheint als der famoseste Kerl, den die ganze antike Geschichte aufzuweisen hat. Großer General (kein Garibaldi), nobler Character, real representative [sic – in English] des antiken Proletariats" ("Spartacus appears to be the most capital fellow that all of ancient history can show for itself. Great general [not a Garibaldi], a noble character, real representative of the ancient proletariat"). Marx mentioned in the same letter that he read about Spartacus in Appian (in Greek) and considered his work to be a very valuable book. Quoted from *Karl Marx–Friedrich Engels: Werke* (Berlin: Dietz, 1974), vol. 30, 159–160; quotation at 160. Cf. H. T. Wallinga, *Der famoseste Kerl: Over Spartacus en zijn opstand* (Utrecht: Faculteit der Letteren, Rijksuniversiteit Utrecht, 1990).– For modern research tools on ancient slavery see Wolfgang Zeev Rubinsohn, *Die großen Sklavenaufstände der Antike: 500 Jahre Forschung* (Darmstadt: Wissenschaftliche Buchgesellschaft, 1993), and especially *Bibliographie zur antiken Sklaverei*, ed. Heinz Bellen and Heinz Heinen; rev.

eth century the legend received a new boost when the cinema turned to telling Spartacus' story, usually with little regard to the historical Spartacus. The cinematic process of myth-making about Spartacus culminated in Kubrick's film. Once Hollywood has appropriated a historical subject, the factual past takes a back seat to the dream factory's power of shaping our imagination. In the words of screenwriter and historical novelist Gore Vidal: "In the end, he who screens the history makes the history."[2] When history has become legend, screen the legend. He who screens the legend keeps the legend alive in the most effective way of all, for, as director Mann once said, "legend makes the very best cinema. It excites the imagination more."[3] As a result, historical films tend to supersede our knowledge of historical facts, not least when lavish spectacles made at million-dollar expense and with the proverbial cast of thousands dazzle our senses. A film like *Spartacus* stirs our emotions to identify ourselves with its hero and his cause. Even better if such a film can be marketed, as was *Spartacus*, with Hollywood's customary hyperbole but also with some justification as "the thinking man's epic."

Throughout the present book and in virtually all publications about *Spartacus*, the film is identified as or referred to as Kubrick's. This is in keeping with a general, and sensible, convention of identifying films by the names of their officially credited directors. Nevertheless, in the case of *Spartacus* we should also be aware of the uncredited contributions by its original director. Anthony Mann provided a brief summary of his work on the film in an interview given shortly before his death in 1967:

> Kirk Douglas was the producer of *Spartacus*: he wanted to stress the 'message' of the picture. I figured the 'message' would be conveyed better by showing *physically* the full horror of slavery. A film has to be visual. Too much dialogue will kill it . . . From that point on, Kirk and I were in disagreement . . . I worked nearly three weeks actually directing and all the opening sequence is mine; the slaves on the mountain, Peter Ustinov [Batiatus] examining Kirk Douglas's teeth, the arrival at the gladiators' school and the opposition of Charles McGraw [Marcellus the trainer]. As for the rest, the film follows my shooting script faithfully right up to the escape.[4]

by Dorothea Schäfer and Johannes Deissler; 2 vols. (Stuttgart: Steiner, 2003). Additional scholarship is cited in several chapters and collected in the bibliography of the present book.

2   Gore Vidal, *Screening History* (Cambridge: Harvard University Press, 1992), 81.

3   Quoted from Christopher Wicking and Barrie Pattison, "Interviews with Anthony Mann," *Screen*, 10 no. 4 (1969), 32–54, at 41.

4   Quoted from Jean-Claude Missiaen, "Conversation with Anthony Mann," tr. Martyn Auty, *Framework*, 15–17 (1981), 17–20; quotations at 19.

The finished film's evident qualities, some of which may be traced back to Mann, and the resonances it has found among viewers, however, tend to disguise a number of considerable shortcomings. An important reason for these is the fact that Kubrick, a fiercely independent-minded *auteur* and an artist obsessed with every detail of his work, had no decisive control over *Spartacus* after replacing Mann and was displeased with the result: "I am disappointed in the film. It had everything but a good story."[5] Kubrick consistently disowned *Spartacus* – unlike all his other films. As he put it in 1968:

> *Spartacus* . . . was the only film that I did not have control over, and which, I feel, was not enhanced by that fact. It all really just came down to the fact that there are thousands of decisions that have to be made, and that if you don't make them yourself, and if you're not on the same wavelength as the people who are making them, it becomes a very painful experience, which it was. Obviously I directed the actors, composed the shots and cut the film, so that, within the weakness of the story, I tried to do the best I could . . . The only film [of mine] that I don't like is *Spartacus*.[6]

We can, of course, sympathize with Kubrick and, now looking back over his complete body of work, understand that *Spartacus* is not really "a Kubrick." The fact that a number of scenes in the screenplay were shortened or eliminated only exacerbates the problem.[7] For example, the scenes dealing with Roman politics are largely unconvincing as they now appear on the screen. The filmmakers faced a dilemma commonly found in many historical films: to make a highly sophisticated system of government whose complexities are familiar only to specialists understandable to a lay audience – or at least convincingly to present an ancient government to modern viewers. This problem is most obvious in the machinations of Senator Gracchus, the antagonist of Marcus Crassus, the film's villain. Gracchus must be shown as being able to manipulate the senate in general and Crassus' protégé and henchman Glabrus in

5   So Kubrick in Joseph Gelmis, "The Film Director as Superstar: Stanley Kubrick," in *Stanley Kubrick: Interviews*, ed. Gene D. Phillips (Jackson: University Press of Mississippi, 2001), 80–104; quotation at 102. This interview was first published as "Stanley Kubrick" in Joseph Gelmis, *The Film Director as Superstar* (New York: Doubleday, 1970), 293–316.
6   Charlie Kohler, "Stanley Kubrick Raps" (interview), *The East Village Eye* (August, 1968), rpt. in *The Making of* 2001: A Space Odyssey, ed. Stephanie Schwam (New York: Modern Library, 2000), 245–257; quotations at 251.
7   On this aspect of the film see in particular Duncan L. Cooper, "Who Killed the Legend of Spartacus? Production, Censorship, and Reconstruction of Stanley Kubrick's Epic Film" in this volume.

particular in order to win a round against Crassus. Gracchus succeeds when he has the senate send arrogant and incompetent Glabrus against Spartacus. Glabrus is duly defeated, and his humiliation causes a serious setback to Crassus. But how likely is it that none of the senators, most of them presumably experienced and wily politicians, sees through Gracchus' strategies whereas audiences, most of them presumably *not* experienced and wily politicians, do – as they must in order to be able to follow the future power struggles of Crassus, Gracchus, and Julius Caesar and the eventual fall of Gracchus? Even in the truncated version of his part that we have now, Charles Laughton gives an unforgettable performance as Gracchus, but viewers who remember him only two years after *Spartacus* in his greatest political role, again as a wily senator but this time an American one in Otto Preminger's political drama *Advise and Consent*, will realize what his Gracchus could have been like if *Spartacus* had indeed had a better story. So the film's assessment by Peter Ustinov, who as Batiatus had a memorable scene with Laughton shortly before Gracchus' suicide, is unfortunately too good to be quite true: "*Spartacus* was a film with an extraordinarily rich mixture and as full of intrigue as a Balkan government in the good old days."[8] If only Ustinov were right! His characterization of Laughton is apt to reinforce viewers' regrets about *Spartacus*: "Laughton [was] the man of concessions, who regarded acting as part art and part whoring. He had sold his soul to Hollywood in a way, but had kept a grip on his impenetrable integrity through thick and thin . . . he was surrounded by things of beauty, which were parts of his soul translated."[9] With only minor substitutions, these words describe Laughton the actor as much as Gracchus the politician, whose sense of beauty the film well illustrates by giving his villa the famous Roman fresco cycle of wall paintings from the Villa of the Mysteries.

Still, Kubrick's mastery of cinematic technique and art could not completely be suppressed, not even on his first project on such a gigantic scale. What one of the actors said about Kubrick is worth keeping in mind:

> Some people thought Kubrick was an odd choice [to direct *Spartacus*] because he had a kind of cynical approach. I thought he was brilliant. He understood human frailty . . . Universal . . . wouldn't give him room to move . . . he always wanted that scope, and he had to really maneuver to

8 Peter Ustinov, *Dear Me* (Boston and Toronto: Little, Brown / Atlantic Monthly Press, 1977), 299. The quotation is the first sentence of his chapter on *Spartacus* in this autobiography.
9 Ustinov, *Dear Me*, 300–301.

get *Spartacus* made. He was a genius with the camera, but as far as I was concerned, Stanley's greatest effectiveness was in his one-on-one relationships with actors . . . Almost everybody treated Kubrick [with hostility or contempt]. They had no idea who they were dealing with. Later on they'd lionize and canonize him at Universal and everywhere else, but not in those days.[10]

As scholars have demonstrated, *Spartacus* fits in with Kubrick's other films in more than its style. One of them concludes:

In representing the rebellious slaves as a concretization of man's efforts to resist dehumanization throughout human history, *Spartacus* fits thematically into Kubrick's total canon of films better than most critics of his work are prepared to admit. Spartacus was vanquished by the technological superiority of Roman military tactics, and man will continue in Kubrick's films . . . to resist being overpowered by his own ever increasing technological advances.

Moreover, *Spartacus* has a further thematic affinity with Kubrick's other pictures in that once more a man has devised an apparently foolproof plan which fails in the end through a mixture of unforeseen chance happenings and human frailty . . . In a Kubrick film human weakness and/or malice along with chance are always standing in the wings ready to disrupt the best-laid plans that his heroes or anti-heroes can devise.

Hence *Spartacus* seems to be more than a marginal film in Kubrick's career, although it could well have been a better picture all around had Kubrick been allowed to exercise the artistic control that he has enjoyed on all of his other films.[11]

One particular scene in *Spartacus* may serve as an illustration of Kubrick's genius with the camera and in the editing room. It is one of the most famous in the entire film and has inspired a variety of imitations, a clear sign of its impact.[12] The idea of human solidarity is a fundamen-

---

10   Tony Curtis and Barry Paris, *Tony Curtis: The Autobiography* (New York: Morrow, 1993), 180–181 and 185.

11   Gene D. Phillips, *Stanley Kubrick: A Film Odyssey* (New York: Popular Library, 1975), 97. Also (largely verbatim) in Gene D. Phillips and Rodney Hill, *The Encyclopedia of Stanley Kubrick* (New York: Facts on File, 2002), 346.

12   David Hughes, *The Complete Kubrick* (London: Virgin, 2000; rpt. 2001), 81–82, and Jon Solomon, *The Ancient World in the Cinema*, 2nd edn. (New Haven: Yale University Press, 2001), 53, list some examples. Not all of them are in a reverent mood, since epic grandeur easily lends itself to parody. Most noteworthy as a satire on Jesus, Spartacus, and the entire genre of Roman and biblical epics is a scene in *Monty Python's Life of Brian* (1979), directed by Terry Jones ("I'm Brian!" etc.). During the broadcast of the 2005 Academy Awards, a commercial for Pepsi Cola digitally incorporated a Roman soldier holding a soda can with Spartacus' name on it, with the predictable result. A tribute of sorts to the ending of Kubrick's film occurs at the end of John Guillermin's *King Kong Lives* (1986), when King Kong dies upon seeing – yes, his new-born son!

tal part of Spartacus' legend and helps explain his worldwide appeal. Its highest expression in the film occurs after the decisive defeat of the slaves by the overwhelming might of the Roman military colossus. Asked to identify Spartacus, the survivors all claim to be him: "I'm Spartacus! I'm Spartacus!"

Kubrick sarcastically expressed some of his frustration with *Spartacus* in his immediately following film when he referred viewers specifically to this moment. In the first scene of *Lolita* (1962), Humbert Humbert asks his nemesis Clare Quilty, who has a white bed sheet draped over one shoulder and arm like a cinematic Roman: "Are you Quilty?" He receives the reply: "No, I'm Spartacus. Have you come to free the slaves or something?" Absurdly, Quilty then proposes "a lovely game of Roman ping pong – like two civilized senators. Roman *ping* – you're supposed to say 'Roman *pong*'." Some *faux*-classical decorations are visible in the background of this scene. Almost a decade later, Kubrick satirized the genre of Roman and biblical epics in one of Alex's fantasies in *A Clockwork Orange* (1971). Nevertheless, the inherent quality of the *Spartacus* scene becomes evident if we turn to two modern parallels, one fictional and one historical. Both involve World War II. The same year in which *Spartacus* was released, Otto Preminger's *Exodus*, an epic about the foundation of Israel in the 1940s and written, like *Spartacus*, by Dalton Trumbo, contained a scene in which a young Jewish girl tells of an incident that had occurred in Denmark:

> When the Nazis marched into Denmark, they ordered every Jew to wear a yellow armband with the Star of David on it . . . The next morning, when every Jew in Denmark had to wear his armband, King Christian came out of Amalienborg Palace for his morning ride. And do you know something? *He* wore the Star of David on *his* arm . . . And you know something else? By afternoon, *everybody* was wearing Stars of David, Jews and Danes and, well, just everybody.[13]

This is a well-known story, told repeatedly and in slightly different versions, but it is not true. By contrast, Frederic Raphael, who wrote the screenplay for Kubrick's last film, *Eyes Wide Shut* (1999), recalls a conversation he had once had with him about *Spartacus*:

13 A late scene in *Exodus* contains another reminiscence of Spartacus' history. To evacuate a small village that is expecting a night attack by a superior enemy, the film's hero has, among other things, fires built to deceive the enemy into thinking that he has more people to fight back than are really present; they then slip away under cover of darkness. Cf. Sallust, *Histories* 3.96 (Maurenbrecher) = 3.64 (McGushin), and Frontinus, *Strategies* 1.15.22.

I singled out the scene where Crassus calls on the slaves to identify the man Spartacus and (supposedly) save their own lives by doing so. I told him how, the previous New Year's Eve, Sylvia [Mrs. Raphael] and I had been on a train to Colchester with a man who had been in a prisoner-of-war camp in Germany. At some point, in 1942 or 1943, the S.S. had paraded all the English prisoners and ordered any Jews to take one step forward. One or two did so. The S.S. officer yelled out that if there were any others, they had better admit it by the time he had counted to three. The menace in his voice somehow alerted the prisoners to what might happen to the few Jews who were being singled out. One, two . . . at the shout of three, *all* the prisoners stepped forward. "Pretty good scene," Kubrick said.[14]

Kubrick's casual comment is in keeping with his attitude to *Spartacus*, but Raphael's anecdote shows that Kubrick's verdict is too harsh. This one moment in *Spartacus* best illustrates its appeal. Through its epic scale and because of its popularity as a film by Kubrick and with an unusually distinguished cast, it has eclipsed all other Spartacus films made before or after.[15] And it has been a major source of inspiration for the one recent film that all by itself brought the genre of Hollywood's ancient epics back to the silver screen decades after their demise. Ridley Scott's *Gladiator*

---

14   Frederic Raphael, *Eyes Wide Open: A Memoir of Stanley Kubrick* (New York: Ballantine, 1999), 13–14.

15   These are: *Spartaco* (1909, dir. Oreste Gherardini?), *Spartaco* (1911, dir. Ernesto Maria Pasquali), *Spartaco* (before 1912, dir. Filoteo Alberini?), *Spartaco* (1912, dir. Roberto Chiosso), *Spartaco: Il gladiatore della Tracia* (1913, dir. Giovanni Enrico Vidali), *Spartaco* (1953, dir. Riccardo Freda; English titles: *Sins of Rome, Sins of Rome: Story of Spartacus, Spartacus the Gladiator*), *Il figlio di Spartacus* (1963, dir. Sergio Corbucci; English titles: *Son of Spartacus, The Slave*), *La vendetta di Spartacus* (1965, dir. Michele Lupo; English title: *The Revenge of Spartacus*), *Il gladiatore che sfidò l'impero* (1965, dir. Domenico Paolella; English title: *Challenge of the Gladiator*), *Spartacus* (2004, dir. Robert Dornhelm; with exteriors filmed in Bulgaria, modern Thrace). All films except for this last, an American television film based on Fast's novel, were produced in Italy. On them cf. in general Maria Wyke, *Projecting the Past: Ancient Rome, Cinema and History* (New York and London: Routledge, 1997), 34–56. Correct information about the silent films, not all of which seem to have survived, is difficult to obtain; sources often contradict each other. The films made in the 1960s have little (or less) to do with Spartacus. Nick Nostro's film *Gli invincibili dieci gladiatori* (1964; literally: "The Ten Invincible Gladiators") was a sequel to Gianfranco Parolini's *I dieci gladiatori* (1963; English titles: *Ten Desperate Men, The Ten Gladiators*) but was marketed outside Italy with Spartacus' name added to its title for greater commercial appeal (in English: *Spartacus and the Ten Gladiators*). The Russian *Spartak* or *Spartakus* (1977), directed by Vadim Derbenyov and Yuri Grigorovich, is the first film of Aram Khachaturian's ballet of 1954, albeit in a condensed version. An adaptation of Arthur Koestler's novel *The Gladiators*, to be called *The Gladiators* or *Spartacus* and to be directed by Martin Ritt from a screenplay by Abraham Polonsky, was abandoned in preproduction. Ritt and Polonsky were both victims of the blacklist.

(2000) exhibits numerous plot and character similarities to *Spartacus*. So *Spartacus* deserves a re-evaluation both critical and sympathetic.

Spartacus: Film and History presents a new assessment of the film from a variety of perspectives. As such, it is a companion volume to the one I have edited on *Gladiator*.[16] But the complex history of *Spartacus*, an integral aspect of the film's qualities and weaknesses, made a somewhat different editorial approach advisable. Films are visual texts. Like works of literature, they tell stories, if predominantly in images and not in words. But as visual narratives films are capable of analysis, interpretation, and criticism from literary points of view. We may term such an approach *film philology*.[17] To do justice to any literary or filmic text, scholars must be closely familiar with it: with its content, contexts, origin, reception, and existing scholarship. Only then can they interpret or evaluate it. Since films are now an integral part of high-school, college, and university curricula, teachers have a special responsibility to know their "texts," for only then can they appropriately incorporate them into their courses. In the case of *Spartacus*, such an approach calls for close familiarity with all the basics of this film's complicated production history, with the different versions in which it was released, and with its eventual restoration.[18] So the present volume opens with two contributions on the production of the film and its subsequent fate, even going beyond its restoration by pointing us to a version that would take us as closely as possible to the original intention of its principal makers. The other contributors examine several historical and film-historical aspects of *Spartacus*. The film should also be seen and evaluated alongside the

---

16   *Gladiator: Film and History*, ed. Martin M. Winkler (Oxford: Blackwell, 2004).

17   Cf. my "Introduction" to *Classical Myth and Culture in the Cinema*, ed. Martin M. Winkler (New York: Oxford University Press, 2001), 3–22, especially 18–21, and my "Altertumswissenschaftler im Kino, oder: *Quo vadis, philologia?*" *International Journal of the Classical Tradition*, 11 (2004), 95–110, at 95–102. For films as texts cf. in particular Raymond Spottiswoode, *A Grammar of the Film: An Analysis of Film Technique* (Berkeley: University of California Press, 1950; rpt. 1973); Peter Wollen, *Signs and Meaning in the Cinema*, 4th edn. (London: BFI [British Film Institute], 1998); Patrick Phillips, *Understanding Film Texts* (London: BFI, 2000); James Monaco, *How to Read a Film: The World of Movies, Media, and Multimedia: Language, History, Theory* (New York and Oxford: Oxford University Press, 2000). Cf. also Kristin Thompson, *Storytelling in the New Hollywood: Understanding Classical Narrative Technique* (Cambridge: Harvard University Press, 1999). All works contain further references.

18   Just as literary scholars base their research and teaching on authoritative editions of their texts, often with commentary and supplemental materials, film philologists are called upon to do the same wherever possible. In the case of *Spartacus*, such an edition is readily available on DVD from the Criterion Collection (#105). It contains extensive supplements and supersedes all other extant versions.

historical record, so translations of the principal sources about Spartacus complement the essays. The ancient texts will guide readers interested in comparing history and film or in tracing the changes that may
occur when the past is adapted to a popular medium of the present. Two
excerpts from the souvenir book of *Spartacus*, an unusual specimen of
such programs, are included as well.[19] By no means does the present
book exhaust the variety of approaches to the historical, cultural, or
textual aspects of *Spartacus* that are possible; they are intended to point
all readers but especially scholars, teachers, and students in the direction of further work on this film and on its historical foundations,
whether ancient or modern.[20]

Historical films – just like historical plays, operas, novels, or paintings
– are by nature fictional to varying degrees.[21] It is therefore necessary to
turn to the question of what the historical Spartacus intended to achieve
with his revolt. Like Hannibal before him, the legendary Spartacus is
often believed to have come close to overthrowing Rome and abolishing
slavery. The Spartacus of our film presents us with an instance of this
view, notwithstanding the extensive discussions, even quarrels, among

---

19   *Spartacus: The Illustrated Story of the Motion Picture Production*, ed. Stan Margulies
(Bryna Productions and Universal Pictures Studios, 1960).

20   Discussions of *Spartacus* may be found elsewhere as well, especially in the follow-
ing works: *1. By classical scholars and historians:* William V. Harris, "Spartacus," in *Past
Imperfect: History According to the Movies*, ed. Mark C. Carnes et al. (New York: Holt,
1995), 40–43; Wyke, *Projecting the Past*, 63–72; Alison Futrell, "Seeing Red: Spartacus as
Domestic Economist," in *Imperial Projections: Ancient Rome in Modern Popular Culture*, ed.
Sandra R. Joshel, Martha Malamud, and Donald T. McGuire (Baltimore and London: Johns
Hopkins University Press, 2001; rpt. 2005), 77–118; Solomon, *The Ancient World in the
Cinema*, 50–57; Urbainczyk, *Spartacus*, 118–130; Marcus Junkelmann, *Hollywoods Traum
von Rom: "Gladiator" und die Tradition des Monumentalfilms* (Mainz: von Zabern, 2004),
150–165 and 391–394 (notes); and Monica S. Cyrino, *Big-Screen Rome* (Oxford: Blackwell,
2005), 89–120. *2. By film scholars:* Derek Elley, *The Epic Film: Myth and History* (London:
Routledge and Kegan Paul, 1984), 109–112; John Baxter, *Stanley Kubrick: A Biography*
(New York: Carroll and Graf, 1997), 1–5 and 123–141; Vincent LoBrutto, *Stanley Kubrick:
A Biography* (1997; rpt. New York: Da Capo, 1999), 166–193 and 534–536 (notes);
James Howard, *Stanley Kubrick Companion* (London: Batsford, 1999), 63–72; Hughes, *The
Complete Kubrick*, 64–85; Paul Duncan, *Stanley Kubrick: Visual Poet 1928–1999* (Cologne:
Taschen, 2003), 58–71, with numerous illustrations.

21   On the often controversial topic of the presentation of the past in the present, and
on *Gladiator* as a specific example, see my comments in "*Gladiator* and the Traditions of
Historical Cinema," in *Gladiator: Film and History*, 16–30, where I provide references
to scholarship on history and film in general. Cf. further my short outline "Quomodo
stemma *Gladiatoris* pelliculae more philologico sit constituendum," *American Journal of
Philology*, 124 (2003), 137–141.

some of its creative personnel over what they called the "large" and the "small" Spartacus. But such a view of Spartacus is anachronistic and does not do justice to the real Spartacus and his people. But then, even the ancients, in retrospect, could not fully understand the reasons why the revolt of Spartacus spread as widely and as quickly as it did and why Spartacus was able to achieve so many victories against great odds. St. Augustine commented on this in his *City of God*, written A.D. 413–426, in the context of an overview of slave wars and civil wars:

> Then followed a slave war and civil wars. What battles were fought, what blood was shed so that almost all the Italic tribes, among whom the Roman empire had the greatest power, could be subdued as if they were the savage lands of barbarians! Now, the way in which the slave war arose from only very few gladiators (that is, fewer than seventy), to what a large number of fierce and cruel slaves it grew, which generals of the Roman people that number defeated, which cities and areas it devastated and how it did so – all this historians have scarcely been able to explain satisfactorily.[22]

Confusion about Spartacus and about his achievements and goals is therefore almost unavoidable. But the consensus of modern historians about Spartacus' goals is significantly different from what the legendary or cinematic Spartacus wants to achieve. I cite two scholars at some length to emphasize this important point. The first is an authority on Roman republican history in general:

> It causes no surprise that Marxist historians and writers have idealized Spartacus as a champion of the masses and leader of the one genuine social revolution in Roman history. That, however, is excessive. Spartacus and his companions sought to break the bonds of their own grievous oppression. There is no sign that they were motivated by ideological considerations to overturn the social structure. The sources make clear that Spartacus endeavored to bring his forces out of Italy toward freedom rather than to reform or reverse Roman society. The achievements of Spartacus are no less formidable for that. The courage, tenacity, and ability of the Thracian gladiator who held Roman forces at bay for some two years and built a handful of followers into an assemblage of over 120,000 men can only inspire admiration . . . But no suggestion emerges anywhere in the sources that the rebels were motivated by idealistic dreams of the equality of slave and free; still less that they aimed at an overthrow and

---

22 Augustinus, *The City of God* 3.26. On this passage cf. Orena, *Rivolta e rivoluzione*, 261–269.

reconstruction of the social order. Their activities pointed toward self-liberation and escape from Italy.[23]

The second scholar is an expert on ancient slavery. He reaches an almost identical conclusion:

> The severities of slavery . . . hardly stand in need of further emphasis. It does, however, require stress that the escalation of the revolt of gladiators into a sustained war of servile resistance cannot possibly have been what Spartacus and his immediate companions had hoped to achieve when they made their escape from Capua . . . The desire to avoid incarceration, to gain liberty, and to take revenge for injuries suffered is comprehensible enough in sheer human terms. But no matter how similarly arduous the living conditions of other slaves, there is no evidence to suggest that Spartacus and his followers . . . purposely set out from the beginning to raise a general rebellion of slaves throughout central and southern Italy. Indeed, the peculiarity of their circumstances [as slave-gladiators], once contrasted with those of other slaves, precludes any such thought . . . The argument might be made that Spartacus had once hoped to exploit the general tendency of slaves to resist servitude by flight and to convert the original revolt of gladiators into a wider slave rebellion. But there is no evidence of such aspirations. There can be no reasonable doubt, therefore, that widespread revolt . . . was not at all the best means by which the glad-iators from Capua might hope to convert their act of flight into a state of permanent freedom, for the greater the rebel numbers, the greater the prospect of Roman retaliation in kind . . . it was the sheer size of the upris-ing itself that made it impossible to render permanent the freedom the slaves acquired by their acts of revolt. Their only option was to withstand Rome's retaliation for as long as was practically possible by resorting to whatever methods of survival could prove effective . . . it becomes impos-sible to view the Spartacan movement as being in any way dominated by abstract or ideological imperatives: freedom from slavery was the intent of the fugitives; the slavery system itself remained unaffected.[24]

These assessments and my preceding observations are intended to serve readers as a framework for their encounter with the essays in this book. It will be readily apparent that there is no complete consensus between

23   Erich S. Gruen, *The Last Generation of the Roman Republic* (Berkeley, Los Angeles, and London: University of California Press, 1974), 20 and 406.
24   Keith R. Bradley, *Slavery and Rebellion in the Roman World, 140 B.C.–70 B.C.* (Bloom-ington and Indianapolis: Indiana University Press, 1989; rpt. 1998), 98–101. Contrast, however, H. T. Wallinga, "Bellum Spartacium: Florus' Text and Spartacus' Objective," *Athenaeum*, 80 (1992), 25–43.

and among contributors. But this will, we hope, be an incentive to readers to approach the Spartacus of history and film from a fresh perspective. The readers we hope for are all those interested, on the one hand, in ancient history and the classical tradition and, on the other, in cinema and its cultural importance. We also address academic readers in these and related areas of the humanities such as modern history and American studies. All contributions are written in non-specialized English and without academic jargon. We annotate and give references where appropriate so that readers can pursue individual topics further on their own. If we succeed in persuading readers to think anew about Roman history and culture and about historical cinema or to watch *Spartacus* or other historical films with greater understanding or appreciation, our book will have achieved its goal.

As editor of this volume I am indebted first and foremost to my contributors for their willing and enthusiastic participation. They formed a veritable *familia academica Spartacia*. I am grateful to independent scholar Duncan Cooper for agreeing to rework and update his fundamental research on *Spartacus* that had originally appeared in the film journal *Cinéaste* and for providing me with copies of materials from the Kirk Douglas Papers. I am also grateful to the editors of *Cinéaste* for permission to use Duncan Cooper's publications in their journal as the basis for his contributions here. I owe another debt of gratitude to Thomas Mann at the Library of Congress in Washington, D.C., for providing me with information about some out-of-the-way sources on American slavery. For illustrations I am once again indebted to William Knight Zewadski, Esq., who allowed me to use a number of film stills from his unique collection. At Blackwell, Al Bertrand, my commissioning editor, deserves thanks for his interest in and generous support of this project from its inception. I also thank Angela Cohen, Annette Abel, and the Blackwell staff for efficiently seeing the book through the production process.

CHAPTER ONE

Who Killed the Legend of Spartacus? Production, Censorship, and Reconstruction of Stanley Kubrick's Epic Film

Duncan L. Cooper

Stanley Kubrick's and Kirk Douglas's *Spartacus*, based on a novel by Howard Fast, purports to tell the true story of a gladiator who, 2,000 years earlier, led a mighty slave uprising which almost succeeded in overthrowing the decaying Roman Republic and its ruthless slave empire. The film represents a breakthrough for left-wing themes in Hollywood cinema after a decade of McCarthyism, not only because of its revolutionary political message but also because blacklisted screenwriter Dalton Trumbo received credit for the screenplay under his own name. This broke the blacklist which had been in effect in Hollywood for most of the 1950s. Efforts by right-wing columnist Hedda Hopper and the American Legion to promote a boycott of the film failed when newly elected President John F. Kennedy publicly endorsed it after attending a screening in Washington, D.C. *Spartacus* went on to become an international box-office hit, winning four Academy Awards and capturing the Golden Globe Award as the Best Dramatic Film of the year.

1. Kirk Douglas vs. Universal Studios: The Battle for Control of *Spartacus*

Author Howard Fast, however, believed that the film did not do complete justice to his book. In an interview accompanying the Criterion

Collection edition of the restored film, Fast commented that aside from the gladiator fight between Kirk Douglas and Woody Strode nothing in the film could compare in dramatic intensity with the corresponding scenes in the novel. In fact, despite his extensive contributions to the film's screenplay, for which Fast never received the credit he deserves, an enormous gap exists between the vision of Spartacus which emerges from his novel and the one projected by the film. Using the little that is known about Spartacus as a basis, Fast molded the gladiator rebel into a mythic hero, a messianic figure engaged in an epic revolutionary struggle to overthrow Roman power in order to restore a legendary Golden Age of primitive tribal communism said to have existed in some distant epoch prior to the advent of human exploitation. For Fast, strict adherence to the known facts was less important than the timeless moral truth that was implicit in the legend of Spartacus. By contrast, the film followed a more conservative reading of the facts. It reduced Fast's gentle Christ-like character to a brawling animal who slowly develops into a likeable tough and then gradually into a sensitive human being and democratic leader. Instead of Fast's visionary who, through the force of his charismatic personality and military genius, was able to weld an amorphous mass of "slaves, deserters, and riff-raff" into a force which managed to defeat nine of Rome's best-trained armies and nearly toppled the Republic, the film presents us with a good man and capable leader to whom everything seems to come easy but whose revolt founders in an orgy of torture and death almost before it has begun.[1] The escape to freedom of Spartacus' wife and new-born son from the carnage of 6,000 crucifixions offers the audience only a few rays of hope for the future, especially if we consider that Rome became an almost worldwide empire that lasted for another 500 years.

Because of this difference between book and film, some admirers of the latter believed that cuts imposed by Universal Pictures and the Catholic Church's Legion of Decency had severely reduced its image of the legendary Spartacus from giant to midget, as it were. These cuts included some gory shots of arms, legs, and heads being cut off in battle, a lengthy scene of a man being drowned in a pot of soup, a shot of blood spurting onto the Roman aristocrat Crassus' face as he slashes the neck of the dying gladiator Draba, and the subtly bisexual "oysters and snails" seduction scene between Crassus and his slave Antoninus. These cuts,

---

1   The quotation is from Appian, *The Civil Wars* 1.14.117; quoted from *Appian's Roman History*, tr. Horace White, rev. E. Iliff Robson, vol. 3 (Cambridge: Harvard University Press / London: Heinemann, 1913), 219.

totaling about five minutes, may also have included at least one battle scene depicting a significant victory for the slave army, whose lack was made evident by numerous lines of dialogue throughout the film which referred directly or indirectly to many such victories. Some lines from Spartacus' speech to the slaves assembled on a beach – "We've traveled a long ways together. We fought many battles, won great victories" – and his lines to his wife Varinia – "But no matter how many times we beat them, they always seem to have another army to send against us. And another." – are two of the most pointed examples.

Thus when it was announced in September 1990 that Universal Pictures was going to release a fully restored version of the film with five minutes of censored footage reinserted, many fans of the film dared to hope that perhaps now, after thirty years, the authentic legendary *Spartacus* might finally appear on screen. An advance press handout ("*Spartacus* Premiere Fact Sheet") by restoration producers Jim Katz and Robert Harris touted their restoration as "a film with an entirely different tone . . . a completely different film [from] the version we're used to" and raised further expectations.

Spartacus already had much going for it: magnificent performances by Laurence Olivier, Charles Laughton, and Oscar winner Peter Ustinov, moving scenes from the pen of Trumbo, spectacular camerawork by Oscar winner Russell Metty, excellent editing by Oscar nominee Robert Lawrence, a stirring musical score by Oscar nominee Alex North, and, of course, the direction by Stanley Kubrick. These elements, combined with Fast's heroic theme of mankind's age-old quest for freedom, make *Spartacus* a powerful and moving historical epic. The meticulous restoration by Robert Harris reinforces the film's impact.

Unfortunately, since Universal had junked almost all the outtakes, trims, and censored scenes of the film in 1975, the restorers could do very little beyond reinserting about five minutes of lost footage to bring *Spartacus* back to its 197-minute pre-censorship version. Thus the restored version is still roughly the same film that audiences saw during its original run in the early 1960s. A few censored scenes have been restored, notably the "oysters and snails" seduction scene, the two quick shots showing the blood and the terror on Crassus' face as he stabs Draba, and a longer version of the scene of devastation after the film's final battle.

On the other hand, several important scenes between Senator Gracchus, the fictionalized leader of the Roman plebeians, and his protégé, the young Julius Caesar, remain missing despite Harris's dedicated efforts to find them. These deleted scenes defined Gracchus' political identity through a sometimes funny depiction of his rather corrupt but nevertheless sincere relationship with his constituents, the common citizens of Rome's fourth ward. They also explained the motivation for Caesar's crucial defection to Crassus and the patricians late in the film. This reason was Gracchus' own defection to Spartacus. Reportedly, Laughton, who played Gracchus, was outraged when he realized that several of his scenes were not going to be used in the film and threatened Kirk Douglas with a lawsuit. Laughton was incensed that the studio was keeping his name on the marquee while reducing his role to what might be called a bit-part senator. Nothing came of the lawsuit, but one of these deleted scenes, in which Gracchus explains the secrets of Roman politics to Caesar as they stroll through the back alleys of the slums of Rome, survived in the film until its July, 1960, press screening but was afterwards cut by the studio for reasons of length.

Even more disappointingly, Harris failed to discover any trace of even one lost battle scene that depicted a major slave victory over the Roman legions. Most modern historians would probably agree that during the course of his rebellion Spartacus defeated nine Roman armies ranging from a few thousand raw militia to tens of thousands of veteran legionaries. But viewers today would search in vain for anything like this astounding military accomplishment. Thus both the real and the legendary achievements of Spartacus and his rebels remain as absent from the restored version as they were from the original censored version.

2. The Perils of Breaking the Blacklist

Little if any blame for this travesty of history falls on the shoulders of the film's director. Then thirty-one years old, Kubrick had very little control over the content of the film, for all final decisions were made by Executive Producer Kirk Douglas, although subject to a veto from Universal. So it is not surprising that, despite the support and assistance he provided the restoration, Kubrick never retracted his public disavowal of *Spartacus*, going so far as to suggest that it be removed from his filmography. "I am disappointed in the film," he mused rather wistfully: "It had everything but a good story."[2]

---

2 Quoted from Joseph Gelmis, "The Film Director as Superstar: Stanley Kubrick," in *Stanley Kubrick: Interviews*, ed. Gene D. Phillips (Jackson: University Press of Mississippi, 2001), 80–104; quotation at 102. This interview was first published as "Stanley Kubrick," in Joseph Gelmis, *The Film Director as Superstar* (New York: Doubleday, 1970), 293–316.

Evidence indicates that Kubrick himself was only too willing to portray the violence, corruption, and moral degeneracy that inevitably results from a long and bitterly contested class war. Kubrick was responsible for the decision to show the final battle on screen and so turned the film into a full-scale epic. According to James B. Harris, his producer and business partner in the 1950s:

> When Stanley read the script, there was no battle scene – it was done in a sort of surrealistic way, with helmets floating down the water with blood stains and battle sounds in the background. Stanley said that you can't make a spectacle movie and not have a battle scene in it. So he talked them into going to the cheapest area, Spain, where he could get all those extras.[3]

Battle montages showing a series of slave victories, something that Trumbo had fought for from the beginning and through three versions of the screenplay, also appeared for the first time in revised script pages in late March, 1959, a month after Kubrick replaced Anthony Mann, the film's original director. Kubrick may have also hoped to temper ex-communist Trumbo's adulation of the working class and enthusiasm for violent revolution with the irony that revolutions often fail more because of the mistakes, moral weaknesses, and corruption of the revolutionaries themselves than as a result of the supposedly overwhelming strength of their adversaries. Lacking the authority to make final decisions, Kubrick engaged the other members of the film's executive committee – screenwriter Trumbo, executive producer Douglas, and producer Edward Lewis – in a running, sometimes acrimonious, debate through four versions of the script over what final form the film should take.

Nor is Anthony Mann to be blamed. Well respected for his 1950s *films noirs* and westerns, Mann supervised, along with Douglas, the four months of pre-production of *Spartacus* and presumably participated in the complete rewrites of the script that were done in the Fall of 1958. After two weeks of shooting the opening sequence in the mines and some of the early scenes in the gladiator school that are still in the film today, Douglas fired Mann. Mann went on to make such acclaimed epic films as *El Cid* (1961) and *The Fall of the Roman Empire* (1964), both of which contain large-scale battle scenes. As producer Lewis remarked in an interview on the Criterion Collection edition of the film: "If it had been up to Tony Mann, we would have used up ten reels for the final battle."

---

3 Quoted from "Stanley Kubrick: A Cinematic Odyssey," *Premiere* (August, 1999), 85–93 and 98–100, at 86.

As his westerns attest, Mann believed, far more than Kubrick, in mythic heroes as the proper subject for film and was a perfect choice to direct *Spartacus*. Mann was interested in legendary characters: "legend makes the very best cinema. It excites the imagination more . . . legend is a concept of characters greater than life."[4] His creative philosophy closely fit Fast's conception for *Spartacus* because Mann believed in "the nobility of the human spirit . . . this is what drama is. This is what pictures are all about. I don't believe in anything else."[5] As for strict historical accuracy, Mann, like Fast, believed that "the most important thing is that you get the feeling of history. The actual facts, very few people know."[6] He could hardly have had any difficulties presenting this story of a larger-than-life legendary hero of old.

Neither can Trumbo be saddled with the responsibility for the film's failure to live up to the novel's potential. Although altering much of its plot and character development in order to conform to the needs of a cinematic treatment, he insisted, through five versions of the script, on retaining Fast's original conception of Spartacus' nearly successful revolutionary challenge to Rome. Nor is Douglas to be blamed. In his autobiography he describes his personal conception of Spartacus, based on Fast's novel:

> Spartacus was a real man, but if you look him up in the history books, you find only a short paragraph about him. Rome was ashamed; this man had almost destroyed them. They wanted to bury him. I was intrigued with the story of Spartacus the slave, dreaming of the death of slavery, driving into the armor of Rome the wedge that would eventually destroy her.[7]

As Douglas's biographer Michael Munn wrote me: "the film was first and foremost Kirk Douglas' vision." Douglas named himself executive producer to "ensure the picture would be made his way."[8] Recent comments by Tony Curtis have confirmed that Douglas wanted to emphasize the love story at least as much as the slave uprising. Disagreements over this basic concept led to Mann's dismissal two weeks into production. However, in his recent comments Douglas stressed his determination to

4   Christopher Wicking and Barrie Pattison, "Interviews with Anthony Mann," *Screen*, 10 no. 4 (1969), 32–54; quotation at 41.

5   Anthony Mann, "Empire Demolition," in *Hollywood Directors 1941–1976*, ed. Richard Koszarski (New York: Oxford University Press, 1977), 332–338; quotation at 337–338. Mann's essay first appeared in *Films and Filming*, 10 no. 6 (March, 1964), 7–8.

6   Mann, "Empire Demolition," 336.

7   Kirk Douglas, *The Ragman's Son* (New York: Simon and Schuster, 1988), 304.

8   Michael Munn, *Kirk Douglas*, rev. edn. (New York: St. Martin's, 1989), 78.

portray the story of "a slave whose vision of freedom almost overthrew the Roman Empire."[9] Special consultant Saul Bass, who designed the film's distinctive title sequence, confirmed to me that during the whole time he worked on *Spartacus* there was never any doubt or wavering about this point in the minds of Douglas, Lewis, Trumbo, or any other member of the production company. As the shooting came to a close, the coming-attractions trailer produced for the film was specifically designed to market *Spartacus* with this theme. The trailer opens with a banner rolling up the screen against the backdrop of the Roman Forum and stating:

IN THE YEAR 70 B.C. ROME – COLOSSUS OF THE WORLD – FACED ITS GRAVEST CHALLENGE

The scene immediately shifts to the inside of a Roman command tent, where Laurence Olivier as Marcus Crassus gravely informs his staff about the seriousness of the situation:

Nine Roman armies have been destroyed – by Spartacus. And our defeat will mean – the fall of Rome.

All other key promotional materials produced for the film – the thumbnail plot summaries, the comic book, the historical pamphlet, the study guide, the souvenir book, the soundtrack album program notes, the paperback edition of the novel – also told the story of a slave revolt which won victory after victory and all but overthrew Rome herself.

However, the three principal filmmakers had to contend with the interference of Universal, their primary financial backer. Studio head Ed Muhl had some very different ideas, leading to what Trumbo described as "a basic conflict of opinion about the dimensions of Spartacus and his struggle, a conflict which has been in evidence from the earliest beginnings of the project."[10] Originally Muhl never conceived of *Spartacus* as a spectacle but as an intimate film that would cost between $3 and $4 million. A personal friend of Trumbo's and the man who deserves much credit for breaking the Hollywood blacklist, Muhl, too, wanted to make an exciting but still historically accurate film. Although he was

---

9   Tony Curtis, taped radio call-in with the author; Marshall Green (assistant director on *Spartacus*), interview with David Chandler, March 25, 1960, 18–19 (for unpublished book *The Year of Spartacus*); audio commentary by Kirk Douglas on Criterion Collection edition of *Spartacus*.
10   Dalton Trumbo, "The Sequence on Vesuvius: Notes", 2.

fascinated by the struggles between liberal and conservative factions in the Roman Senate, transparent analogues to contemporary American politics that Trumbo had inserted into the script, Muhl told me: "Deep ideas are nice to have in a picture. But what counts is audience appeal."

In response to Douglas' concept of *Spartacus* Muhl further remarked to me: "it's understandable that Kirk would want to build up his own part but that's not what the picture was about." He concluded: "We did what was possible under the circumstances . . . You know that phrase, 'the art of the possible'." His attitude probably hardened when late in 1959 persistent rumors of new Hollywood hearings by the House Un-American Activities Committee began to surface and a full-scale right-wing attack on the film began after Walter Winchell revealed that blacklisted writer Trumbo was the author of the screenplay.[11] *Spartacus* was the first truly independent production financed by Universal, but in the end Muhl's cautious approach prevailed because he and the studio held the trump card: the legal right to make the final cut.

Although Douglas still claims that *Spartacus* represents the fulfillment of his personal vision, he was ultimately forced to go along with most of Muhl's wishes because, by insisting that Trumbo be given official credit for the screenplay, he had set the film on a perilous collision course with the political right and the Hollywood blacklist. He wrote in his autobiography:

> That night it all suddenly became very clear. I knew what name to put on the screen [as the author of the screenplay] . . . The masquerade was over. All my friends told me I was being stupid, throwing my career away. It was a tremendous risk. At first nobody believed me. Dalton did . . . The blacklist was broken.
>
> [Director] Otto Preminger called me from New York . . . He was amazed that I was using Dalton Trumbo's name openly.
>
> Soon after, he held a press conference announcing that Dalton Trumbo would be the writer of [Preminger's film] *Exodus*.
>
> I wasn't thinking of being a hero and breaking the blacklist . . . I was just thinking, how unfair for someone to say, "Put my name on it. Let me get the credit for someone else's work."[12]

Douglas and Trumbo were fully aware of the risks involved if *Spartacus* did not earn back well over the $12 million that the studio had invested in it. Trumbo wrote in one of his letters that, if the film had failed, "I, for

---

11   On this see especially *Additional Dialogue: Letters of Dalton Trumbo, 1942–1962,* ed. Helen Manfull (1970; rpt. New York: Bantam, 1972), 493–494.

12   Douglas, *The Ragman's Son,* 323–324.

one, would never have been able to work again, and those who do not yet work openly would have even a slighter chance than I of making it."[13] Therefore, as he himself acknowledged, in the climate of the late 1950s the characters in *Spartacus* had to espouse ideas far less radical than he would have liked in order to save the film from destruction at the hands of both conservative and liberal anti-communist critics. Trumbo told David Chandler in an interview:

> TRUMBO: You see, the bloody fight to express ideas, even mild ones, is really recurrent and it will happen again in a different form, maybe more severely, maybe less severely. The pressure is always on and we writers do discipline ourselves, we do censor ourselves. For example, you know how carefully I have to write a script, particularly if my name is going to be on it.
> CHANDLER: I thought you were very bold in *Spartacus*.
> TRUMBO: Well, I thought I was very restrained . . . because I realized that a thing which any other writer would say and [that] would never be thought of or analyzed or would never be significant or noticed, when I say it, it becomes highly significant – smuggling in propaganda and doing all sorts of things, so you see I consider this a very mild script.[14]

If Trumbo himself saw the necessity of self-censorship in order to break the blacklist, it is easy to understand why Muhl insisted on toning down the film still further at the last moment, even if this meant a serious weakening of its dramatic impact by reducing the legendary stature of its protagonist to run-of-the-mill proportions. In the pithy words of Tony Curtis: "Universal was being so heavy handed about everything including production values . . . *Spartacus* cost $12 million and was the most expensive picture Universal had ever made. It ended up grossing $14 or $15 million but they were scared shitless at the time."[15]

3. Trumbo's Struggle for the Large Spartacus

Douglas' battle with the studio was only lost at the eleventh hour, when the film was being readied to be shown to the press. That battle had

---

13   *Additional Dialogue*, 575.
14   Trumbo–Chandler interview of August 2, 1960 (*The Year of Spartacus*, 56–57).
15   Tony Curtis and Barry Paris, *Tony Curtis, The Autobiography* (New York: Morrow, 1993), 180 and 185.

begun with the very inception of the project, the first drafts of the script. Despite his determination to exercise extreme caution, it was Trumbo, along with Fast, who fought most consistently for a film which would remain faithful to the novel's essential message: man's capacity, in all ages of history, to rise and overthrow tyranny and oppression. From the beginning of his work, Trumbo waged a stubborn campaign to include scenes, or at least a battle montage, which would depict some of Spartacus' great victories over the Romans. On Fast's advice he added an enormous five-page montage to his first draft of July 15, 1958. This montage, narrated by Gracchus, traced the whole course of the war and included many of Spartacus' most important victories. Similarly, and also on Fast's recommendation, the relatively brief treatment of Spartacus' first victory over Glabrus and the garrison of Rome was greatly expanded to a major sequence encompassing four scenes and costing an estimated $300,000. At the same time the final battle was de-emphasized: the audience was to hear the sounds of battle but not see the action. Following the novel, emphasis would be placed on the bloody aftermath to underscore Spartacus' great victories but to downplay his defeat.

Other forces were at work, however, as the film moved towards production. By the third draft, known as the Final Screenplay and dated December 9, 1958, the huge battle montage had disappeared and the battle with Glabrus had been reduced to a narration while plans were under way for a detailed rendition of the final battle. To counterbalance this, the story was now told in flashback and opened with a speech by Crassus to his officers in which he refers to nine Roman armies destroyed by Spartacus and warns of the possible fall of Rome.

The filmmakers had to finish the Roman sections of the script first in order to attract the British actors. They then had to rush into production in order to beat another film company which was also preparing a film about Spartacus, this one based on Arthur Koestler's novel *The Gladiators*. For these reasons the sections of the script dealing with the slaves were still unfinished and in need of extensive rewriting when shooting began on January 27, 1959. By the end of May, 1959, as the script was again being revised, Trumbo, with Kubrick's approval, was able to insert first one and then four of his proposed battle montages depicting seven or eight slave victories. These montages were calculated to lend credibility to a plot change inspired by Kubrick in which the over-confident slaves abandon their chance to escape on the waiting pirate ships and instead try to overthrow the whole slave system by marching on Rome. Trumbo believed these battle montages were crucial to the success of the film. In a memo he wrote:

And this brings us down to a basic conflict of opinion about the dimensions of Spartacus and his struggle: a conflict which has been in evidence from the earliest beginnings of the project. Through three versions of the script I have fought against the idea of diminishing the scope of Spartacus' activities, against shortening to the point of absurdity the length of time in which he held the field, against the idea that he was a mere escapee who won a few encounters against provincial garrisons instead of a great military leader who for four years running defeated the finest legions and the greatest armies Rome could put in the field against him. You cannot have a Roman story in which Spartacus motivates the actions of the most powerful men in Rome and shakes Roman society to its very foundations, and then go to a Spartacus story in which Spartacus is merely the head of a large gang of runaway convicts. Thus far the larger concept of Spartacus' power and ability, and of the scope of his military ventures, has won through; not I feel because I really convinced anyone of the dramatic necessities of my view, but rather because it takes nine months to make a baby and a man who has to stay in the field for nine months obviously has to be doing something.[16]

Trumbo was still blacklisted, but his work on the screenplay of *Spartacus* was the worst-kept secret in Hollywood. Still, the pretense had to be maintained that Edward Lewis was writing the script. Trumbo was banned from the lot, unable to be present on the set when Douglas and Kubrick made last-minute changes to the script and, generally speaking, removed from the decision-making process. In another memo he complained bitterly about the script changes that had been forced upon him while production was under way:

It is almost a year now since I began to write this script. Since then I have turned out hundreds upon hundreds of pages and well over 200,000 words. In its more primitive stages, before the underlying theory of the script was challenged, before an unremitting attack on the political meaning and the intellectual content of every scene was begun, the script was able to attractive five top stars, several millions of dollars from a studio, and even to generate a little excitement, a certain enthusiasm.

Since that time I have written ceaselessly to try to make the script as good as at least a few people thought it was in those first remote days of its conception . . . Many scenes have been improved. Other scenes, I regret to say, have been diminished . . .

For the past three months the script has been written by a committee rather than by a writer. Everything has been thrown at me: hostile

16   Trumbo, "The Sequence on Vesuvius: Notes", 2.

Koestlerian ideas derived from quite another book: rhetorical speeches and character gems from the newly discovered Fast script which should have been read months and months ago; psychiatric observations which I have found to be of immense value; the rival opinions of actors; the director's opinion (possibly correct) that the words don't matter anyhow so long as they're simple, and that any attempt with speech to provoke thought or illuminate intellectual, political, or moral concepts simply confuses the audience; a widespread conviction that complexity has no place on the screen, and that simplicity is best brought out by action alone; every possible attempt at swift and easy solutions to the problem of a script which is essentially complex and therefore is bound to have a certain complexity of motives (as you have discovered in ten versions of the climax) . . .

I have gone through a process of inquisition on this script that rivals any torment devised by a committee of Congress. The difference is that one can tell the committee to go fuck itself and stop the ordeal, whereas considerations of friendship, mutual respect, professional obligation, and . . . artistic commitment and devotion, prevent such an escape from present circumstances.

I am prepared to admit that democratically the votes of a full-time actor, a full-time director, and a full-time producer are worth three times the dissent of a full-time writer. They are also worth three times the vote of a competent secretary, which is what I have lately become.

[However], there are moments in the history of the drama when the vote of one full-time writer outweighs and outnumbers the votes of any three who are so fully occupied in other professions that they are for the present, unable themselves to do the writing . . . if there is no better method, let us go back to the old fashioned idea that by and large the best man to invent a story and write a script is a writer.[17]

Trumbo was finally smuggled onto the studio lot to view the film's first rough cut. What he saw provoked in him such a negative reaction that over the next seventy-two hours he wrote an eighty-page "Report on *Spartacus*" in three parts. In it he summarized what he called "The Two Conflicting Points of View on Spartacus," which had underscored the entire debate over the last year. Then, in a lengthy section entitled "Scene-by-Scene Run-Through," he analyzed all the film's weaknesses caused by innumerable on-set rewrites done without his knowledge or consent. He pleaded to be allowed to write a series of retakes that he said would either make or break the film.

---

17   Trumbo, "Last General Notes on Spartacus," 1–2 and 5.

For want of a better term, Trumbo labeled the two conflicting views of Spartacus as "The Large Spartacus" and "The Small Spartacus." The premise of the Large Spartacus was that Spartacus' revolt was a major rebellion which shook the Roman Republic to its foundations, involved a series of brilliant military campaigns and the defeat of the best soldiers Rome could put in the field, and was finally put down by the over-whelming might of three Roman armies. The premise of the Small Spartacus was that the revolt was more on the scale of a jail-break and subsequent dash to the sea, that there were no important slave vic-tories, and that the rebellion was put down by only one Roman army.

Trumbo then listed an entire series of other conflicting conceptions about the film and its main character that flowed from these basic prem-ises. He made it clear that he believed only one of these conceptions could be right and that the right choice was the Large Spartacus. With con-siderable justification he asserted that the conscious intention of the executive committee through all three preliminary drafts of the screen-play had been to construct a film around the concept of the Large Spartacus. In his view, the basic problem with the film was a slow turn toward the Small Spartacus through the endless rewrites of the final screenplay after shooting had begun. He pleaded with the committee to embrace the Large Spartacus "without any reservations . . . otherwise we shall be utterly lost."[18]

After reading the Report, Douglas was asked by Kubrick how Trumbo had liked the film's first rough cut and replied: "He *didn't* like it! And he's right."[19] Douglas still refers to Trumbo's Report as "the most brilliant analysis of movie-making that I have ever read."[20] Much to Kubrick's chagrin, Douglas and Lewis decided significantly to revise the film even though this would entail a considerable additional expense. The key players' contracts were extended and a large number of revised or new scenes containing Large-Spartacus dialogue were shot starting in November, 1959. These included the two scenes with the pirate envoy Tigranes Levantus, Spartacus' speech to the rebels after their return to the gladiator school, his speech to the assembled slaves on the beach near Brundisium, and the last dialogue and confrontation between Spartacus, Antoninus, and Crassus.

On the question of the battle montages, however, Trumbo apparently failed fully to persuade Douglas and Universal. At this time, in August of

---

18 Trumbo, *Report on Spartacus*, section I: "The Two Conflicting Points of View on Spartacus," 6–7.
19 Quoted from Bruce Cook, *Dalton Trumbo* (New York: Scribner, 1977), 272.
20 Douglas, *The Ragman's Son*, 325.

1959, more money had been obtained from Universal for battle scenes, and it had been decided to move the production to Spain to shoot the final battle and a number of other scenes with the help of the Spanish army. The question was whether or not the battle montages showing the slave army's victories were also going to be shot. As editor Robert Lawrence told me: "the idea [of shooting full-blown additional battle scenes] was discussed, but it was never actually done" because the money was not forthcoming from Universal. As part of an agreement between Douglas's company, Bryna Productions, and Universal Studios, six days of scenes with slave victories were to be filmed in Spain as part of a total of twelve days of battle scenes, at an estimated cost of half a million dollars. However, when Douglas came back with Trumbo's proposals from his Report for a large number of additional scenes, the deal was renegotiated. The new agreement called for a total of twenty-two days of shooting in Spain at an estimated cost of nearly a million dollars, although the number of shooting days for battle scenes was cut down to six, enough to accommodate the final battle but not the early slave victories. The studio argued that if the slaves' victory scenes were too good they could detract from the impact of the final battle, but if they were lackluster they would detract from the quality of the film as a whole. Douglas had to fall back on the idea of a brief animated battle map to dramatize these slave victories. The studio was opposed even to this minimal reference to Spartacus' series of victories and wanted to opt for a map without any battles.[21] Saul Bass was commissioned to design this alternate map and produced several different versions which, he told me, were "very elaborate at first, then later much simpler." Bass was told that his map was to be cut into segments to be used as inserts for a big montage containing marching and dialogue but no battles. As editor Lawrence told me: "We had maps with battles and maps without battles because some people wanted one kind and some people wanted the other."

In an appendix to an "Outline of the scenes to be shot in Spain," Trumbo made a final plea for the shooting of full-scale battle montages:

> During the march from Luceria to Metapontum a dozen important battles were won by Spartacus and the slaves. I understand that a map is to be used, with some pictorial device superimposed to indicate the sequence of victories. Not knowing exactly how it is to be done, I have not indicated battle montage or explosive physical scenes to indicate these victories [in

21 "*Spartacus*: Present Edited Continuity of Completed Picture" (October 2, 1959), Seq. No. 54; Appendix ST [Studio], ST-15; "*Spartacus*: Revised Music Notes" (November 5, 1959), 12, Reel 16.

this outline]. These are left to the invention of the director. But I think they should be taken into serious consideration, for we should let our audience know that a sequence of victories rather than two battles produced the slave threat to Rome.[22]

In December, 1959, a significant amount of battle footage became available for additional battle scenes. Kubrick returned from Spain with film of the final battle. Studio executives were awed by what Douglas called "incredible footage of the [final] battle, so wide that he'd had to shoot from almost half a mile away."[23] These scenes, shot from 100-foot-high towers, depict the Roman army deploying into battle formations and the slave army charging down a bluff into them. But the filmmakers never used additional footage of the slave army's charge that was shot from another ground-level camera located a short distance from the base of this bluff. So this footage was available as a master shot for another major battle scene. Furthermore, the studio rejected the accompanying close-in fighting scenes that involved nearly five hundred extras as "boring and conventional" and ordered a series of retakes with gory shots of severed arms, legs, and heads. Thus by refusing to use the nearly one minute of close-in Spanish fighting scenes in the final battle, they made them available for possible use in a battle montage or another major battle sequence.[24]

Still more footage became available in early February, 1960, when second-unit director Yakima Canutt finished directing five days of these retakes that included the slave army rolling its flaming logs into the Romans and numerous other fight scenes featuring Kirk Douglas, Tony Curtis, John Ireland (Crixus), and Nicholas Dennis (Dionysius). After viewing the rushes, Douglas expressed his disappointment with his own scenes to Canutt. They were, he said, "not too good. I should have had scenes like the ones you shot with Curtis and Ireland. They looked

22   Trumbo, "*Spartacus*: Material to be Shot in Spain," 31.

23   Douglas, *The Ragman's Son*, 326.

24   Sources: "Outline for Battle Sequence" (August 13, 1959); "*Spartacus*: Present Edited Continuity of Completed Picture" (October 2, 1959), Seq. No. 73; Appendix SP [Spain], SP-12; "Continuity Breakdown" (October 15, 1959), "Added Scenes–Spain," 51–55 (Scenes 1–38); "*Spartacus*: Music Notes, Revised II" (January 21, 1960) by Kubrick (Reel 22, Ft. No. 000–441); "*Spartacus*: Daily Production Report" (November 25 and December 14, 1959); letter From Fred Banker to Charles Block of Globe Photos on Bill Nunley's *Spartacus* layout (March 10, 1960), containing promotional profile of propman-armorer Nunley; "Proposed List of Gory Shots Tying to Battle Sequence As Outlined by S. Kubrick" (January 4, 1960); *Spartacus* Teaser Trailer; my interviews with Melville Tucker, Saul Bass, Robert Lawrence.

great."[25] To round out the final battle and remedy Douglas's problem, two more days of battle scenes were shot in mid-March, including several retakes with him. Editor Lawrence told me: "We had hundreds of feet of [additional] battle scenes. But some people wanted it in the picture and some people didn't."

4. The Battle Over the Editing

Evidence I have collected over several years strongly suggests that Trumbo and Douglas were determined to build their film around the Large Spartacus but that Universal deliberately censored this concept during and after the editing process in order to keep *Spartacus* within acceptable and long-established limits of the country's political climate. Despite vigorous objections by Trumbo, Douglas, and Kubrick, Universal's attitude resulted in the elimination of nearly a dozen dialogue and action sequences that would have indicated that Spartacus' rebellion might actually have succeeded in destroying Rome. These cuts included such slave victory scenes as the "Battle of Luceria," the "Battle Map Metapontum," and the lengthier "Battle of Metapontum." Four additional sequences were slated for elimination but later restored thanks to the determined resistance of the filmmakers and the fortuitous opposition of the Catholic Legion of Decency. Unlike conventional cuts imposed by studio censors for language, sex, violence, and nudity, these political excisions were intended wholly to eliminate Trumbo's concept of the Large Spartacus and replace it with the Small or, at best, a "Medium" Spartacus.

With millions of dollars, inflated egos, and dearly held political convictions at stake, every big-budget film is a compromise among writer, director, producer, and studio. In the case of *Spartacus*, the struggle between Douglas and studio boss Ed Muhl over the final content of the film became so bitter that even thirty years later Muhl agreed to speak with me only on the condition that we would not discuss conflicts between the personalities involved. For his part, Douglas complained bitterly in his autobiography about studio interference in several films his production company, Bryna Productions, produced with Universal's financial backing and distribution. More than a quarter century after *Spartacus* Douglas was still so frustrated with the studio censors'

25   Yakima Canutt and Oliver Drake, *Stuntman: The Autobiography of Yakima Canutt* (1979; rpt. Norman: University of Oklahoma Press, 1997), 194.

elimination of the "oysters and snails" scene that he reproduced it in its entirety in the chapter on the making of the film in his autobiography.[26]

According to Muhl, Universal watched *Spartacus* closely "because it needed watching." The studio appointed Marshall Green as assistant director to keep a close eye on Kubrick while Muhl's right-hand man, Universal's creative director Mel Tucker, viewed all the dailies, worked closely with producer Lewis, conferred frequently with Muhl himself, and even accompanied Kubrick to Spain to keep the young director within budget. As Muhl told me, when necessary he himself directly intervened to assert his ultimate authority. *Spartacus* underwent sweeping changes during the editing process, particularly in the section between the beginning of the slaves' trek across Italy and the end of their victorious march at the seaport of Brundisium. According to supervising editor Irving Lerner, the struggle over the final content of the film became so intense that Universal executives, in an unprecedented move, periodically came into the editing room and ordered him to reinstate or delete individual scenes, thereby overriding Douglas's instructions. As a result, a number of scenes, particularly those featuring Charles Laughton, went in and out several times. The process of arriving at a final cut on which Lerner, Douglas, Kubrick, and Muhl could even temporarily agree dragged on for so long that Lerner was finally forced to quit *Spartacus* in order to begin directing, as scheduled, a film of his own.[27]

In January, 1960, the filmmakers made their opening move. They inserted a six-second battle scene, the "Battle of Luceria" that depicted Spartacus' first great victory over the Roman army, into the film after the first big slave march from Mt. Vesuvius to Luceria.[28] At the same time they decided to include the Battle Map, using the rejected battle footage from Spain as well as titles naming the sites of a series of great slave victories.[29] To this end they inserted a ten-second sequence, probably containing more Spanish battle scenes, titled "Battle Map Metapontum" that followed the slaves' second march from Luceria to Metapontum.[30]

There is also some evidence to suggest that following Canutt's five days of shooting in early February, the filmmakers decided to use a much

26   Douglas, *The Ragman's Son*, 303–334 ("The Wars of Spartacus").

27   Irving Lerner, uncredited supervising editor on *Spartacus*, in June 29, 1960, interview with David Chandler (*The Year of Spartacus*, 3 and 17).

28   "*Spartacus*: Music Notes, Revised II," (Reel 18, Ft. No. 000–009).

29   "*Spartacus*: Revised Final Screenplay" (January 16, 1959, with revisions through March 27, 1959), Scene 248-E.

30   "*Spartacus*: Music Notes, Revised II" (Reel 18, Ft. No. 521–536).

longer battle-map montage in place of the Battle of Luceria and the Battle Map Metapontum. In a post-production scheduling memorandum dated February 12, 1960, to Muhl, Universal's creative head Mel Tucker, producer Lewis, and editor Lawrence, Universal Editorial Department Chief Sid Lund requested: "the number, design and timing of the map inserts for the battle sequences should be finalized as soon as possible." Lund does not specifically remember this memorandum but, as he told me, if it made such a reference, "then the facts at the time had to support it." However, some time over the next two months Kubrick seems to have developed doubts about using Trumbo's concept of battle montages with map inserts to dramatize Spartacus' series of victories over the Romans. This device had been employed in quite a number of historical films. Kubrick, who had successfully campaigned for a full-scale rendition of the final battle, probably concluded that using the available battle footage in a full-blown version of Spartacus' great victory at Metapontum and combining it with the original ten-second battle map would be a far more effective way to engage the audience in the slave army's struggles against the Roman legions.

The post-editing music notes of April 13, 1960, drafted right after the edited version of the film had been shown to the Universal executives from New York, reveal that the six-second Battle of Luceria had by then been dropped from the film, the ten-second Battle Map Metapontum had been reinstated, and a new scene depicting the Battle of Metapontum had been slated to be inserted as part of a series of major changes between the beginning of the slaves' victorious campaign at Mt. Vesuvius and their arrival at the sea. This new battle sequence, for which composer North wrote a pencil sketch score entitled "Battle of Metapontum," is cited by its cue without the usual description of the accompanying action but with the annotation "Not in as yet." The march into Metapontum features scenes of thousands of slave soldiers parading through the town. Later, in the existing scene at the Roman baths, several senators express their shock and incredulity when they learn of the loss of 19,000 men at Metapontum. To be used in conjunction with this dialogue and action, the Battle of Metapontum had to have been on a grand scale.[31]

Over the next six weeks a number of cut scenes and sequences were reinstated, and the revised film was screened again for the top Universal

31 "*Spartacus*: Music Notes" (April 13, 1960), Reels 16B and 17B; interviews with North's collaborator Mark McGurty and orchestrators Henry Brandt and Sid Raiman. McGurty immediately recognized the music cue title "Battle of Metapontum" and commented that "it was a whole lot longer than eight seconds."

publicity people. These reinserted sequences included the crucial Balcony Scene, in which Gracchus permanently alienates Caesar by suggesting that, to judge from his unprecedented record of success, Spartacus might well defeat Crassus and perhaps take Rome itself, a prospect he prefers to the death of the Republic at the hands of Crassus. But by the end of April, the Battle of Metapontum had been eliminated from the film.

At the filmmakers' insistence, an eight-second version of the Battle Map Metapontum was completed in time for June previews. This version included Saul Bass's map and a series of titles superimposed over scenes from the film, possibly those from the deleted six-second Battle of Luceria. Production assistant Stan Margulies, who oversaw the production of the new battle map, could not recall whether these scenes consisted of marching or of battle sequences, although a battle map without battles is a bit of a contradiction. As he told me, his inclination is that the titles represented the sites of Spartacus' important victories.[32]

Significantly, the Final Shooting Script of September 14, 1959, composed after principal shooting had been completed, the Revised Music Notes (April 13, 1960), the Continuity for the Final Preview on June 20, and the Continuity for the version shown to the press on July 26, all indicate that the two legions sent against the slaves were ordered to intercept and destroy them, in the words of Senator Gracchus, "at the city of Luceria," the site of the second slave camp scene and of the bathing scene in which Varinia informs Spartacus that she is pregnant. In the version of September 14, 1959, Gracchus' speech to the senate was combined with an earlier senate scene and came before the Luceria camp scene. It tied in directly with the Battle of Luceria sequence which was inserted immediately before that scene in January, 1960. But in the later versions the Battle of Luceria was deleted and Gracchus' speech was split off from the earlier senate scene and inserted shortly after the Luceria camp scene. But Luceria represented the starting point of the march south that the Battle Map Metapontum illustrated. Similarly, both the music notes and the continuity later referred to a major Roman defeat at Metapontum, over a hundred miles south of Luceria and on the slaves' way to Brundisium. Clearly the filmmakers intended the Metapontum map to dramatize a series of slave victories in just the way that Trumbo had indicated in his Revised Final Script of March 27, 1959, leading up

32   Letter from James Pollak, National Screen Service, to Stan Margulies (May 27, 1960), as told me by Margulies.

to the climactic Battle of Metapontum.[33] Composer North devoted the first six seconds of his cue entitled "Metapontum Triumph" to four crescendos that probably corresponded to titles flashed on the screen that named the sites of slave victories. These comprise the music for the Battle Map and can still be heard as the opening bars of the film's overture.[34]

After the Final Previews the film was handed over to Universal. Before the press screening on July 26, 1960, the studio unilaterally eliminated the Metapontum Map and the Balcony Scene as part of a series of forty-two wide-ranging cuts and trims, made, as Muhl told me, "for content, not for length."[35] Some time after the press screening, Gracchus' words to the senate about sending two legions to intercept Spartacus "at the city of Luceria" were overdubbed by another actor to become "the city of Metapontum." This change reduced the slave army's series of four or five victories to one, which was itself never shown. With the cutting of the Battle Map Metapontum and the Battle of Metapontum, the entire triumphal march into Metapontum that followed was rendered meaningless and the last vestige of the true magnitude of Spartacus' achievements was eliminated.

The studio cuts might have met with more determined resistance if all the filmmakers, except for Douglas, had not departed for new projects and were probably unaware of what was taking place. Still, editor Lawrence sensed that *Spartacus* was long even for first-run theaters and might be cut by the studio. He was horrified at what he discovered later: "all my notes, all the script notes: Gone. Gone. They were just thrown out. All the trims, all the should-we-or shouldn't-we stuff, all the 'Stanley says hold onto it but Kirk doesn't like it.' All that kind of stuff, beautifully labeled and ready: Gone."[36] Composer North was still on the scene and protested against the damage the cuts were doing to a number of his

33 "*Spartacus*: Final Shooting Script" (September 14, 1959; this is actually a cutter's continuity in the form of a script), Scene 248-Z; "*Spartacus*: Music Notes" (April 13, 1960), Reel 17A; "Combined Continuity on *Spartacus*" (June 20, 1960), Reel 9A, page 3 no. 19; "Continuity and Dialogue on *Spartacus*" (July 26, 1960), Reel 8B, page 3 no. 20.

34 According to Gordon Thiel, director of the UCLA Music Library, in interview with me; Alex North Manuscripts, UCLA Music Library: *Spartacus*, Orchestrated Score for "Metapontum Triumph" music cue; Overture on Criterion Collection edition.

35 Cf. "*Spartacus*: Music Notes" (April 13, 1960), Reel 17B; "Post-Final Preview Cutting Sheet," item 32; "Combined Continuity on *Spartacus*" (June 20, 1960), Reel 9A, page 3 no. 19 (25 ft. = 16 2/3 seconds); "Continuity and Dialogue on *Spartacus*" (July 26, 1960), Reel 8B, page 3 no. 20 (13 1/2 ft. = 9 seconds); cut = 11 1/2 ft. = 7 2/3 seconds.

36 Quoted from Henry Sheehan, "The Fall and Rise of *Spartacus*," *Film Comment*, 27 no. 2 (March–April, 1991), 57–58, 60, and 63; quotation at 60.

music cues. When he learned that additional cuts were being made he dictated the following scathing telephone message to producer Lewis:

> Since we spoke there have been additional cuts in Kitchen No. One, Forest Meeting and Luceria Camp [scenes]. This complete disregard and disrespect for me and for my contribution by persons not qualified in any artistic levels [are] an insult to my abilities. The illogical picayune cuts force me to suggest you hire a butcher and remove my name from screen credits. With my background and reputation I do not intend to participate in amateur night.[37]

Ten days after the press screening and following eight months of deliberation, the studio, encouraged by a favorable ruling from the Screenwriters Guild, announced that Trumbo would receive credit as the sole author of the screenplay. Universal thus became the first major studio openly and, as events would prove, successfully to challenge the blacklist.

5. Covert Censorship of *Spartacus*

At the same time that almost all of Spartacus' historically significant actions were being eliminated, almost all the reactions to them were eliminated as well. These cuts not only reduced the film's dramatic impact but in some cases also seriously damaged its internal logic, as the following examples demonstrate.

Spartacus Bargains with the Pirate Tigranes after the Battle of Luceria

This added scene, written by Trumbo as part of the retakes and originally inserted after the first big slave march from Vesuvius to Luceria, contained the following lines, addressed by Tigranes to Spartacus:

> Of course it pleases Roman vanity to think you're noble. They shrink from the idea that a slave can beat them. Keep on winning and they'll elevate you to the rank of a prince! . . . The party of Gracchus is in difficulty because the Senate can find no one to defeat you. Therefore the party of Crassus delights in every victory you win . . . But you – you can't actually believe you're going to win? With the endless armies Rome can muster

---

37   Quoted from North's typed telephone message to Lewis.

against you? . . . Surely you understand you're going to lose. You have no chance. The world is too small for you. Every power on earth will fight you. Even the enemies of Rome will turn against you if you show promise of success . . . They'll butcher you to the last man, woman and child."[38]

A few days after being shot, this scene was shifted back to just before the slaves' first battle on Mt. Vesuvius. Nearly all the dialogue was replaced by retakes or eliminated.[39]

Discussion of the Battle of Metapontum

This sequence, the opening section of the scene in the Roman baths, contained the following dialogue by Roman senators about the defeat at Metapontum:

LAELIUS: What news from Metapontum?
SYMMACHUS: Heralds are crying the news now. We lost nineteen thousand men including Commodius and all his officers!
LAELIUS: Nineteen thousand! . . . It takes us five years to train a legion. How can this Spartacus train an army in seven months? There's something wrong. Something very wrong.

Eliminated from the film's first rough cut, this sequence was restored as a result of an eloquent plea by Trumbo in his Report. It survived as the only specific reference to a major slave victory that is still in the film today.[40]

Spartacus' Speech to the Slaves by the Sea

A cutting sheet dated March 2, 1959, reads "dialogue out" in reference to Spartacus' lines:

38 Trumbo, "Retakes, With Notes and Old Scenes For Comparison" (October 1959), 22, and 24–27.
39 *Spartacus*: daily production reports of January 22, 25, 28, and 29, 1960; "*Spartacus*: Music Notes, Revised II," Reel 18, Ft. No. 000; "*Spartacus*: Present Edited Continuity of Completed Picture" (October 2, 1959), Seq. No. 53; Trumbo, "Report on *Spartacus*," section II, 32.
40 Trumbo, "Report on *Spartacus*," section II, 42–43; "Projection Room Notes: Running With Mr. Douglas" (November 12, 1959); *Spartacus*: "Roman Bath Sequence"; "Dialogue Continuity on *Spartacus*" (April 18, 1960), Reel 17, page 3.

We've traveled a long ways together. We fought many battles. Won great victories. Now instead of returning to our homes across the sea, we must fight again . . . I'd rather be here, a free man among brothers, facing a long march and hard fight, than to be the richest man in Rome. Fat with food he didn't work for, and surrounded by slaves.[41]

The heart of Spartacus' speech to the slaves, these lines ultimately remained in the film despite the initial order to cut them. But without the battle scenes to which they refer, most of their impact was lost.

The Panic in Rome

A sequence depicting defeated legionaries limping back into Rome while a terrified citizenry begins to flee the city was meant to convey the fact that Spartacus' revolt reached such proportions that it precipitated a panic. This in turn led to the installation of a quasi-dictatorship, the beginning of the end of Roman democracy. As a result of Trumbo's Report, this sequence was reinstated on the "Present Edited Continuity of Completed Picture" as one of the Added Studio Scenes to be shot as part of the retakes approved at a top-level studio meeting on October 10, 1959. It appeared three weeks later on the "Revised Music Notes" of November 2, 1959, marked "Scene Missing." It is unclear whether it was ever actually shot. It never appeared in studio documents again.[42]

The Senate Appoints Crassus

A scene intended to follow the preceding contained dialogue in which the senate offers Crassus the command against the slaves and warns him that, if he does not accept, Rome will fall to Spartacus. To this prospect Crassus reacts with indifference. Shot, according to Trumbo, as part of the retakes, the scene was never used.[43]

---

41   "*Spartacus*: Cutting Notes" (March 2, 1960); "Speech on Beach" (Reel 19); "Dialogue Continuity on *Spartacus*," Reel 19, pages 1–2.

42   "*Spartacus*, 2nd Draft Screenplay" (September 22, 1958), Scenes 256 and 259–260; Trumbo, "Report on *Spartacus*," section II, 45; "*Spartacus*: Revised Music Notes" (November 5, 1959), 13 (Reel 17); "*Spartacus*: Present Edited Continuity of Completed Picture" (October 2, 1959), Seq. No. 66; Appendix ST [Studio], ST-19.

43   *Additional Dialogue*, 562. A still photograph with caption appears in *Photoplay Studies*, 25 no. 4 (August, 1960), 18.

The Balcony Scene

In a scene which follows Crassus' assumption of power, Gracchus tells an increasingly outraged Caesar: "This Spartacus has quite a talent when it comes to handling an army . . . He's developed such a bad habit of winning that Crassus may not be able to cure him of it . . . If Spartacus wins I intend to ask the Senate to emancipate his whole army." Eliminated from the film's first rough cut, this scene was belatedly restored as a result of Trumbo's "Report" and went in and out several times. Its final elimination by the studio after the Final Previews destroyed the whole motivation for Caesar's defection from his mentor and from republican democracy to Crassus and imperial dictatorship.[44]

The Original Prologue

Part of the first rough-cut flashback version of *Spartacus* contained Crassus' long address to his staff officers on the eve of the final battle. It included these lines: "Nine Roman armies have been destroyed by Spartacus . . . and our defeat will mean the fall of Rome." Cut along with the rest of Crassus' original speech when the flashback was eliminated, these lines were considered to have enough audience appeal to be used as the opening scene of the film's trailer, where they still can be heard.[45]

Spartacus and Varinia's Last Night Together

Spartacus confesses his fear of impending defeat to Varinia:

VARINIA: They've never beaten us yet.
SPARTACUS: No. But no matter how many times we beat them, they always seem to have another army to send against us. And another. Varinia, it's as if we've started something that has no ending.[46]

---

44 "*Spartacus*: Final Shooting Script" (September 14, 1959), Scene 284; Trumbo, "Report on *Spartacus*," section II, 45; "*Spartacus*: Present Edited Continuity of Completed Picture" (October 2, 1959), seq. no. 67–68; Appendix ST, ST-15; "*Spartacus*, Music Notes, Revised II," Reel 20, Ft. No. 237.11; "Dialogue Continuity on *Spartacus*" (April 18, 1960), Reel 19, page 1; "Dialogue Continuity on *Spartacus* (Incorporating Changes)" (June 3, 1960), Reel 18B, pages 2–3; "Combined Continuity on *Spartacus*" (June 20, 1960), Reel 10A, pages 4–5; "Continuity and Dialogue on *Spartacus*" (July 26, 1960), Reel 10A, page 4; "Post-Final Preview Cutting Sheet," item 31.
45 "*Spartacus*: Final Shooting Script," Scene 8.
46 "*Spartacus*: Final Shooting Script," Scene 273.

This is the only specific statement in the film about Spartacus' series of victories that the censors never attempted to cut. It may have resulted from Trumbo's growing uncertainty about the ultimate fate of the modern proletarian revolution. Its tone of hopelessness meshed nicely with the studio's view, despite its unwelcome candor.

The Final Battle

A crucial reaction shot from this sequence remains in the film, in which a visibly dazed and frightened Crassus heaves a surreptitious sigh of relief at the appearance of his allies, Pompey and Lucullus. However, in contradiction to the filmmakers' express written intentions, long-shot and medium-shot takes rather than the close-up take of this shot were used. This obscured Olivier's subtle performance during the film's climactic moments and destroyed the basis for Crassus' lingering anxiety after his victory.[47]

Crassus Walks among the Dead Slaves

This scene originally contained lines expressing Crassus' shock and disbelief at the sight of the mutual love between the fallen slave men and women, a closeness that banished their fear of death and transformed them into a force which he senses will ultimately prevail over the power of Rome. The cutting of these lines without their author's knowledge during the initial filming of this scene provoked some of the bitterest charges of bad faith in Trumbo's entire Report. But despite his vehement protests, they were excluded from subsequent retakes.[48]

A large number of scenes from the first half of the film presaging great military success for the slave army survived beyond the Final Preview. They included "Spartacus' Speech to the Gladiators" after their return to the gladiatorial school, "Spartacus' Greeting to New Recruits on Mt. Vesuvius," "Spartacus Bargains with the Pirate Tigranes" (Second Version), "Spartacus Confronts the Defeated Glabrus," and "Glabrus Reports Back to the Senate." Furthermore, as indicated above, a number of scenes from the second half of the film that built upon or recapitulated the great slave victories also survived, including the triumphal

---

47   *Spartacus*: "Daily Production Report" (December 28, 1959); "*Spartacus*: Additional Shots Beyond The Script Requirements" (December, 1959).

48   "*Spartacus*: Revised Final Screenplay" (January 16, 1959, with revisions through June 1, 1959), Scenes 321–323; Trumbo, "Report on *Spartacus*," section II, 46–47.

"March into Metapontum," "Caesar Discusses Metapontum," "Spartacus' Speech on the Beach" at Brundisium, and "Spartacus and Varinia's Last Night Together." Taken together, they outline the Large Spartacus, the rebel slave who almost defeated Rome. The only remaining source that powerfully illustrates them was the Battle Map Metapontum, which encapsulated in six seconds the action to which the dialogue in all these scenes refers. Once the studio cut that map, the filmmakers' underlying conception of *Spartacus* disappeared.

6. The Attempted Overt Negation of the Film's Message

Not satisfied with the elimination or neutralization of nearly all of the scenes that affirmed the idea of the Large Spartacus, the studio also appears to have forced radical changes in key dialogue in order to make its message unmistakable. Thus, during the last days of 1959, the last scene between Spartacus and Antoninus, in which the key historical question posed by the film is addressed, was retaken. Here is the original:

ANTONINUS: Could we have won, Spartacus? Could we ever have won?
SPARTACUS: Just by fighting them we won something. When even one man says 'No, I won't,' Rome begins to fear. And we were tens of thousands who said it. That was the wonder of it.[49]

In the retake Spartacus replies in the negative, providing an explicit statement of the almost hopeless message which the film still delivers today: "No. That was the wrong fight. We were doomed from the beginning. But it was a beautiful thing."[50] Editor Lawrence remarked about this to me: "this scene was redone because some people wanted the film to express this idea whereas other people wanted to express the original idea." No revolutionary leader could ever have expressed such defeatist ideas, and it is highly unlikely that Trumbo wrote these lines, not least because they completely contradicted Spartacus' subsequent defiant prophecy to Crassus. Referring to the fallen Antoninus, he declares: "Here's your victory. He'll come back. He'll come back and he'll be millions!"

49 Trumbo, "Retakes; With Notes and Old Scenes For Comparison" (October, 1959), 69–70.
50 "Dialogue Continuity on *Spartacus*" (April 18, 1960), Reel 26, page 1; "Combined Continuity on *Spartacus*" (June 20, 1960), Reel 12B, page 5.

The original version of this scene was ultimately restored.[51] Prompted by audience reaction, the filmmakers made a number of changes in Douglas' scenes after the final previews; this may be one of them. But simultaneously a hastily revised version of the film's voice-over prologue was introduced. It contained a new downbeat conclusion:

> Here [in the mines] under whip and chain and sun he [Spartacus] lived out his youth and early manhood and dreamed the death of human servitude. The historians of ancient Rome have recorded the death of his dream, and the utter destruction of his life and all his hopes. Yet his name still lives. And the last vestiges of slavery disappear before our eyes. And the defeat of Spartacus has become the victory of man.[52]

Shortly before the premiere, objections from the Catholic Legion of Decency forced the studio to restore the original prologue, with a new upbeat if anti-historical opening referring to Christianity as a historical force "destined to overthrow the pagan tyranny of Rome." This is the prologue we now have. It ends by reminding the audience that the cause for which Spartacus fought was ultimately victorious by describing Spartacus as "dreaming the death of slavery, two thousand years before it finally *would* die."

7. The Price of Breaking the Blacklist: From Primitive Rebellion to Middle-Class Respectability

Trumbo and Douglas failed to save any of the scenes depicting Spartacus' great victories. Plot and action are the crucial elements in a motion picture, and the plot of *Spartacus* is that of the Small Spartacus. Just as Trumbo predicted, after a promising beginning the result was not only a depressing film but, in large sections, a boring one. As the film's souvenir book states, *Spartacus* is about the life of a "man who led an inspired crusade for freedom against the most powerful state on earth, defeating in bloody battle nine of its best trained armies," but only one of those victories, the tiniest one at that, is ever shown.

---

51   "Continuity and Dialogue on *Spartacus*" (July 26, 1960), Reel 12B, page 4.
52   "Dialogue Continuity on *Spartacus*" (April 18, 1960), Reel 2, page 1; "Combined Continuity on *Spartacus*" (June 20, 1960), Reel 1B, page 1; "Continuity and Dialogue on *Spartacus*" (July 26, 1960), Reel 1B, pages 1–2; program notes on original soundtrack album of *Spartacus*.

Whatever its artistic weaknesses, *Spartacus* went on to break box-office records worldwide. Right-wing opposition from John Wayne and Hedda Hopper helped deny it a nomination for Best Picture, but the film was nominated for six Academy Awards and won four as well as the Golden Globe Award for Best Dramatic Film of the Year. Some of its negative reviews, particularly the devastating one by influential Bosley Crowther in *The New York Times*, show just how close the frightened and duplicitous studio executives came to ruining their own film. According to *Variety*, his review left the Universal bosses "stunned and almost in a state of shock" because he dismissed *Spartacus* as "heroic humbug" that is "pitched about to the level of a lusty schoolboy's taste" and concluded: "too many people, too many cooks had their ladles in this stew, and it comes out a romantic mishmash of a strange episode in history."[53] The film was ultimately saved by the public and by a handful of American liberal critics, who deplored the blacklist and knew what was at stake. But then and now most people would probably agree with film historian John Baxter, who later wrote: "In his novel, Howard Fast had seen Spartacus, the slave revolutionary, as the affirmation of man's ability in all eras to resist dehumanisation . . . But [in the film] Spartacus achieves nothing. His movement flounders in an orgy of torture and death for which Trumbo's hint that his protest will be heard centuries in the future seems a meagre justification."[54]

Kubrick's bitter comment that the film "had everything but a good story" is quite apt. Even Crowther praised the opening gladiatorial training sequence as "lively, exciting and expressive, no matter how true to history it is." But, he went on to complain, "the middle phase is pretentious and tedious, because it is concerned with the dull strife of politics," and we see "an endless amount of simulation of political rivalry in Rome, in which the senators and generals are more confusing and less amusing than those in Washington." Crowther picked the final battle as his favorite sequence. But he concluded that *Spartacus* then "slides off into an anticlimax, wherein a great deal more is made of Miss Simmons' post-war predicament than of the crucifixion of 6,000 captured slaves." The bland banality of large sections of the film fully justifies Kubrick's own disavowal of it. The only exciting scene in the middle of the film is Spartacus' victory over Glabrus and the garrison of Rome. But it is a battle without combat. From all appearances, the slaves overrun a

53 Bosley Crowther, "Screen: Spartacus Enters The Arena," *The New York Times* (October 7, 1960); Entertainment section, 28. Further quotations from this review appear below.
54 John Baxter, *Hollywood in the Sixties* (New York: Barnes, 1972), 159–160.

Roman camp that is virtually deserted and already in flames. Violence, particularly successful violence by the oppressed, has been written out of it.

This was clearly not the kind of story Trumbo wanted to tell. In the first scene between Spartacus and Tigranes his dialogue is calculated to create the suspense needed to sustain the second half of the film. Can Spartacus and the slaves hope to overcome the formidable natural obstacles that block their path as they cross one third of the length of Italy? Can they survive the lethal dangers inherent in "fighting a major battle in every town," as Trigranes says? Is not their cause, as Tigranes contends, doomed from the beginning, or can they make it to the sea and freedom? If so, it will be a miracle. And that is just what Trumbo wanted to say, that Spartacus' heroic campaign was a miracle of the human spirit. The rest of the film was to consist of scenes switching back and forth among the love story, the slave community, and the Roman political struggle, punctuated by a series of bitter battle scenes and the slaves' successive victories over larger and larger Roman armies. Against overwhelming might, they reach Brundisium and, hopefully, freedom. But the intervention of Crassus frustrates their plan. To further his political ambitions, Crassus bribes the pirates, and the slaves are left in the lurch. They must now face the greatest test of all, the combined might of three Roman armies. In the final battle the slave army, resisting the Romans heroically, is destroyed. The aftermath reinforces the bond between the slaves and the man who has led them through their struggle when the survivors refuse to betray Spartacus to the Romans at the price of their own crucifixion.

This was Trumbo's epic plot line, not what we have today. Trumbo saw Spartacus at the outset as almost an animal, an angry, brawling, rebellious slave, reacting to insult and abuse with primitive violence, which erupts in the revolt of the gladiators. Like Fast's, his Spartacus experiences personal growth as he rises to the leadership of the rebellion and deepens his romantic relationship with Varinia. Gradually he begins to understand the hopes and needs of others and finally identifies himself with oppressed humanity's yearning for freedom. Trumbo wanted to make Spartacus into a living symbol of man's passion for freedom:

> We have given Crassus a love of something much bigger than himself: an emotion: his love of Rome. It is for Rome (and his concept of himself in relation to Rome) that all his thought and energy is expended. Just so Spartacus must have a love, an emotion that transcends himself and Varinia: his hatred of slavery, his passion for freedom for them all. We have

given Crassus his passion: but the Small Spartacus has denied Spartacus *his* passion.[55]

But Trumbo could not make Spartacus' ideals apparent through his dialogue. Kubrick's preference for a more visual conception of the character, combined with a desire to put some limits on Trumbo's left-wing predilection, produced a political film with scarcely any politics in it.

The elimination of almost all violent conflict frustrated Trumbo's purpose and sealed the fate of the Large Spartacus. In the early parts of the film Trumbo was able to take Spartacus from a primitive rebel into a charismatic leader with a warm, loveable personality. But what is missing is the original Spartacus, that angry rebel against injustice. Where is the mine slave who hamstrung an overseer with his teeth, the gladiator who desperately fought for his survival in the arena, the enraged rebel who drowned his trainer in a vat of soup, bashed in the brains of one legionary, and stabbed another in the throat? Where are the anger and the passion that are his defining qualities? Spartacus could demonstrate his hatred of injustice and his passion for freedom only in moments of confrontation. But the film eschews all violent confrontation for most of its running time. Spartacus never draws his sword in anger until late in the final battle. The heroic gladiator has practically been emasculated. Instead of fighting arms in hand alongside his men, he rides in on a horse after a battle is virtually over or watches from afar until an emergency forces him to join the fray. He sets tasks for others to perform while he does the thinking. His followers obey him without question. His relationship with Varinia, who is reduced to the status of a supportive wife and mother, becomes conventional. Spartacus seems to have risen from his lowly status only to attain middle-class respectability.

Neither Trumbo nor Kubrick intended to turn Spartacus into a Hollywood cliché. His character was supposed to develop into a mature democratic leader. But without something substantial for him to do, his rival, Crassus, becomes a much more compelling personality almost until the film's final conflict.

8. The Film Builds to an Anticlimax

How the final battle was handled illustrates the two conflicting views of *Spartacus* because, by this time, the slave army itself has become the main

55 Trumbo, "Report on *Spartacus*," section II, 11.

protagonist of the story. Either we view the slaves as innocent and help-less victims of Roman genocide and so perceive Spartacus as a benighted Pied Piper unwittingly leading them to their doom, or we view them as fallen heroes, warriors in a noble cause who, through their heroic sacri-fice, have transcended their own time and place to reach immortality.

Trumbo, of course, fought for the latter alternative. Initially he had argued against showing the final battle on screen. The audience, he maintained, will already know the outcome; what really counts is the aftermath. But once the decision had been made to eliminate the battle montages showing Spartacus' victories, it was inevitable that the final battle scene would have to be included. As Kubrick argued, without at least one major battle this epic would be a complete bore and a box-office bomb.

Thus, while continuing his fight to insert battle scenes or montages, Trumbo also struggled to make the facts surrounding Spartacus' defeat into an even greater measure of his power and importance. In actual history, Crassus suffered several defeats at the hands of the slaves, even resorted to decimating his troops, and wrote to the senate requesting the recall of his rival Pompey from Spain and of Lucullus from Thrace. The clear implication was that without them he could offer no guarantees about the outcome should Spartacus march on Rome. Later, however, his fortunes began to improve as a result of divisions within the slave army. Word reached him that Pompey had crossed the Alps into Northern Italy, and Crassus, according to the ancient biographer Plutarch, was "press-ing forward into action with greater speed than safety" before Pompey "would come and rob him of his glory." As a result, he came perilously close to defeat. During the battle he was forced to show himself in the front lines. Plutarch remarks: "even his best friends thought him, in the words of the comic poet, 'The bravest warrior everywhere but in the field.'"[56] Plutarch also reports that in the battle a heroic Spartacus was

> pushing his way towards Crassus himself through many flying weapons and wounded men, he did not indeed reach him, but slew two centurions who fell upon him together. Finally, after his companions had taken to flight, he stood alone, surrounded by a multitude of foes, and was still defending himself when he was cut down.[57]

56 Plutarch, *Comparison of Nicias and Crassus* 3.2 and 6; the quotations are taken from *Plutarch's Lives*, tr. Bernadotte Perrin; vol. 3 (Cambridge: Harvard University Press / London: Heinemann, 1916; several rpts.), 431 and 433. Cf. Plutarch, *Crassus* 11.2 and 7–8.
57 Plutarch, *Crassus* 11.7 (quoted from Perrin, 349).

The historian Appian even adds that Spartacus, wounded in the thigh and down on his knees, continued to defend himself against his attackers but was eventually killed.[58] The ancient writer Athenaeus says flatly that if Spartacus had not been killed in this battle with Crassus he would have posed a major threat to the Romans.[59]

Taking a few liberties with history, Trumbo insisted that the slave army be overcome by the combined might of the three armies of Crassus, Pompey, and Lucullus rather than by Crassus alone. His objective was to make clear that, had the armies of Pompey and Lucullus failed to arrive in time, Spartacus would have defeated Crassus and perhaps taken Rome. In the concluding section of the film, the feelings and actions of all the main characters, especially Crassus, are predicated on this fundamental premise. The dialogue that Trumbo wrote to precede the final battle was meant to lend credibility to this idea. Following his original Final Screenplay, the first rough cut of *Spartacus* was constructed in the form of a flashback from the eve of this battle, with an opening scene, now appearing late in the film, of Crassus and his aides galloping into the Roman army camp. Inside his command tent, Crassus receives his officers' briefing and surprisingly informs them that all dispositions are to be changed. He then launches into a summary – known as the film's Original Prologue – of the course of the war up to this point. His words were the film's definitive statement of Spartacus' historic stature:

> Nine Roman armies have been destroyed by Spartacus because they went out to fight slaves. Unless I am able to persuade you that the enemy we engage tomorrow is as formidable and skillful as any that you have met in your entire military career . . . then we too shall be defeated. And our defeat will mean the fall of Rome. The question is this: Why has a rabble of slaves been able to destroy the best troops the world ever saw? To answer that question you must understand that rabble. And most particularly, you must understand the man who commands them.[60]

Crassus informs his officers that he has been collecting information about Spartacus since the outbreak of the slave revolt and starts to recount what he knows of the life of the slave leader, beginning with his years spent as a youth in the mines. The scene then shifts to these mines, and the film's story begins. Late in the film, the action returns to Crassus' tent as he finishes his account and dismisses his staff.

58   Appian, *The Civil Wars* 1.14.120.
59   Athenaeus, *The Sophists at Dinner* 6.272–273.
60   "*Spartacus*: Final Shooting Script" (September 14, 1959), Scene 8.

During the rewriting and re-editing that followed the acceptance of Trumbo's Report, it was decided to eliminate the flashback and to open the film directly in the mines with a new voice-over prologue. The original opening was shifted and combined with its continuation late in the film. At Trumbo's insistence, Olivier returned to shoot some new lines for this scene in which he referred to the anticipated arrival of Pompey and Lucullus.

Even as other new scenes containing Large-Spartacus dialogue were being filmed, the "nine Roman armies" dialogue from the Original Prologue was eliminated from the scene just described. Reportedly this was done because the story told up to that scene could stand on its own without a verbal introduction. However, as we have seen, during further editing that story was deprived of its essential elements, the Battle Map and Battle of Metapontum that showed the destruction of those nine armies. The result was a complete reversal of the tone and meaning of the film as it builds to its climax. Instead of anxious expectation, we get assurance of an easy victory. This nearly ruins all of Olivier's efforts in this and the succeeding scene to reveal Crassus' anxiety and frustration. His second-in-command declares: "Sir, I think we can pledge you the most glorious victory of your career!" In itself this amounts to a back-handed testimonial to the historic stature of Spartacus. But Crassus slams the table with his rod and roars back at him: "I'm not after glory! I'm after Spartacus! And, gentlemen, I mean to have him. But this campaign is not alone to kill Spartacus . . . It is to kill the *legend* of Spartacus." Then, sensing that it may already be too late to destroy that legend, Crassus dismisses his officers and falls into a despondent funk, only to be roused by the arrival of Batiatus. Olivier's performance, which helped Peter Ustinov win his Oscar, is lost on an audience which remains almost completely unaware that Spartacus has achieved anything of historic significance.

Without Crassus' enumeration of and reaction to the slave army's accomplishments, most of the suspense now dissolves. The result is a foregone conclusion. All the time, money, and effort expended to film the only real battle in *Spartacus* are largely wasted because, as Trumbo predicted, the audience knows perfectly well what the outcome is going to be. In this context, Crassus' rueful references to the legend of Spartacus become ludicrous. The attempt to make the battle more exciting by having it appear during its opening moments that the slaves are winning falls flat because there are no close-ups of Crassus reacting with fear as his battle plans go awry when the slaves put his advance guard to flight, break through his lines, and engage his legionaries one on one. The appearance of the armies of Pompey and Lucullus almost immediately after the fighting has begun quickly kills any hope – equally on the part of the slaves and of the viewers – that Spartacus' army might somehow still win.

Trumbo's idea about three Roman armies was a dramatic device, devoid of historical validity but designed to explain to the audience how a heroic slave army, led by a genius like Spartacus and fighting in a noble cause, could finally be vanquished after destroying nine Roman armies. The elimination from the film of any depiction or even mention of these nine Roman disasters made this device backfire. Instead of serving as a measure of Crassus' fear of the slave army, the vast extent of the forces he mobilizes against them simply demonstrates the overwhelming superiority of Roman military power which no rebellion, no matter how inspired or justified, can hope to challenge. This fatalistic vision is the very opposite of the theme of Fast's novel and Trumbo's script: that no empire, regardless of its power, can ultimately prevail over the force of man's passion for freedom.

9. The Film's Greatest Performance Is Destroyed

The elimination of the Battle of Metapontum, the Battle Map, and the Original Prologue not only gravely weakened the dramatic impact of the final battle but also thoroughly undermined the motivation for Laurence Olivier's subtle portrayal of Crassus. Crassus embodies the delusions of grandeur of the decadent Roman aristocracy, based on its military conquests, and its fear of the human spoils of those conquests, the slaves. This fear remains dormant only as long as the victims accept their fate. As soon as some form of rebellion or resistance develops, however, it surfaces. Those supposedly safe and powerful realize that they have become vulnerable, so they are determined ruthlessly to crush any form of opposition. This is part of the explanation for the paradox of how a military power that had conquered large parts of the world could have nearly been destroyed by the most pathetic victims of that conquest.

The slave owners also believe in their natural superiority over other races as evidenced particularly on the battlefield. For them, power becomes its own justification. Moreover, slave owners whose entire existence is bound up with the violent conquest of other peoples and with the exaction of obedience through intimidation lose their ability to give and receive genuine affection. The price for their grandeur is the loss of the power to love or to be worthy of love. As Varinia reminds Crassus, love cannot be bought or compelled by force but must be given freely.

These barely concealed tensions come to a head during the final battle. As a modern historian summarized Crassus' campaign some time ago:

> Crassus . . . was sent with six legions against Spartacus. His mission was not an easy one, and he was frequently outgeneraled by the slave; but after suffering several humiliating defeats he destroyed the main body of Spartacus' troops. The last survivors of the slave revolt attempted to escape from Italy but were destroyed by Pompey, who came upon them as he was returning from Spain. Pompey thereupon claimed credit for saving Rome. This claim intensified the jealousy that had separated Crassus and Pompey . . . Moreover, military defeat at the hands of a slave brought a stigma that Crassus could never forget and that darkened his mind for many years to come.[61]

So Trumbo intended the final battle to be *the* traumatic event which sends Crassus into a rampage of senseless cruelty and a pathetic attempt to compete with Spartacus for the love of Varinia. But the film fails to realize Trumbo's intention because there is nothing to convey the idea that Crassus experienced any fear during that battle. It has close-ups of Spartacus directing his army and fighting, but the feelings and reactions of Crassus are absent from this climactic confrontation between the film's two main antagonists.

During the shooting of the retakes following Trumbo's Report, two new shots of Crassus and his staff watching the battle were filmed: the first when the slaves ignite their rolling barricades, thus upsetting the Roman battle plan; the second at the arrival of Pompey and Lucullus that turns the tide against the slaves. The medium close-ups obscure Crassus' anxious reactions to these decisive moments. Here Trumbo missed the opportunity to characterize the real motivation of Crassus' fear. Instead, he spent his efforts on some lines to be said by Crassus about the heroism of the slave women and the love among the slaves. Trumbo believed that the message of these lines was crucial, so he was horrified when, without his knowledge, they were cut from the script:

> I cannot find words to tell you my horror that Olivier's lines relative to the slave women fighting alongside their men and dying in the battle, and to

---

61   Joseph Ward Swain, *The Ancient World*, vol. 2: *The World Empires: Alexander and the Romans After 334 B.C.* (1950; rpt. New York: Harper and Row, 1962), 304–305.

the quality of love among slaves which is to him, such a profound mystery, were not even shot.

If, after all the effort that went into the writing of what could have been an absolutely superb moment . . . a moment essential to the intellectual and spiritual comprehension of what this film is about . . . if these were cut from the script before shooting, and if no one consulted me about the cut (which no one did) then I charge bad faith ...

For the cutting of these lines before they reach film represents a final and irrevocable step in the total elimination of women from this film; the total downgrading of the moral and heroic quality of the slave rebellion: in the castration of Spartacus as a character of any consequence in the film: in an obsession with the Small View of Spartacus as almost to represent a conspiracy, a vulgar conspiracy to kill any distinction which this film might have had.

If we have these lines on film they should by all means go back into the picture.[62]

Kubrick preserved part of what Trumbo was trying to convey. As the camera tracks across the battlefield, the peace and serenity on the faces of the dead slaves, many of them locked in a last embrace, powerfully conveys their nobility, courage, and love.

Trumbo intended Crassus, coming face to face with the heroism and nobility of the slaves in their finest hour, to become frightened and angry. He recoils from the contrast between their simple humanity and the emotional barrenness of his own life, an emptiness he has tried to suppress through his compulsive struggle for wealth and power. His victory has not brought him any peace of mind. Crassus also senses that, without the arrival of Pompey and Lucullus, the slaves might well have defeated him. Trumbo's Crassus was meant to struggle with a new sense of the criminal, morally indefensible, and ultimately doomed social system he has just barely managed to preserve. But in this struggle he fails. In his final confrontation with Spartacus and his utter contempt, Crassus loses all his illusions. He now believes that Spartacus and what he represents will eventually win. In the defiant face of his adversary Crassus sees the future destruction of the edifice of power that he identifies with. Faced with the genuine greatness of Spartacus, his own delusions of grandeur shrink to insignificance.

As originally released and even as restored, the film conveys hardly any of this. Olivier's performance has been robbed of all psychological motivation at key moments. Trumbo's concentration on Crassus' lines as

62 Trumbo, "Report on *Spartacus*," section II, 46–47.

he surveys the dead slaves resulted in a lack of attention to Crassus' much more palpable fear of Spartacus and the slaves while they were alive. This misplacement of emphasis probably stemmed from Trumbo's confusion about the primary cause of the terror that the slave revolt inspired in the Roman ruling class. His emphasis on the moral and psychological threat the slaves posed to Rome rather than on the danger of the Romans' destruction flowed from his underlying belief that, short of a general uprising, the slave army never had a chance at ultimate victory. Trumbo made this explicit in a dialogue between Crassus and Caesar, trying to transform the slaves' crushing defeat into some kind of moral victory:

CRASSUS: I want no grave, no marker for him. His body's to be burnt and his ashes scattered in secret.
CAESAR: Did you fear him, Crassus?
CRASSUS: Not when I fought him. For I knew he could be beaten. But *now* I fear him. Even more than I fear you.

But these lines turn the filmmakers' intentions and history on their heads. The fear inspired by Spartacus when he was alive remained in the minds of his adversaries for generations after his death. The film's emphasis on the moral and symbolic dimension of Spartacus' challenge derives from the hidden message of non-resistance and otherworldly resignation that is implicit in the Prologue with its assertion that only Christianity would overthrow slavery.

The historic legacy of Spartacus and the underlying theme of Fast's novel and Trumbo's screenplay affirmed a faith that remains true today, as we know in the wake of the Vietnam war and the war in Afghanistan against the Soviet Union: that oppressed peoples can rise to challenge all-powerful empires and win. Sadly, the film as released delivered the opposite message: that those who dare to rebel will be crushed. *Spartacus* leaves us with some faint hope for the future, as Varinia and Spartacus' newborn son escape to freedom. Universal produced a film that pleads with the audience to remember the truth about what Spartacus dreamed of while burying the truth about what he actually achieved.

10. From Restoration to Reconstruction

The restoration of *Spartacus* at a length of 197 minutes appeared in 1991. Perhaps, if director Stanley Kubrick had gained enough control during production to include his plot enhancements concerning the political struggles within the slave community between idealistic Spartacus and opportunistic Crixus, the film's story might have cohered and succeeded better. But executive producer Kirk Douglas, not Stanley Kubrick, was the real auteur of *Spartacus*, and in the end Douglas canceled these additions at the urging of screenwriter Dalton Trumbo. Douglas's and Trumbo's own heroic conception for *Spartacus* was in turn later reduced by Universal Studios.

Viewers and scholars may differ on whether the restored film as it stands today adequately conveys Douglas's concept of Spartacus as "the slave whose vision of freedom almost overthrew the Roman Empire." There is a significant body of dialogue in the film which gives that impression by anticipating or referring to Spartacus' great military victories over the Romans. However, the nearly complete absence of the battle action to which this dialogue refers seriously weakens the film's impact. In the words of its restorer, Robert Harris: "if we are speaking of the Large and the Small [Spartacus], then if you want the Large Spartacus, you've got to have the battle montage [showing the slaves' victories]."[63] The inclusion of deleted battle scenes, such as the Battle of Luceria, the Battle of Metapontum, and the Battle Map Metapontum, in the restored version of the film would have improved it significantly by injecting excitement into its middle section and strengthening its historical image of Spartacus.

The last two decades have seen numerous restored versions of classic films which included some lost or censored footage that had not been part of the final cut or of the version in wide distribution after the premiere. There have also been restored versions that were termed "directors' cuts," in which the director chose to add scenes to a new version that had never appeared in the original, either because of cuts imposed by the studio or because budgetary constraints prevented them from being shot. Some directors' cuts have significantly improved some of these films, which now more clearly express their creators' intentions.

The restoration of *Spartacus* contained some lost scenes, particularly a homoerotic seduction scene. These added scenes, together with the beautifully restored cinematography and soundtrack, enhanced the film as a work of popular art and ensures its future preservation in a form close to its original release. But for *Spartacus*, the question of whether or not to attempt a true director's or, in this case, auteur's cut, takes on

---

63 Quoted from interview with me and Gary Crowdus.

particular importance. Many of the film's admirers hoped that the 1991 restoration would serve as a director's cut. Restorer Harris had hoped to use many deleted scenes which, however, were never found because almost all of the many scenes cut from *Spartacus* had been destroyed and because the negative of the Final Preview version had been cut in dozens of places early in the process of making the black and white separations that Harris later used for his restoration.

If Harris had found any of the lost battle scenes, he would undoubtedly have included them. There have been some unconfirmed rumors that some lost scenes were clandestinely rescued and sent for safekeeping to a now deceased archivist at a major national film library. But the chances that any further lost or unused footage would be uncovered seem remote. Even if Douglas had considered joining the growing list of directors and auteurs who have produced personal versions of their films, there appeared to be almost no additional footage which could be used to construct such a cut.

Faced with similar situations, many directors have inserted new scenes which were not shot at the time the original film was made. In some cases they were produced especially for the director's cut, as in the case of Steven Spielberg's *Close Encounters of the Third Kind: The Special Edition* (1980; original version, 1977), with a Collector's Edition prepared by Spielberg following in 1998. Most famously, George Lucas made significant changes for a redone version of his first *Star Wars* trilogy. For the restoration of *Spartacus* the missing sound for the "oysters and snails" scene was re-dubbed by Tony Curtis and Anthony Hopkins, the latter standing in for the deceased Laurence Olivier. For some films new scenes were borrowed from other films. The 2004 television remake of *Spartacus*, directed by Robert Dornhelm, contains numerous battle scenes, but the different aspect ratios of the two films and the different looks of Kubrick's and Dornhelm's battle scenes rule out any borrowing for a reconstruction of the original *Spartacus*.

Such awkward measures are no longer necessary for a reconstruction of *Spartacus*. The key to bringing the filmmakers' original conception back to the screen is the reconstruction of the six-second Battle of Luceria from the working version of January, 1960, and the eight-second Battle Map Metapontum from the Final Preview version. Such a reconstruction has become practicable because the final seven seconds of battle footage which closes the teaser trailer of the film, footage which was originally meant to be used in the final battle, appears nowhere in the film we have today. This footage consists of a one-second close-up of

Spartacus signaling his army to attack, followed by about six seconds of footage showing the front ranks of the charging slave army from the Roman legions' point of view. These scenes may have been used as the opening master shots of the now lost Battle of Metapontum. Their only drawback is the majestic letters of the title *Spartacus*, which appear one by one across the screen during the final five seconds of the shot of the slave attack. But computer restoration programs can remove these letters and fill in the resulting blank spaces with convincing projections of the preceding and succeeding footage. The same programs can extend the attack shot for as many more seconds as required by looping back to a point near its beginning. The resultant scene could be inserted as a reconstructed Battle of Luceria, immediately followed by a reconstructed Battle Map Metapontum, from Saul Bass's original design, that shows the slaves' line of march south from Luceria to Metapontum. The map would be superimposed over a re-run of the slaves' charge in the background. The eight-second score for the Battle Map Metapontum that opens the film's overture, with its four crescendos, could provide musical accompaniment. The first four of the five titles from the Battle Montage in Trumbo's "Spartacus: Revised Final Screenplay," with changes through March 27, 1959 (Scene 248-D), all naming the sites of Spartacus' great victories –

LUCERIA
CANUSIUM
VENUSIA
POTENTA
METAPONTUM

– could be flashed on the screen in time with the musical crescendos. Finally, the closing phrase of Gracchus' preceding speech ("and assign two legions to intercept and destroy Spartacus at the city of Metapontum") are to be replaced by the original version from the final preview (". . . at the city of Luceria"). The resulting sequence of fifteen seconds is to be inserted between Gracchus' speech and the opening of the current triumphal sequence which already bears the on-screen title METAPONTUM. The film's intermission, which was shifted several times during the editing, is to come immediately after the march into Metapontum. This focuses the audience's attention on the zenith of Spartacus' successes and builds up his image, especially in anticipation of his coming confrontation with Crassus.

Insertion of the reconstructed Battle of Luceria and Battle Map Metapontum provides the minimum action necessary to resuscitate Douglas's Large Spartacus. It also permits the addition of the vital opening scene from the trailer, taken from the film's original rough cut, in which Crassus tells his staff officers: "Nine Roman armies have been destroyed . . . by Spartacus. And our defeat would mean the fall of Rome." This fits easily into the current section of the scene in which Crassus turns to face his staff and so replaces his present lines: "Spartacus has every reason to believe that he has outdistanced the pursuing armies of Pompey and Lucullus." The restored dialogue also feeds logically into his next lines:

> However, there are passes through the Apennines unknown to any man. It may fortify your courage to know that the army of Pompey is encamped some twenty miles to the west of us and that the army of Lucullus is approaching this position by forced night march.

All this provides the rationale for the succeeding dialogue about Crassus winning the most glorious victory of his career and killing the legend of Spartacus.

This reconstructed sequence conveys Douglas's and Trumbo's vision of the historical stature of Spartacus, brings his character into clearer focus, provides credibility for Crassus and Batiatus in their next scene, and creates the necessary suspense as the action leads up to the final battle.

In addition, there are three reaction shots of Crassus during the final battle, done as medium or long shots, which put him too far away from the viewers for Crassus' anxiety to be noticeable. Computer technology can bring these shots closer in order to express Douglas's concept that, had Pompey and Lucullus not arrived in time, Spartacus might have won. They also allow the audience fully to comprehend Olivier's performance in the aftermath of the battle, particularly in Crassus' final confrontation with Spartacus. To give the reconstruction a distinctive look, the original drawings done for the film's souvenir book can be used as backdrops for the overture, intermission, and walkout music.

This reconstruction deepens the dramatic impact of every scene in the film, softening its pessimistic tone and endowing it with a more uplifting meaning. As Robert Harris told me, he tried his best to restore the complete 202-minute Final Preview version of *Spartacus* "because a minute can make a big difference. A single line of dialogue can change the whole meaning of a story line." Since "*Spartacus* is a film right on the edge of greatness," as editor Lawrence told me, the difference between merely good and truly great could be very small. The reconstruction proposed here may reveal what impact *Spartacus* could really have had and what was lost when it fell victim to various censors' scissors.[64]

64 I would like to express my gratitude to Gary Crowdus, founding editor of *Cinéaste*, where the first version of this essay appeared. Without his guidance and encouragement, my work on *Spartacus* would not have seen the light of day.

CHAPTER TWO

Dalton Trumbo vs. Stanley Kubrick: The Historical Meaning of Spartacus

Duncan L. Cooper

In his "Report on *Spartacus*," Dalton Trumbo complained bitterly about the rewriting of many of his slave scenes without his knowledge or consent. He felt these rewrites were responsible for the slow turn in the script from the Large to the Small Spartacus. Still blacklisted and working in secret, Trumbo was unable to be present on the set or on location during the shooting of his scenes. Trumbo speculated that most of these rewrites had been done on the set at the last minute as part of a covert campaign by Stanley Kubrick radically to alter the nature of the script.[1]

Actually, it appears that many of these rewrites were done by Howard Fast in collaboration with Kubrick at Kirk Douglas's request and by Kubrick himself. But whatever their differences with Trumbo over the development of the slave story, it is difficult to believe that Fast or Kubrick could have been willing participants in the gross distortion of history that *Spartacus* became. The hallmark of Kubrick's conception of the film was fidelity to bitter realism, which spared the illusions of neither the left nor the right. In response to an interviewer's question whether there was any relationship between his interpretation of antiquity in *Spartacus* and

---

1 On the subject of this chapter see also Natalie Zemon Davis, "Trumbo and Kubrick Argue History," *Raritan*, 22 (2002), 173–190, and *Slaves on Screen: Film and Historical Vision* (Cambridge: Harvard University Press, 2000; rpt. 2002), 17–40 and 140–143 (notes; a chapter on *Spartacus*).

his parody of the inauthentic Hollywood sword-and-scandal epics in *A Clockwork Orange* (1971), Kubrick replied:

> None at all. In *Spartacus* I tried with only limited success to make the film as [historically] real as possible but I was up against a pretty dumb script which was rarely faithful to what is known about Spartacus. History tells us he twice led his victorious slave army to the northern borders of Italy, and could quite easily have gotten out of the country. But he didn't, and instead he led his army back to pillage Roman cities. What the reasons were for this would have been the most interesting question the film might have pondered. Did the intentions of the rebellion change? Did Spartacus lose control of his leaders who by now may have been more interested in the spoils of war than in freedom? In the film, Spartacus was prevented from escape by the silly contrivance of a pirate leader who reneged on a deal to take the slave army away in his ships. If I ever needed any convincing of the limits of persuasion a director can have on a film where someone else is the producer and he is merely the highest-paid member of the crew, *Spartacus* provided proof to last a lifetime.[2]

Kubrick wanted to illustrate the violence, brutality, and corruption of both masters and slaves. Late in the shooting he submitted a list of some seventeen "gory shots" to be included in the film's battle scenes. Only a handful were approved by Douglas and actually shot; these were later censored. By revealing the terrible sacrifices that any war imposes on the combatants, Kubrick hoped to raise the question of whether a noble goal like freedom can justify its human cost. His intent may have been to counteract Trumbo's glorification of the slaves' rebellion, but he could not effectively do so without recounting the fundamental truth about the events of the Servile War, a truth which other members of the film's executive committee seemed quite willing to set aside.

Trumbo, for his part, fought stubbornly for his conception of the Large Spartacus, which he believed to be an accurate reflection of history. Nevertheless, his passionate, eloquent arguments were undermined by his own insistence on the inevitability of Spartacus' defeat once the slaves' chance of escape from Italy was blocked. Paradoxically, this insistence derived from Trumbo's reluctance to confront another reality: the failure of revolutions often derives as much from the weaknesses and mistakes of the revolutionaries as it does from the strength of their opponents. It thus appears that the main issue dividing Trumbo and Kubrick

2 Quoted from Michel Ciment, *Kubrick: The Definitive Edition*, tr. Gilbert Adair and Robert Bononno (New York: Faber and Faber, 2001; rpt. 2003), 151.

was not the question whether or not to downplay Spartacus' military victories but rather whether or not to identify the slaves' own incapacity to cope with their newly won freedom as the ultimate cause of their defeat. This question of the "relative immaturity" of the masses as they make the transition from one era of history into the next during a revolution is the theme of Arthur Koestler's Spartacus novel *The Gladiators*. At the same time that Kirk Douglas's Bryna Productions was beginning work on *Spartacus*, another film company was preparing a film based on Koestler's novel. That film, to be directed by Martin Ritt and starring Yul Brynner as Spartacus and Anthony Quinn as Crassus, was also being scripted by a blacklisted screenwriter, Abraham Polonsky. Polonsky's script was sent to Laurence Olivier, Charles Laughton, and Peter Ustinov at the same time as Trumbo's. They chose the latter. Nevertheless, Ritt and Brynner forged ahead with their plans. Douglas was able to beat them only by getting into production first, but with an unfinished script in which the slave story and the main character were only roughly drawn. Later, as that story was being reworked and rewritten, Kubrick wanted to introduce some provocative ideas from Koestler's novel into their script based on Fast's.

Trumbo, however, was adamantly opposed to these changes. In a memo he distinguished the first long-standing campaign by the film's executive committee to diminish the military stature of Spartacus from a subsequent campaign orchestrated by Kubrick personally to diminish the moral stature of the revolt as a whole:

> Thus was the first campaign against the stature of Spartacus defeated. Then I began to see a second campaign to diminish the character get under way, directed, my dear Stanley Kubrick, by you. Stanley read Koestler. Koestler is a man who was for years bewitched by the idea that he was going to make a revolution, that he was going to lead the dear people in a vast freedom movement. But the revolution didn't come off because the people, in their immense stupidity, didn't see fit to follow Mr. Koestler. Koestler has spent all the years of his life since that fatal moment of rejection by the people in denouncing the common herd, which had so little comprehension of his excellence as a leader. His thesis is simple: the people are stupid, corrupt and altogether responsible for their own miseries. Leaders, on the other hand, are the elite of mankind, tragically frustrated, tragically pulled down and destroyed by the decadence and vulgarity of the very rabble they sought to lead to freedom. Thus Koestler has rationalized the stupidities of his own youth by placing them on the backs of the gross mob, which refused to recognize his virtues . . . The point is not whether the Koestler theory is philosophically or historically right or

wrong: it is rather that all theories are debatable, and that the Koestler theory is directly antithetical to the theory of the script of *Spartacus* . . . I think it is dead wrong to transmit any part of Koestler into *Spartacus*. Nevertheless, the Koestler theory still pops up, not as a "conspiracy" but as a conviction on Stanley's part, and I think we must accept it, or reject it, since it is impossible to compromise with it.[3]

Specifically, Trumbo was attacking Kubrick's proposal of a plot enhancement in which a rebellion by Crixus against Spartacus leads up to the former being hanged. Crixus was one of the leaders of the slave rebellion who led a group of 20,000 to 30,000 slaves in a breakaway movement from the slave army. The quick annihilation of Crixus and his men by the Romans placed Spartacus and the remaining slaves in a fatally weakened position. In the proposed script change, Spartacus learns of the plot to split the slave army and, despite some personal misgivings, hangs Crixus as a traitor.

Kubrick, following Koestler, wanted Crixus' rebellion to be motivated by a desire to remain in Italy in order to pillage and loot. Trumbo, following Fast, wanted to ascribe to Crixus the noble but suicidal goal of marching directly on Rome in order to overthrow the entire slave system. Neither Kubrick nor Trumbo seems to have disagreed with the fundamental premise that Spartacus resorts to the execution of Crixus in order to abort his rebellion and maintain unity. Neither of them seems to have been bothered that, in both novels, Spartacus refuses to take such repressive measures and Crixus leads an initially successful movement. Trumbo argued for the greater drama inherent in his version of this script change, referring to a modern parallel:

> Let us remember that the conflict between Stalin and Trotsky was more dramatic than the conflict between, let us say, Lenin and the Tsar. Why, because Stalin and Trotsky had the same objective, while Lenin and the Tsar had different objectives. Because war between brothers is more dramatic and more tragic than any other kind.
>
> The way I have written the part is this: Spartacus and Crixus share the same goal (freedom). They differ as to how they may reach their goal (escape via Brundisium versus the capture of Rome). Their conflict is of the highest moral order, it is a classic tragedy. Spartacus [ultimately] is compelled to execute Crixus for the good of the whole.[4]

---

3   Dalton Trumbo, "The Sequence on Vesuvius: Notes," 2–3.
4   Trumbo, "The Sequence on Vesuvius," 5.

In arguing for Crixus as a left-wing extremist, Trumbo tried to avoid the second big question surrounding the idea of revolution, a question posed at the time of his writing by the revelations of Khrushchev's speech to the Communist Party's Central Committee that denounced Stalin: Is there not a strong tendency for the leaders of any revolution to supplant the old rulers as a new exploiting class and to establish a new dictatorship to protect their gains? This issue had already been raised in the film in the scene in which Spartacus intervenes to prevent Crixus from having two captured Romans fight to the death as gladiators. The continuation of this conflict between a Crixus who wants to use his power for his own advantage and a Spartacus who has a new vision for people to live together in human brotherhood would have added depth to the superficial, even starry-eyed, portrait of the slave community which the film now provides.

Trumbo goes on in his memo to make an eloquent but unconvincing plea to eliminate the use of any of Koestler's ideas. His summary of Koestler's position in *The Gladiators* is fair, but his attempt to explain it by a personal attack on Koestler's frustrated elitism is not. Koestler wrote in his autobiography that "the amorphous, inarticulate, semi-barbarian horde [of the slave army] . . . is the real hero of the book, milling down the highways of Italy, sacking its cities, defeating the disciplined legions of Rome." Like Fast, Koestler pays tribute to the slaves by asserting "that the Slave Army came within an ace of conquering Rome . . . thus altering the whole course of history."[5]

Then why did their revolution go down in defeat? To Koestler, as he explained in a postscript to *The Gladiators*,

> Spartacus was a victim of the "law of detours," which compels the leader on the road to Utopia to be "ruthless for the sake of pity." Yet he shrinks from taking the last step – the purge by crucifixion of the dissident Celts [led by Crixus] and the establishment of a ruthless tyranny; and through this refusal he dooms his revolution to defeat.[6]

Koestler saw the utopian community founded by Spartacus as a model for an isolated socialist revolution in a backward, underdeveloped country like Russia. His slave heroes cannot be expected to understand the sacrifices which Spartacus demands of them any more than the

---

5   Quoted from Arthur Koestler, *The Invisible Writing: The Second Volume of an Autobiography: 1932–40* (1954; rpt. New York: Macmillan, 1969), 326 and 322.

6   Arthur Koestler, *The Gladiators*, tr. Edith Simon (1939; rpt. New York: Macmillan, 1967), 317.

Russian peasants could understand the collectivization of agriculture or forced industrialization. But Spartacus has too much compassion for his followers to choose a Stalinist course, so he dooms his revolution to certain defeat.

By rejecting Koestler, Trumbo ignored the fact that Howard Fast also attributed Spartacus' defeat to the moral weakness of the slave class as a whole, caused by a lifetime of ruthless repression, and to the splits within the slave army. Late in Fast's novel, an old slave woman tells Crassus: "Spartacus said to us, rise up and be free! But we were afraid. We are so strong, and yet we cower and whimper and run away." Thus, as Fast wrote: "the masses of slaves who peopled the Roman world would not or could not rise up and join [Spartacus]."[7] For Trumbo, on the other hand, the strength of Rome rather than the weakness of the slaves made Spartacus' revolution impossible:

> Koestler was interested in the weaknesses, the vices, the degeneration and demoralization of the slaves, our interest is in showing their strength, their increasing morale and unity to the very end, when the last of them is crucified. Stanley [Kubrick] has said that he wants Crixus as a raider because he wishes to show the demoralization of the slaves. This would be valid if our story established that the demoralization of the slaves led to their defeat. But in our version the demoralization of the slaves could not possibly lead to their defeat because a hundred thousand of them stood to the death in defense of their freedom and of each other. The slaves in our story were defeated by Rome, not by their own weaknesses. Koestler may be right that they were actually defeated by their own demoralization and inability to cope with freedom, but he was right only for Koestler's book . . . the one they couldn't make a movie of. He is wrong for our book . . . the one we are making a movie of . . . the slave demoralization [is] derived from an historical point of view which is highly dubious, since it discounts altogether the fact that Spartacus and a hundred thousand men could scarcely be expected to defeat Rome and the Roman empire and the known world. That was why Spartacus lost . . . not because the slaves are too stupid to be free; and that is what we're dramatizing in this script. Not the reverse.[8]

In contrast to Trumbo's apparently pessimistic stance, Koestler and Fast had taken a more hopeful, positive view of Spartacus' chance at victory. As Fast's Crassus confesses to his fellow aristocrats on two separate occasions:

7   Howard Fast, *Spartacus* (New York, 1951), 284 and 272. Originally, Fast published his novel himself.
8   Trumbo, "The Sequence on Vesuvius," 4 and 6.

You will hear it said that the Servile War was a small thing. It's quite natural that such a view should be taken, since it profits Rome little to tell the world what a job we had with some slaves. But here . . . we can dispense with legends. No one ever came as close to destroying Rome as Spartacus did. No one ever wounded her so terribly.

If Spartacus ever had under his command anything like the three hundred thousand men he was supposed to have led, then we would not be sitting here today . . . Spartacus would have taken Rome and the world too. Others may doubt that. But I fought against Spartacus enough times not to doubt it. I know. The whole truth is that the mass of the slaves of Italy never joined Spartacus. Do you think if they were made of such metal, that we would be sitting here like this on a plantation where the slaves outnumber us a hundred to one? Of course, many joined him, but he never led more than forty-five thousand fighting men – and that was only at the height of his power. He never had cavalry, such as Hannibal did, yet he brought Rome closer to her knees than Hannibal ever did – a Rome so powerful that it could have crushed Hannibal in a single campaign.[9]

Trumbo was understandably desperate to remain faithful to the heroic theme of Fast's novel and to keep out of the film Kubrick's and Koestler's doubts about mankind's moral and intellectual capacity to abolish class oppression. However, in pursuit of this goal he affected a different kind of historical pessimism that we can only call disingenuous. His reliance on the overwhelming power of Rome to explain the inevitability of Spartacus' defeat contradicts his own insistence on his hero's military accomplishments. How could Spartacus' revolt have shaken Rome to its very foundations, as Trumbo maintains, if it was doomed from the beginning? If there never was a chance of victory, then why bother dwelling on Spartacus' victories as a symbol of hope in the first place? Trumbo could not have been unaware of what Alexander, Hannibal, or Julius Caesar had accomplished with armies half the size of the one he ascribed to Spartacus. He was also well aware that in Fast's and Koestler's novels, as in the historical accounts, breakaway movements by portions of the slave army played a major part in leading to its final defeat. In contrast to his former comrades Koestler and Fast, could Trumbo really have believed that, absent these internal splits, Spartacus never had a chance?

Like Fast, Trumbo had left the Communist Party by the time *Spartacus* was being made, in part because he had come to realize that a writer cannot serve a political ideology without losing his artistic integrity. In an interview with David Chandler for a book to promote the film, he

9   Fast, *Spartacus*, 191–192 and 220.

avowed that he no longer believed in the perfectibility of man or in the Leninist dictum that the ends justify the means. But apparently habits of thought stemming from his years in the party were still clouding his judgment. Blaming the failures of modern revolutions on hostile capitalist powers and not on the mistakes or corruption of their leaders has remained a standard practice for left-wing apologists. Trumbo's analysis of the failure of an ancient revolution illustrates this. His insistence that Spartacus be the sole and absolute leader of the revolt rather than the spiritual and intellectual soul of a collective leadership, his anxiety to avoid the question of the corruption of the leaders of revolutions, and his inadvertent justification of Stalin's purges of Old Bolsheviks as necessary to preserve unity, as he does by describing the assassination of Trotsky as the result of a conflict between two brothers who had shared the same goals but espoused conflicting strategies to reach them – all this points to Trumbo's enduring authoritarian leanings and indicates that his analysis has more in common with Koestler's than he might have admitted.

Like Trumbo, Koestler and Fast believed that, at least initially, not enough slaves had joined Spartacus to make his victory possible. Like Trumbo, they also believed that under those circumstances extremely severe measures to preserve unity might be the only way to keep the chance for future victory alive: a split in the slave army would almost inevitably lead to disaster, as it ultimately did. Thus, Trumbo really differs from Koestler and Fast not about the immediate cause of Spartacus' defeat but about the ethical question of whether, or to what extent, the end – the survival of the revolution – justifies the means: the purge of all dissident elements and the institution of a ruthless dictatorship. Despite Spartacus' unwillingness to take such repressive measures and his consequent defeat, the recent collapse of the Communist bloc, which had been founded upon the principle that the end does justify the means, suggests that Koestler may have been right after all when he concluded that hope for the future lies with the birth of a new movement whose members will "preach that only purity of means can justify the ends."[10]

Ultimately, the message Fast and Trumbo were trying to convey in the film was the opposite of the cynical view that, despite Spartacus' successes, "almost" counts for nothing in history and that isolated popular revolutions led by idealistic minorities will always be doomed to defeat. The real, intended but ultimately frustrated, theme of the film is that

---

10   Arthur Koestler, *Darkness at Noon*, tr. Daphne Hardy (New York: Macmillan, 1941), 260.

Spartacus nearly managed to destroy Rome. That he should have failed is hardly surprising; that he came as close as he did is almost miraculous. In contrast to Koestler's and Kubrick's pessimism, their film was meant to signify that no oppressive power can remain standing once a sufficient number of people are determined that it should fall. That determination to win freedom remains as alive today as when Spartacus' revolt began.

Koestler's views may have been too extreme to fit into a popular film, but Kubrick's desire to confront the real moral and political dilemmas inherent in violent social change, to recognize the temptations for personal aggrandizement that inevitably attend the rise to power of a previously oppressed class, to depict political conflicts within the slave camp that parallel those on the Roman side – in sum, to inject political realism into the film – this could have made *Spartacus* a much profounder work than what it became.

CHAPTER THREE

Spartacus, Exodus, and Dalton Trumbo: Managing Ideologies of War

Frederick Ahl

Two Hollywood films appeared in 1960 which touched on subjects involving sensitive political issues of the time: Stanley Kubrick's *Spartacus* and Otto Preminger's *Exodus*. Both are about wars, one ancient and generally forgotten, one modern but part of a causal nexus extending back to antiquity. Both are partisan in their points of view. And both have scripts written by Dalton Trumbo, the author of one of the most acclaimed of all anti-war novels, *Johnny Got His Gun* (1939), whose narrator and hero is an ordinary American soldier hideously crippled during World War I. This essay tries to trace how Trumbo, the passionate denouncer of war, became himself both the victim of, and a partisan voice in, the ideological struggles of the mid-twentieth century. For he did not only write the scripts for the two war films named above, which vied with each other for the top ratings at the box office in 1960 and 1961, but also for Victor Fleming's *A Guy Named Joe* (1943), a celebration of the role of the fighting American soldier and the very antithesis of *Johnny Got his Gun*.

The timing of the publication of *Johnny Got His Gun* could hardly have been more awkward for Trumbo: it appeared just days before the outbreak of World War II in Europe. Although the prospect of a new war was looming as Trumbo was writing his novel, the dominant memory of World War I was still what most critics saw as its pointless carnage. That had been the war to end all wars and, in the eyes of most, had brought death, mutilation, and misery to tens of millions with little obvious advantage to anyone. *Johnny* sold out quickly, and a reprint seemed in order. But Trumbo, surprisingly, refused to allow one. *Johnny* was not reprinted until 1946, and Trumbo did not add an explanatory "Introduction" until a new edition appeared in 1959. Then he reflected on the pressure he had faced during the war from the political right to authorize a reprint. He was subjected, he says, to a campaign of "fiercely sympathetic letters denouncing Jews, Communists, New Dealers and international bankers" on the grounds that these groups had suppressed his novel "to intimidate millions of true Americans who demanded an immediate negotiated peace." The four groups he mentions are the standard Nazi trinity of demons, with President Franklin D. Roosevelt added for an American flavor. Trumbo thus gives the impression that he was under pressure chiefly from Nazi sympathizers, who had practical reasons for wanting to keep America out of the war to ensure a speedier German victory. *Johnny* was to provide the perfect morally and politically clean underpinning to justify American neutrality. "Nothing," Trumbo claims, "could have convinced me so quickly that *Johnny* was exactly the sort of book that shouldn't be reprinted until the war was at an end."[1]

The first person to censor Trumbo's publications, then, was Trumbo himself. While he never renounced the total pacifism of *Johnny* and indeed reaffirmed it in a 1970 "Addendum" to his introduction, he suppressed his pacifist authorial voice in favor of a strongly pro-war rhetoric for the duration of World War II. Of course one may reasonably argue that this war involved clearer moral issues than World War I and that under the circumstances failure to oppose Hitler's ruthless aggression was tantamount to abetting his cause. This rationale must have seduced Trumbo into writing the numerous film-scripts favoring war that he wrote after 1939. But to do so when one has just published a pacifist novel that argues the collective injustice of all war is problematic. And to re-issue a pacifist novel, suppressed during the war, after the war is over is somewhat disingenuous.

Once an avowed pacifist concedes, in effect, the moral propriety of war under certain circumstances, he enters a hopeless semantic jungle. One can attempt to distinguish between wars of aggression and wars of defense. But one does not always have the knowledge necessary to make an informed decision. The official discourse of a nation's internal politics frames almost all wars as defensive, and critical background information

---

1   Quoted from the reprint of Dalton Trumbo, *Johnny Got His Gun* (New York: Bantam, 1970), p. 3 of the unpaginated Introduction.

is usually kept classified and beyond public scrutiny. It's easier to persuade the public that one is fighting a just war when the line between truth and propaganda is blurred by the government and the news media. If most citizens are persuaded that their country is free and that foreigners are not, oppression is necessarily what occurs elsewhere. This point was made with heart-rending eloquence 2,500 years ago by Euripides in *Iphigenia in Aulis*, when a young woman is trying to explain to herself and to her desperate and angry mother why her beloved father is about to kill her as a sacrifice to ensure his own military glory over a foreign foe: "The foreign world is collective slavery, but Greeks are free individuals" (1400–1401).

In Trumbo's explanation for his self-censorship, the expression "true Americans" is pointed. It alludes to what was to become and remain the most powerful classifier in twentieth-century American political rhetoric: "un-American." ("Patriotic" runs a close second.) In 1937, during Roosevelt's administration, the United States Congress had established the House Un-American Activities Committee (HUAC), which evolved over the next two decades into a kind of modern Inquisition before which ideological heretics of selected types could be summoned for questioning. If they failed to cooperate, they could be jailed or, if foreign-born, stripped of their citizenship and deported. It was particularly sinister that the congressional response in the days of crisis preceding World War II was to force a general consensus on what was *not* American rather than to undertake the more complicated task of suggesting what it meant to *be* American.[2] For the committee could select a given activity in utter isolation from all other factors and make it the sole criterion of un-American behavior, while totally ignoring, for example, the entrenched racism that blighted American society of the day.

At the outset, HUAC investigated various political activities. World War II differed from World War I in that, from the earliest days, ideological issues were at the forefront. Italian Fascism, German Nazism, and Soviet Communism established themselves by harnessing the passions and discontent of the majority to overwhelm powerful minorities. All envisaged a radical restructuring of society. And all were anti-capitalist. Karl Marx, an exiled German living in London, had denounced the oppressiveness of capitalism decades before World War I. His theories

---

2 Aljean Harmetz, *Round Up The Usual Suspects: The Making of Casablanca: Bogart, Bergman, and World War II* (New York: Hyperion, 1992), 246, notes that studio boss Harry Warner used the heading "Our Ism . . . Americanism" to head the editorial page of the *Warner Club News* for years; the book contains a chapter under that heading (240–251).

provided the underpinning for the Russian Revolution in October, 1917, which overturned the country's existing order to create what was in theory a workers' state. The Nazi movement in Germany and the Fascist movement in Italy, though sharing these anti-capitalist sentiments, did not threaten all elements of the monied classes immediately but only, at least for the moment, the Jews and the Communists. Consequently, Communism was widely viewed by the propertied classes in the United States (aside from those who were Jewish) as the most threatening, for the Great Depression had left many Americans receptive to the idea of such radical economic change. But there was no need to insist on too close a distinction in the early days of World War II since Germany and Russia were, at first, allied with one another.

In 1941, however, after the Japanese attack on Pearl Harbor, America joined Britain in the war against Nazi Germany. The struggle against what the conservative establishments in both countries really feared, Communism, was put on hold for the time being. Once the Soviet–Nazi Pact ended, the Soviet Union was a useful ally until the war was won. Even the ultra-right had to ease up on its anti-Soviet invective. This temporary lull lured writers of the American left, like Trumbo, into a trap: that of professing their Communism and praising the patriotic fervor of Soviet resistance to the Nazis. But neither Winston Churchill nor the American right forgot that the Soviet Union represented the major long-term threat to the ruling classes. As the Allies began winning the war, HUAC focused almost exclusively on Communism. Its investigations persuaded a sufficiently large section of the American public to accept that anyone who was, or could be represented as, a Communist was an actual or potential traitor. HUAC encouraged citizens to watch one another for signs of latent Socialism and in effect authorized employers to fire employees involved in unions or in leftist activities or statements. J. Edgar Hoover and the FBI stood ready to investigate. Faced with public humiliation and ruin, most people held their tongues. Some turned informer.

It was not until after the war was over that HUAC summoned Trumbo to appear. By this point he was Hollywood's best-known and most sought-after scriptwriter. Indeed, one could hardly criticize his patriotic service in American war-time propaganda. He served as a war correspondent with the US Army Air Force and wrote the script for Mervyn LeRoy's *Thirty Seconds over Tokyo* (1944), a film commemorating the first token American air attack on Japan in 1942 that was a prelude to the raids on Hiroshima and Nagasaki. He wrote the script at the time when Britain's Royal Air Force set about the destruction of major German cities with a verve and efficiency as chilling as it is understandable. True, there was general public enthusiasm for the devastating Allied aerial bombardment of Germany. Indeed, the word "blockbuster," the war-time slang for the huge bombs used by the RAF to destroy entire city blocks, is still current as a term of approval to describe a spectacularly successful movie. Yet how, after the massive RAF onslaught upon Hamburg and other German cities in 1943, the author of *Johnny Got his Gun* could agree to write the script for *Thirty Seconds over Tokyo* is, to me, unfathomable. What is more fathomable, however, is that the Nazis declared that the saturation bombing of Germany was a savage attack on civilians and retaliated in kind as much as they could. They began by allowing the killing of downed Allied pilots although they had hitherto rejected this policy already practiced by the Japanese. But since they had not been able to launch any major air attacks on England for two years, they had to wait for the V1 and V2 rockets, which now became a top priority. More ominously the Allies, sensing victory, in 1944 approved the Morgenthau Plan, "under which post-war Germany would be stripped of its industry and converted into an agricultural nation."[3] So Germans could see the saturation bombing not just as wartime strategy but as demolition work in preparation for a new, depopulated, and agricultural Germany. They knew that Henry Morgenthau, Jr., was America's leading financier. He was Roosevelt's Secretary of the Treasury from 1934 until 1945, and he was Jewish. And this further strengthened the Nazis' already virulent anti-Semitism. It was Kurt Vonnegut, Jr., and not Trumbo who was to bring the horror of Allied saturation bombing to the attention of the American public in his 1969 novel *Slaughterhouse Five.*

After World War II, HUAC aimed at eliminating any chance that the Socialism sweeping Europe might sweep America, too. It was not just the Soviet Union that frightened them but the troubling outcome of Britain's first post-war elections, which rejected Churchill and his Conservative Party in favor of Clement Atlee and the socialist Labour Party. Here was proof that the radical left could triumph in an election, not just by revolution. Since the United States could not very well denounce its own closest ally, the Committee blurred the distinction between Socialism and Communism and focused on the latter, with huge success. Over the long term, it disempowered the American left as the voice of American workers and empowered the right as the voice of American populism. The public at large came to accept that Communism and Socialism were

3   The summary from which I quote is at the Treasury Department's official website: http://www.treasury.gov/education/history/secretaries/hmorgenthaujr.shtml. For Morgenthau's own perspective see his *Germany Is Our Problem* (New York: Harper, 1945).

un-American. By the time HUAC got to Trumbo in 1947, he was "un-American" by definition because he was a Communist.

Restrictions on free thought and free speech produce results. They have been applied by every kind of regime, political or religious, throughout history because almost all candidates for power have the establishment and maintenance of their own position and ideology as their first concern. Gaining power in any system is easier if the public is blinkered and can be relied on to look in only one or, more subtly, two pre-approved directions, for that gives them the illusion of choice. It is better still if you can frighten people into putting their own blinkers on. Then, if you are an outsider trying to break into the world of power, you cater to what a sufficient percentage of those who are politically active want, believe, or hate. It is irrelevant that you can't fool all of the people all of the time. You just have to fool enough of the people enough of the time.

Given Trumbo's history of published invective against HUAC and the bosses of capitalism, it is not at all surprising that he was called before HUAC, convicted of contempt of Congress for refusing to cooperate with its inquiries, and sentenced to a year in prison. And Tim Palmer is surely correct when he argues that it was Trumbo's articles in the Hollywood trade press that provoked HUAC rather than his film scripts.[4] The only surprise, really, is that HUAC waited until September, 1947. Trumbo, along with nine other Hollywood writers, was placed on a blacklist by a group of Hollywood executives and producers who vowed in what is known as the Waldorf Statement that these men would receive no further employment in the film industry. Trumbo had silenced his own pacifism. Now HUAC and the frightened administrative elite of Hollywood tried to silence his voice altogether.

After serving nine months of his sentence, Trumbo emerged from prison. He moved for a few years to Mexico. His name began to disappear from the public eye as a scriptwriter but was kept visible in other publications, including a reprint of *Johnny Got His Gun* in 1952 at the time of the Korean War. Yet HUAC was more successful in suppressing his name than his voice in the world of film. Despite the blacklist, HUAC's activities did not have quite such disastrous consequences for writers as they did for Hollywood's performing artists who had fallen victim to their inquisition. The ban, in fact, took no account of the laws of the capitalist marketplace. Hollywood producers still wanted to make films. First-class scripts were in high demand but in short supply. Further, Trumbo

4   On this see Tim Palmer, "Side of the Angels: Dalton Trumbo, the Hollywood Trade Press, and the Blacklist," *Cinema Journal*, 44 no. 4 (2005), 57–74.

felt he could not afford to stop work as a scriptwriter. That was how he earned his living. There was, then, a community of interests between independent producers, less affluent than their counterparts at the studios, and banned screenwriters. The blacklist produced a black market which enabled independent producers to purchase the services of blacklisted writers at discount prices. A single script earned Trumbo more than the annual salary of a schoolteacher or factory worker. Both sides, in effect, went underground. Trumbo continued to write prolifically, using a variety of pen names and passing scripts off as composed by friends rather than by himself. He was the author, for instance, of the original story for William Wyler's *Roman Holiday* (1953) and Irving Rapper's *The Brave One* (1957). Both won Academy Awards for what Trumbo had contributed, although he could not be identified.

Commercial publishers, given the political climate, wouldn't touch Howard Fast's novel *Spartacus* in 1950. The FBI advised against publication. Angus Cameron, the editor-in-chief of Fast's usual publisher, had been forced to resign because he, too, was under scrutiny for publishing left-wing manuscripts.[5] Fast, however, refused to be defeated and published *Spartacus* at his own expense in 1951. It was a huge success nationally and internationally and was translated into more than fifty languages. Fast had done exactly what dissident Soviet writers were doing with their own works that the Communist Party had banned, but on a much grander scale. It was, paradoxically, a triumph of American capitalist entrepreneurship by a now well-to-do Communist. For, as powerful as were the forces of hate and prejudice that HUAC unleashed, they could not overcome the impetus to make money. Fast could thumb his nose at those who had sought to suppress him.

Not all Americans in high places saw Communist writers like Fast and Trumbo in the same way as did HUAC. Presidents Truman and Eisenhower took a very different view. A revised directive issued by the State Department in February, 1953, to the International Information Administration (IIA), established by President Truman the previous year and supervising, among other things, the Voice of America radio broadcasts, declared:

> The reputation of an author affects the active utility of the material. If he is widely and favorably known abroad as a champion of democratic causes, his creditability and utility may be enhanced.

5 Cf., e.g., Eric Homberger, obituary for Howard Fast, *The Guardian* (March 14, 2003), at http://books.guardian.co.uk/news/articles/0,,914007,00.html. See also John J. Simon's obituary for Angus Cameron, *The Guardian* (November 20, 2002), at http://books.guardian.co.uk/obituaries/story/0,,851096,00.html.

> Similarly, if – like Howard Fast – he is known as a Soviet-endorsed
> author, materials favorable to the United States in some of his works may
> thereby be given a special creditability among selected key audiences.[6]

The IIA saw Fast as very useful to national goals, pointing out, discreetly
but firmly, that he was not a Soviet propagandist as HUAC suggested, but
a writer known for championing democratic causes who said some nice
things about America. The IIA surely had a point in suggesting such an
approach. The Soviet Union had been jamming Voice of America broadcasts since 1948 because of its uniformly anti-Communist stance. And
one's propaganda, which we in the United States tend to call "information," won't persuade people who can't listen.

Clearly the IIA relished Fast's achievement. The classified State
Department directive was, however, leaked to Senator Joseph McCarthy,
the most vocal member of HUAC. He promptly accused the IIA of encouraging subversion. The success of Fast's rebellion and its support by the
executive branch of the government drove McCarthy and his successors
wild with rage. In less than three weeks, the State Department was forced
to accept a total ban on books, music, and paintings produced by "communists, fellow travelers, et cetera." And "in the madness that followed,
nervous librarians discarded and even burned books placed on what
appeared to be a State Department blacklist."[7]

McCarthy and HUAC saw in Soviet Communism a total threat to the
existence of their idea of world order. They were afraid that they would
lose the struggle. So they wanted to crush even the slightest trace of
Communist ideology. The Executive Branch assumed that the battle
could be won or that some kind of coexistence could be negotiated over
time and saw in writers like Fast an opportunity to build bridges of
understanding. But it had now lost a critical battle. As a result, the United
States continued on a program of enforcing ideological orthodoxy by
playing on public fears and prejudices and by suppressing or intimidating those who opposed them, no matter how highly placed. But just as
McCarthy underestimated the doggedness of a few of his opponents,
so the intellectuals vastly underestimated the long-term results of
McCarthy's actions.

By the late 1950s HUAC was running out of control under the leadership of McCarthy until he met his match in Edward R. Murrow. And

---

6   Quoted from Thomas C. Reeves, *The Life and Times of Joe McCarthy: A Biography* (1982;
rpt. Lanham: Madison Books, 1997), 479.
7   Reeves, *The Life and Times of Joe McCarthy*, 480, with the sources cited in his notes
53–54.

in 1959, Trumbo broke cover with a new edition of *Johnny Got His Gun*,
which included the introduction from which I have quoted above. The
following year, during the close contest for the presidency between
Richard Nixon and John Kennedy, Nixon's neutrality on the issue of the
blacklist was secured and Kennedy's support for the ending of the ban
guaranteed. Kirk Douglas and Otto Preminger were now free to allow
Trumbo's name to be listed in the credits of *Spartacus* and *Exodus*. Congress remained silent and Kennedy himself crossed the picket lines to
attend *Spartacus*. The blacklist, though its effects were still felt for years
to come, was no longer enforceable on a national political level. In the
long run, then, the breaking of the blacklist was a paradoxical triumph
of capitalist economics over both capitalist and Communist ideology.[8] In
1957, attempts to maintain the blacklist degenerated into farce, but the
thirteen years during which it had been maintained were a grim era
for many, including Trumbo. And the legacy of fear did not end when
Trumbo's name appeared on the credits for *Spartacus* and *Exodus*. Five
years after the blacklist ended, Kenneth Macgowan's influential *Behind
the Screen: The History and Techniques of the Motion Picture* was published.[9]
There is not a word in the book that offers the slightest hint that there
ever had been a HUAC, a blacklist, or the Hollywood Ten. The two chapters on censorship deal exclusively with the control of sexual imagery
and language in films, and Dalton Trumbo is cited only once (on page
243) for his negative criticism of Russian camera techniques in 1933.

Of the two films that brought Trumbo's name back to the screen in
1960, *Spartacus* is the better known nowadays. *Exodus*, a box-office
success in its day, was based on Leon Uris's novel, which had been a
best-selling novel since before World War II, even more spectacularly
successful than *Spartacus*. Its subject appeared, at the time, to be
uncontroversial in the United States: the establishment of Israel. There
are obvious parallels between the two film scripts, written by the same
author at approximately the same time even if they treat historical events
separated by more than two millennia. In an internet interview given in

---

8 Jeffrey P. Smith, "'A Good Business Proposition': Dalton Trumbo, *Spartacus*, and the End
of the Blacklist," *The Velvet Light Trap*, 23 (1989), 75–100, gives a detailed and incisive
account of the process. Cf. Palmer, "Side of the Angels," 67–70.

9 Kenneth Macgowan, *Behind the Screen: The History and Techniques of the Motion Picture*
(New York: Dell, 1965; rpt. 1967). What changes, if any, were made to the text between
Macgowan's death in 1963 and the book's publication and copyright registration by his
estate in 1965 is not clear since the book lacks the prefatory notice customary in a posthu-
mous publication. Macgowan's latest reference to a specific date (on page 327) is to January
1, 1964 (i.e., after his death).

2000, however, Howard Fast, who was originally to write the script for *Spartacus* and who had delivered a screenplay, says that producer and star Kirk Douglas called him to Hollywood to write some twenty-seven scenes to integrate the footage he had on the basis of Trumbo's script.[10] But we must balance Fast's claims against the fact that Douglas appears to have called upon Trumbo to work with the script when Fast's own original screenplay had proved unworkable.[11]

The case for filming *Exodus* seemed pretty straightforward from a financial point of view. What presumably attracted Preminger to Trumbo as writer was his concern to take some of the Zionist edge off Uris's bestseller and perhaps his personal ambition to be the first to place a blacklisted writer in the credits. The revelations about the Holocaust and the pictures from the Nazi death camps had so greatly shocked the European and American worlds that there was widespread sympathy for and admiration of Israel. Indeed, the establishment of Israel had been, in some form or other, on the Allied agenda since at least 1942. Trumbo, who was not Jewish, was a good choice for the job because of his socialist ideals since his involvement could mute leftist critics who shared the Soviet view that the foundation of Israel was not a good idea. The West's sympathy for Israel was still on the rise when *Exodus* appeared and did not peak until well after the Six-Day War in 1967.

Exodus was *the* novel and *the* film commemorating the resurrection of Jewish dignity and culture from the ashes of the Holocaust, the reincarnation of a long-disembodied soul. *Exodus*, however, tells a story that was then, and still is, in progress. It was written by a Jewish author about Jews who were repeating the exploits of Moses and his people and returning to what their religion told them was their rightful ancestral land. If we are Jewish, *Exodus* is about us and the fulfillment of a Zionist dream. The film takes our sympathy for granted. If we are not Jewish but Anglo-Saxon Protestants, the largely non-Jewish cast makes us feel comfortable: these are people like *us*. Trumbo was careful not to overwhelm us with too many Jewish markers or stereotypical characters. Never has a film about Jews been made with such a Midwestern-looking cast, headed by the only partly Jewish Paul Newman in the prime of his beauty. But if we are Arabs, we seethe, although Trumbo toned down Uris's Arab caricatures. So the vision of *Exodus* has been highly susceptible to the unpre-

---

10   Quoted from transcript of "Spartacus: An Interview with Howard Fast" (June 28, 2000) at http://www.trussel.com/hf/ancient.htm.

11   Described by Kirk Douglas, *The Ragman's Son* (New York: Simon and Schuster, 1988), 306–310.

dictable course of events and the shifting tides of public opinion about Israel. For the movie's accommodation of Judaism to a kind of Viking-warrior aesthetic for European and American consumption gives an unintended visual confirmation of the Palestinian stereotype of Israel as an alien Western colony planted in Palestinian land, as a kind of almost-Christian crusader state peopled by Jews who don't look or behave at all like those whom Palestinians were seeing around them before 1948.

Further, the foundation of Israel created a new group of dispossessed people, the Palestinian Arabs. There were those who felt that claiming rights to land once held by ancestors in the remote past was a dubious proposition. Remedying old injustices with new injustices meant the displacement of grievances from one group to another. The dispossessed Arabs were convinced that they were being made to pay the price for the double anti-Semitism of the West, which had no use for either Jews or Arabs. Besides, it was becoming evident that highly placed interests in Britain and the United States had had their own reasons for planning the establishment of Israel. During World War II neither country had encouraged large-scale immigration of displaced Jews into its own territories and had on occasion even turned away such desperate refugees as had managed to escape the Nazis. There were millions, not thousands, of Jews to be accommodated. Since it was clear to the Allies as they started to win the war that they could not resettle the Jews in their European homelands, they harnessed Jewish Zionism to their carriage and planned for the settlement of a grateful, well-educated, European population on the coast of the Middle East. Such settlement was more problematic to the British than to the Americans since Palestine was a British Mandate. Jewish settlement caused immense problems for the British government when matters got out of control.

The Morgenthau Plan for the de-industrialization of post-war Germany is a reminder that Britain and America had not learned their lesson from the First World War. They knew that leaving a defeated enemy in ruins was an invitation to further conflict. The plan opted for a solution that was little more than a modified version of what the ancient Romans had done to Carthage and Corinth: the total dismemberment of the vanquished opponent. Fortunately the plan was abandoned in 1947 through fear of a Europe left too open to Soviet expansion and was replaced by the Marshall Plan, one of the most enlightened strategies a victorious alliance has ever devised for a defeated enemy. But by then it was too late. In 1944, highly placed Nazi officials had begun to grasp that defeat was unavoidable and that Churchill was insisting on unconditional surrender. The Morgenthau Plan seemed to validate the official Nazi view of Jewish menace to German culture. To the Nazis, it was part of a Jewish plot, aided by British and American capitalists, to obliterate their Germany for ever. There is a curious passage pertaining to this issue in the diary of Joseph Goebbels, Hitler's Minister of Propaganda, for May 26, 1943:

> An interesting report tells about the conference at Casablanca. According to this report it was decided that the Anglo-Saxon powers would create a national home for the Jews in Palestine after their eventual victory. This national home is to take care of 20,000,000 Jews. These Jews are to engage chiefly in intellectual and managerial tasks; the work is to be done, as decided in Casablanca, by middle European and especially German workers. For this a large-scale resettlement would be necessary that would, to a certain extent, depopulate Central Europe. It isn't hard to imagine what's going on in the brains of these plutocratic statesmen who are dependent upon the Jews; but we also know what we must do to protect the German people against such a fate.[12]

I find no trace of such a proposal among available documents pertaining to the Casablanca Conference. The number of Jews to be resettled seems too large to be accounted for exclusively by Goebbels' own sense of the Jewish population of the Reich, and even a very low ratio of workers to managers yields a total number to be resettled at double the population of England at the time. There seem to be four possibilities: 1) that the report is Goebbels' fiction; 2) that it represents a real, presumably suppressed, report; 3) that Goebbels is exaggerating a real report that has been suppressed; 4) that it is disinformation supplied to him by parties unknown. David Irving's detailed if controversial biography of Goebbels is unconscionably silent about this diary entry.[13] It is clear from the tone of Goebbels' diaries in 1943 that he knows that the war is going badly and that defeat is likely. He is also aware of Churchill's demand for Germany's unconditional surrender, and he appears to have some advance knowledge of the nature of the Morgenthau Plan which was not officially set forth until over a year later. He hints that the Final Solution is to be the German response to the threat that the Allies intend to establish a huge state in Palestine in which Germans provide the labor

---

12   *The Goebbels Diaries: 1942–1943*, ed. and tr. Louis P. Lochner (1948; rpt. Westport: Greenwood Press, 1970), 398. The conference took place in Casablanca between January 14 and 24, 1943, with Roosevelt, Churchill, and Stalin in attendance.

13   David Irving, *Goebbels: Mastermind of the Third Reich* (London: Focal Point Publications, 1996), refers to the conference only once, and unhelpfully, on page 742.

and Jews the management and brains while Germany itself is reduced to a pre-industrial society.

Whether Goebbels' perception of Allied intentions is right or wrong is impossible to assess, since many critical documents from the period will remain classified for another half century. But we cannot eliminate the possibility that Goebbels' perception of Allied intentions, however unfounded and paranoid, triggered the most monstrous phase of the Holocaust. Germany was going to prevent at least one part of its post-war annihilation by preemptive action of its own. There would be no Jews left to go to Palestine and build a powerful new land while non-Jewish Germans tilled farmlands. The closer defeat loomed, the more feverishly the Nazis killed the Jewish internees.

It is a terrible indictment of Allied myopia that their analysts failed to think their way into the Nazi frame of reference and envisage the scope of potential counter-measures, since the savage treatment of Jews in the Third Reich and the doctrinaire anti-Semitism of the Nazi leadership had become well known by 1943. So there is a nightmare scenario if one answers the old legal question *Cui bono?* – Who profits? – in the context of political expediency. The full story of *Exodus* is yet to be told and will probably never be told. If truth is war's first casualty, it may also be its last.

Spartacus, however, seemed at the time a more complicated case. Spartacus himself was too menacing a figure for the ancient Romans to consider a hero, and most of our historical information about him derives from ancient Greek rather than Roman authors. He remains a threat to the governing elites of the world today. Your enemies are the people working for you, an ancient proverb ran: *quot servi, tot hostes.*[14] Spartacus was the historical proof that these people could rise and menace any society which had wealthy employers and mistreated employees, even though his rebellion was ultimately crushed. The fear lingered that such an uprising might succeed some day, against all odds. Quite aside from the October Revolution, the General Strike in Britain in 1926 had raised just such a specter of popular revolution.

The ruling classes in Britain and America had no interest in making Spartacus a heroic model. Besides, he was a slave – someone who had no business being an epic-style hero – and too low-class and dangerous an opponent to be dignified with heroic status. He was not brought into the

---

14   References to and variants of this proverb may be found in A. Otto, *Die Sprichwörter und sprichwörtlichen Redensarten der Römer* (1890; rpt. Hildesheim and New York: Olms, 1988), 319–320 (number 1637).

center of Roman history until Karl Marx and his followers put him there and until somewhere there was a society which established itself, at least in theory, by bringing about the revolution that Spartacus failed to accomplish (and probably did not try to bring about). Russia's October Revolution turned Spartacus into a hero. Political and ideological tracts were linked to his name as were even soccer teams such as Moscow Spartak – appropriately, since he had started his rebellious career as a gladiator in public arenas.

It is therefore surprising that the best-known modern accounts of Spartacus should be in English, not in Russian – until one recalls that those who brought Spartacus into the English language were Jewish artists with central European backgrounds: Arthur Koestler and Howard Fast wrote the novels about Spartacus, and the film was produced by Kirk Douglas and directed by Stanley Kubrick. No less surprising is the fact that the film appeared when the American cultural and literary world was staggering from public persecution of socialists by HUAC. For there was no mistaking the leftist origins of the modern Spartacus tradition, and anxieties about Castro's recent overthrow of the Batista dictatorship in Cuba and the Civil Rights movement within the United States troubled the American extreme right. But the horrendous experiences of European Jews during the 1930s and 1940s had given them a special sense of community with the plight of Spartacus and his fellow slaves. For Jews had been treated as a community apart in many European countries, not fully citizens, not Christian, considered not fully human. They had been used for slave labor by the Nazis until they could no longer work, then destroyed with even less dignity and on an infinitely larger scale than Crassus could have imagined in his wildest dreams. Here, indeed, is the crucial difference between the plight of the Jews in Auschwitz and the gladiators in Capua. The Nazi goal was the extermination of Jews, the labor camp a means of extracting what value could be extracted from them while they still lived. But slaves were a major engine of the Roman economy. In *Spartacus*, Batiatus' gladiators represent a financial investment whose loss spells ruin for him. And when the Romans are obliged to kill their slaves, they are destroying their own property and their own establishment.

In *Spartacus*, then, a diverse group of oppressed people from different lands escapes slavery. After initial successes it is unable to leave the land of its captivity and is exterminated. In *Exodus*, a similarly diverse group, which has come close to extermination, finds a new home in Palestine. What differentiates the two stories is not just the failure of one and the tentative (though possible) success of the other but the fact that the

Exodus group has a cultural coherence within itself and is connected to our own society, to Hollywood, and to the author of the original novel in a way that the *Spartacus* group is not. How could a mostly non-Jewish American audience be lured into caring about what happened to a Thracian slave in the remote past?

The publicity agents thought they knew. The magical buzzword dominating the advance publicity was "freedom."[15] And, as reviews attest, that publicity was successful in suggesting to the public how it should think about the themes of *Spartacus*. Hopes for the success of *Spartacus* rested mainly on the gamble that a controversial bestseller would become a hit at the box office and that the presence of Dalton Trumbo in the credits would not drive audiences away. A market research report commissioned by the producers determined that Trumbo's presence in the credits would deter only twelve and a half percent of those who knew who Trumbo was, would not bother fifty percent, and would actually entice thirty-seven and a half percent to see the film.[16] The story has an earlier setting than most of Hollywood's Roman epics: the 70s B.C., when Rome was still an oligarchic republic, not an autocracy. There was still a forum for political dissent within Roman ranks. Julius Caesar's star was only beginning to rise. The antagonists, Spartacus and Crassus, were not among the small number of Roman historical names familiar to audiences of the day unless they had read the novel. And since the setting is two generations before the birth of Christ, there are no Christians to make it a drama of religious faith of the kind that had brought audiences to LeRoy's *Quo Vadis* (1951) or to Henry Koster's *The Robe* (1953). Like most film epics about ancient Rome, *Spartacus* focuses on the conflict between a powerful elite and the dispossessed poor and enslaved. In the usual Hollywood manner, it frames that conflict in terms of a struggle not so much between citizen groups of different social classes within one society but between two separate and unintegrated societies and ideologies, of which one has been utterly subjected to the other. It thus avoids overt suggestions of a Marxist class conflict. The nature of the story reminds us, as do the ancient historical accounts, that the varied ethnic and cultural background of Spartacus' host makes its energy inherently unstable.

Spartacus is, paradoxically, full of visual symbols of Christianity yet adamantly silent about religion. There is not a word to indicate that Spartacus or any of the slaves subscribe to any religious creed at all.

15   Smith, "A Good Business Proposition," 92–95.
16   Smith, "A Good Business Proposition," 90.

Both novel and film present a world without consciousness of the divine whatsoever. Yet the eye of the camera yields a film made in the full aware-ness that the Christianity of its audience will dictate how the visual imagery is understood, especially in the climactic scene when the hero is crucified. There Kubrick's camera leads us through a series of images recalling familiar representations of the crucified Christ but shorn of any explicit sense of resurrection or of a life beyond the grave. This is mortal man dying for his fellow mortals in the knowledge that the future lies only with his equally mortal infant son. This sequence is the sanctifica-tion of heroic humanism, of a courage and virtue that does not depend on any assumption of the sufferer's divinity or on any expectation or hope of eternity. The Marxist notion that one does not have to subscribe to a religious code to be moral is scrupulously maintained, as one would expect in a novel and script written by Marxists. But producer and direc-tor know that, regardless of how clearly the film makes the point that crucifixion was a common form of execution in Roman times for lower-class criminals by emphasizing the huge numbers of slaves crucified after their defeat and capture, audiences will see any crucifixion in terms of the death of Christ. For the Christian church, once it came to power in Rome, in effect outlawed crucifixion and thereby marked it as exoteric, holy, and unique. It found other and no less painful modes of eliminat-ing those it condemned. Since the consensus of ancient sources is that Spartacus died in battle, his elevation to the cross can have no purpose other than to evoke comparisons with Christ.

Had Spartacus been hanged or beheaded, or had he simply died in battle, his death would not have acquired such an aura of sanctity. *Spartacus* relies heavily on the Christian imagery of crucifixion to secure our attention for a hero whose purpose was more secular, social, and at least potentially revolutionary. In *Spartacus*, it is Crassus who serves an abstract master or, rather, mistress: Rome. We might, for a moment, feel that Fast, Trumbo, Kubrick, and Douglas are parodying American secu-larized Christianity. To counterbalance any such sense, however, Douglas had cast Laurence Olivier, whose very English, theatrical enunciation and aristocratic manner are far distant from the strident vulgarity of a Joe McCarthy.

Because almost all films are cooperative creative ventures, the origi-nal author, the producer, the director, and the scriptwriter are forced to make compromises. Material from other sources and similar works gets incorporated here and there. Thus the end product is often less satisfy-ing to any one of its creators than it is to an audience that views it as a whole and integrated work. A Christian audience, for example, might well go away from the film with the notion that *Spartacus* is a kind of Christian allegory and Spartacus a sort of proto-Christ. Yet Spartacus' relationship to the Roman establishment is very different from Christ's. Spartacus is a slave who cannot be free without rebelling and challenging the secular world. Once free, he becomes a military and social threat to Rome. Christ, by contrast, was of free and distantly noble lineage (even if we leave God out of the picture). It appears from Christian texts that he could have lived contentedly, if obscurely, if only he had not challenged and thus threatened the religious and local authorities. These secured the acquiescence of the Roman procurator in their condemnation of him and made the Romans his executioners.[17] I find it hard to imagine that any of the creators of Spartacus had a vested interest in making him a proto-Christ, though the more business-minded would not have wanted to preclude this if it would help box-office receipts. Only Trumbo himself had a Christian background as a Christian Scientist. The others were Jewish. The draft of a 1959 letter from Trumbo to Pablo Picasso suggests that Trumbo saw *Spartacus* as a political rather than a religious allegory:

> The theme of the film, for which I take full responsibility, is simple and, I feel, curiously appropriate to our times: in waging a life-and-death struggle to keep Spartacus and his followers enslaved, the senate and people of Republican Rome inevitably produced the conditions for their own enslavement under a dictatorship of the right.[18]

By asking Picasso, whose *Guernica* is perhaps the most powerful of all pictorial representations of civil war, to provide a drawing to illustrate *Spartacus*, Trumbo underscores the intensity of his concern for the political substance of what he is essentially claiming as his film. He speaks in a language surely calculated to kindle the sympathies of a fellow artist in exile, whose masterpiece was itself at the time in exile from a Spain ruled by the last of Europe's Fascist dictators, General Franco. In Trumbo's mind Rome is clearly an allegory of the United States, and Crassus, despite Olivier, is symbolic of American political power. Most striking to

---

17   It is puzzling that the Romans, usually sticklers for legal niceties, should have executed a man who assiduously avoided challenging Rome's authority, who was not tried in their courts, and whom their own procurator had declared innocent and pointedly refused to condemn. Later Christian documents, such as the Apostles' Creed, are more emphatic about Pontius Pilate's role in the execution.

18   Quoted from Natalie Zemon Davis, "Trumbo and Kubrick Argue History," *Raritan*, 22 (2002), 173–190, at 185.

me is that Trumbo sees the film not so much as Spartacus' struggle for freedom as the struggle of the imperial republic in which he lives to prevent Spartacus and others from achieving freedom. And those threatened by Rome are not just people such as Spartacus that it seeks to hold in bondage, but the citizens of Rome themselves, who, without realizing it, are destroying their own freedom as they suppress that of others. Ultimately, Julius Caesar waits to make Rome a fiefdom for himself and his successors, though he adopted a popularist rather than what we would now call a right-wing program. And that, I think, is the force of the prologue, which announces: "The age of the dictator was at hand, waiting in the shadows for the event to bring it forth." That event was, as Trumbo sees it, the crushing of Spartacus' rebellion. Roman determination to maintain, and success in maintaining, a slave society led logically to an expansion of slavery and further diminution of freedom. "Spartacus destroyed the republic that would not give him freedom," the sympathetic Roman senator Gracchus observes.

Although British and American historians of ancient Rome are never likely to accept such a Marxist reading of Roman history, the fact remains that, less than a century later and after decades of civil war, the Roman people lost the right to vote for their consuls, who were thenceforth appointed by the emperor. Republican government of any kind was dead for the next millennium. Frustration with the oppressiveness of Roman imperial rule contributed, it is true, to the subsequent appeal of Christianity at many levels of ancient society. Christianity, however, did not seriously challenge the institution of slavery until the nineteenth century. Further, it encouraged the ideal of subservience to a single God, slavery to whom – a phrase usually softened to "service to whom" – is perfect freedom. Its leaders created a powerful political force by encouraging the rejection of secular aspirations among the people, by offering them the promise of eternal salvation in the afterlife if they accepted the faith's doctrine without question, and by making martyrdom the most desirable goal in this life. Further, by encouraging the faithful to sign over their worldly wealth to the Christian community, the church acquired huge economic resources. So by the time Christianity became the official religion of the Roman Empire, the ordinary people had been trained not only to accept placement in whatever social class they were assigned to, but to subordinate themselves intellectually as well as economically and politically to serve a new set of rulers acting in the name of a single god. Doctrinal disputes over how this god was to be defined led to the various splits within the Church and the foundation of Islam.

Curiously enough, HUAC was to have its own special role in redefining Christianity. If Trumbo had compromised pacificism by becoming a

Communist and a writer of war films, HUAC compromised Christianity by making the rejection of Communism and the acceptance of capitalism fundamental to the American identity. Early Christians had disavowed worldly possessions and accepted the obedience imposed by faith, as even their opponents admitted:

> They scorn all possessions without distinction and treat them as community property; doctrines like this they accept strictly on faith. Consequently, if a professional sharper who knows how to capitalize on a situation gets among them, he makes himself a millionaire overnight.[19]

For centuries the Church forbade Christians the lending of money at interest although people, as always, needed to raise money in a crisis. The Church allowed stateless Jews to take on the reviled function of money-lenders, with ultimately grim consequences. By the time the Church lost the power to enforce its rule, Jews were the dominant force in international banking.

In America, the official atheism of Marx and of Soviet Communism allowed politicians to force upon the public a theologically ruinous equation between godliness and capitalism, which flouts some of the most fundamental teachings of the Gospels. The United States became a reverse of Soviet orthodoxy. To be a true American you had to deny Socialism to prove you believed in God. To be a Soviet Socialist you had to deny God. Once Howard Fast, when asked by HUAC whether his loyalty was only to the United States of America, answered:

"No, sir."
"You have another loyalty?"
"Yes, I do."
"And this loyalty supersedes your loyalty to the United States of America?"
"Yes, sir, it does!"
"Would you care to name this entity?"
"Gladly. I call it 'God.'"[20]

If one had substituted the Soviet Union for the United States and asked Fast exactly the same question in Moscow, the same answer might, with more understandable logic, have sent him either to jail or

---

19   Lucian, *Death of Peregrinus* 13; quoted from *Selected Satires of Lucian*, ed. and tr. Lionel Casson (1962; rpt. New York: Norton, 1968), 369. Lucian was writing shortly after A.D. 165.
20   Quoted from Fast's obituary by Daniel Gavron, "A Fast Friend," *Ha'aretz* (March 15, 2003).

to a re-education program. But his answer did not save him from an American jail in 1950.

To return, then, to Trumbo's letter drafted to Picasso. If there were remnants of the soul of the disappointed Christian lurking beneath the Communist in him, they showed themselves in his struggle to idealize Spartacus, make him morally clean, write him large, while Kubrick wanted to endow Spartacus with more commonplace traits, and make him small. The film's final version fortunately gives us elements of both. To Trumbo's disgust, Kubrick had the defeated Spartacus spit in Crassus' face. Perhaps Trumbo would have rather had Spartacus turn the other cheek. For the nobility of Spartacus' sacrifice as the film presents it lies in what seems more than Christ-like about his leadership. To save him from crucifixion his followers claim they are Spartacus; they do not betray him. His love for and dedication to others and his determination to share the death of his fellow slaves when he has the chance to secure a safe escape for himself is not based on any knowledge or hope of divinity or resurrection. He is giving up his one and only life.

Insofar as *Spartacus* is an allegory of the contemporary world, the Romans are, in Trumbo's terms, the affluent of America. Only America's poor, no more than a third of the population, would even consider joining a Spartacus. In most other Hollywood epics, Rome is a paradoxical and fluid blend of *us* and *them*. The Middle-Eastern headscarves worn by Jews and newly converted Christians in William Wyler's *Ben-Hur* (1959), for instance, make their wearers appear uncomfortably different from us. Theirs is a world of disempowerment and suffering, with which we don't really identify even if we think we ought to. And the idea of turning the other cheek and enduring the abuse of the arrogant is anathema in our official culture. The communalism of the early Christians has been set aside in favor of an aggressive militarism, capitalism, and secular self-advancement of the kind epitomized in the ancient Rome we see on our screens. This Rome is the raw power of worldly might that menaces the "good guys," but it is also the seductive dark side of our own aspirations.[21]

Spartacus and *Exodus* were released at a pivotal moment in American history and culture, when it seemed that a decisive corner had been turned. *Spartacus* showed its colors boldly. Displaying blacklisted Trumbo in the credits was an act of defiance which challenged the censors to

---

21   On this cf., for example, William Fitzgerald, "Oppositions, Anxieties, and Ambiguities in the Toga Movie," in *Imperial Projections: Ancient Rome in Modern Popular Culture*, ed. Sandra R. Joshel, Margaret Malamud, and Donald T. McGuire, Jr. (Baltimore and London: Johns Hopkins University Press, 2001; rpt. 2005), 23–49.

oppose it. It is hard for young people now to understand the courage it took to stand up to, much less defy, the pressures that the HUAC inquisition put on the entire film industry and to grasp the extent to which actors, film historians, reviewers, and publishers tried to keep the attention of HUAC and the FBI away from them. If one sees, as I do, a disappointed idealism underlying Trumbo's script for *Spartacus*, it is perhaps that of a writer who has been forced to survive by compromising his pacificism, concealing his identity, watching others collect Oscars that are rightfully his, and looking with some apprehension at the America he perceives as he emerges to reclaim his authorial identity. For while Trumbo's Jewish colleagues managed to retain their religious and cultural sense of themselves over years of persecution, he, like many other Christians with leftist political beliefs, had become alienated and excluded from his religion which had merged with HUAC's capitalist credo in America and which was largely silenced in Western Europe where it had lost moral authority by faltering under Nazi pressure.

The American left, like Spartacus, could enjoy only a temporary triumph in a land whose ruling elite had by the early 1970s reestablished the control that had seemed to be slipping away. Much the same happened in antiquity during the forty years after Spartacus' death. Rome consolidated its control of the Mediterranean. It still had some unresolved issues with the rulers of Iran (ancient Parthia), whom it had failed to defeat and whom Crassus died fighting, and some troubles in the Balkans. But Rome faced no major external attacks. The price it paid, however, was the usurpation by Julius Caesar and his dynasty of its right to govern itself, the creation of a powerful executive branch of government backed by a large professional army under direct imperial command, and a professional administration that was responsible not to the senate and people but to the head of state. Trumbo may have suspected that the same fate was in store for the United States. That is what makes *Spartacus* a major political text for its time, not simply a dramatization of an important uprising in the remote past.

Now, over forty years after *Spartacus*, America imagines itself standing alone on what had once been Rome's pinnacle, surrounded by a sea of paradox. Soviet Communism is comatose or dead. Red, the traditional color of Socialist banners, symbolic of popularism, and abandoned by the American left during the "Red Scare" of the 1940s and 1950s, has now been taken up by the right wing. Communist China is the world's most successful capitalist enterprise and one of its most abusive employers. Socialism is mortally wounded in Britain and elsewhere in the corporate European Union. And the damage done to the spiritual authority of Christianity in America by its annexation to economic capitalism may well prove irreparable. Thus Spartacus, both man and movie, have a poignancy now that they lacked in the heady days of the film's release. Yet in terms of thematic relevance, they have so far weathered the years better than *Exodus*, because the tale of Spartacus is not about the apparent triumph of social justice but about the dogged pursuit of a dream of social justice which has a moral validity despite its defeat, and in its defeat.

CHAPTER FOUR

Spartacus: History and Histrionics

Allen M. Ward

Stanley Kubrick's *Spartacus* has become a classic among cinematic epics set in the ancient world. A large budget provided all the elements for success: a superb cast, moral passion, intelligent and thought-provoking dialogue, detailed costumes and sets, beautiful photography, scenic grandeur, and, most importantly, a compelling story. From a strictly historical point of view, however, the film is problematic. Generally, filmmakers assume that audiences are not primarily interested in the actual facts when they view historical films.[1] Therefore their makers believe that it is necessary to provide mainly the impression, atmosphere, and feeling of history, not the kind of accuracy demanded from an academic historian writing on the same topic.[2] Consequently, it is hard not to agree with Jon Solomon that precise concerns with historical accuracy in a film like *Spartacus* are the petty preoccupations of "Ph.D.'d scholars."[3]

---

1 Cf. Martin M. Winkler, "*Gladiator* and the Traditions of Historical Cinema," in *Gladiator: Film and History*, ed. Martin M. Winkler (Oxford: Blackwell, 2004), 16–30, at 16–24. – I thank Nina C. Coppolino of Providence College for her generous help in critiquing my text for publication.
2 Jon Solomon, *The Ancient World in the Cinema*, 2nd edn. (New Haven and London: Yale University Press, 2001), 73 (caption to fig. 41).
3 Solomon, *The Ancient World in the Cinema*, 53.

But as a professional historian who realizes that the visual media more than any other modern medium shape the public's perception of the past, I wish that the makers of historical films took their inevitable, even if unintentional, role as historical educators more seriously.[4] In fact, it seems rather condescending to assume that the general public is not interested in the accuracy of historical films. A good story is essential, but the first question I am often asked after the final credits have rolled is: "How accurate was it?"

Certainly, some poetic license must be granted to artists, novelists, playwrights, and filmmakers to create vivid and dramatic portrayals or interpretations of actual people and events. Nevertheless, it would be desirable if creative artists showed greater concern for historical sources and did not contradict them more than necessary to meet their legitimate ends. A skilled and reasonably conscientious filmmaker should be able to make a historical movie not only entertaining and relevant to the present but also faithful to what is known about the time and people portrayed. Indeed, it is easy to check the historical record by consulting standard reference works, major sources in translation, and trained historians. In particular, the ancient historical record – sometimes, no doubt, itself fictional – is often more dramatic and entertaining than the modern fictions that filmmakers frequently introduce. By these criteria, then, *Spartacus* earns a decidedly mixed review for historical accuracy, whether the ultimate responsibility for a particular failing lies with Howard Fast, who wrote the novel on which the film is based, with Dalton Trumbo, the blacklisted Hollywood writer who wrote the original script, or with numerous others who introduced changes during production.[5]

---

4 On visual media and the past see, for example, Martin M. Winkler, "The Roman Empire in American Cinema after 1945," in *Imperial Projections: Ancient Rome in Modern Popular Culture*, ed. Sandra R. Joshel, Margaret Malamud, and Donald T. McGuire, Jr. (Baltimore and London: Johns Hopkins University Press, 2001; rpt. 2005), 50–76, at 51; and Mark C. Carnes, "Introduction," in *Past Imperfect: History According to the Movies*, ed. Mark C. Carnes et al. (New York: Holt, 1995), 9–10. Marcus Junkelmann, *Hollywoods Traum von Rom: "Gladiator" und die Tradition des Monumentalfilms* (Mainz: von Zabern, 2004), 150–165 and 391–394 (notes), provides a historian's perspective on *Spartacus*.

5 A comparison of Howard Fast's 1951 novel *Spartacus* with Kubrick's film reveals many major differences in historical details. For the roles of Trumbo and others in shaping the final version of the film see especially the contributions of Duncan L. Cooper in the present volume; cf. further Alison Futrell, "Seeing Red: Spartacus as Domestic Economist," in *Imperial Projections*, 77–118, at 97–99, and Theresa Urbainczyk, *Spartacus* (London: Bristol Classical Press, 2004), 122–125.

On the positive side, the film does have a solid historical core.[6] It conforms to the ancient accounts that in the late 70s B.C. Italy was wracked by a great slave revolt that was touched off when a charismatic enslaved gladiator named Spartacus and a number of comrades broke out of the gladiatorial training school run by Lentulus Batiatus at Capua.[7] The movie plausibly locates the beginning of the breakout in the kitchen of the gladiatorial school because, as Plutarch reports, the escapees seized cleavers and roasting spits from some kitchen for their initial weapons.[8] Although it is difficult to keep count in the melée that, quite realistically, accompanies their escape in the film, the initial number of escapees seems accurate or at least is not greatly exaggerated. While one source gives the low figure of "30 or more," others range from 64 to 78, with 74 being the most frequent.[9]

After their breakout, the slave-gladiators in *Spartacus* generally reflect the ancient accounts as they overcome local troops, confiscate weapons, gather followers from the surrounding countryside, and take refuge on the slopes of Mt. Vesuvius, where they continue arming themselves as they conduct local raids and defeat the first forces that the Roman Senate sends against them.[10] The film hints at further victories recounted in much more detail by the ancient sources as the slaves try to escape from Italy. Then, as history records, Marcus Licinius Crassus obtains a command from the senate to bring the massive resources of the Roman Republic fully to bear against the rebels.[11] In the meantime, Spartacus has negotiated with a representative of Cilician pirates for transport from

6   Acknowledged, e.g., by historian William V. Harris, "Spartacus," in *Past Imperfect*, 40–43, at 42.

7   The most important ancient sources are collected and translated in Brent D. Shaw, *Spartacus and the Slave Wars: A Brief History with Documents* (Boston and New York: Bedford / St. Martin's, 2001).

8   Plutarch, *Crassus* 8.2.

9   Florus, *Epitome* 2.8.3, gives the low count; 74 appears in Orosius, *History against the Pagans* 5.24.1 (erroneously given as 64 in Shaw, *Spartacus and the Slave Wars*, 151), and 64 in Velleius Paterculus, *History of Rome* 2.30.5. Appian, *The Civil Wars* 1.14.116, says "about 70." "80 lacking 2" is the number in Plutarch, *Crassus* 8.2 (erroneously 72 in Shaw, 131), while Sallust, *Histories* 3.90 (Maurenbrecher) = 3.60 (McGushin), Livy, *Periochae* 95, Frontinus, *Strategies* 1.5.21, and Eutropius, *Breviarium* 5.7, all agree on 74.

10   Plutarch, *Crassus* 8.2–9.3; Appian, *The Civil Wars* 1.14.116; Orosius, *History against the Pagans* 5.24.1; Velleius Paterculus, *History of Rome* 2.30.5; Florus, *Epitome* 2.8.3–4; and Frontinus, *Strategies* 1.5.21.

11   Plutarch, *Crassus* 10.1; Appian, *The Civil Wars* 1.14.118; Livy, *Periochae* 96; Florus, *Epitome* 2.8.12; Orosius, *History against the Pagans* 5.24.5; Velleius Paterculus, *History of Rome* 5.30.6.

Italy by ship, and he and his now huge following of fugitive slaves and peasants reach the sea after a harrowing march through the wintry Apennines. The pirates, however, prove faithless, and the desperate fugitives, hemmed in on all sides by advancing Roman armies, make a heroic but futile stand against Crassus and his well-trained legions, with horrific casualties on both sides.[12]

The movie also manages to convey some important general truths about late Republican Rome. First is the brutality that Roman society often exhibited. The opening sequence conveys a correct impression of the brutal conditions under which slaves worked in Roman mines. The film also gives a good sense of the brutality endured by gladiators and the pleasure that spectators took in the violent games of death for which they were trained. The extensive use of crucifixions as brutal object lessons to terrorize other slaves into acquiescing to the domination of their masters is no figment of Trumbo's or Kubrick's imagination but was a common occurrence in Roman life, even if the numbers whom Crassus had crucified at once were unusual.

The highly personal nature of Roman Republican politics also comes through well. Although Gracchus, a fictional character, and Crassus represent different modern political ideologies, their personal rivalry for power and influence is much more conspicuous because of the dislike that they express for each other in their maneuverings for power. Their intense animosity not only produces good drama but also reflects the personal conflicts characteristic of the era that produced Marius and Sulla, Cicero and Clodius, and Pompey and Caesar.

The film also effectively portrays the pervasive role of rhetoric and oral communication in Roman life. Lentulus Batiatus feels compelled to give a formal speech from his balcony to the newly arrived gladiators, gray-haired senators who look as if they had just stepped out of a Roman portrait gallery orate in debate on the senate floor, great set speeches before mass audiences sharply delineate the social and ideological contrasts between Crassus and Spartacus, and the slave Antoninus, a singer of stories, gives voice to the longings of the poor and downtrodden around the slaves' campfire.

Costumes and sets show an admirable striving for authenticity. One major gaffe, however, reveals how art can create fictions that crowd out

---

12   This scenario is loosely based on Plutarch, *Crassus* 9.5, 10.3–4, and 11.5–7; Appian, *The Civil Wars* 1.14.120; Florus, *Epitome* 2.8.10–14; and Orosius, *History against the Pagans* 5.24.6–7.

historical reality in the modern imagination. The film shows the seats of the Senate House arranged in semi-circular tiers. The set is copied from a famous series of frescoes done between 1882 and 1888 by the Italian painter Cesare Maccari (1840–1919) in the Salone d'Onore in Rome's Palazzo Madama, home of the modern Italian Senate. The most frequently reproduced scene of Maccari's images shows the infamous conspirator Catiline in 63 B.C., sitting abandoned and dejected in the foreground at the end of the second row while Cicero excoriates him in his *First Catilinarian Oration*. This painting has been reproduced so often in Latin textbooks and histories of Rome that it has even shaped the presentation of the Republican Senate in some non-fiction books on ancient Rome.[13] Although the Curia Hostilia, the Republican Senate House at the time of Spartacus, has not survived, subsequent senate houses were always rectangular. In view of the Romans' deep-seated traditionalism, there should be no doubt that the interior plan of Emperor Diocletian's version, centuries later and still standing today for all to see, with its central door opening out onto the Roman Forum in one end, a dais at the opposite end, and rows of benches along the sides, reflects the basic layout of its predecessors.[14]

The houses of wealthy or well-to-do characters like Crassus, Gracchus, and Lentulus Batiatus are modeled on the sumptuous townhouses and villas excavated at Pompeii and its environs which date from the late first century B.C. until the eruption of Vesuvius in A.D. 79.[15] Members of the wealthy Roman elite and their imitators aspiring to power in the late Republic occupied similar homes in Rome, many of them on the Palatine Hill, where they were submerged under later imperial palaces.[16] In an admirable attempt to re-create the appearance of such homes for *Spartacus*, set designers copied not only the architecture of houses from Pompeii but also authentic furnishings and decorations. For example, a wall in Gracchus' house displays reproductions of the famous series of wall paintings in the Villa of the Mysteries, originally constructed in the

---

13   Most recently, it is the model for a small picture in a brochure addressed to classics teachers to urge them to incorporate into their courses the twelve-part television series *Rome* (2005), produced by HBO. I thank Lara Langer of the Metropolitan Museum of Art, New York City, for help in identifying the artist and location of the frescoes.

14   Cf. Alfonso Bartoli, *Curia Senatus: Lo Scavo e il Restauro* (Roma: Istituto di Studi Romani, 1963), 3.

15   Cf. Henri Stierlin, *The Roman Empire: From the Etruscans to the Decline of the Roman Empire*, tr. Suzanne Bosman (Cologne and New York: Taschen, 2002), 100–123.

16   Lawrence Richardson, Jr., *A New Topographical Dictionary of Ancient Rome* (Baltimore and London: Johns Hopkins University Press, 1992), 279–282, s. v. "Palatinus, Mons."

second century B.C., that date to about 60 B.C. and depict women parti-
cipating in some Dionysiac rite.[17] The upper level of the walls in the room
where Lentulus Batiatus entertains Crassus and his party at a private
showing of gladiators is decorated with gladiatorial scenes similar to
those depicted in mosaics from Leptis Magna in Libya and others now in
the Galleria Borghese in Rome. The colonnaded garden in which Crassus
inspects a group of slaves is an authentic representation with Grecian
columns, marble and bronze statuary, and even a mosaic copied from an
original found in Rome.[18]

This garden is part of a sumptuous suburban villa. Whether Crassus
actually owned such a luxurious dwelling in either Rome or its suburbs
at the time of Spartacus' revolt is unclear. His notorious acquisition of a
pleasant suburban villa at a very favorable price may have taken place
just about that time, but we do not know whether he kept it for himself
or turned it over for a quick profit as he usually did with real estate.[19]
Later, in 56 B.C., Crassus had a house at Rome in a very expensive neighborhood on the Palatine near an area where two houses had been sold
for huge sums in recent years.[20] In 73, however, he may have still been
living in the much less lavish accommodations in which he had lived
with his father and two married brothers before they died.[21] By the time
of Spartacus' revolt, Crassus had profited handsomely from being on
Sulla's winning side at the Battle of the Colline Gate in 82 and then from
his subsequent activities as a real-estate developer and entrepreneur.
Nevertheless, he seems to have been careful not to waste money by living
lavishly in the manner of many of the nabobs to whom he sold real
estate.[22]

---

17   Cf. Stierlin, *The Roman Empire*, 118–119.

18   Solomon, *The Ancient World in the Cinema*, 57 (figs. 28–29); cf. Stierlin, *The Roman Empire*, 101–111.

19   On this cf. my *Marcus Crassus and the Late Roman Republic* (Columbia and London: University of Missouri Press, 1977), 74–75.

20   Cicero, *On Behalf of Caelius* 9 and 18; cf. Richardson, *A New Topographical Dictionary of Ancient Rome*, 125, s. v. "M. Licinius Crassus Dives"; Pliny the Elder, *Natural History* 36.103; Cicero, *Letters to Atticus* 1.13.6. Cf. Ward, *Marcus Crassus and the Late Roman Republic*, 47 and 55.

21   Plutarch, *Crassus* 1.1; cf. Ward, *Marcus Crassus and the Late Roman Republic*, 47 and 55.

22   Plutarch, *Crassus* 2.5. Cf. Ward, *Marcus Crassus and the Late Roman Republic*, 62–74, and Bruce A. Marshall, *Crassus: A Political Biography* (Amsterdam: Hakkert, 1976), 15. The story that Crassus had a private fire brigade that would refuse to douse a fire until the building's owner and threatened neighbors had sold to Crassus on the spot is a modern invention.

Crassus may not have sought a more impressive dwelling in Rome until 70 B.C., when he had reached the consulship. At that point in life, a man sought to advertise his success in climbing the social and political ladder. Cicero, buying from Crassus, did so in 62 after his consulship of 63, as did M. Valerius Messalla Niger during his consulship in 61.[23] Even if Crassus had been living in his less luxurious old family home in 73, it would have exhibited a level of comfort and quality far above the conditions in which ordinary citizens lived. That is the historically valid point that the film emphasizes in its depiction of the homes inhabited by Crassus, Gracchus, and even Lentulus Batiatus, a man of far lower rank who aspired to be like them by enriching himself as a trainer and purveyor of gladiators.

The reconstruction of Batiatus' training school at Capua and the costumes and combat of the gladiators are historically more accurate than what many other movies have exhibited. One anomaly is each gladiator's little "queue" or *cauda* ("tail"), which resembles the one worn by Japanese sumo wrestlers or samurai and is supposed to mark a man as a gladiator. It seems to have no textual and little visual evidence to give it historical support.[24] The training school, however, with appropriate modifications for the less elaborate establishment run by a private entrepreneur, seems to conform to the picture developed from the excavations of the Ludus Maximus, the training school attached to the Colosseum in Rome. The kitchen area even has an accurate reproduction of a typical Roman grain mill, which consisted of a large conical stone base and a hollow truncated conical stone that fitted, small end down, over the top of the base and was turned like a capstan by horizontally projecting wooden arms to grind grain which was placed in the wide opening at the top. The major historically questionable item in the school is the large rotary training device with staggered upper and lower blades. While a slave turns it by pulling on a rope wrapped around a drum at the top, a

---

23   Cicero, *Letters to His Friends* 5.6.2; Ward, *Marcus Crassus and the Late Roman Republic,* 202 and note 11.

24   The filmmakers may have been misled by the tail-like projection on the back of some fancy gladiatorial helmets like the one in Toronto's Royal Ontario Museum or the one that seems to stick out from under the helmet of a *secutor* ("pursuer") on the Colchester Vase in England, but most depictions of helmeted or bareheaded gladiators unambiguously show no such thing. The charioteers showing the colors of Rome's four circus factions in mosaic panels now in the Museo Nazionale Romano have some kind of tail-like projections sticking up behind their caps, but charioteers were not gladiators. Cf., however, Vincent LoBrutto, *Stanley Kubrick: A Biography* (1997; rpt. New York: Da Capo, 1999), 170, on the hair design for Spartacus and the gladiators in the film. Cf. further Junkelmann, *Hollywoods Traum von Rom,* 131–132.

trainee alternately has to jump over and duck under the blades to avoid having his lower legs amputated or his head cut off. There is no evidence for this device, but it aptly illustrates the kind of ingenuity that the Romans applied to providing spectacles in the arena.[25]

When Crassus has Lentulus Batiatus put on a private showing of gladiators, *Spartacus* fairly accurately presents the gladiators fighting in pairs with different kinds of equipment. The lack of the two referees usually present at Roman fights is a failing, but Spartacus, a Thracian by birth, appropriately fights armed as a Thraex ("Thracian"), while his opponent appears as a *retiarius*, a net man armed with a fishnet and trident.[26] Both men, following known practice, have one arm protected by armor. Neither has helmet or greaves (shin guards), although a Thraex would have had them later in the Empire. Unfortunately, Spartacus fights with a strange-looking sword that has a short and narrow blade on each side of its longer and wider central one instead of with the curved scimitar that was the distinctive weapon of a Thraex. In 73 B.C., however, all of the elaborate protocols of the imperial period will not yet have evolved, so that the scene as a whole does not do violence to what we know about that time.

Similarly, the film fairly re-creates some aspects of the military history of the period. The emphasis on Glabrus' failure to build a fortified camp underscores the basic principle that Roman soldiers were supposed to build one every time they stopped marching even for one night.[27] One might argue that some of the equipment and details of armor better reflect the early imperial army, for which there is much more visual evidence, but it would have been difficult to represent arms and armor of the late Republic more authentically.

Unfortunately, the great battle that resulted in Spartacus' disastrous defeat depicts the formation of a Roman legionary army that was based on the tactical unit of the maniple in the mid-second century B.C. and not on the cohort of around 70 B.C. Although cohorts are frequently mentioned earlier in the film, one of Crassus' subordinate officers even

---

25   Cf. Strabo, *Geography* 6.2.7; Pliny the Elder, *Natural History* 36.116–120.

26   On the arms and conventions of gladiatorial combat see Marcus Junkelmann, "*Familia Gladiatoria*: The Heroes of the Amphitheatre," in *Gladiators and Caesars: The Power of Spectacle in Ancient Rome*, ed. Eckart Köhne and Cornelia Ewigleben; tr. Anthea Bell (Berkeley and Los Angeles: University of California Press, 2000), 31–74. For all aspects of gladiatorial equipment and combat as well as modern recreations see Junkelmann, *Das Spiel mit dem Tod: So kämpften Roms Gladiatoren* (Mainz: von Zabern, 2000).

27   Cf. Lawrence Keppie, *The Making of the Roman Army: From Republic to Empire*, new edn. (Norman: University of Oklahoma Press, 1998), 36–38.

refers to the then-obsolete maniple, and the maniples of the two legions that Spartacus and his men watch being deployed are drawn up in three staggered ranks to form what some military historians call a quincunx, a formation like the five on our dice. Although this impressive army performs a number of precision drills that awe the slaves (and the viewers) and show them what a well-oiled killing machine it was, these particular drills seem to reflect mid-second-century b.c. maneuvers rather than those of Crassus' day.[28] Sadly, the slave rebels' use of huge rolls of flaming straw against the Romans is totally unhistorical. Appian does mention that at one point the rebels hurled bundles of dry sticks into a ditch and set them on fire to hinder the construction of Roman siege works, but that is a far cry from what the movie depicts.[29]

It would be pointless, however, to complain that at the time of the battle Crassus commanded not two but eight legions, the number actually mentioned when Gracchus discusses the senate's offer of a command to Crassus. Nominally, they would have amounted to 40,000 men, but 25,000 to 30,000 is a more likely number after deduction for casualties and desertions.[30] It would have been prohibitively expensive to field this many extras. Still, an accurate re-creation of the cohort-based organization and tactics of two legions would have convincingly conveyed a sense of the Roman state's overwhelming organized might that Crassus brought to bear against Spartacus' irregulars and would have been no more expensive than the anachronisms actually employed.

Much worse is the misrepresentation of the particular circumstances that forced the slaves' final confrontation with Crassus. It is true that a Lucullus had arrived with a Roman army at Brundisium. That was Marcus Terentius Varro Lucullus, whose army the senate had recalled from the province of Macedonia. Nevertheless, his troops did not join Crassus' legions for the final battle.[31] Pompey, moreover, had not landed

---

28   For the evolution of the Roman legion see Keppie, *The Making of the Roman Army*, 19, 33–36, 38–39, 63–67, and 173–174. Keppie, 39, cites this battle scene from *Spartacus* as a depiction of the second-century b.c. manipular legion in action. Under the heading "Training + Tactics = Roman Battle Success," the film's souvenir program – *Spartacus: The Illustrated Story of the Motion Picture Production*, ed. Stan Margulies (Bryna Productions and Universal Pictures Studios, 1960) – devotes two pages to a textual description, with diagrams, of this kind of fighting. They are reprinted, with additional editorial comments, in the present volume.

29   Appian, *The Civil Wars* 1.14.119.

30   Cf. Appian, *The Civil Wars* 1.14.118.

31   Plutarch, *Crassus* 11.2; Appian, *The Civil Wars* 1.14.120. Appian here misidentifies him as his brother Lucius Licinius Lucullus, who was still fighting Mithridates in the province of Asia.

another army at Rhegium. He was on his way back by land over the Alps from Spain and was nowhere near southern Italy.[32] Even those historical circumstances, however, were enough to make both Spartacus and Crassus want to confront each other quickly. Spartacus would have had no chance against three skilled commanders in Italy, and Crassus did not want anyone else to get credit for defeating Spartacus.

Spartacus has many other particular historical inaccuracies, some of which combine a lack of respect for history with a desire to imbue a historical story with contemporary significance. First of all, there are several problems with the characters who appear in the film. As our sources make clear, a third leader accompanied Spartacus and Crixus in the escape from Capua. He was Oenomaus, who, along with Crixus, initially led those identified as Gauls and Germans.[33] Oenomaus never appears, and Crixus is always portrayed as Spartacus' dedicated lieutenant right up to the famous scene after the last battle when he is one of the first to stand up and call out "I'm Spartacus!" According to Sallust, however, there was a major disagreement between Crixus and Spartacus early on: Spartacus sensibly wanted to escape as soon as possible from where the slaves were, but Crixus and the Gauls and Germans imprudently wanted to fight the Romans head on or at least stay to raid and plunder.[34]

The only hint of any such disagreement appears in the scene when the gladiators return to the abandoned school of Batiatus. Noble Spartacus scolds Crixus and the others for acting like Romans in making prisoners fight like gladiators and persuades them that their goal should not be aimless raiding but to fight their way to Brundisium and to escape by sea. Crixus quickly and enthusiastically adopts Spartacus' plan and remains by his side. The sources, however, indicate that Crixus and Oenomaus either agreed to disagree with Spartacus or, more positively, made a strategic division of forces and split off with the Gauls and Germans to form a second rebel army, that Oenomaus was soon killed, and that Crixus became the leader of the Gauls and Germans until he, too, died in battle and was succeeded by Castus and Gannicus.[35]

32   Cicero, *On Behalf of the Manilian Law* 30; Plutarch, *Crassus* 11.2–5 and 7–8, *Comparison of Crassus and Nicias* 3.2, and *Pompey* 21.1–2; Appian, *The Civil Wars* 1.14.119.

33   Appian, *The Civil Wars* 1.14.116; Eutropius, *Breviarium* 5.7; Florus, *Epitome* 2.8.3; Orosius, *History against the Pagans* 5.24.1. Ignoring the anachronism of its excellent description of the second-century B.C. Roman army, the film's souvenir program also insists that both Lucullus and Pompey joined up with Crassus for the final battle.

34   Sallust, *Histories* 3.96 and 98 (Maurenbrecher) = 3.64 and 66 (McGushin); cf. Plutarch, *Crassus* 9.5–6.

35   Orosius, *History against the Pagans* 5.24.1–4; Appian, *The Civil Wars* 1.14.117; Livy, *Periochae* 96 and 97; Frontinus, *Strategies* 2.5.34; Plutarch, *Crassus* 11.3.

Even Spartacus, whose role is the most historical, often appears in ways the sources do not support. Physically, Kirk Douglas may be a little undersized to represent a man whose great bodily strength both Plutarch and Sallust stress, yet he does have a commanding presence that communicates the great spirit they praise.[36] Unfortunately, the film's illiterate "son and grandson of slaves" who was sold before his thirteenth birthday to work in the mines, as the narrator tells us at the beginning, bears no resemblance to the Spartacus of the sources except that he is identified as a Thracian. Plutarch says that in sagacity and refinement Spartacus was more Greek than Thracian, high praise that no Greek like Plutarch would have given to an illiterate slave-born miner.[37] Athenaeus' statement that Spartacus was "a slave, a Thracian by birth" refers only to his status at the time of his escape.[38] There is nothing to contradict Appian and Florus, who present Spartacus as a freeborn Thracian who had once fought as a paid auxiliary for the Romans and then, having turned against them – becoming a "deserter and bandit," in Florus' words – was captured and condemned to be sold into slavery as a gladiator.[39]

Indeed, that scenario fits the particular historical circumstances very well. In the late second century B.C., the Romans had already annexed part of western Thrace to Macedonia. Other Thracian tribes had remained free and probably supplied auxiliaries for the Roman armies in Macedonia, whose governors waged a number of campaigns against local tribes in the 70s. Then, to counter the growing threat of Mithridates VI, king of Pontus, to Bithynia on the eastern border of Thrace, the Romans began to push into free Thrace. That could have driven Spartacus to desert the Romans and fight against them.

The movie goes too far in romantically making the humble Spartacus into a paragon of natural virtue in contrast with the brutal, rich, and vice-ridden Romans.[40] There is absolutely no evidence that Spartacus ever dreamed of eliminating slavery. The ancient world embraced slavery as part of the natural order of things. Most ancient thinkers never questioned it.[41] Even the New Testament, the body of texts sacred to the soon-to-arise new religion invoked by the opening narrator, unquestioningly

---

36   Plutarch, *Crassus* 8.2; Sallust, *Histories* 3.91 (Maurenbrecher) = 3.61 (McGushin). Florus, *Epitome* 2.8.8, also stresses Spartacus' strength.
37   Plutarch, *Crassus* 8.2.
38   Athenaeus, *The Sophists at Dinner* 6.272–273.
39   Appian, *The Civil Wars* 1.14.116; Florus, *Epitome* 2.8.8; cf. Plutarch, *Crassus* 8.2, and Varro in Flavius Sosipater Charisius, *Ars Grammatica* 1.133 (Keil).
40   Cf. Harris, "Spartacus," 42.
41   Athenaeus, *The Sophists at Dinner*, 6.272, mentions a few noteworthy exceptions.

accepts the existence of master and slave.[42] Sallust, a contemporary of Spartacus, does imply that Spartacus was one of the few "prudent people" with "free and noble minds" in the slave army and portrays him as trying repeatedly, if vainly, to restrain the baser instincts of the majority of his men who were bent on rape, murder, and arson.[43] Other sources, however, clearly contradict the film's scene in which Spartacus castigates his men for making Romans fight as gladiators. Florus and Orosius explicitly assert that Spartacus used Roman prisoners as gladiators in funeral celebrations.[44] Appian is probably referring to one of these funerals when he says that Spartacus sacrificed 300 Roman prisoners on behalf of his dead friend Crixus.[45] Appian also reports that Spartacus crucified a Roman prisoner to inspire his followers by reminding them of the fate that awaited them if they did not win.[46]

We might be tempted to reject these stories as pro-Roman sources trying to make the Romans look better by blackening their enemy, but there is nothing improbable about the accounts.[47] Florus even speculates that Spartacus was trying to wipe out the stigma of having been a gladiator by being a giver of gladiatorial shows instead.[48] Indeed, Spartacus' reported actions reflect the behavior of a man operating within the cultural norms of his own time. After all, gladiatorial contests were supposed to be sacrifices of blood to sustain the dead, and Crassus had imposed the murderous punishment of decimation on at least one of his own cohorts after a cowardly performance in battle as an object lesson to those who might be tempted to turn tail and run in future battles.[49] In fact, to make Spartacus more believable, Kubrick wanted to have Spartacus conform less to modern moral standards, in contrast to Trumbo's more ideological vision.[50]

The opening scene, which shows Spartacus being brutalized as a slave carrying heavy loads of rock at the desolate site of a Roman mine in Libya, is completely unhistorical in its particulars. There was no Roman province of Libya until the reign of Diocletian (A.D. 284–305). Even

42   Pointed out by Harris, "Spartacus," 43. Cf. Matthew 10.24–25 and 25.14–30; Luke 12.47; 1 Peter 2.18.
43   Sallust, *Histories* 3.98 (Maurenbrecher) = 3.66 (McGushin).
44   Florus, *Epitome* 2.8.9; Orosius, *History against the Pagans* 5.24.3.
45   Appian, *The Civil Wars*, 1.14.117.
46   Appian, *The Civil Wars*, 1.14.119.
47   Harris, "Spartacus," 43, raises the possibility of propaganda against Spartacus.
48   Florus, *Epitome* 2.8.9.
49   Ward, *Marcus Crassus and the Late Roman Republic*, 88.
50   Cf. Futrell, "Seeing Red," 98.

Cyrene, the previous name for Roman Libya, did not become a Roman province until 74 B.C., one year before Spartacus' rebellion. Neither is the area known for any mines, but if it were and Lentulus Batiatus had, by some miracle, found his way there, he could not have come upon a strong mature man who had been sold off to work in the mines before his thirteenth birthday. Such a boy would have died long before from the harsh conditions under which ancient slaves labored in mines.

As for Batiatus himself, the only fact known besides his name is that he did run the gladiatorial school from which Spartacus escaped. Therefore, there is nothing to prevent him from playing the role that Peter Ustinov memorably assumes in the rest of the movie. Much the same can be said for Spartacus' wife Varinia, at least after she and Spartacus are reunited after the gladiators' escape. Plutarch is the only source for her existence. He says that she was with Spartacus before he became a gladiator and that she escaped from Capua with her husband, but he gives her no name.[51]

One thing is certain, however: Spartacus' wife would not have been called Varinia. That is the feminine form of the Roman name Varinius, which belonged to one of the early Roman commanders against Spartacus.[52] Plutarch clearly says that Spartacus' wife was a Thracian from the same tribe as he was. Therefore she could not have been from Britannia, as Varinia, played by British actress Jean Simmons, tells Crassus she is. She should have had a Thracian name. Plutarch identifies her as a "prophetess subject to Dionysiac frenzies," so that Diaskentha, the feminine form of the Thracian name "Child of God," would have been appropriate. It is fittingly exotic without being hard to pronounce.[53]

Pity poor Gaius Claudius (or Clodius) Glaber, the hapless commander who disgraced himself when Spartacus made a surprise attack on him and the 3,000 men whom he had brought to besiege Spartacus on the slopes of Vesuvius.[54] His name is somewhat confused in the sources, but

51 Plutarch, *Crassus* 8.3.
52 Appian, *The Civil Wars* 1.14.116 (with the wrong *cognomen*); Frontinus, *Strategies* 1.5.22; Sallust, *Histories* 3.96 (Maurenbrecher) = 64 (McGushin); cf. Livy, *Periochae* 95 (with misspelling "Varenus").
53 Plutarch, *Crassus* 8.3.
54 Plutarch, *Crassus* 9.1–3; Frontinus, *Strategies* 1.5.21; Florus, *Epitome* 1.2.4; Orosius, *History against the Pagans* 5.24.1. Appian, *The Civil Wars* 1.14.116, mistakenly calls him Varinius Glaber. Livy, *Periochae* 95, gives him the more famous Claudian *cognomen* Pulcher. For his rank and for other sources concerning his name see T. R. S. Broughton, *The Magistrates of the Roman Republic*, vol. 2: *99 B.C.–31 B.C.* (1952; rpt. Chico: Scholars Press, 1985), 109 and 115 note 1, and T. Corey Brennan, *The Praetorship of the Roman Republic* (Oxford and New York: Oxford University Press, 2000), vol. 2, 431.

the movie turns it into Marcus Publius Glabrus and makes him into the commander of the non-existent "Garrison of Rome." As Crassus rightly points out to him in the film, it was illegal for armed troops to enter Rome. The only exception was on the most temporary basis to celebrate a major military victory. Emperor Augustus first established what might be called a garrison for Rome: nine cohorts of the elite Praetorian Guard and three urban cohorts of regular soldiers. These latter cohorts, plus three cohorts of the Praetorian Guard, were the first troops ever permanently stationed in Rome. Whatever troops the historical Gaius Claudius Glaber commanded in 73 B.C. were not regular units but were hastily recruited on his way south.[55]

Spartacus greatly exaggerates Gaius Julius Caesar's physical appearance and political status. Suetonius says that he was tall, with slender limbs and fair skin.[56] All of the surviving ancient portraits show Caesar to have had rather sharp and angular features, so that he would not have looked much like bronzed and well-muscled John Gavin. Obviously Caesar could not have received command of Rome's non-existent garrison in the absence of the historical Glaber. Moreover, contrary to the movie, he was not yet even a senator but had begun his formal political career only shortly before the start of Spartacus' revolt. In 74 B.C. he had been appointed legate to M. Antonius Creticus, father of Mark Antony, in the ongoing war against piracy; in 73 he had returned to Rome upon being co-opted into the prestigious priestly college of pontiffs. Shortly thereafter he was elected military tribune for either 72 or 71. Therefore he could have served under Crassus in the war against Spartacus.[57] That would have given Trumbo a fine historical opportunity to hint at a future dictatorship with its attendant foreshadowing of modern Fascism instead of unhistorically making Crassus the vehicle of that message.

Laurence Olivier, on the other hand, bears an uncanny resemblance to a bust that some scholars have identified as a portrait of Marcus Licinius Crassus, the wealthy Roman who defeated Spartacus and crucified 6,000 survivors along the Appian Way from Capua to Rome.[58]

---

55   Cf. Appian, *The Civil Wars* 1.14.116.

56   Suetonius, *Julius Caesar* 45.1.

57   Harris, "Spartacus," 42, rejects Caesar's presence out of hand, but it is not impossible; see Ward, *Marcus Crassus and the Late Roman Republic*, 110–112.

58   This bust is in the Ny Carlsberg Glyptotek (inv. no. 749). A photograph appears in the exhibition catalogue *Kaiser Augustus und die verlorene Republik*, ed. Mathias René Hofter (Mainz: von Zabern, 1988), 317. For the uncertainty of the attribution see the review by R. R. R. Smith, *Journal of Roman Studies*, 79 (1989), 214.

Unfortunately, the rest of Crassus' portrayal is wildly inaccurate. Crassus and the other leading men of Rome were not all patricians. Unfortunately, modern English usage equates the word "patrician" with high-ranking hereditary aristocrats in general. Before 367 B.C., a small group of wealthy families whose ancestors bestowed on them the hereditary designation of patrician generally did monopolize Rome's highest-ranking positions. After 367, when members of wealthy non-patrician families regularly gained access to the highest offices, patrician families were no longer the only members of the ruling elite. The members of this elite were now designated as *nobiles* ("notables"), regardless of their patrician or non-patrician birth. Caesar was a patrician, but Crassus came from one of the non-patrician families who had made it into the highest ranks of the Roman elite.[59] Indeed, more of the senators in Crassus' day were non-patricians like him than patricians like Caesar.[60]

Equally invalid is the idea that there was anything like a "patrician party," a term Crassus uses in a conversation with Caesar. No political parties in the modern sense of the word existed at all. While like-minded men or those with a common interest might work together informally, there were no formal political organizations with registered members, official ideologies, and institutionalized leadership. Politics centered much more on rival personalities and ambitions as individuals struggled to achieve status as prominent leaders of the Republic.

Therefore there is no question that Crassus wanted to become the recognized leading man at Rome, as did Pompey and Caesar, his eventual partners in their opportunistic coalition known as the First Triumvirate of 60 B.C. He was, however, no law-and-order, proto-Fascist general itching to become dictator, as he appears in *Spartacus*.[61] Crassus always worked within the existing Republican framework in the period after Sulla's dictatorship (82–80 B.C.) and had no wish to overthrow the system that would validate the status he desired. He never had the non-existent titles "First General of the Republic," "Father and Defender of Rome," or "First Consul." Historically, he had no legions under his command to bring into the city as Glabrus suggests or to give up when he shares Glabrus' disgrace. It was Crassus' very lack of recent military

59   Ward, *Marcus Crassus and the Late Roman Republic*, 47–53; Marshall, *Crassus*, 16.
60   In general cf. T. P. Wiseman, *New Men in the Roman Senate 139 B.C.–A.D. 14* (London: Oxford University Press, 1971).
61   Cf. Harris, "Spartacus," 43.

glory that threatened his ability to compete for election to the consulship, and that is why he sought the command against Spartacus.[62]

It is also supremely ironic that *Spartacus* portrays Crassus as luxury-loving, amoral, and bisexual. (This last aspect, made explicit in the film's "oysters and snails" scene, had been excluded from the film's originally released version.) Crassus was notorious for his wealth, but not because he lived lavishly. As noted above, although he eventually built on the Palatine a house appropriate to his status, he did not squander his money on numerous luxurious homes and country villas. Instead, he was famous for his moderate lifestyle and preferred to invest his wealth as productively as possible.[63] What was scandalous about him was the way in which he became rich. Early on, he had profited from Sulla's proscription lists, even illegally, it was said.[64] Later, he took too much personal interest in making money, something that was considered to be beneath the dignity of a Roman noble. Plutarch gives the scandalous example that Crassus bought valuable properties at fire sales – literally so – and then resold them at a handsome profit after a large gang of skilled slaves whom he maintained had rebuilt or remodeled the buildings that had burned down.[65]

Despite his reputation for avarice, however, Crassus had the cleanest reputation of all his peers in regard to his familial and sexual life. Rumors about Caesar's bisexuality abounded.[66] Pompey had a series of wives in politically opportunistic marriages and divorces.[67] Crassus, on the other hand, dutifully married Tertulla, the widow of a childless brother. They raised at least two well-regarded sons together, and there is no hint of any later divorce or other marriage despite some malicious rumors about Tertulla's fidelity.[68] Moreover, at the very public trial of Marcus Caelius in 56 B.C., Cicero would have been laughed out of court if he

---

62   Ward, *Marcus Crassus and the Late Roman Republic*, 64 and 82–85; Marshall, *Crassus*, 30–31. If Crassus had held a military command as a praetor in 73 B.C., it seems likely that Plutarch would have noted it. Brennan, *The Praetorship of the Roman Republic*, vol. 2, 433, thinks that he may have held a minor command as an ex-praetor in 72 before receiving the command of the war against Spartacus.

63   Plutarch, *Crassus* 1.1, 2.4–6, and 3.1.

64   Plutarch, *Crassus* 2.3 and 6.6–7.

65   Plutarch, *Crassus* 2.4.

66   Suetonius, *Julius Caesar* 49.1–52.3; Catullus 57.

67   Suetonius, *Julius Caesar* 50.1; Plutarch, *Pompey* 4.2, 9.1–3, 42.7, 47.6, and 55.1–2; Cicero, *Letters to His Friends* 5.26.

68   Cf. Ward, *Marcus Crassus and the Late Roman Republic*, 55–56 and 291–292; Marshall, *Crassus*, 12–13.

had been exaggerating too much when he referred to "Crassus' irreproachable house."[69]

Gracchus, Crassus' populist opponent in the senate, did not exist at all. The name recalls Tiberius and Gaius Sempronius Gracchus, the two martyred popular reformers from the last third of the second century B.C. It took four generations for any of the Sempronii Gracchi to reach prominence again, and no one with the *cognomen* Gracchus was an important senator at the time of Spartacus' uprising.[70] As we shall see, however, there was a historical personage who could easily have provided the model for Charles Laughton's Gracchus. Neither Antoninus, Tony Curtis's slave character, nor Tigranes Levantus (better: Levanticus), Herbert Lom's stereotypically Oriental ambassador from the Cilician pirates, is a known person, but they are not contradicted by what we know, and each is a historically appropriate character. Slaves like Antoninus were common as teachers and entertainers in upper-class Roman homes. Even as an exaggerated stereotype, Tigranes reflects the Greco-Roman view of people from lands bordering the eastern Mediterranean. Historically, Spartacus had to have dealt with someone like him who represented the pirates. These invented characters are perfectly appropriate for historical fiction.

The film also excellently depicts the number and variety of Spartacus' followers as documented in the ancient sources and creatively imagines the complexity of the rebels' encampments and the difficulty of their treks over the length and breadth of Italy. On the other hand, it goes too far in turning the makeshift community of slaves and desperately poor peasants into a proletarian utopia in which, despite some hardships, the children are well nourished and loved, happy peasants dance around campfires, and leaders work in harmonious camaraderie. Appian does state that people flocked to Spartacus because he parceled out the loot from his raids in equal shares. Still, the film would have made the fugitive slaves and peasants and their leaders more heroic if it had depicted the harsh conditions, desperate struggles, and internal tensions they had to confront more realistically.

69   Cicero, *On Behalf of Caelius* 9.
70   There was no Sempronius Gracchus in the senate between the death of C. Sempronius Gracchus in 121 B.C. and the appearance of the T. Sempronius Gracchus who was identified as a quaestor designate on a coin of 37 B.C.; cf. Broughton, *The Magistrates of the Roman Republic*, vol. 2, 476, and vol. 3: *Supplement*, 190. A promising young orator named Tiberius Sempronius Gracchus was a paramour of Julia, daughter of Augustus, who exiled him in 2 B.C. (Tacitus, *Annals* 1.53).

An abbreviated chronology further diminishes the heroic achievement of Spartacus and the rebel masses. Historically, approximately two years passed between the start of Spartacus' rebellion in 73 B.C. and the final battle in 71. By the time the praetor Varinius had replaced the hapless Glaber and he and his officers had fought a number of engagements with Spartacus in 73, it was already late autumn, probably around November. Therefore, most likely the rebellion started in July or August.[71] Crassus took over late in 72 and finished in about six months, so that the last battle would have occurred around April of 71 and the rebellion would have lasted a total of about 22 months.[72]

In the movie, no more than a year can have elapsed from the time of the gladiators' breakout at Capua to the crucifixion of Spartacus at the end. Having fled Capua, Spartacus seems, quite reasonably, to spend a couple of months gathering more and more followers and training an effective army before Glabrus' arrival. Just before Spartacus ignominiously defeats Glabrus, Tigranes appears in Spartacus' camp and strikes a deal whereby the Cilician pirate fleet would transport the fugitives out of Italy from the port of Brundisium on the other side of the peninsula seven months later.[73] Upon defeating Glabrus, the slaves make a harrowing march over the Apennine Mountains in winter. Then, after a short respite during which Varinia announces that she is going to have a baby in the spring, they raid places like Metapontum to collect more loot to pay the pirates. They reach Brundisium at the appointed time only to have the pirates leave them in the lurch. Not long after that Spartacus is forced into the climactic battle with Crassus, during which Varinia miraculously survives while giving birth to Spartacus' son. It could not be more than about a month later when Spartacus is crucified on the Via Appia outside the walls of Rome and Varinia, with the help of Gracchus and Batiatus, escapes from Crassus with her baby to set off for a new life as a freedwoman in Aquitania.

This abbreviated chronology makes it impossible for the film to give its viewers a strong sense of the numerous humiliations that Spartacus and his forces inflicted on the Romans. Modern political considerations led to a conscious distortion of history. Trumbo wanted to show more of Spartacus' victories, but the executives at Universal Studios were anxious

---

71   Sallust, *Histories* 3.96 (Maurenbrecher) = 3.64 (McGushin). Cf. Ward, *Marcus Crassus and the Late Roman Republic*, 83 note 1.

72   Appian, *The Civil Wars*, 1.14.121. Cf. Ward, *Marcus Crassus and the Late Roman Republic*, 97 note 41.

73   Throughout *Spartacus*, the cast has great difficulty in pronouncing the city's name. Most of the time it comes out as "Brindusium."

to avoid arousing the ire of conservative Americans with too much proletarian revolution and wanted scenes of the slaves' military victories
kept to a minimum.[74] Whatever ideological angle Trumbo might have
pursued, he was right in this case. According to our sources, over approximately two years the rebels won at least thirteen battles and plundered
at least four major cities. It greatly diminishes the historical Spartacus
not to give audiences a better idea of the rebels' extraordinary success
under his leadership.

The film would have been much more exciting and spectacular if it
had shown Crassus' elaborate attempt to isolate Spartacus somewhere
in the toe of Italy by building a great fortified rampart and ditch, which
Spartacus finally breached in a daring nighttime attack.[75] It would not
have been difficult to construct an appropriate set for this. Even the two
battles whose details are actually shown do scant justice to Spartacus'
ingenuity and heroism. In the film's surprise attack on the misnamed
Glabrus, Spartacus and his men simply rush Glabrus' unfortified camp
on foot and horseback, but, as described by Plutarch and others, the
attack on the historical Glaber was far more worthy of Hollywood
scriptwriters. Spartacus and his men cleverly plaited ladders out of wild
vines that grew on Vesuvius, they stealthily scaled down the precipitous
cliffs separating them from the Romans below while one man stayed
behind to toss down their weapons, and they surrounded Glaber's unpro-
tected camp before anyone was aware of the danger.[76]

Spartacus looks even more like a Hollywood hero than does Kirk
Douglas in Plutarch's description of the last battle. Instead of meeting
the Roman attack on horseback, Spartacus refused to mount his steed,
a symbol of aristocratic generalship, when it was brought to him before
the battle. Dramatically proclaiming that he would have plenty of horses
if he won and no need of one if he lost, he killed the animal with a thrust
of his sword. Then he rushed fearlessly into the fray on foot and almost
reached Crassus before he was cut down.[77] With a little research, a
scriptwriter could have created a screenplay that better reflects the

---

74   Futrell, "Seeing Red," 98 and 117 note 52.
75   Plutarch, *Crassus* 10.4–6; Appian, *The Civil Wars* 1.14.118–120; Frontinus, *Strategies*
1.5.20. It is improbable that the siege works stretched for the 600 stades (ca. 35 miles) that
Plutarch claims, but they were still a massive undertaking. See Ward, *Marcus Crassus and
the Late Roman Republic*, 89–90 note 20; Patrick McGushin, *Sallust: The Histories*, vol. 2
(Oxford: Clarendon Press, 1994), 150.
76   Plutarch, *Crassus* 9.1–3; Frontinus, *Strategies* 1.5.21; Florus, *Epitome* 2.8.4.
77   Plutarch, *Crassus* 11.6–7. Much of this description and that of Appian, *The Civil Wars*
1.14.120, may be rhetorical commonplaces.

ancient sources and does not contradict the historical particulars while yielding an equally dramatic, entertaining, and uplifting film story. Below, I outline the plot of such a film.

Instead of opening with a bogus scene at a Libyan mine, this movie begins with Spartacus, a Thracian who has formerly fought as an auxiliary for Rome but now opposes the expansion of Roman power into his tribal land. He and his recent bride Diaskentha are captured and sold to Lentulus Batiatus, who has use for both of them at his gladiatorial training school. Not only is Spartacus humiliated by having his wife work as a kitchen slave while he is forced to train as a gladiator, but he is predictably outraged when Batiatus and his overseer, the Marcellus character of Kubrick's film, sadistically goad him by assigning her as a sexual favor to Crixus. Honorably and wisely, Crixus refuses to violate her. When he and fellow slave Oenomaus manage to convince a murderously enraged Spartacus that his wife is unharmed, the three become fast friends and begin plotting to organize a breakout of all those gladiators not suspected of being informants. We also see, much as in Kubrick's movie, interspersed scenes of training, the daily life of the gladiators, and a private show requested by the wealthy Crassus to celebrate the elevation of his young friend Julius Caesar to the college of pontiffs. Crassus, always on the lookout for skilled slaves, notices Diaskentha's grace and intelligence. Batiatus, who now considers her a liability, happily sells her to him. When Spartacus finds out, his loose-tongued anger reveals to an informer that an escape plan is afoot. When the three friends discover this informer talking to Marcellus in the kitchen, they and about seventy others jump into action, kill Marcellus, outfight the guards, rescue Diaskentha, and escape to Vesuvius.

We now cut to Rome and a more authentic representation of the Senate House. The senate is meeting to deal with the crisis after local forces have failed to capture the rebels. The ambitious praetor Crassus, whose vast wealth largely rests on slave labor, does not want to interrupt his business and political affairs to take up a command against a few marauding fugitives, but his less accomplished fellow praetor Gaius Claudius Glaber does. Crassus, wishing to acquire more political allies as he looks toward running for the consulship, works to obtain the command for Glaber. One of the consuls-elect for 72 B.C., the populist politician Lucius Gellius, backs Varinius, another praetor. In the process Gellius engages in some populist rhetoric by pointing out that many poor farmers also support Spartacus. They do so because it is hard for them to survive in the face of the great landowners and their huge slave-run estates, whose brutal working conditions drive many additional slaves to revolt. In the end, however, the rich Crassus successfully pulls strings for Glaber.

Since little is known about Glaber and Varinius and their political relationships, a writer of historical fiction is perfectly free to create such a scenario. Moreover Gellius, who was about 63 years old in 73 B.C., is an excellent historical analogue to the character of the unhistorical Gracchus in Kubrick's film. He had studied oratory under Gaius Papirius Carbo, who had been a supporter of the reformist Gracchi brothers who had served on Tiberius Gracchus' land commission.[78] Although Carbo eventually turned against Gaius Gracchus, Gellius, during his impressionable teenage years, would have known Carbo principally as a follower of the Gracchi, and this probably shaped Gellius' populist leanings. The *cognomen* Publicola ("Favoring the People") no longer appears to belong to Gellius, but his adopted son bore it. The name is an indication of the family's populist orientation.[79]

The real Gellius had been praetor in 94, but for twenty-two years his career had been blocked by the rise of the conservative Sulla and his political heirs. Their hold on power was challenged by younger men willing to take a populist stance.[80] One of those people was Pompey, with whom Gellius had served in 89 B.C. under Pompey's father during the war with the Italian Allies, the Social War, as it is generally called, of 91–88 B.C. Gellius now seemed to favor Pompey, whose own ambitions were bringing him into conflict with Sulla's political heirs in the senate and soon would form a direct challenge to Crassus' bid for prominence.[81] Gellius is therefore the perfect character to provide a dramatic opponent to Crassus in a film.

As our imagined movie continues, Glaber's ignominious defeat is a setback for Crassus and allows Gellius to have Varinius put in charge of the slave war. Now it is possible to show Spartacus' defeat of Cossinius, one of Varinius' officers who, according to Plutarch, suffered the comic embarrassment of almost being captured while bathing before he was killed.[82] Next, Spartacus' reputation soars during a series of battles, in one of which Oenomaus perishes. The series culminates with the capture of Varinius' lictors and Varinius' horse right from under him.[83] To save

78   Cf. Ward, *Marcus Crassus and the Late Roman Republic*, 24.
79   On the *cognomen* see E. Badian, "The Clever and the Wise," *Bulletin of the Institute of Classical Studies*, Supplement 51 (1988), 1–11, at 8 note 11.
80   See Ward, *Marcus Crassus and the Late Roman Republic*, 24–25.
81   On this cf. Ward, *Marcus Crassus and the Late Roman Republic*, 24 and 91–102.
82   Plutarch, *Crassus* 9.4–5.
83   Plutarch, *Crassus* 9.5; Appian, *The Civil Wars* 1.14.116 (despite the confusion of names).

time and avoid repetition, the film could show these battles as a quick montage of short scenes but with some attention on the death of Oenomaus and the capture of Varinius.

Then we see the arduous trek over the snowy Apennines to the relatively safe eastern side of the Italian peninsula, from which Spartacus hopes to march north to the Alps in the spring and to escape from Italy. There, a long simmering dissension comes to a head between those who want to follow Spartacus' plan and those, particularly the Gauls and Germans, who want to stay and plunder Italy under Crixus. Diaskentha, whose prophetic powers would have brought her respect in ancient society, mediates their dispute and points out the strategic and logistical advantages that separate forces would have. The two leaders, remaining friends, agree to split their followers into two armies. Spartacus spends the rest of the winter preparing for a spring march to the Alps.

Back in Rome, Lucius Gellius, now consul, argues that he and his colleague, Gnaeus Cornelius Lentulus Clodianus, can bring this unfortunate war to a satisfactory conclusion and then make reforms to prevent another outbreak. Crassus, seeing the war as an opportunity for himself, argues that unlike him they have no meaningful military experience, but the senate defers to their rank. Having recruited two consular armies of two legions each, the consuls march east as soon as possible in the spring to engage the two rebel armies. Gellius' army manages to kill Crixus and inflict a crushing defeat on the Gauls and Germans in the Garganus region. Lentulus blocks Spartacus in the north so that Gellius can take him in the rear. Spartacus boldly seizes the initiative, smashes Lentulus first, then wheels around and defeats Gellius. Again, a quick succession of brief scenes can cover the military action.

Spartacus honors Crixus with a great funeral that includes 300 gladiatorial duels to the death by Roman prisoners. On this occasion he delivers a great speech about his hatred of the Romans and about the slaves' fight to be free. In another series of vignettes, he and his followers march north. They defeat Cassius, the proconsul of Cisalpine Gaul, at Mutina and, realizing that they are not strong enough to risk fighting the large number of veteran troops still in the rest of the province, return south. Now they quickly defeat the forces of the two consuls regrouped in Picenum and then capture the port city of Thurii, which Spartacus uses as a base for resupplying his army and preparing for a direct attack on Rome itself. There he learns that Diaskentha is pregnant.[84]

84   The confusion in the relevant sources permits my reconstruction of events in the preceding three paragraphs: Plutarch, *Crassus* 9.5–7; Appian, *The Civil Wars* 1.14.117; Livy, *Periochae* 96; Orosius, *History against the Pagans* 5.24-3–7; Florus, *Epitome* 2.8.8–11.

In the meantime, Crassus seizes the opportunity to humiliate his opponent Gellius by persuading the senate to recall both consuls and to put him in sole command of the war, which he offers to finance on his own. With this commission he hopes to build up a following of loyal veterans large enough to offset the one that Pompey will soon be bringing back from Spain. Crassus even enlists a number of opportunistic aristocrats as staff officers, among them his friend Caesar, newly elected as a military tribune. Crassus hires six veteran legions and sets up camp in the vicinity of Picentia astride the road from Rhegium to Rome, the main road that is closest to Thurii if one went from there to Rome. While whipping his legions into shape, Crassus summons Lentulus Batiatus to brief him on Spartacus.[85]

In late winter to early spring, Spartacus and his whole army march west from Thurii to the road for Rome. Crassus orders his legate Mummius to circle around Spartacus' rear but not to engage him. Mummius' subsequent disobedience and defeat need only be reported to Crassus and not shown on the screen, but Crassus' punishment of the most cowardly 500-man cohort of Mummius' troops would make a dramatic statement about the nature of Roman power. This punishment is decimation: one tenth of the cohort is selected by lot and clubbed to death by the rest.[86]

After that brutal lesson, Crassus' legions defeat a detachment of the rebels and pursue Spartacus, who flees south to the Straits of Messina. There he negotiates with Cilician pirates to transport his men to Sicily, which had been the scene of massive slave rebellions over the last sixty years. Spartacus hopes to open up a new front against Rome on Sicily.[87] The pirates, however, betray him, and he desperately tries to cross the straits on crudely constructed rafts. Bad weather and the notoriously tricky currents wreck this venture.[88] By now Crassus has had his men construct a huge ditch and a rampart fortified with palisades across the neck of the promontory on which Spartacus' forces are encamped. A

---

85   Plutarch, *Crassus* 10.1, confuses Picenum with Picentia. Cf. Ward, *Marcus Crassus and the Late Roman Republic*, 86 note 11.

86   Plutarch, *Crassus* 10.1–3; Sallust, *Histories* 4.23 (Maurenbrecher) = 4.18 (McGushin). Appian, *The Civil Wars* 1.14.118; Florus, *Epitome* 2.8.12. Either Appian or his source exaggerates the number of men executed. Polybius, *Histories* 6.38.1–3, first describes the practice of decimation in the Roman army.

87   Plutarch, *Crassus* 10. 1–3; Appian, *The Civil Wars* 1.14.118. Shaw, *Spartacus and the Slave Wars*, 79–129, provides the sources for the Sicilian slave wars.

88   Sallust, *Histories* 4.30–31 (Maurenbrecher) = 4.26–27 (McGushin); Florus, *Epitome* 2.8.12.

series of rapid cuts back and forth between the activities on the two sides would effectively indicate the passage of time.

Spartacus becomes desperate to break Crassus' siege. He crucifies a Roman prisoner to unnerve the Romans and to remind his followers of what will happen to them if they should fail. On a dark night during a late spring snow squall, Spartacus' men hurl anything that they can find into the ditch and set fire to the palisade with bundles of burning branches. Thus they break the Roman blockade and flee to the surrounding mountains, from where they make a dash toward Brundisium, the port in which they hope to commandeer ships and escape from Italy.[89]

Unfortunately, however, they learn that Marcus Terentius Varro Lucullus, whom the senate has summoned to return with his army from Macedonia, is now landing at Brundisium. Hoping to panic Crassus, who wants to end the war before Pompey returns from Spain, the slaves again split their forces and head toward Rome. Castus and Gannicus lead one group, Spartacus heads the other. In response, Crassus splits his forces. Spartacus, seemingly unstoppable after a hard-won victory over the contingent left to cover him, learns that he immediately has to face Crassus' fresh troops, who have annihilated Castus and Gannicus. The decisive battle is imminent. Spartacus plunges his sword into his horse. He dies, heroically fighting on foot.[90]

Kubrick has been criticized for having his Spartacus survive to be crucified later, despite Appian's explicit testimony that Spartacus died in battle and that his body was never found.[91] That testimony does not force a screenwriter to jettison what Jon Solomon has rightly identified as the most satisfying part of *Spartacus*.[92] If Spartacus' body was never found, there is no proof that he did not survive. The story of his death could have been a ploy to protect his identity in the hope that he might escape and continue the fight. Spartacus might have survived to become one of those anonymously crucified along the Appian Way.[93] Therefore it is not too much to imagine the scene in which all the survivors reply "I'm Spartacus!" to Crassus' offer of sparing the rest if only they identify Spartacus.

Trumbo's script stretches credulity, however, by not having Crassus use Batiatus to identify Spartacus when his other ploy has failed. After all, Crassus had detained Batiatus in the Roman camp for this very

---

89   Appian, *The Civil Wars* 1.14.120.
90   Plutarch, *Crassus* 11.2–7.
91   Cf. Harris, "Spartacus," 42.
92   Cf. Solomon, *The Ancient World in the Cinema*, 53.
93   Appian, *The Civil Wars* 1.14.120.

purpose. Our version could have Crassus flog Batiatus out of his camp before the battle because Batiatus insists on trying to obtain the right to sell all potential captives despite Crassus' plan to crucify them. Batiatus need not be present in our script to identify Diaskentha, since Crassus had earlier paid close enough attention to her to want to buy her from Batiatus. She could more realistically give birth a day or two before the battle and be in hiding in a nearby cave. Crassus discovers her as he happens to pass and hear the baby's cries. He takes her and the child to Rome, not because he lusts after her as in the film but because, in the absence of Spartacus himself, they are the greatest trophies that he can display in his victory celebration. Afterwards, they would be killed according to Roman custom.

Gellius, affronted and envious, conspires with a peeved Batiatus to steal these symbols of Crassus' victory and spirit them out of Rome to freedom. Without dictatorial powers, Crassus is not the kind of enemy who could force the popular Gellius into committing suicide. Instead, Gellius savors his personal triumph over his rival in the private luxury of his home while Batiatus (now guilty of theft, even treason) and Spartacus' wife and infant son make their way to the Via Appia and get past Crassus' troops, who are quartered outside Rome to await his victory ovation.[94] Diaskentha bids her wrenching farewell to the dying Spartacus, who is hanging anonymously on his cross. The three fugitives set off south down the Via Appia toward the port of Puteoli, from which they will take ship for new lives in the free city of Massilia.

In this way, history and histrionics could dramatically complement each other. Audiences could enjoy the kind of grand and thought-provoking epic that has made Kubrick's *Spartacus* a classic. At the same time they would have a memorable narrative of people and events that closely matches the historical record.

---

94 Cf. Ward, *Marcus Crassus and the Late Roman Republic*, 98 and note 45; Marshall, Crassus, 33–34.

CHAPTER FIVE

Spartacus, Rebel Against Rome

C. A. Robinson, Jr.

EDITOR'S NOTE: The following text is a composite of two versions of an essay written by a well-known classical scholar for the souvenir program book of *Spartacus*. The original version was entitled "Spartacus – Rebel or Hero?" This title was changed to "Spartacus, Rebel Against Rome" for the published version, which was significantly shortened. As a result, a few brief passages were transposed to different places, and occasional changes in punctuation became necessary, too. Below, such passages have been restored to their original versions. The composite text here given incorporates in italics all passages excised from the original. Insignificant changes in punctuation and capitalization that resulted from the editing process have not been marked, but all substantive variants are recorded. A few spelling errors have been silently corrected. The original's divisions into paragraphs, occasionally different from the published version, have been restored. Textual variants that in some cases replace the original's usually longer versions appear below in square brackets and are indicated by ALT. The original version is preserved in Box 37 of the Kirk Douglas Papers deposited at the Wisconsin Center for Film and Theater Research, part of the Wisconsin Historical Society Archives in Madison, Wisconsin. Some of its pages have brief handwritten annotations. A few of these are small revisions, most likely the author's; others are indications for cutting the text for length. These latter appear to be the author's as well; for that reason, such cuts and a few other minor word changes are not incorporated here. (They are not important for the argument.) Most of the textual cuts made for the published version, however, are not marked on the original; presumably, they were done without the author's involvement. The primary purpose of the cuts is to present readers of the souvenir book with a cleaner and easier-to-grasp image of Spartacus. Some of the passages that were excised or, in some cases, skillfully condensed seem to have been considered too discursive or too detailed about the historical background. Other passages were cut because they give information that contradicts the story of the film. In several places these cuts result in a characterization of Spartacus and his revolt that differs from the original's. The composite that follows will facilitate comparison of the original with the published version and with the finished film.

Such is the vanity of man that there is an understandable tendency to overemphasize the magnitude of his present-day achievements, forgetting that they are no more than a minute addition to the mosaic of fulfillment. Take the eternal struggle for freedom and human dignity; watch each day's turn of events and the shouting headlines they inspire. Then reflect that the torch of liberty was kindled before the dawn of recorded history and has been carried forward through the ages by dedicated men *and passed on to new bearers when older hands faltered and dropped away, as in an everlasting relay race.*

History has been kind to some of these torch-bearers, fickle to others. One man, for example, who led an inspired crusade for freedom against the most powerful state on earth, defeating in bloody battle nine of its best trained armies, was almost expurgated from history. His was no ordinary rebellion, but an organized revolt against established custom and authority which aroused a fear so deep among the proponents of the existing order that two generations were to pass before men could speak calmly of the experience. This extraordinary and quite heroic man was named Spartacus. *The rebellion he was destined to lead developed into the greatest revolt of slaves in ancient Roman history.*

Spartacus came from Thrace, a land in north-eastern Greece long noted for its vigorously independent ways. As a youth he *served in the Roman army, deserted, became a brigand,* was captured and brought to Rome, where [ALT.: *Here*] he was sold as a slave. *The story goes that while Spartacus was waiting in the capital to learn his fate a snake coiled itself around his face one night as he slept. His wife was with him, and she, being a prophetess fired with Bacchanalian frenzy, said that the omen portended formidable power for Spartacus, but that it would not end happily for him.*

It was in this fashion that Spartacus wound up at Capua, a great city in Campania, as the area around the Bay of Naples was called. Being strong and brave, he was put into the school at Capua where gladiators were trained, for the urban masses of Rome insisted not only on cheap food but also on entertainment. *And what more exciting sport can be imagined than that of man fighting man, unless it be that of a man, or rather groups of men, fighting wild animals? The Romans had both kinds of entertainment, until finally they became so brutalized (as will always happen in such things) that the gladiators were given no chance at all against the beasts and were thrown at them bound hand and foot.*

The famous revolt in the first century before Christ began with one type of slave – the gladiators – but it quickly attracted all manner of men in Italy who hoped to improve their lot. Since they came from the lowest class of society, they were, most of them, uneducated, wild, and brutal, but some of them had been, once upon a time at least, decent ordinary men and women. They had been scooped up quite indiscriminately by pirates who kidnapped them and sold them into slavery or by the Roman armies as they advanced the imperial frontiers further and further around the Mediterranean Sea. If now they were cruel, their oppressors had themselves to thank for the hateful conditions that make men desperate.

This was not the first time in Roman history that slaves had risen up against their masters, but it was by all odds the best organized revolt and the most intelligently led and therefore the most dangerous. The accounts given by the ancient writers concerning Spartacus – by Livy, the great historian, by Plutarch, the famous biographer, and by Sallust and Appian, *two other historians* – emphasize the horrible conditions under which slaves lived out their lives and their determination to win freedom with Spartacus. *That most reactionary of Roman aristocrats, Cato, advised in his book on agriculture that slaves should be worked like animals and then thrown out on the rubbish heap to die. Little wonder, then, when they saw freedom within their grasp, that the slaves should have fought with a desperation that inspired terror throughout Italy and the neighboring island of Sicily.*

Ancient history provides no figure with whom Spartacus can be properly compared. We marvel at the engineering *and building* accomplishments of the ancient world, constructed without benefit of modern technological knowledge and implements. Surely the rebellion led by Spartacus was no less a miracle of leadership engineering. He was a slave, with no organized government behind him, no group of trained soldiers at his beck and call, no stores of weapons and food on which to draw. Rebellions, then *as* [ALT.: *and*] now, almost invariably started with these necessities assured, with leaders trained in command functions. Beginning with nothing, Spartacus organized his armies, forged his armor, gathered in the food, planned the strategy and, what may seem quite surprising, normally did all that he could to protect innocent people from the revenge of his men. *Plutarch tells us that Spartacus was more like a Greek than a barbarian and in his humanity and intelligence was far above the status of a slave.*

Other leaders in ancient history, of course, inspired their followers with the same passionate devotion that Spartacus elicited. In an earlier day, Alexander the Great of Macedon and Hannibal of Carthage, and not long after Spartacus, Julius Caesar, the most remarkable of all Romans, were idolized by their men, but they all had long-established governments behind them. Spartacus, a mere slave and a gladiator, organized a motley crew of many races into a *dread and* powerful army of 90,000 men, but the cement that held them together was not the carefully planned campaign of a regular government but *the* hatred of their lot, hatred of their oppressors, the desire for freedom and the hope of returning to their native lands.

Spartacus supplied the spark, the brains, the sustained counsel that almost succeeded. At first, the Roman government did not take the uprising seriously, but it is impossible for us (with all our hindsight) to say that the bid for freedom was altogether doomed from the beginning. Escape home was entirely within the realm of possibility, and surely that was sufficient. Improvement in the condition of slaves was the very least that might be expected and actually became a fact, even though the rebels eventually lost. Such fear did they inspire.

But one thing was not possible, and that was the permanent overthrow of the Roman government. The Romans had lost many an army in the past; in fact, in one day at Cannae Hannibal killed at least 60,000 men. If Spartacus had killed Crassus, the general (or praetor as he was called) that Rome finally sent against him, another general and other armies would have been found. Indeed, this same Crassus lost his life later on in the Syrian desert fighting against the Parthians. And yet Rome remained and went on to further conquests.

All this heightens the struggle of Spartacus. His minimum goal – escape from Italy and freedom of some sort, at least – slipped his grasp at the end, quite true. The fault was not his, however, but his followers', who at a critical moment and in the fashion of nomads broke up into groups, each following its own inclinations.

But the [ALT.: The] true measure of Spartacus is to be seen against the backdrop of his adversary. *By the first century* B.C., *the period of Spartacus, the Roman Republic had built a mighty Empire.* [ALT.: Rome was a world power.] The turning point in its development, *from the headship of an Italian federation to that of a world power* [ALT.: from Republic to Empire] dated from *the glorious* [ALT: its] victory over Hannibal just before 200 B.C. [ADDED SENTENCE; CF. BELOW:] Its continued conquests brought tremendous internal problems.

Hannibal's conqueror, Publius Cornelius Scipio – "Africanus," as he was dubbed – held a magnificent triumph in Rome, amid the rejoicing of a populace that had lived so long under the threat of annihilation. And then Rome went on to further conquests. Sicily, Sardinia and Corsica had already been turned into provinces. Spain, North Africa, Macedonia, Greece and Asia Minor were soon added. Eventually, of course, this great Empire came to include Gaul (modern France) and Britain, the lands along the Rhine and Danube Rivers, Syria as far as the Euphrates River, Palestine, and Egypt.

Meanwhile, tremendous problems developed in Italy, which were to account for the conditions confronting Spartacus and his followers. Thousands of small farmers *had been* ruined by the *war with Hannibal. They sold* [ALT.: farmers, ruined by the wars, sold] their land to rich neighbors, thus commencing the growth of vast plantations worked by *gangs of slaves, while they themselves gravitated to the city* [ALT.; CF. BELOW: the captured prisoners-of-war who formed the huge slave population]. *There was also the fact that in the course of its expansion Rome captured thousands upon thousands of prisoners who were sold as slaves. The general confusion brought on by Rome's marching armies was such that pirates from time to time also renewed their ancient trade, so that at moments life was quite uncertain in the eastern Mediterranean world. This was a world that had known the ways of civilization for two thousand years. Even the little island of Delos in the Aegean Sea became a notorious center for the slave trade and boasted that it could handle ten thousand slaves a day.*

It is obviously all too true that Rome's glorious victory over Hannibal created severe problems at home. Rome was a world power – eventually it became practically the only civilized power, as it conquered the ancient world. But the small farmer who had fought so well for Empire was now ruined, a member of the idle city proletariat. What was worse, he and his fellows were the citizens, members of the Assembly that governed both the city of Rome and its Empire. What real interest did they have in the welfare of the provincials or even in improving their own positions?

We may be certain of this, the slave was a forgotten man [ALT.: The slaves were the forgotten men in Roman society], with no legal status whatever. *Some were, however, slightly more fortunate than their brothers. A body slave or a household slave was considered luckier than one who was shackled to a plow or confined to the dark bowels of an iron mine or some sun-broiled marble quarry. These household slaves were bought by their masters on the basis of their superior intelligence or comeliness and it was not unknown for a master to give them their freedom as a reward for faithful performance of duties.*

Another category – like that of Spartacus himself – was selected for a bittersweet existence in the gladiatorial arena. Since most contests were staged to the death, the less hardy gladiator would be killed off early in his career, giving him sweet surcease from the brutality and horrors of slavery. The hardier and more nimble and skillful gladiator could with luck survive for years before meeting death at the business end of a sword or a Thracian dagger. But these gladiators represented a mere handful of the slaves. The others were treated as beasts of burden; worse, in fact, because they were more plentiful.

If the two top social classes at Rome – the senatorial and the capitalist – cared little for the lowly masses, the slave had no hope at all. Nor did he have any regard for the wonderful traditions of ancient Rome or any desire to cultivate the stern Roman qualities of duty and devotion to the state which had created this great Empire. His thoughts, naturally, were of himself.

We can understand, and perhaps excuse, those Romans who gave their first attention to the free poor and not to the slaves. Though there was much opposition on the part of most rich Romans, two brothers did try to do just this. Tiberius and Gaius Gracchus, for so the brothers were called, tried to revitalize the moral fabric of the Roman state by moving the urban rabble back to the land or by planting them in colonies abroad. The rich were in no mood to give up the farms which their fathers and grandfathers had long held, and they resisted by riot and murder first one Gracchus and then the other.

And so the attempt at reform failed, and Rome entered upon a century-long revolution during which one famous general after another – Marius, Sulla, Pompey, Julius Caesar, Antony, Augustus – tried to seize the supreme power in the state. It was Julius Caesar's grandnephew, Augustus, who finally brought the Roman Republic to an end and introduced a period when Emperors, and not citizens, ruled.

It was during the reign of the first Emperor, Caesar Augustus, that Jesus Christ was born. And in other ways, too, it was a notable period, for the civilized world was commencing an era of peace and prosperity that was to endure two and a half centuries. But the revolution that inaugurated this amazing era had been long and terrible, and few things had been more terrifying than the revolts of slaves. Their position had become unendurable, and they were determined to act here and now.

If, as we have said, the revolt in Italy under Spartacus was the best organized, it was not the first. There had been other rebellions of slaves, and Spartacus was wise enough to profit by their mistakes. The first two major strikes for freedom had taken place in neighboring Sicily, a land full of various peoples, but chiefly Greeks. It was a rich and ancient land, now part of the Roman provincial administration. In the half century after Hannibal's defeat the Romans had made a quarter of a million people prisoners of war and had sold them as slaves. Further conquests and breeding at home produced other thousands, and now they were scattered across the vast estates of Sicily and Italy.

Representatives of all the nationalities of the known world could be seen, but most of the slaves in Sicily had their origins in the eastern Mediterranean.

The owner of slaves, in Roman antiquity, had complete power over them, even that of life and death, he could scourge, torture and crucify them. He even encouraged quarrels among them so that they might not join in plotting against his own life. The gangs of slaves often worked chained together, and at night they slept in filthy, crowded dungeons.

[ALT. TO PRECEDING ITALICIZED PASSAGE:] Their owner had complete power over them, even that of life and death. He could scourge, torture and crucify them. He even encouraged quarrels among them so that they might not join in plotting against his own life. The slaves often worked chained together, and at night they slept in filthy, crowded dungeons. They were treated as beasts of burden; worse, in fact, because they were more plentiful.

The slaves had no hope at all. Little wonder, then, when they saw freedom within their grasp that they fought with a desperation that inspired terror throughout Italy.

[CONTINUATION OF PRECEDING ITALICIZED PASSAGE:] *The slaves on the cultivated farms were the worst treated, because they could be most easily supervised. The shepherds, by the very nature of their task, had to roam with the flocks and consequently were allowed more freedom. Nevertheless, we can imagine with what fear they were viewed. Here were thousands of strong and desperate men, hating their owners, and yearning for freedom. Travelers were often robbed and murdered, women were raped, and for long periods in the second century B.C. both property and life were in constant danger.*

Then, suddenly in 135 B.C., the storm broke in Sicily. A Syrian slave, named Eunus, was the leader. He called himself King and his concubine Queen. At first only a few hundred hardy souls joined him, then with increasing success thousands of slaves deserted their masters and adopted a career of plunder and murder. The fatal mistake of Eunus (which Spartacus was careful to avoid) was the belief that he could keep on defeating Roman armies. He should have tried to escape home; instead he thought he could permanently hang on to Sicily. Eventually he was overthrown and his revolt collapsed.

The danger of slave revolts persisted, however. Indeed, in 104 B.C. a second and more terrible rebellion of slaves broke out in Sicily. They could not have chosen a better moment from their own point of view. The Romans were fully occupied in Italy with a dangerous invasion of Germanic tribes from the north. These were the famous Cimbri and Teutons, who struck an awful fear into every Roman breast. It was not until the Romans had beaten back the Germans that they were able to dispatch respectable forces to Sicily, where for three years the whole way of life had been threatened. Once again tens of thousands of desperate men – both slave and free – flocked to their leaders, Salvius and Athenion.

But, as was always the case, Roman arms finally triumphed, the leaders of the revolt and many of their followers were killed, and thousands of prisoners were brought to Rome to grace the celebration. But when they were ordered to amuse the Roman populace by fighting wild beasts, they chose to die in combat with one another, that they might at least have the satisfaction of dying like warriors. Their conqueror, the Roman consul Aquilius, was captured later on by King Mithradates, a powerful enemy of Rome in Asia Minor. Mithradates had the opinion that Aquilius was a greedy man and so he poured molten gold down his throat.

The slave revolts in Sicily had almost succeeded. Might not another man, with better brains and some luck, win out against the armies of Rome, no matter what their power, especially if he adopted as his major aim escape from Italy? In 73 B.C., Spartacus saw his chance and struck. He and seventy others broke into a kitchen at Capua and stole knives and spits and then fled in the direction of Mt. Vesuvius, *that beautiful volcano which was to bury Pompeii and other cities a century and a half later under its ash and lava.*

The men who had broken out *of the school at Capua* were more than ordinary slaves, for they were trained gladiators, accustomed to fight and kill. *Moreover, the origins of most of them were not in the civilized Asiatic East, as had been the case in Sicily.* They were dangerous Thracians and Gauls, Cimbri, Teutons and other Germans, brave and hardy European warriors [ALT.: Europeans] all. *In the beginning, the command was divided between the Thracian Spartacus and two Gauls, Crixus and Oenomaus.*

Now, at this time, there was no police force in Italy. Consequently, the Roman government had to send regular soldiers against the gladiators, a small force, at first, because the uprising was not regarded seriously. [ALT. TO PRE-CEDING TWO SENTENCES:] The Roman government sent a small force of regular soldiers against the gladiators at first, because the uprising was not regarded seriously. The Roman troops were defeated and stripped of their arms – *bronze breastplates and greaves, leather shields, iron swords, spears, and javelins. Then the gladiators hurried to the top of Vesuvius and took up their position beside the crater. On every side were steep and slippery precipices, except at one spot, where the way was narrow and difficult. This was the point that the new Roman commander decided to guard, but the gladiators pulled up the wild vines growing round about them, made them into ladders and so got down the cliffs without the Romans knowing of it. Then they turned on the Romans and crushed them.*

The victory gave Spartacus *and his followers still* more arms, and *they* [ALT.: his followers] stole horses to form a cavalry unit. But now so many recruits were joining him that he had to put special men to work forging their weapons; still others were detailed to find food. And yet more thousands – wild shepherds, runaway slaves, the oppressed poor – flocked to Spartacus' cause, willing to fight *hard* for their freedom.

When he had overthrown still other Roman armies, Spartacus conceived the sound idea of marching north, through the whole length of Italy, to the Alps. The plan would then be to cross the mountains, when each man would escape home as best he could. This was far more practicable than imagining, as the Sicilian slaves had done, that they could ever establish themselves as free men in the perpetual shadow of Roman arms. But all the successes puffed up the followers of Spartacus, and they were so confident of themselves that they went about Italy ravaging the land and wasting valuable time.

So now the Roman Senate sent both consuls – Gellius and Lentulus – against the insurgents. Gellius caught the rebel leader, Crixus, and a plundering contingent of Gauls and Germans off their guard, away from Spartacus, and slew them. Not much later Spartacus overwhelmed both consuls, and to avenge the end of Crixus he made three hundred Roman prisoners fight in pairs to the death. On the overthrow of another Roman army, even Roman soldiers deserted to Spartacus.

Here was a dangerous and able leader of desperate men on the loose in Italy. Murder, rape and looting followed in their wake, though Spartacus exerted himself to protect the innocent. Spartacus' personality and genius for leadership and military victory, however, kept the ever-growing army together. Seventy, eighty, ninety thousand men were banded together in a fighting organization, bent on freedom.

[ALT. TO PRECEDING ITALICIZED PASSAGE:] Army after army was sent against him, only to be crushed. Even Roman soldiers deserted to Spartacus, whose personality and genius for leadership and military victory kept the ever-growing army together.

The march continued northward, almost as far as the Alps. Then suddenly the over-all strategy changed. The plan of crossing the Alps was abandoned, and the gladiators and all their followers turned back south again. We cannot be certain of the reason for this. Was there dissension in their ranks? Had they been in Italy so long that despite their suffering they could not bear to leave? Did they think that they might capture Rome itself, or at any rate continue on their career of looting?

It is a good guess that Spartacus saw the difficulties involved, for a successful crossing of the Alps would not necessarily guarantee freedom – escape from Italy, yes, but after that, what? Much of the world immediately beyond the Alps, and especially eastward toward Thrace, held Roman armies that would continue to harry the fugitives. Much better, so Spartacus probably reasoned, was to march south, cross to Sicily, where tens of thousands of slaves, full of memories of their near-success against Rome, would rise up and join them. Perhaps then they might be invincible.

However that may be, the Roman government now [ALT.: Finally, the Roman government] took vigorous action *against an enemy that seemed to be spreading terror and destruction at will.* Marcus Licinius Crassus, who had served with distinction under the dictator Sulla, was appointed *praetor and given* [ALT.: praetor, given] extraordinary powers to crush the rebels.

This Crassus, *as it happens,* was much more than a military figure. For one thing, he was the richest man in the world; and for another, he yearned for political power. He saw clearly that this would not be possible without military glory, because *these were days when* military machines and their commanders counted for *far* more than statesmen and ballots. *Crassus' chief rival at the time was already a military hero – Pompey the Great, vain, pompous and honorable. He had won spectacular military victories in Africa and Spain.*

Neither Pompey nor Crassus was destined to become strong enough to make himself master of the Roman state alone. They had to ally themselves with a third man, Julius Caesar, who, in addition to his commanding intelligence, had tremendous popularity with the Roman masses. The unofficial but famous union of these three men – Pompey, Crassus and Caesar – became known as the First Triumvirate; despite the orations of Cicero and the opposition of other Republican patriots, the Triumvirate contributed mightily to the end of Republican Rome. This happened a little later, after the war with Spartacus was concluded.

Meanwhile, on his appointment as praetor, Crassus bestirred himself to win victory as speedily as possible, before Pompey should return to Italy covered with military laurels. Crassus added his six legions to the remnants of the four legions who had served under the unhappy consuls. This gave him a large force of over 20,000 men, but recent defeats had unsettled Roman morals. Therefore, Crassus separated off a Roman contingent of several hundred men that had performed particularly poorly and resurrected an old custom known as decimation; that is to say, every tenth man was singled out at random and killed. Discipline, however, was restored.

With great speed Crassus pursued Spartacus southward, into the very toe of Italy, facing Sicily. Spartacus' plan, as we have said, was to cross over to

Sicily, raise the slaves in rebellion and see what the future might bring. He had the good fortune to find some pirates in the straits of Messana, and these he paid to transport himself and his men to the island. But the pirates, in the fashion of their kind, vanished when they had been paid.

[ALT. TO PRECEDING ITALICIZED PASSAGE:] To win victory as speedily as possible, Crassus pursued Spartacus southward, into the very toe of Italy. There Spartacus found some pirates in the straits of Messina, and these he paid to transport himself and his men to Sicily. But the pirates vanished when they had been paid.

Crassus now thought *that* he had Spartacus cornered *in the narrow toe of Italy, where the supply of food would quickly run out. To trap the gladiator in, Crassus built a wall and dug a ditch right across the peninsula, thirty-seven miles long, from sea to sea. But on a stormy night Spartacus filled up part of the ditch with earth and boughs and trees and escaped. He* [ALT.: but Spartacus eluded the trap,] headed for the *great* port of Brindisi, in the heel of Italy, *whence* [ALT.: where] he might pass across the Adriatic Sea. But, as luck would have it, a Roman army was just then returning from Greece, and Spartacus was forced to turn north.

For more than two years the rebel army, made up of so many diverse elements, had held together. But now dissensions developed in the ranks. Two Gauls, Castus and Cannicus [Gannicus], *broke away from Spartacus and were destroyed by Crassus. The loss of several thousand men was a grievous blow to Spartacus, but still he persisted. Crassus, for his part, pressed with all his might, for he had recently learned that Pompey was about to arrive in Italy from Spain, and the last thing he wanted to do was to share victory with his rival.*

And so it came about, in 71 B.C., that the armies of Spartacus and Crassus met in mortal combat *in southern Italy. Plutarch, the biographer of Crassus, tells us that on the fateful day Spartacus' horse was led up to him. The determined gladiator drew his sword and killed the animal, saying "If I win the battle today, I shall have a great many better horses of the enemy, and if I lose, I shall have no need of this one." Thereupon, sword in hand, he made directly for Crassus and barely missed him. He did, however, kill two centurions that came to Crassus' rescue. Then Spartacus' men began to fall, Spartacus among them. His body was never found. All the slaves that stood their ground perished then and there.*

Crassus had [ALT.: and Crassus] won a decisive victory. *To be sure, several thousand slaves escaped and fled northward, but never again would Rome be threatened by a slave war.* Six thousand slaves were captured and crucified, and their crosses were set up along the Appian Way from Capua to Rome. Five thousand more *slaves* continued in their flight towards the Alps, but *just at that moment* Pompey *arrived in northern Italy and* wiped them out. *Pompey wrote a letter to the senate saying that Crassus had indeed conquered the slaves in a pitched battle, but that he had brought the war to an end. Pompey was awarded with the honor of a magnificent triumph in Rome, while Crassus, to his bitter disappointment, had to rest content with the lesser honor of an ovation.*

The war was over, but the memory of the terrible fear it had instilled lasted on. Steadily, the Romans improved the *living conditions and* treatment of their slaves. *More free men were required by law to be hired on the great plantations to lessen the danger of large slave concentrations and revolts. Six short years after Spartacus' death, there was born in southern Italy a son of a freedman who was destined to be one of Rome's greatest and most wonderful poets. This was Horace, an ornament of the Augustan Age together with Virgil and Livy. The freeing of slaves* [ALT.: and the freeing of slaves] became a common custom *at Rome, until finally the clever and able freedmen filled up the Roman imperial bureaucracy. With the establishment of the Emperors, however, foreign conquests came pretty much to an end, and with them the capture of prisoners of war and their enslavement. Slavery thenceforth counted for less and less in the imperial economy, for house-bred slaves are notoriously expensive. Still, the institution continued and was not vigorously attacked in antiquity until the triumph of Christianity.*

Spartacus lost his bid for freedom, his army of oppressed malcontents, *which he so skillfully organized,* was utterly destroyed, and everyone tried to forget. A terrible episode in history had come to an end. But further generations of slaves could be grateful for the heroic sacrifice which made their own lot better. And the generality of mankind, forty years after Spartacus, was able to settle down *with the Emperor Augustus* to a period of prosperity never before equaled, and to an era of peace that is thus far the longest on record.

CHAPTER SIX

Training + Tactics = Roman Battle Success

EDITOR'S NOTE: The following text was first published in the souvenir program book for *Spartacus*. It is here reproduced without the accompanying extreme long-shot of the Roman army deployed in battle formation before the decisive encounter with the slave army. This scene, filmed in Spain, gives an indelible impression of how the Roman military machine at its mightiest may have appeared to its enemy. The scene's visual impact is best appreciated if it is viewed as it was intended to be viewed: on a huge cinema screen.

A few verbal anachronisms in the text like "the Empire" and "robot formation" are negligible. But the description of Roman battle tactics is anachronistic because such a battle formation was outdated by the time of Spartacus' revolt. On this and on a few other assertions made in this text cf. the contribution by Allen Ward in the present volume. Diagrams illustrating the development of Roman legionary formations and battle tactics may conveniently be found in John Warry, *Warfare in the Classical World: An Illustrated Encyclopedia of Weapons, Warriors and Warfare in the Ancient Civilisations of Greece and Rome* (1980; rpt. Norman: University of Oklahoma Press, 1995), 111, 112, 153, and 187. The first of these, in full color, is instructive for the battle in *Spartacus*. Cf. also Lawrence Keppie, *The Making of the Roman Army: From Republic to Empire* (1984; rpt. Norman: University of Oklahoma Press, 1998), 38–39 (section entitled "The Legion in Battle," with mention of *Spartacus*).

The text appeared in the souvenir book without identification of its author. On a different page the book refers, with Hollywood hyperbole, to the film's historical expert, who probably designed or at least helped design the final battle sequence, in the following terms:

Vittorio Nino Novarese, historical and technical adviser on the film, was able to answer, as a matter of course, questions on what the Romans ate for breakfast, the training of a gladiator and the ceremonies of the Senate. A professor of history, costume and decor at Rome's State School for Cinematographical Studies, a world authority on ancient military history, he spent 18 months insuring the authenticity of the motion picture.

Elsewhere, the souvenir program lists and describes a number of locations used for filming *Spartacus* and reports Novarese's impression of one of these:

> The terrain of Thousand Oaks, California, . . . is a topographical carbon copy of the land rolling south and west from Rome and Capua toward the Tyrrhenian Sea.
>
> Even the film's historical and technical adviser, Vittorio Nino Novarese, was hard put to find differences between Thousand Oaks and his native Italy. ("Ah, yes," he said, "Rome has come to California.")

Training + Tactics = Roman Battle Success

THE INVINCIBILITY of the Roman legions, like their superior roads, aqueducts and public buildings, was the result of careful planning and meticulous attention to detail. The combination of sound tactics, thorough organization of supply and logistics, and five years of training for each soldier provided the Empire with an endless stream of triumphs. This motion picture shows, for the first time in film history, the maneuvers which conquered the world.

The infantry was the basic branch of the military organization, and the legion was the basic unit. Comparable to a modern regiment, the legion had 3600 men and was further divided, for command purposes, into ten cohorts (battalions), 30 maniples (companies) and 60 centuries (platoons).

Battle experience proved that the Roman soldier, carrying full battle gear, could fight at peak efficiency for only 15 minutes, and all combat plans were based on this fact. A cohort of 360 men was divided into six 60-man waves, each wave fighting 15 minutes and resting for 75. Thus it was possible for fresh troops to enter the battle constantly and keep unremitting pressure on the enemy. The fighting period for a single cohort was estimated at $10^1/_2$ hours.

A legion usually deployed its cohorts in checkerboard fashion, three rows deep, making it possible for fresh troops to take their place on the battle line without leaving too large a gap in depth. The men were spread six feet apart, giving the legion a front of 2,000 feet.

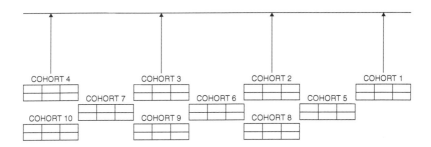

There was a fixed pattern of attack, and each line of soldiers was assigned specific tasks. Little was left to chance. Experience had shown the Romans that a running soldier, heavily armed, would tire quickly. To avoid the danger of having fatigued soldiers start actual combat, the order to attack was given at a precise moment. If the enemy was in a defensive position, the trumpets sounded when the Romans were 360 feet away. If the enemy was advancing, the attack signal came when 750 feet separated the two forces. In either case, the distance to be covered prior to contact was about the same. Cohorts 1, 2, 3 and 4 advanced while the other battalions waited in place. When they were approximately 200 feet away, the soldiers in the first two rows ran forward, javelins in position for throwing.

1. When these two rows closed the gap, they threw their javelins at the front ranks of the enemy, then drew their swords and rushed in for hand-to-hand combat.

2. While they were doing this, the next three rows of soldiers moved up to the firing line [*sic*] and hurled their javelins to the rear of the enemy force, adding to their confusion and making it difficult for the foe to bring up reserves.

3. These three rows then joined their comrades in the man-to-man combat. Simultaneously, the second platoons of cohorts 1, 2, 3 and 4 advanced one-third the distance toward the battle and took up positions to cover any emergency.

4. If the first or second attack wave seemed to be succeeding, cohorts 5, 6 and 7 rushed into the combat in an effort to secure a quick and decisive triumph. The remaining three cohorts – 8, 9 and 10 – were still held in reserve, in case the enemy rallied or in case their apparent retreat turned out to be a trap.

The strength of the Romans, fighting in robot formation, was their undoing against Spartacus, who had trained his men in guerilla tactics and surprise attacks. Fighting against odds of two to one, the gladiator general and his army still managed to win victory after victory with their unorthodox methods.

But the greatest tactics could not prevail against a force which combined all the legions of Crassus, Pompey and Lucullus. In this decisive battle, there were ten Romans for each slave soldier. Spartacus was never out-generalled, only out-numbered.

CHAPTER SEVEN

The Character of Marcus Licinius Crassus

W. Jeffrey Tatum

Even before Marcus Licinius Crassus makes his first appearance in Stanley Kubrick's *Spartacus*, the announcement of his approach to the gladiatorial school of Lentulus Batiatus excites an anxiety approximating servility on the part of the school's owner. The very mention of Crassus' name reduces Batiatus to his characteristic and comic deviousness and fawning. Then Batiatus informs the viewers about something his household already knows: "Crassus has expensive tastes." Enter the Roman, riding a white steed and resplendent in elegant white garb delicately set off by golden brocade and lavender wrap. He is accompanied by three distinguished friends: Helena, apparently his lover, her brother Glabrus, and Glabrus' new wife Claudia. At first we see Crassus only from a distance, the most striking element in his posh procession.[1] He becomes more accessible, however, after he has entered Batiatus' house, discovered the bust of his political opponent Gracchus, and leers at Varinia with such blatant absorption that his host is moved to inquire: "Is there anything wrong, your nobility?"

---

1 The style of Crassus' introduction recalls the initial appearance of Spartacus, simply one of many slaves, and so constitutes the first of the film's many collations of its two central characters. Cf. Peter Hanson, *Dalton Trumbo, Hollywood Rebel: A Critical Survey and Filmography* (Jeffrerson and London: McFarland, 2001), 138–141 and 145–147. – I am grateful to Angela Aslanska, Monica Cyrino, and Laurel Fulkerson, each of whom improved this paper considerably.

Crassus has brought his guests to Capua to entertain the newlyweds with an expensive gift: they are to watch two pairs of gladiators fight to the death. This proposition unnerves Batiatus, who at first refuses: "We never fight them to the death." Crassus calmly observes: "Today is an exception." He cuts short further remonstrations from Batiatus with an enormous payment, playing on the latter's evident greed with which Crassus is apparently long familiar. The Romans are served wine. Again he stares at Varinia with marked sexual interest, although he covers this by asking about her education. This conversation contains the film's first close-up of Crassus, emphasizing his sexual fascination with the slave woman. Crassus then purchases her from Batiatus for a huge sum. Helena, hardly insensitive to it all, is naturally provoked. When she accuses Crassus of failing to give her brother a proper wedding present, he reveals that he has arranged for Glabrus to become commander of the garrison at Rome, an arrangement, we learn, that Crassus had made by purchasing the Roman Senate and outfoxing Gracchus.

Crassus' visit to Batiatus' gladiatorial school attracts viewers' attention largely for its subsequent scene in the amphitheater that culminates in the combat between Spartacus and a fictional black gladiator and the latter's death. But the sequence matters also for its delineation of Crassus' character. The story of *Spartacus* is largely constructed around the oppositions between Crassus and Spartacus and Crassus and Gracchus, a structure that tends to make the patrician general the natural focus both for our appreciation of the senator's tainted devotion to popular liberty and the slave's pure devotion to freedom. In particular, the contrast between Crassus and Spartacus, achieved most effectively in Kubrick's cross-cutting of the Roman dictator's speech to his legions with Spartacus' appeal to his slave "brothers" before their final battle, remains fundamental to the film's drama. Both of Crassus' rivals will fail, but each will have the consolation of achieving a moral victory. In this, the film's action and morality reflect contemporary sensibilities, and Crassus is central to its meaning.

His character is immediately evident, even from his initial appearance. He is immensely rich and a spendthrift; money is a means to pleasure and power. While he is not entirely shameless – he later reproves Glabrus by insisting that "one of the disadvantages of being a patrician is that one is occasionally required to act like one" – he is unembarrassed in the open display of his lover. Nor does he disguise his erotic fascination with a slave girl in the presence of his mistress and peers. In short, he is sensual and acquisitive. His political ambition is evident from the start. His gift to Glabrus will, he makes clear, come at a cost, and he is explicit in his hostility to the Roman mob and its champion Gracchus and in his contempt for the senate, a body available for purchase much as he purchases Varinia. The film, as its prologue and the episode at Batiatus' school make plain, blames slavery on all of Roman society. But Crassus, with his singular superiority of station and in Laurence Olivier's commanding presence in the part, immediately comes to represent the pinnacle of the Roman slave system. The toady Batiatus greets Crassus as "most noble radiance, first general of the republic, father and defender of Rome." But there is little doubt that Crassus, deeply implicated in the inhumanity of slavery, desires much more. At the end, he has become dictator of Rome.

The contrasts between Crassus and Gracchus are obvious enough. The one is patrician, the other low-born, as scenes, later deleted and lost, revealed in which Gracchus visits the neighborhood of his birth and acts as patron to the urban poor. Crassus is a militarist, Gracchus a politician who has succeeded in climbing to the top. He is fat and ugly; Crassus, handsome and fit. Being Romans, they are debased, a necessary perspective in this film. But Gracchus' foibles are less reprehensible than those of Crassus. The latter desires sexual domination of Varinia and Antoninus and is repellent to both. Gracchus, who enjoys sexual relations with several of his slave women, is affectionate and well liked by his household. Just before his suicide he frees his slaves, who clearly mourn him. This was more apparent in the longer version of Gracchus' suicide, in which he remarks to one slave that he expects to see her "in paradise."

Crassus and Gracchus are inevitable political adversaries. Gracchus represents a tarnished version of democratic ideals. When a supporter of Crassus impugns his integrity during a stormy senatorial debate, he proclaims: "I'll take a little republican corruption along with a little republican freedom. What I won't take is the dictatorship of Crassus." On this point Gracchus feels so strongly that he is willing to make common cause with Spartacus' rebellious slaves. Immediately after Crassus has demanded the dictatorship as his price for leading Rome's legions against Spartacus, Gracchus informs his protégé Julius Caesar that he has arranged for the slave army's escape from Italy, a sordid but necessary tactic if Rome is to preserve its freedom from Crassus' designs. In a scene that was cut from the film before its release but that followed Crassus' assumption of the dictatorship after foiling Gracchus' scheme to allow Spartacus to make his way out of Italy, Gracchus tells Caesar: "if Spartacus wins, I intend to ask the senate to emancipate his whole army." This revelation motivates Caesar to betray his mentor and defect to Crassus.

Even more crucial to the film's plot, however, is that Crassus is the antithesis of Spartacus. They occupy exactly opposite positions in Roman society. The one aims at a dictatorship that will return Rome to the strict social stratification of the past, while the other is a liberator who endeavors to establish a humane, liberal, and egalitarian community and whose principal importance, as the film's prologue and ending make inescapably clear, is for the future. The two also differ in less obvious ways. Their different relations to the young slave Antoninus makes this evident. Spartacus enjoys a close friendship with Antoninus, a singer of songs and teacher of the classics. Spartacus values Antoninus' intellectual attainments. Antoninus reads messages for Spartacus, who is illiterate, and so helps the slave rebels' cause in a practical way. Beyond this, Spartacus is touched when Antoninus recites his poetry and confesses to Varinia his admiration for literature and his disappointment in his own ignorance. Near the close of the film, as Antoninus is dying, each expresses his love for the other. By contrast, Crassus, although fully aware of Antoninus' erudition, only values Antoninus for his handsome physique and makes him his body servant. In the "oysters and snails" scene, Crassus employs a perverted form of Socratic dialogue to seduce Antoninus.

In matters of sex and love, Spartacus and Crassus diverge from each other most strikingly. When Varinia is assigned to Spartacus for sex in the gladiatorial school, he reveals that he has never had a woman. He stares at her naked body and, by placing his hand around her throat, implies his mastery over her. The repulsive voyeurism of Batiatus and his gladiatorial trainer incite Spartacus' outraged insistence that he is not an animal. Nor, adds Varinia, is she, and Spartacus respects her for this. The scene, unusual and no doubt difficult to watch for contemporary audiences, reveals yet another side of the inhumanity of slavery but also conveys Spartacus' self-control and gentleness in circumstances in which Varinia could not have expected a shred of decency; hence her subsequent attraction to Spartacus. Once liberated, they fall in love and become a family. Their relationship demonstrates Spartacus' virility and provides the audience with "interludes of Middle American domesticity."[2]

His love for Varinia may even be the catalyst for Spartacus' act of rebellion.[3] Friendship and love remain the exclusive property of the slaves throughout the film. This is clearest in the case of Spartacus, whose first action is to rush to the aid of a slave who has collapsed in the

2   Quoted from Derek Elley, *The Epic Film: Myth and History* (London: Routledge and Kegan Paul, 1984), 112.
3   Cf. Elley, *The Epic Film*, 112.

mines. In the gladiatorial school Spartacus succeeds in winning the friendship of Crixus. In his command of the rebellion he earns the love of all his "brothers." Each of them is willing to be crucified in his place after they have lost the final battle with Crassus' legions. Spartacus' relationship with Varinia carries the film beyond standard romance by representing the expectations of middle-class American life as the ultimate fulfillment of the slaves' struggle for freedom. When we see, somewhat unrealistically, a number of the slaves who have been killed in the battle lying on the ground in close familial embraces, the images are intended to reveal that tyranny is the enemy of love.

If Spartacus is an ideal, first as a virgin and then in marriage, Crassus is a libertine. There is no hint that he is a husband or father, for children and families are wholly absent from this film's sterile Roman world.[4] Instead, he is with a lover to whom he is anything but devoted. He also inclines to slaves, female and male. But like Spartacus, he is not a rapist. He does not take Varinia against her will and unsuccessfully attempts to seduce Antoninus. Both cases reveal what Crassus really wants: willing capitulation. This is parallel to his desire for political power. In words that contain an explicitly sexual analogy, Crassus anticipates his political success: "I shall not violate Rome at the moment of possessing her." His true appetite is for a compliant world, as he tells Antoninus – and reveals to us, the viewers – immediately after trying to seduce him. Looking out over the city of Rome, with the cohorts on the march, Crassus says:

> There, boy, is Rome. There is the might, the majesty, the terror of Rome
> . . . No man can withstand Rome, no nation can withstand her . . . There's
> only one way to deal with Rome, Antoninus: you must serve her, you must
> abase yourself before her, you must grovel at her feet, you must – love her.

The immediate flight of Antoninus, who has vanished when Crassus turns from gazing at the marching column, indicates his understanding of Crassus' remarks. But there is a deeper pathology in Crassus' sexual identification with Rome: his narcissism. When Crassus had rejected the suggestion that he occupy Rome with his legions in the words already quoted, his equal infatuation with Rome and power brought a sardonic comment from Gracchus: "This republic of ours is something like a rich widow. Most Romans love her as their mother, but Crassus dreams of marrying the old girl – to put it politely." Oedipal dreams often signify a will to power.[5] But Crassus' passion for Rome stems from his moral mor-

---

4   Andrew Sodrowski, "'Something Like a Rich Widow': Spartacus and the Protestant Work Ethic," *Latent Image* (2003), at http://pages.emerson.edu/organizations/fas/latent_image/issues/2003–01/printed_version/Spartacus.htm.
5   Examples appear in Herodotus, *The Histories* 6.107, and Suetonius, Caesar 7.2.

bidity. This travesty of love is shown up by Varinia's and Antoninus' devotion to Spartacus and forms an important element in the slaves' moral victory over the Romans in general and over Crassus in particular. As Derek Elley well put it: "When the pair [Spartacus and Crassus] come face to face . . . Crassus' behaviour is as much that of a cuckolded lover as a frustrated general, his scream a terrifying expression of inadequacy."[6]

Crassus' comments to Antoninus and his subordination to a dominant Rome in analogy to his own desired sexual domination of Antoninus conjure up Crassus' all-consuming but entirely self-directed passion. The Crassus of *Spartacus* demands the obedience and conformity that we attribute to modern totalitarianism. In the totalitarian state of George Orwell's *Nineteen Eighty Four*, to take the most obvious example, subordinated citizens must learn to love Big Brother. Crassus embodies the modern urge, familiar from right- and left-wing ideologies, to eradicate the individuality and identity of others for the sake of a single individual's conception of order. Crassus calls his dictatorship "order," an idea he reprises in his final confrontation with Gracchus. Crassus' handsome physique reveals the appeal of such totalitarianism, while his narcissism and warped sexuality are meant to cause the film's viewers a greater feeling of repugnance than could be incited by allegorical or political abstractions like Big Brother or Roman corruption. Turpitude of this stature and impact on those Crassus deals with far exceeds the comparatively benign level of vice and corruption in Gracchus and stands as the very opposite of Spartacus' moral purity. The extreme autocracy of Crassus is defined by its degree of difference from Gracchus' sickly republicanism and from the wholesome freedom championed by Spartacus.

So the rebellious slave is virtue personified while Crassus lends flesh and blood to the representation of tyranny along modern lines. This kind of dichotomy is familiar from earlier Hollywood "toga movies" and shows mid-twentieth-century American middle-class values and pretensions.[7] In such films pagan Rome is in fundamental opposition to Christian and American virtues, an antithesis that, like the pairing of Rome and slavery in *Spartacus*, establishes a reductive grid on which to arrange certain American assumptions: equality, liberty, and a wholesomely decent morality. It is less a religious assertion than a gesture toward the

---

6   Quoted from Elley, *The Epic Film*, 111.
7   See especially William Fitzgerald, "Oppositions, Anxieties, and Ambiguities in the Toga Movie," in *Imperial Projections: Ancient Rome in Modern Popular Culture*, ed. Sandra R. Joshel, Margaret Malamud, and Donald T. McGuire, Jr. (Baltimore and London: Johns Hopkins University Press, 2001; rpt. 2005), 23–49.

genre of Hollywood's Roman epics that *Spartacus* commences with an invocation of Christianity even before its arrival in history and concludes with the unmistakable Christian image of Spartacus on the cross.[8] The oppressed are the good, the oppressors the bad, and American audiences know that the good will win in the end because they are themselves the living proof of it: Manifest Destiny begins in Greco-Roman antiquity. And so Spartacus is decent, faithful to his wife, worried about his son's future, and inspiring to his friends. He is the very enactment of the Protestant work ethic: for American men in the audience, he is the quintessence of what each imagines himself to be.[9]

Yet certain anxieties can insinuate themselves into this simple polarity. In Batiatus' amphitheater, the black gladiator Draba defeats Spartacus for the delectation of Crassus and his entourage but refrains from killing Spartacus; instead, he hurls his trident at Crassus and is killed. The camera angle suggests an identity between the Romans and the viewers: Draba throws his weapon at both alike. Here the film pointedly equates slavery with the New World's enslavement of Africans and with the social reality that in 1960 continued to deny civil rights to black Americans. Draba's corpse, left hanging upside down in the gladiators' barracks, evokes the horrors of lynching. A potentially disturbing element in the film is the casting of wholesome American actor John Gavin as Julius Caesar, which undermines any New-World innocence because Crasssus predicts Caesar's dictatorship, the one fact of Roman history familiar to all modern audiences.

But the Crassus of *Spartacus* is by no means the Crassus of antiquity. Nor is he the Crassus of Howard Fast's novel or of *The Gladiators*, Arthur Koestler's novel about Spartacus. Does that matter? After all, it has never been necessary that period films bear a close relationship to the history they appropriate, nor do most viewers insist on an explanation for a film's divergences from the book that inspired it. But in this instance our appreciation of *Spartacus* increases if we pay attention to the particular respects in which its characterization of Crassus goes

---

8   Critics regularly remark on the oddity of the film's introduction of Christianity, an anachronism that plays no part in Fast's novel. However, C. Osborne Ward, *The Ancient Lowly: A History of the Ancient Working People from the Earliest Known Period to the Adoption of Christianity by Constantine*, vol. 1 (1889; rpt. New York: Franklin, 1970), 329, describes Jesus as Spartacus' natural and successful successor in the struggle against slavery. Ward's work had first appeared in 1888 and was Fast's Marxist historical source: "There . . . I found the story of Spartacus"; quoted from Howard Fast, *Being Red: A Memoir* (1990; rpt. Armonk and London: Sharpe, 1994), 276.

9   Sodrowski, " 'Something Like a Rich Widow.' "

against historical fact and against Crassus' literary re-creations. Our understanding of the significance of Crassus in *Spartacus* depends on what is *missing* from the film's portrayal of him. Put differently, this Crassus constitutes a kind of correction of previous historical and literary depictions of him.

The historical Crassus was rich and greedy. A major theme of Plutarch's biography of Crassus is his avarice, emphasized at the beginning and stressed again in Plutarch's comparison of Crassus with Nicias, the former's Greek parallel.[10] Even among his contemporaries Crassus' wealth was proverbial, as was his willingness to acquire it by any means whatsoever. Crassus' attitude toward money – his keenness to profit from activities disreputable for a Roman noble – aroused criticism, because the senatorial aristocracy of Rome, who required wealth and were fond of increasing their share in it, held strict principles about its acquisition. Wealth was to be obtained by inheritance and expanded by agriculture and by the spoils of war. There were other forms of profiteering such as mining, lending money, tax farming, and trade, but these had to be left to the knights, prosperous Romans below the senatorial order who did not compete for public office or hold provincial commands. Senators were held to a higher standard. For instance, legislation was passed in 218 B.C. that severely restricted the participation of senators and their sons in shipping and trade, and senators were prohibited from investing in Roman tax-farming corporations (the publicans of New Testament notoriety). These restrictions were often circumvented, but it was essential that such sordid dealings be kept as quiet as possible.[11] Crassus, however, simply discarded these inhibitions: he accumulated wealth by aggressively profiting from the misfortunes of others; by real-estate speculation and construction; by investing in mines; by legacy hunting; by training and hiring out slaves skilled in all manner of service; by money-lending and by making deals with tax-farming corporations. Wealth earned by these means was offensive to aristocratic Roman sensibilities. Although his money made Crassus influential and powerful, his business

10 Plutarch, *Crassus* 1–3 and 6.5 and *Comparison of Nikias and Crassus* 1.1–5. On Crassus' character see Bruce A. Marshall, *Crassus: A Political Biography* (Amsterdam: Hakkert, 1976), 13–17, and Allen M. Ward, *Marcus Crassus and the Late Roman Republic* (Columbia and London: University of Missouri Press, 1977), 68–82.

11 Cf. in particular Cicero, *On Duties* 1.150–151 and on this Andrew R. Dyck, *A Commentary on Cicero, De Officiis* (Ann Arbor: University of Michigan Press, 1996), 331–333, with abundant further references. On senators in business see E. Badian, *Publicans and Sinners: Private Enterprise in the Service of the Roman Republic* (Ithaca and London: Cornell University Press, 1972; rpt. 1983), 101–107.

practices attracted obloquy both in antiquity and in subsequent accounts composed by modern historians.[12]

Yet however much his contemporaries disapproved of Crassus' greed, they admired his conduct. He avoided extravagance and kept a modest home, into which he invited common folk whom he cultivated in a manner very much like the film's Gracchus:

> Crassus was generous with strangers, for his house was open to all . . . When he entertained at table, his invited guests were for the most part plebeians and men of the people, and the simplicity of the repast was combined with a neatness and good cheer which gave more pleasure than lavish expenditure . . . He pleased people also by the kindly and unaffected manner with which he clasped their hands and addressed them. For he never met a Roman so obscure and lowly that he did not return his greeting and call him by name.[13]

Crassus' personal morality was of the highest fiber. He was faithful to his wife, and his devotion to his son was much admired. Even Cicero, who loathed Crassus not least for his avarice, could appeal in court to the well-known fact of Crassus' morally immaculate family life, what Cicero once called his *castissima domus* ("very chaste household").[14] As Plutarch put it: "The Romans . . . say that the many virtues of Crassus were obscured by his sole vice of avarice."[15] A similar point was made by the earlier Roman historian Velleius Paterculus:

> Although Crassus was, in his general character, entirely upright and free from base desires, in his lust for money and his ambition for glory he knew no limits, and accepted no bounds.[16]

It can scarcely be doubted that the ancients would not have recognized the Crassus of *Spartacus*.

---

12   On Crassus' business techniques see Plutarch, *Crassus* 2.2–3.3, and Ward, *Marcus Crassus and the Late Roman Republic*, 68–82. On Crassus' influence cf. Sallust, *The Conspiracy of Catiline* 48.5; on his reputation in antiquity and among modern historians see Ward, 1–4.

13   Plutarch, *Crassus* 3.1 and 3; quoted from *Plutarch's Lives*, tr. Bernadotte Perrin; vol. 3 (Cambridge: Harvard University Press / London: Heinemann, 1916; several rpts.), 321.

14   Cicero, *On Behalf of Caelius* 9.

15   Plutarch, *Crassus* 2.1; quoted from Perrin, 315.

16   Velleius Paterculus, *Compendium of Roman History* 2.46.2; quoted from *Velleius Paterculus: Compendium of Roman History* and *Res gestae divi Augusti*, tr. Frederick W. Shipley (Cambridge: Harvard University Press / London: Heinemann, 1924; several rpts.), 151.

Modern communists' appropriation of Spartacus and his rebellion in political discourse and historical research made it natural for Howard Fast to focus on the capitalist quality of Crassus' reputation. Although Fast's novel is suffused with anachronisms, its author was well aware of the commercial restrictions imposed on the Roman nobility and of their success in evading them.[17] His Crassus is neither markedly political nor ideological; in the novel, Gracchus and Cicero are the practical and ideological forces of Rome. Instead, Crassus is an officer who is also an industrious businessman. Fast characterized him as "the great financier and general" (235). He despises Batiatus, who is rich and formidable and not at all the buffoon of the film, because Batiatus will "do anything for money"(52). Crassus is always on the lookout for good investments and rejects agriculture and warfare as insufficiently profitable. He prefers manufacture – in this instance, of perfumes (293–297) – for which he rejects slaves as not useful enough. As he explains (297):

> "A slave eats your food and dies. But these workers turn themselves into gold. Nor am I concerned with feeding and housing them."
> "Yet," Caius speculated, "they could do as Spartacus did –"
> "Workers revolt?" Crassus smiled and shook his head. "No, that will never be. You see, they are not slaves. They are free men. They can come and go as they please. Why should they ever revolt? . . . No. As a matter of fact, all through the Servile War, we never stopped our ovens. There is no bond between these men and slaves."

In Fast's novel Cicero and not Crassus insists on the crucifixion of the slaves after the war. This is largely because of the limitations of his economic vision: for Cicero it is unfortunate that the prosperity of Rome depends on slave labor despite the ill consequences of such a system. But Crassus has seen the economic future; to him the proto-communism of the slaves represents a return to "the way it was in the old times" (166). The extent of his terrible profiteering is only hinted at: Crassus, although criticizing the crucifixions as a waste, later describes the death of Spartacus to young Caius in a remarkable formulation: "So he went out the way he came, out of nothing into nothing, out of the arena into the butcher shop" (35). Caius in turn is reminded of a conversation with

---

17   Cf. Howard Fast, *Spartacus* (1951; rpt. Armonk and London: Sharpe, 1996), 26–27. Below, parenthetical page references are to this edition, which preserves the first edition's pagination. Alison Futrell, "Seeing Red: Spartacus as Domestic Economist," in *Imperial Projections*, 80–97, discusses Spartacus in communist discourse and provides further references. On Communist Party criticisms of Fast's novel see Andrew Macdonald, *Howard Fast: A Critical Companion* (Westport and London: Greenwood Press, 1996), 97–98.

a Roman knight in the sausage business. He, too, described the crucifixions as wasteful before revealing that, with the assistance of Caius's uncle, he had "managed to buy a quarter of a million pounds" of the dead slaves' flesh: "I smoked them, minced them, and mixed it with pork, spice and salt" (17–18). Caius avoids learning the truth about Crassus: "What the general said recalled to Caius the conversation with the sausage maker, and it was on the tip of his tongue to raise the question. But then he thought better of it" (35).

Fast's Crassus combines avarice with private immorality. He seduces Caius and rapes Caius' sister; his own household is unhappy, and his son hates him. As does the film it inspired, Fast's novel relies upon an important polarity, the distinction between the patricians and Spartacus. Spartacus' moral elevation and purity, emphasized again and again, entail the depravity of the patricians, of whom Crassus is the most attractive and talented and consequently the most frightening.

With *Spartacus*, Kirk Douglas's Bryna Productions beat a rival project for a film about Spartacus based on Koestler's novel. One of the many controversies that arose during the making of Kubrick's film was the director's attempt to introduce into Dalton Trumbo's screenplay aspects of Koestler's novel, in which the portrayal of Spartacus was significantly different. Koestler's Spartacus and his rebellion ultimately succumbed to shortcomings that demonstrated the moral failure of both the oppressed and the oppressors. To Trumbo, the debate over how best to characterize Spartacus was essential to his view of the film and led him to caricature Kubrick's vision of Spartacus as the "Small Spartacus," a figure that he juxtaposed unfavorably to his own heroic construction, the "Large Spartacus." But like Fast, Koestler drew his Crassus in sharp strokes. Crassus enacts capitalist principles and is utterly incapable of seeing the world in any but economic terms.[18]

Neither the moral profiteer of antiquity nor the debased capitalist general of Fast's and Koestler's novels emerges in Trumbo's screenplay. To some degree perhaps this can be attributed to the process of simplification required to transform Fast's sprawling novel into a movie of manageable proportions. Trumbo's Batiatus, for instance, is distilled from the novel's *lanista* and another character. For the sake of unity and ultimate plot resolution in the contest between Crassus and Spartacus, it is the general himself and his lover who visit Capua to view a gladiatorial display. Fast had Caius and his lover Bracus, each dispensed with in the film, make the journey and enjoy the spectacle, whose

18   Arthur Koestler, *The Gladiators*, tr. Edith Simon (New York: Macmillan, 1939; rpt. 1965), 276–293.

purpose lacks an obvious point. In Fast's version, Crassus and Spartacus never meet.

But dramatic concentration of Fast's novel can only be a partial explanation of Crassus' conversion from capitalist to autocrat; after all, simplification of plot need not entail an absence of complex characterization. Here we must take into account the various creative, political, and commercial pressures that influenced the conflicts over the film's screenplay. Most attention has been devoted to the debate over Spartacus' character, not Crassus'. Although the film was made amid extreme controversy, and although Trumbo could rightly complain of considerable alterations made to his script and to his vision of the film's essential story, all subsequent debating and rewriting took as its point of departure some version of his screenplay, whose fundamental design emphasized the contest between the "Large Spartacus" and Crassus. The character of Crassus was apparently little changed in the creative development of *Spartacus*, so Trumbo's vision had an advantage over the others, not least because it was bolstered by the requirements of dramatic unity and balance.

This competition among artistic visions could not escape commercial considerations, which were themselves implicated in the political atmosphere of the time. In these circumstances, the more universal a story, the safer it was to tell it and enhance a movie's appeal. As Edward Lewis, the film's producer, puts it in his commentary on a DVD release of *Spartacus*, "there was never any talk of trying to use this as a vehicle to expound any political position . . . it's about slaves who are overthrowing the yoke of oppression, that's what it's about . . . that's what makes it contemporary for all time." Lewis goes on to emphasize that Trumbo's screenplay was from the start an exercise in dramatic storytelling, not in polemic: "he was looking for stories that made great movies." Now there is no denying that the film recalls and comments on the shameless authoritarianism of McCarthyism and its effects. But it was also easy for audiences not to hear this voice in *Spartacus* and to see only the same unreflecting affirmation of American values as in other toga movies of the period. After all, Crassus' personal immorality, partially preserved from Fast's Crassus and standing in vivid contrast to Spartacus' middle-American wholesomeness, unmistakably marked out the Roman as essentially anti-American. This was by no means accidental. Ed Muhl, the head of Universal Studios, insisted: "Deep ideas are nice to have in a picture. But what counts is audience appeal."[19]

---

19   Muhl to Duncan L. Cooper; quoted from Cooper, "Who Killed the Legend of Spartacus? Production, Censorship, and Reconstruction of Stanley Kubrick's Epic Film" (above, in this volume, 21).

This was a reality that did not elude Trumbo. In an interview he confessed: "The pressure is always on and we writers do discipline ourselves, we do censor ourselves . . . I realized [in writing *Spartacus*] that a thing which any other writer would say and [that] would never be thought of or analyzed or would never be significant or noticed, when I say it, it becomes highly significant – smuggling in propaganda and doing all sorts of things, so you see I consider this a very mild script."[20] In a letter to fellow blacklisted writer Alvah Bessie, Trumbo celebrated the profits of *Spartacus* and *Exodus*, his next project, as "a victory for every blacklisted person," recognizing that, had they flopped, "I, for one, would never have been able to work again, and those who do not yet work openly would have even a slighter chance than I of making it."[21] For varying reasons, then, but none unconnected with commercial consequences, *Spartacus* adhered to the political discourse acceptable from the mass media of its time.

One necessity of that containment was the elimination of Crassus' capitalism. This was not an effect of overt censorship but instead an artistic decision not to criticize American capitalism in the film. The depiction of Crassus also avoids even a hint of what Robin Wood has called the "Rosebud syndrome": "money isn't everything; money corrupts; the poor are happier. A very convenient assumption for capitalist ideology: the more oppressed you are, the happier you are."[22] Crassus' immense wealth, whose acquisition is never a topic in the film, simply is an attribute of his aristocratic station. False, then, to the historical Crassus and to the literary figure in Fast or Koestler, this Crassus has become the embodiment of Roman decadence, an Old-World representation of tyranny that underscores the New-World quality of Spartacus' struggle for freedom.

This construction of Crassus' character admirably suited Trumbo's purposes. Throughout the late fifties, Trumbo had labored to eliminate the Hollywood blacklist that had blighted his career as a screenwriter.[23] He was never unaware of the importance of public opinion for the

---

20   Quoted from August 2, 1960, interview of Dalton Trumbo by David Chandler for unpublished book *The Year of Spartacus*, 56–57.

21   *Additional Dialogue: Letters of Dalton Trumbo, 1942–1962*, ed. Helen Manfull (1970; rpt. New York: Bantam, 1972), 575.

22   Robin Wood, *Hitchcock's Films Revisited*, rev. edn. (New York: Columbia University Press, 2002), 290. The use of capitalist mogul William Randolph Hearst's lavish estate at San Simeon, California, as Crassus' home is a possible exception to this claim.

23   Cf. Jeffrey P. Smith, " 'A Good Business Proposition': Dalton Trumbo, *Spartacus*, and the End of the Blacklist," *The Velvet Light Trap*, 23 (1989), 75–100.

restoration of his reputation. The profitability of *Spartacus* was within his calculations from the start of his composition of its screenplay. Hence his safe script, which allowed Stan Margulies, the publicity director for Bryna Productions, to observe about the American Legion's hostility to *Spartacus*: "I think it [the Legion's criticism] provides us plenty of room to defend the picture – if a defense should be needed – on the grounds of its content rather than on contributing personnel."[24] So Bryna Productions distributed study guides and souvenir books that stressed the movie's dramatization of "the struggle for freedom, both physical and spiritual," of "human rights and dignity," and of "man's eternal desire for freedom." Such formulations, as Maria Wyke has noted, fitted nicely with anti-communist Cold-War rhetoric and diminished the potential to identify the communists' class struggle with Spartacus' struggle against Crassus' Rome.[25] It was no surprise, then, that *The Hollywood Reporter* could insist that there was "nothing more subversive in 'Spartacus' than [is] contained in the Bill of Rights and the Fourteenth Amendment" or that the Daughters of the American Revolution hailed *Spartacus* as "a lesson in freedom and man's sacrifice in the name of it."[26] This publicity was influential and effective, if based on the straightforward morality of Trumbo's script. Its conservatism depends largely on the uncomplicated contrast between Crassus and Spartacus. Only if we turn our attention to what Crassus so pointedly was *not* in the movie do we recognize in this film a remarkable exemplar of the sheer force of capitalism in American society during the mid-twentieth century. Indeed, the success of *Spartacus*, replete with screenplay credit to Trumbo under his real name rather than, as before, pseudonymously, transformed Trumbo from an enemy of the people into an American hero.[27]

Despite the contemporary climate of communist discourse and its use of the Spartacus legend as a means of ennobling and encouraging the class struggle against modern capitalism, *Spartacus* from its inception endeavored to translate this story into another toga movie celebrating American values. *Spartacus* shows its audiences the struggle of freedom against totalitarianism in unambiguous terms. Although they are urged to reflect on the condition of civil rights in the United States and perhaps to ponder the complicity of (some of) their ancestors in the institution of

24 Letter from Stan Margulies to Kirk Douglas, quoted from Smith, "'A Good Business Proposition'," 92.

25 Maria Wyke, *Projecting the Past: Ancient Rome, Cinema and History* (New York and London: Routledge, 1997), 72; cf. Smith, "'A Good Business Proposition'," 92–93.

26 Both quotations from Smith, "'A Good Business Proposition'," 92.

27 Cf. Smith, "'A Good Business Proposition'," 93–94.

slavery, viewers are given no reason to recognize any disturbing dimension to capitalism. The historical Crassus, who combined personal rectitude with relentless profit-taking and an avoidance of luxuriousness, came too close to the Protestant work ethic to be a villain suitable to such a purpose in the simple moral universe of *Spartacus*. Nor was Fast's or Koestler's Crassus suitable for this, although they supplied the requisite wickedness. In order to preserve the moral world view of the toga movie and to avoid the introduction of the class struggle at any serious level, *Spartacus* had to reject the historical and literary antecedents of Crassus and change his characterization accordingly. If *Spartacus* was to turn a profit on its twelve-million-dollar investment, the enemy of middle-class American values could hardly be depicted as a capitalist.

The reductive nature of the plot enhances the film's universality and opens the door to the film's appropriation by the left and by the right. The release of *Spartacus* initially brought severe criticism from the American right, whose ire was chiefly directed against the employment of blacklisted writers and not the content of the film. An attempted boycott was shattered when John F. Kennedy crossed a picket line to attend a screening. Thereafter the movie could be viewed, and was viewed, as "a Cold War sermon in historical guise."[28] Leftist interpretations of the film are also possible.[29] But these are less immediately obvious insofar as the film's genre and historical context are concerned. And viewers indifferent to the Cold War or to the class struggle undoubtedly find *Spartacus* appealing as a simple slave's struggle against a master's overwhelming power. And today, many value it as a work by a director who was later to turn into a worldwide cult figure.

Critics of *Spartacus* regularly concentrate on the character of Spartacus and his portrayal by Kirk Douglas as the main factor for the success or failure of the film. But no viewer can fail to be engaged by its Crassus, who is the focus of antagonism both within Rome (in his political fight against Gracchus) and in the Romans' contest with the slave rebellion. Nevertheless, Crassus' character, although animated by Laurence Olivier's compelling performance, is, in the end, simply Spartacus reversed: an exponent of tyranny decked out in vices so ostentatious that they could not fail to disgust middle-class American audiences. Crassus is the "bad guy" whom audiences know they could themselves never become. He personifies excess and European totalitarianism, but nothing

---

28   Wyke, *Projecting the Past*, 71.
29   Examples are John Baxter, *Stanley Kubrick: A Biography* (New York: Carroll and Graf, 1997), 133–134, and Futrell, "Seeing Red."

American. So, to American viewers, there is nothing in this Crassus that is immediately disturbing or unsettling. The idea that capitalism, which mid-century Americans associated with freedom and the moral vision of Protestantism, could still be complicit in the oppression of others is entirely absent from *Spartacus* for the very reason that it has been excised from Crassus' characterization. It is no small irony that this left-wing venture, which employed the talents of two leading communist writers and even broke the blacklist, became a simple tale in which the values of America's Main Street were given comfortable heroic stature. The result was a blockbuster that can have raised no one's consciousness. A mild script indeed.

CHAPTER EIGHT

Roman Slavery and the Class Divide: Why Spartacus Lost

Michael Parenti

Given the grinding poverty and social misery endured by the ordinary people of Rome, why did they fail to make common cause with the slave population, especially when the latter moved toward insurgency with the strength of numbers as when they were led by someone like Spartacus? This question informs the present inquiry.

1. Oligarchy and Poverty

When Spartacus and his brave hearts launched their rebellion in 73 B.C., Rome was a Republic. This is easily forgotten when people today read about his struggle. Nor does Stanley Kubrick's movie dwell upon that fact, choosing instead to show – correctly so – that actual rule in Rome was by an aristocratic oligarchy embedded in the senate. To be sure, the common people, the plebs, exercised a sporadic influence with agitations in the streets and in the Forum. On occasion, with enough organization and turnout and with the right leadership from inspired tribunes or some other *populares*, men of the people, they might carry the day on one or another measure in the Tribal Assembly. But it was the senate, dominated by an inner circle of ultraconservative noblemen (*nobiles*), that determined foreign policy, appointed provincial governors, and held the purse strings of the Republic. In brief, the

Republic's political system permitted the wealthy few to prevail on most, if not all, issues.

For those at the bottom of the social order, life was a mean struggle. The mass of the propertyless *plebs urbana*, the urban population, and their country cousins, the landless *plebs rustica*, lived from hand to mouth under material conditions that often were akin to slavery. The city-dwelling commoners, the Roman *proletarii*, were piled into thousands of poorly lit inner-city tenements. These dwellings were sometimes seven or eight floors high, all lacking toilets, running water, and decent ventilation. The rents for these fetid warrens were usually exorbitant, forcing the poor to double and triple up, with entire families cramped into one room. Tenants who escaped the typhoid and fires that plagued the slums still lived in fear of having these structures collapse upon them, as happened all too frequently. The ingenuity for which Roman architecture is known was not lavished upon the domiciles of the indigent.

As is true of many societies before and since, in ancient Rome the very material wretchedness that the poor endured was treated as evidence of their moral and personal deficiencies. In the minds of the well-to-do, the plebs were the authors of their own poverty and had only themselves to blame for their woes. That darling of classicists through the ages, Marcus Tullius Cicero, was tireless in his disparagement of the lower classes. He was part of an already established tradition when he described the *plebs urbana* as "the city's dirt and filth" and as "a wretched and starving rabble" or as the "the city scum" and an "inexperienced mass." He acknowledges that they are starving but sees it as their own fault. And whenever the people mobilized against class injustice, they became in Cicero's mind that most odious of all creatures, a mob.[1]

As in any plutocracy, in the Roman Republic it was a disgrace to be poor and an honor to be rich. Those of the opulent class, living parasitically off the labor of others, were hailed as men of quality and worth while the impecunious, who struggled along on the paltry earnings of their own hard labor, were considered vulgar and unworthy. Though he wrote during the time of emperors, the satirist Juvenal might as well have been speaking of Republican society when he observed: "Men whose domestic poverty is an obstacle to their qualities do not easily rise, but at Rome any such attempt is even tougher."[2]

---

1   Cicero, *To Atticus* 1.16.11 and 1.19.4; *Philippics* 2.116, cf. 8.9. For a recent introduction to the subject under discussion on these pages cf. Thomas Habinek, "Slavery and Class," in *A Companion to Latin Literature*, ed. Stephen Harrison (Oxford: Blackwell, 2005), 385–393.

2   Juvenal, *Satires* 3.164–166.

2. Common Cause Between Plebs and Slaves

Why then did the Roman plebs, this wretched and impoverished populace, not ally itself with the slaves? Together they would have composed
a powerful and potentially irresistible tide. First, we should note that in
fact there actually were times when plebeians made common cause with
slaves. Many of Rome's working people were themselves ex-slaves or the
sons of ex-slaves. Some of the *proletarii* regularly worked alongside
slaves, as at certain construction sites, and were inclined to feel a
common sympathy with the servile population on basic issues. For good
reason did Cato the Younger, dearly beloved by today's conservatives, fear
restiveness among the poorest citizens, for they were often the ones who
could stir up all the people.[3]

   An incident of A.D. 61, reported by Tacitus, is worth noting.[4] The city
prefect had been murdered in his bedchamber by one of his slaves.
According to ancient custom, when a master was killed by a *servus*, all
servi in the household had to be put to death. This was to insure that all
the guilty parties were punished, including those who may have secretly
collaborated or who looked the other way and knowingly failed to report
the plot. Total extermination sent a message to the servile population
that *all* of a master's slaves were personally responsible for his safety. But
the city prefect's household had some four hundred *servi*, including
women and children. The threatened mass execution of such a number,
many of them entirely innocent, evoked angry protests from the Roman
citizenry, who assembled outside the Senate House. The senate's decision
to go ahead with this mass execution was delayed by a crowd of people
armed with stones and torches. Emperor Nero had to call out the troops
to line the route along which the condemned were to pass. The moral
outrage expressed by the protestors signaled a sympathetic bond between
impoverished slaves and the impoverished plebs.

   Bonding between poor commoners and slaves was possible because of
the conditions of labor created by the prevailing mode of production.
Much of agriculture consisted of *latifundiae*, vast plantations upon which
concentrated numbers of the *plebs rustica* and even greater numbers of
servi labored almost as an undifferentiated mass under the exploitative
dominion of overseer and plantation owner. Being part of the same formidable workforce toiling shoulder to shoulder, as it were, plebs and
slaves sometimes found it possible to act in unison. Spartacus himself

---

3   Cf. Plutarch, *Caesar* 8.3–4.
4   Tacitus, *Annals* 14.42–45.

won some support from poorer elements within the free population during his rebellion. Starting out as a slave in a gladiatorial school in Capua, he and seventy-eight other men escaped and over time grew into an army of seventy thousand. They were able to build such a formidable force in part because many freedmen and other free commoners joined their ranks along with thousands of fugitive slaves.

Despite all this, we cannot deny that unity of action between slaves and impoverished Roman subjects was the exception rather than the rule. There were far more Roman subjects in the ten legions needed to crush Spartacus than in his own army.

3. The Myth of the Idle Poor

Down through the ages, historians have characterized the Roman *proletarii* as an idle demoralized rabble who lived parasitically off free handouts of bread and circuses. With their stomachs kept full by the dole and their minds and spirits distracted by a continual array of arena spectacles, the plebs had no reason to make common cause with rebellious slaves. They had devolved into selfish idlers, bought off by the authorities.

Contrary to this image propagated by past and present historians, dole recipients did not live like parasites off the "bread" they received, which actually was a sparse wheat or corn allotment used for making bread and gruel. The people's tribune C. Licinius Macer once pointed out the insufficiency of this dole in a speech to the *plebs*: "five measures [per man], . . . which really can be no more than prison rations. For just as that meager supply keeps death away from prisoners but completely weakens them, so this small amount does not relieve you from domestic cares."[5] Macer understood that people cannot live by bread alone, not even at the basic physiological level. The plebs also needed money for rent, clothing, cooking oil, and other necessities, including additional food. Most of them had to find work, low-paying and irregular as it might be. The bread dole often was a necessary supplement, the difference between survival and starvation, but it was never a total sustenance that allowed people to idle away their days. In any case, we might question why so many scholars have judged the Roman people to be venal and degraded just because they demanded affordable bread and were concerned with having enough to feed themselves and their children.

5   Macer's speech is preserved by Sallust, *Histories* 3.48; quotation at 3.48.19.

As with bread, so with circuses. There is no denying that the games, chariot races, and gladiatorial contests – the few amusements available to the poor at no cost – helped them forget their grievances for a spell, acting as popular distractions not unlike televised sporting events today. The emperors seemed to have been well aware of the diverting function that the arena spectacles served, which explains why they maintained them regardless of cost.[6] The games were the major spectator sports of rich and poor alike. Probably a higher proportion of wealthy nobles and equestrians frequented them, seated in reserved front-row stalls that afforded them the best view, than did common people. The rich had the time and leisure to attend. In the Colosseum, and presumably in earlier amphitheaters, the front rows were reserved for magistrates, foreign dignitaries, and senators. The rows directly behind them were set aside for the upper social classes, with additional seats for priests, military officers, and other special groups. Women were segregated, consigned to the worst seats at the very top. And behind them was standing room for the impoverished *proletarii*.[7]

To suggest that the plebs failed to make common cause with slaves because they were pampered layabouts is to ignore the grimmer class realities prevailing in ancient Rome. Still there is no denying that bread and circuses, especially bread, did in some limited and dismal way blunt the desperation that the plebs faced every day, helping them to see themselves as at least a notch above the slaves.

4. Clients and Mercenaries

One way the nobles maintained their influence over the populace was by recruiting large numbers of the plebs into their private service. Forced by sheer poverty, many indigents sold their services and loyalties for modest sums. The patronage that the rich extended to their paid followers (*clientelae*) served the oligarchy well. Influential patrons spent many a morning at home in audience to a throng of followers who came to press for a favor, pass on useful information, receive an assignment, pay their respects, and secure a meager handout of money or food. The

6   On the importance of organized spectacles in ancient Rome see, e.g., Roland Auguet, *Cruelty and Civilization: The Roman Games* (1972; rpt. New York: Barnes and Noble, 1998); Donald G. Kyle, *Spectacles of Death in Ancient Rome* (London and New York: Routledge, 1998); and Alison Futrell, *Blood in the Arena: The Spectacle of Roman Power* (Austin: University of Texas Press, 1997; rpt. 2000). All contain additional references.

7   Lionel Casson, *Everyday Life in Ancient Rome*, rev. edn. (Baltimore and London: Johns Hopkins University Press, 1998), 104.

democratic tribune Macer tried to shake the commoners into taking action against the plutocracy and admonished them: "like sheep, you, the multitude, have submitted yourselves to the service and enjoyment of some individuals. You have been stripped of everything that your forefathers left you except that you yourselves now choose your masters with your ballots just as you once chose your defenders."[8]

The patronage system wedded portions of the lower class to the uppermost stratum. As social historians have long noted, patronage created relationships of personal dependence.[9] It gave Roman political life its private armies and lasting semi-feudal character. The affluent patrons used their clientele as voting blocs, electoral campaign workers, ready-made gangs of counter-agitators, and even death squads. These armed cadres of what historian Theodor Mommsen called "bludgeon boys" were used in times of crisis to beat and assassinate oppositional popular forces and their leaders. Such arrangements had an intimidating and demoralizing effect on popular democracy. One is reminded of the comment by nineteenth-century American tycoon Jay Gould: "I can hire one half of the working class to kill the other half."

Aside from these private armies, the ranks of the Roman army itself were composed of men of modest means, whose small holdings or dire poverty made them willing recruits. Many fought with the promise of a land allotment or the lure of war booty. Various complements were drawn not only from the *proletarii*, first allowed to bear arms during Marius' rule, and from the rural populations of the Italian peninsula but also from far-flung colonies. These provincial units did not always make the most reliable troops, but, when facing insurgent slaves, they served well enough.

5. The Slave Menace and Racist Ideology

Of crucial import was the way the slave population was repeatedly demonized by the ruling elites as a murderous alien menace to Rome and to

8 Sallust, *Histories* 3.48.6.
9 Cf., e.g., Max Weber, *The Agrarian Sociology of Ancient Civilizations*, tr. R. I. Frank (1976; rpt. London and New York: Verso, 1998), 281. Weber's book first appeared in 1891. Recent studies of Roman patron–client relationships in Republic and Empire, with additional references, are Richard P. Saller, *Personal Patronage under the Early Empire* (Cambridge: Cambridge University Press, 1982; rpt. 2002); *Patronage in Ancient Society*, ed. Andrew Wallace-Hadrill (London and New York: Routledge, 1989; rpt. 1990); and Koenraad Verboven, *The Economy of Friends: Economic Aspects of* amicitia *and Patronage in the Late Republic* (Brussels: Latomus, 2002).

all its citizenry. Hence the Roman proverb: "So many slaves, so many enemies."[10] In 63 B.C., Cicero publicly accused Catiline, a nobleman, of conspiring with armed slaves and plebs to torch Rome and launch the destruction of the Roman people. Describing a case of slaves turning against their master, Pliny the Younger referred to the "dangers, indignities, and mockeries" that slaves impose on their supposedly kind masters, for their "brutality" leads slaves to murder and rebellion.[11] The Roman historian Florus saw Spartacus' rebellion not as a monumental struggle for liberty but as a disgraceful undertaking, perpetrated by slaves and led by gladiators, "the former people of the lowest class; the latter, of the worst."[12] Cicero readily discredited any popular action by charging that *slaves* were involved. Thus he denounced the disturbances that erupted in the wake of Julius Caesar's assassination as being perpetrated by "slaves and beggars."[13] That a slave is a lowly human being or subhuman barbarian is a theme readily found in various ancient texts.[14] In the minds of many Romans, slaves were substandard in moral and mental capacity, barely a notch or two above animals.

In the generation after Spartacus, the *popularis* Publius Clodius, an ally of Julius Caesar, actually recruited the poorer citizenry, freedmen, and slaves in an attempt to rebuild people's organizations (*collegia*) and put them on a paramilitary basis as a means of defense against the plutocrats' death squads. The senate oligarchs repeatedly tried to drive a wedge between Clodius and the citizenry by alleging that his followers were made up exclusively of slaves and criminals. In a speech, Cicero referred to the supporters of Clodius as "city scum and slaves."[15] Privately, Cicero denounced Clodius as a scoundrel of the worst sort: "he runs from street to street and openly offers the slaves the hope for freedom . . . and he uses slaves as advisers."[16]

All slavocracies develop a racist or caste ideology to justify their oppressive and dehumanized relationships. In Rome, male slaves of any

10   Seneca, *Moral Epistles* 47.5.
11   Pliny the Younger, *Letters* 3.14.5.
12   Lucius Annaeus Florus, *Epitome of Roman History* 3.20.1–2 (= 2.8.20.1–2).
13   Cicero, *To Atticus* 14.10.1.
14   One of the earliest ancient statements on slavery is voiced by the slave Eumaeus, who had been born a king's son, in Homer's *Odyssey*: "Zeus . . . takes away one half of the virtue / from a man, once the day of slavery closes upon him" (*Odyssey* 17. 322–323); quoted from Richmond Lattimore, *The Odyssey of Homer* (New York: Harper and Row, 1965; several rpts.), 261.
15   Cicero, *Against Piso* 9. I discuss Clodius in *The Assassination of Julius Caesar: A People's History of Ancient Rome* (New York and London: The New Press, 2004), 76–77.
16   Cicero, *To Atticus* 4.3.2.

Figure 1 The opening shot of *Spartacus*. The desert of Libya filmed by original director Anthony Mann in Death Valley. Universal.

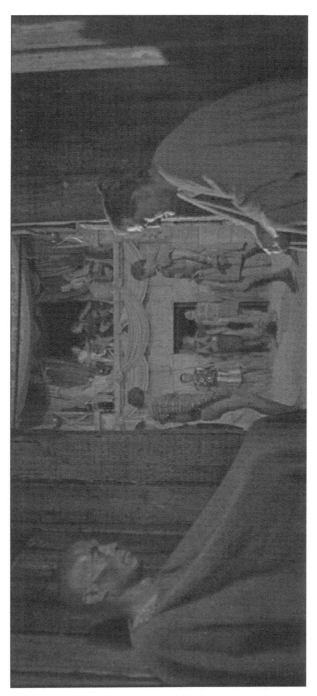

Figure 2 Draba and Spartacus shortly before their duel. Universal.

Figure 3 Lobby card of the duel between Draba and Spartacus. The William Knight Zewadski Collection.

Figure 4 Lobby card of Spartacus after his first victory over the Romans. The William Knight Zewadski Collection.

Figure 5   Crassus' arrival at his villa, filmed at William Randolph Hearst's San Simeon. Universal.

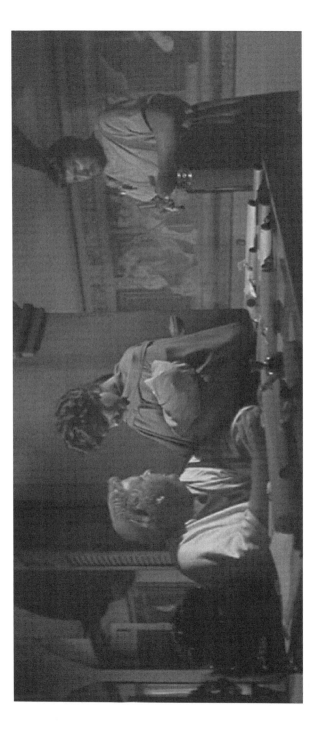

Figure 6 Batiatus and Varinia, with Spartacus' child, bid farewell to Gracchus immediately before Gracchus' suicide. The frescoes of the Villa of the Mysteries are visible in the background. Universal.

Figure 7 Spartacus' address to his people on the mountainside. Universal.

Figure 8 The Sermon on the Mount in Nicholas Ray's *King of Kings* (1961). Metro-Goldwyn-Mayer.

Figure 9   The Roman legions arrayed for battle. Director Stanley Kubrick put his cameras on elevated platforms half a mile away from the 10,000 Spanish soldiers recruited for this sequence. Universal.

Figure 10 Spartacus moments before the decisive battle. Film still autographed by Kirk Douglas. The William Knight Zewadski Collection.

Figure 11   Varinia finds Spartacus dying on the cross in the film's last sequence. Universal.

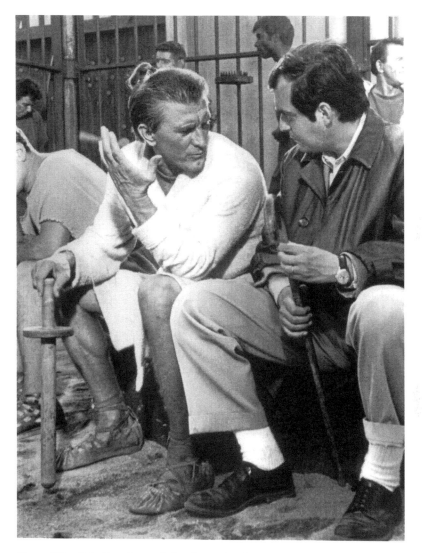

Figure 12 Kirk Douglas and Stanley Kubrick on the set of the gladiatorial school. The William Knight Zewadski Collection.

Figure 13 Kirk Douglas in heroic pose in a promotional photograph. The William Knight Zewadski Collection.

Figure 14 One of the most arresting images for *Spartacus* appears on this German poster of a blond Spartacus dueling with Draba before a blood-red background. The heroic nudity is a tribute to the tradition of classical art. The same image was used in 1962 for the cover of the American mass-market paperback of Arthur Koestler's *The Gladiators*, but with a different background.

Figure 15 American poster for Michele Lupo's *La vendetta di Spartacus* (*The Revenge of Spartacus*, 1965), one of several Italian films inspired by and cashing in on *Spartacus*. The medallions of the principal actors are patterned on those for Kubrick's film. The William Knight Zewadski Collection.

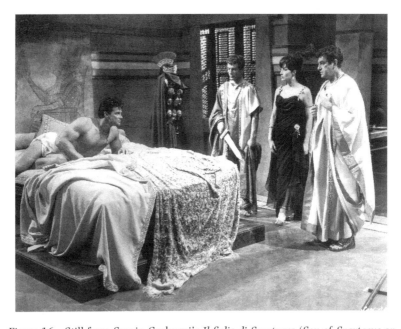

Figure 16 Still from Sergio Corbucci's *Il figlio di Spartacus* (*Son of Spartacus* or *The Slave*, 1963). Muscleman Steve Reeves (l.) is the titular hero. The William Knight Zewadski Collection.

Figure 17 A typical moment in gladiator cinema, here from Michele Lupo's *Gli schiavi più forti del mondo* (*Seven Slaves against the World*, 1964). The film's plot is indebted to that of *Spartacus*. The William Knight Zewadski Collection.

Figure 18   This still from Nunzio Malasomma's *La rivolta degli schiavi* (*The Revolt of the Slaves*, 1961), a loose remake of Alessandro Blasetti's *Fabiola* (1951), shows that not all Italian epics have to shun comparison with the Hollywood product. The William Knight Zewadski Collection.

age were habitually addressed as *pueri* ("boys"). A similar degrading appellation was applied to slaves in ancient Greece and in the pre-Civil War United States, persisting into the segregationist South of the twentieth century. Slaves in ancient Rome were mostly foreigners, so it was easy to portray them as a barbarian menace in addition to attributing to them an innate inferiority. Spartacus himself was a Thracian, and most of his followers were foreigners. The Roman oligarchs lost no opportunity to keep plebs and slaves apart by playing up their ethnic divide. Cicero was part of a long-standing tradition when he stoked ethno-class prejudices in regard to slavery. He assured his audiences that Jews and Syrians were "nations born to slavery," that is, they had an inborn proclivity for servitude.[17] They were not of the same cut as real Roman citizens.

That most slaves were from alien stock in Spartacus' day further fueled the Romans' tendency to loathe them as wastrels and brigands, troublesome contaminants of respectable society. Ethnic and class biases conveniently dovetailed, making it that much easier to demonize the slave population in the eyes of many ordinary Romans.

6. The Ruling Ideology

Ruling-class rapacity rarely parades in naked form. Those ensconced at the social top utilize every advantage in money, property, education, organization, and prestige to maintain their ideological hegemony over the rest of society. They marshal a variety of arguments to justify their privileged position, arguments that are all the more sincerely embraced for being evidently self-serving. But ideology is not merely a promotion of class interest. The function of ruling-class ideology is to disguise narrowly selfish interests by wedding them to a loftier and all-encompassing view of society.

First and foremost, the Roman oligarchic clique represented its privileges and interests as being tantamount to the common good. It claimed a community of interest with all of Rome's citizens. The aristocrats professed to be protectors of everyone's welfare. The laws they promulgated and the rulings their magistrates put forth served not only themselves

---

17   Cicero, *On the Consular Provinces* 10; cf. *For Flaccus* 65. Cf. further Livy, *From the Foundation of the City* 35.49.8 and 36.17.5, adduced and discussed by Moses I. Finley, *Ancient Slavery and Modern Ideology*, ed. Brent D. Shaw (expanded edn.; Princeton: Wiener, 1998), 187 and 245–246 note 99.

but every Roman – or so they would have the public believe. It followed that the well-being of the Republic and of the entire society depended on the public service rendered by those prominent few who presided so wisely and resplendently over affairs of state, those whose high station itself gave proof of a selfless and deserving excellence.

Secondly, ruling-class protagonists repeatedly warned that any leveling forces were a threat to all and that the rebellious elements among the servile population were out to kill not only their masters but all free Romans. The oligarchs portrayed mass agitation not as righteous resistance to injustice but as divisive and destructive to Rome itself, the work of unscrupulous, unstable, aggrandizing, bloodthirsty demagogues who inflame popular passions and mislead the multitude. It is quite likely that Spartacus' army of slaves was portrayed in these terms, certainly by the third year of their campaign when they fought their way down from Cisalpine Gaul to "threaten" Rome itself.

Finally, slaves were in fact a class apart from Roman citizens. Although common citizens might be nearly as impoverished as slaves, they could still think of themselves as Romans, able to vote and voice their sentiments in the Forum, endowed with certain rights and liberties, circumscribed as these might be, and able to make their own day-to-day decisions and to sell their labor on the "free" market rather than themselves being marketed like chattels.

In a word, the nobles maintained their influence mostly with their wealth, social prestige, and the protection and patronage they extended to their paid clientele, along with the threats and actual applications of force they employed with their armed squads and with the Roman army. Their ability to enlist the efforts of the many in causes that served the interests of the few extended into elections and the functions of magistrates, censors, and other governing interests. *Because* they were poor, the commoners could readily be recruited and easily led – or misled – by the rich. They could be given many little tasks and responsibilities for meager payoffs but no real power or social standing. In any case, most ordinary Romans were far too involved in the daily struggle for survival to risk joining in a common cause with rebellious slaves. They were too busy trying to make a living to make revolutionary history.

In sum, the Roman ruling class did what just about every ruling class before and since has done: it kept the populace divided against itself and tied in some way to those at the top; it played upon national loyalties and survival fears; it stoked ethnic prejudices and class bigotry; and it conjured up images of a reputable citizenry that was being victimized by pernicious slaves and the lumpenproletariat – not unlike the way in which the middle and working classes in modern societies are made to fear and resent a marginalized underclass. For all the variations in characters and costumes, and the differences in historical circumstances, the basic scenario is a familiar one. Well before Spartacus and his rebels were finally crushed by Roman legions, they had been isolated and outdone by the cultural and ideological hegemony of the oligarchy.

CHAPTER NINE

The Holy Cause of Freedom: American Ideals in *Spartacus*

Martin M. Winkler

"Four score and seven years ago our fathers brought forth on this continent, a new nation, conceived in Liberty, and dedicated to the proposition that all men are created equal." With these words President Abraham Lincoln began the Gettysburg Address on November 19, 1863. In the course of his short speech he referred to the "great task remaining before us": the abolition of slavery and "a new birth of freedom."[1] In the spirit of Lincoln, the title of a modern history of the American Civil War is *Battle Cry of Freedom*.[2]

---

1   On the Gettysburg Address and its echoes of classical antiquity cf. Garry Wills, *Lincoln at Gettysburg: The Words That Remade America* (New York: Simon and Schuster, 1992; rpt. 1993). Lincoln's text is at Wills, 263. On Lincoln cf. Merrill D. Peterson, *Lincoln in American Memory* (New York and Oxford: Oxford University Press, 1994; rpt. 1995). On the importance of the Civil War for the development of American democracy and the abolition of slavery see now especially Sean Wilentz, *The Rise of American Democracy: Jefferson to Lincoln* (New York: Norton, 2005).

2   James M. McPherson, *Battle Cry of Freedom: The Civil War Era* (New York: Oxford University Press, 1988; rpt. 2003). The title of a recent study by a professor of American religious history indicates that the Americans have a primarily moral, even sacred, perspective on this war: Harry S. Stout, *Upon the Altar of the Nation: A Moral History of the American Civil War* (New York: Viking, 2006). For some critical comments on this book see the review essay by McPherson, "Was It a Just War?" *The New York Review of Books* (March 23, 2006), 16 and 18–19.

Freedom and *liberty* are quintessential terms for the way Americans have understood themselves and their history since the days of the American Revolution. Patrick Henry proclaimed "Give me liberty or give me death," and Thomas Jefferson spoke of "the holy cause of freedom."[3] This is in spite of the fact that those who declared all men to be created equal could themselves own slaves, a circumstance that elicited a rather sharp comment from Samuel Johnson: "how is it that we hear the loudest yelps for liberty among the drivers of negroes?"[4] Johnson put his finger on the sorest spot in American history.

The Americans patterned their new republic on that of ancient Rome.[5] The Roman republic has long been the best-known slave-holding society of the pre-modern West, but it was also the culture generally revered as a model for new political and social developments during the Enlightenment and later. With Rome as their model, Americans could own slaves and still regard themselves as preservers and defenders of liberty at home and abroad.[6] After increasingly heated debates over

3 Jefferson's words are in his "Response to Address of Welcome by the Citizens of Albemarle" in Virginia (February 12, 1790); quoted from Thomas Jefferson, *Writings*, ed. Merrill D. Peterson (New York: Library of America / Viking, 1984), 491.

4 Quoted from Samuel Johnson, "Taxation No Tyranny; an Answer to the Resolutions and Address of the American Congress" (1775), in *The Yale Edition of the Works of Samuel Johnson*, vol. 10: *Political Writings*, ed. Donald J. Greene (New Haven and London: Yale University Press, 1977), 411–455; quotation at 454. Cf. Greene's comment on this at 454 note 9. On the wider context see now Simon Schama, *Rough Crossings: Britain, the Slaves and the American Revolution* (2005; rpt. New York: Ecco, 2006), and Gary B. Nash, *The Forgotten Fifth: African Americans in the Age of Revolution* (Cambridge: Harvard University Press, 2006).

5 On this subject see, e.g., Meyer Reinhold, *Classica Americana: The Greek and Roman Heritage in the United States* (Detroit: Wayne State University Press, 1984); Susan Ford Wiltshire, *Greece, Rome, and the Bill of Rights* (Norman: University of Oklahoma Press, 1992); and Carl J. Richard, *The Founders and the Classics: Greece, Rome, and the American Enlightenment* (Cambridge and London: Harvard University Press, 1994). All contain further references.

6 Cf. Eugene N. Genovese, *The Slaveholders' Dilemma: Freedom and Progress in Southern Conservative Thought* (Columbia: University of South Carolina Press, 1992; rpt. 1995), 5: "The proslavery theorists never tired of proclaiming that the greatness of ancient Egypt, Israel, Greece, and Rome had been based on slavery, and the reading of ancient history and literature seemed to confirm the proclamation." Cf. also *Slavery Defended: The Views of the Old South*, ed. Eric L. McKitrick (Englewood Cliffs: Prentice-Hall, 1963); *The Ideology of Slavery: Proslavery Thought in the Antebellum South, 1830–1860*, ed. Drew Gilpin Faust (Baton Rouge: Louisiana State University Press, 1981; rpt. 1985); Larry E. Tise, *Proslavery: A History of the Defense of Slavery in America, 1701–1840* (Athens and London: University of Georgia Press, 1987); and Elizabeth Fox-Genovese and Eugene D. Genovese, *The Mind of the Master Class: History and Faith in the Southern Slaveholders' Worldview*

slavery, the secession of thirteen slave-owning states from the Union and after more than a year and a half of Civil War, American slaves officially became free with Lincoln's Emancipation Proclamation of January 1, 1863. In the twentieth century, Americans defended freedom abroad in both world wars and defeated Fascism and Nazism. When a new totalitarian enemy, Soviet Communism, began to affect Americans, the resulting Cold War had its domestic corollary in McCarthyism, which extended even to Hollywood.[7]

(Cambridge: Cambridge University Press, 2005), 249–304 (chapter entitled "In the Shadow of Antiquity"). See also Richard, *The Founders and the Classics*, 95–98 and 241 (slavery as an "antimodel"). For a comparison of Roman and American slave systems see, e.g., Barry A. Crouch, "'Booty Capitalism' and Capitalism's Booty: Slaves and Slavery in Ancient Rome and the American South," *Slavery and Abolition*, 6 (1985), 3–24. On the legal background see especially Alan Watson, *Roman Slave Law* (Baltimore and London: Johns Hopkins University Press, 1987) and *Slave Law in the Americas* (Athens and London: University of Georgia Press, 1989; rpt. 1990), and the following essays in *Slavery and the Law*, ed. Paul Finkelman (Madison: Madison House, 1997): Alan Watson, "Seventeenth-Century Jurists, Roman Law, and Slavery" (367–377); Jonathan A. Bush, "The British Constitution and the Creation of American Slavery" (379–418); Alan Watson, "Thinking Property at Rome" (419–435); and Jacob I. Corré, "Thinking Property at Memphis: An Application of Watson" (436–451). In general cf. also David Brion Davis, *The Problem of Slavery in Western Culture* (1966; rpt. New York: Oxford University Press, 1988), *The Problem of Slavery in the Age of Revolution, 1770–1823* (1975; rpt. New York: Oxford University Press, 1999), and *Inhuman Bondage: The Rise and Fall of Slavery in the New World* (New York: Oxford University Press, 2006), 27–47 and 336–340 (notes; chapter entitled "The Ancient Foundations of Modern Slavery"). Cf. James Oliver Horton and Lois E. Horton, *Slavery and the Making of America* (New York: Oxford University Press, 2005; rpt. 2006).

7   For recent studies of McCarthyism see *McCarthyism: The Great American Red Scare: A Documentary History*, ed. Albert Fried (New York: Oxford University Press, 1997); Ellen Schrecker, *Many Are the Crimes: McCarthyism in America* (1998; rpt. Princeton: Princeton University Press, 1999); *The Age of McCarthyism: A Brief History with Documents*, ed. Ellen Schrecker, 2nd edn. (Boston: Bedford / St. Martin's, 2002); and Ted Morgan, *Reds: McCarthyism in Twentieth-Century America* (New York: Random House, 2003; rpt. 2004). Tom Wicker, *Shooting Star: The Brief Arc of Joe McCarthy* (Orlando: Harcourt, 2006). Cf. also Stephen J. Whitfield, *The Culture of the Cold War*, 2nd edn. (Baltimore and London: Johns Hopkins University Press, 1996). For various perspectives on McCarthyism in Hollywood see Stefan Kanfer, *A Journal of the Plague Years* (New York: Atheneum, 1973); Lillian Hellman, *Scoundrel Time* (Boston: Little, Brown, 1976; rpt. 2000); Larry Ceplair and Steven Englund, *The Inquisition in Hollywood: Politics in the Film Community, 1930–1960* (1980; rpt. Urbana: University of Illinois Press, 2003); Victor Navasky, *Naming Names* (1980; rpt. New York: Hill and Wang, 2003); Nancy Lynn Schwartz and Sheila Schwartz, *The Hollywood Writers' War* (1982; rpt. New York: McGraw-Hill, 1983); Brian Neve, "HUAC, the Blacklist, and the Decline of Social Cinema," in Peter Lev, *Transforming the Screen 1950–1959* (New York: Scribner, 2003), 65–86 and 319–322 (notes); and Thomas Doherty, *Cold War, Cool Medium: Television, McCarthyism, and American Culture* (New York: Columbia University Press, 2003; rpt. 2005).

The most conspicuous kind of film that Hollywood had begun making after World War II was historical epics, chiefly in reaction to the rise of television. These films began to thrive when several technical innovations were introduced to make the cinema screen more attractive than the tiny black-and-white screen in American living rooms. The cinema is the best mass medium to express political, cultural, and social issues, and historical films reflect the period of their making at least as much as they deal with the past.[8] Concerning American cinema set in antiquity, a scholar has pointed out:

> The favorite epic story . . . concerns a persecuted group secretly supported by God: Jews, Christians, and occasionally slaves. Their oppressors are Egyptians, Romans, patricians. It is the colonies against the mean mother country . . . I am not attributing sneaky allegorical motives to the makers of these movies, I am just saying that there aren't all that many models for a big confrontation between a powerful (but doomed) tyrant and a virtuous victim whose virtue, in the end, will reap rich historical rewards. This is the encounter that takes place again and again in epics, and it seems natural that American moviemakers should, no doubt unconsciously, fall back on a popular version of their country's birth.[9]

Stanley Kubrick's *Spartacus* conforms to this general pattern. I will here examine *Spartacus* in regard to the specifically American qualities with which the filmmakers endowed their titular hero and his story. In the popular American imagination, the history of Rome is inextricably linked to the early history of Christianity. So a religious component is present even in a film like *Spartacus* that is set decades before the birth of Jesus. In its presentation of Spartacus as a messianic protagonist, the film expresses a dual emphasis on freedom and religion that is more important than any of the political analogies that it contains and more

8 On cinema as society's seismograph cf. my comments in the "Introduction" to *Classical Myth and Culture in the Cinema*, ed. Martin M. Winkler (New York: Oxford University Press, 2001), 3–22, at 8 note 7. J. Hoberman, *The Dream Life: Movies, Media and the Mythology of the Sixties* (New York and London: The Free Press, 2003; rpt. 2005), is a detailed study along such lines and refers to *Spartacus* throughout.
9 Michael Wood, *America in the Movies; or, "Santa Maria, It Had Slipped My Mind"* (1975; rpt. New York: Columbia University Press, 1989), 184. Before *Spartacus*, the Paris of Robert Wise's *Helen of Troy* (1956) had urged his beloved to escape with him as the only way to end her status as a virtual slave in Sparta and obtain her liberty. The trend continues in recent cinema: Antoine Fuqua's *King Arthur* (2004), despite its name more of a Roman than a medieval film, justifies its simplistic tale of endless gore with the hero's quest for freedom.

revealing about how Americans see themselves.[10] The film's prologue alerts viewers to the connections between freedom and religion. I approach *Spartacus* from the point of view expressed in this prologue, here placed in the context of comparable prologues heard in 1950s American films about Rome.

1. Prologues

The first film set in ancient Rome that was produced in Hollywood after 1945 is Mervyn LeRoy's *Quo Vadis* (1951). Its prologue reveals the way audiences are to interpret the story of Nero and the early Christians and provides the model for other films made in the 1950s. Over images of a legion returning to Rome victorious, with booty and slaves, the omniscient narrator tells us the correct attitude with which to follow the story. Looking back on the past with a modern consciousness, he provides a bridge between contemporary and ancient times. I quote only those of the narrator's words that express the film's general theme of tyranny, liberty, and religion, omitting those others that reflect more topical overtones.[11] The prologue of *Quo Vadis* is a blueprint for the narrative perspective of *Spartacus* almost ten years later:

> Imperial Rome is the center of the empire, an undisputed master of the world. But with this power inevitably comes corruption . . . Rulers of conquered nations surrender their helpless subjects to bondage. High and low alike become Roman slaves, Roman hostages. There is no escape from the whip and the sword. That any force on earth can shake the foundations of this pyramid of power and corruption, of human misery and slavery,

10   I refer readers interested in political interpretations of *Spartacus* to John Baxter, *Stanley Kubrick: A Biography* (New York: Carroll and Graf, 1997), 133–134; Maria Wyke, *Projecting the Past: Ancient Rome, Cinema and History* (New York and London: Routledge, 1997), 56–72, and Alison Futrell, "Seeing Red: Spartacus as Domestic Economist," in *Imperial Projections: Ancient Rome in Modern Popular Culture*, ed. Sandra R. Joshel, Margaret Malamud, and Donald T. McGuire, Jr. (Baltimore and London: Johns Hopkins University Press, 2001; rpt. 2005), 77–118, at 97–111. Hoberman, *The Dream Life*, 1–36 and 410–413 (notes), examines political, cultural, and cinematic contexts of *Spartacus* in a chapter entitled "Remaking History, A.D. 1960." Hoberman discusses the similarities of *Spartacus* to two other large-scale epics of the same year, John Sturges' *The Magnificent Seven* and John Wayne's *The Alamo*. In both, an outnumbered group of plucky heroes fight for the righteous cause of freedom against oppressors. In the one, half of the heroes die; in the other, all.

11   I examine these in "The Roman Empire in American Cinema After 1945," *The Classical Journal*, 93 (1998), 167–196, at 172–184; slightly revised in *Imperial Projections*, 77–118, at 55–65.

seems inconceivable. But thirty years before this day a miracle occurred. On a Roman cross in Judaea, a man died to make men free, to spread the gospel of love and redemption. Soon that humble cross is destined to replace the proud eagles that now top the victorious Roman standards. This is the story of that immortal conflict.

The narrator then refers to "the Antichrist known to history as the Emperor Nero," thereby clinching the viewers' required attitude. To those in the audience who remember their history lessons, his double reference to Roman corruption and the alliterative image of Rome as a "pyramid of power" that will topple just as the legionary eagles will fall from their height implies not only the imminent overthrow of Nero but also the eventual fall of Rome – both due to the rise of Christianity, which will emerge triumphant after and despite the crucifixion of Jesus. Jesus' death, shown during the prologue in a flashback, appears as a defeat only to unregenerate pagans; we in the audience, of course, know it for what it really was: the triumph of the meek and good over the haughty and evil.[12] Jesus dies for our spiritual freedom in *Quo Vadis*; in his own film, so will Spartacus.

The same perspective recurs in Henry Koster's *The Robe* (1953), the first film to be released in the widescreen format that would come to predominate epic filmmaking from now on.[13] The studio considered a religious and Roman topic more suitable to introduce its new technology than a film with a contemporary story. (Jean Negulesco's widescreen comedy *How to Marry A Millionaire* had gone into production before *The Robe* but was released after it.) The protagonist of *The Robe* is an aristocratic Roman who with his fiancée converts to Christianity; both die for their faith rather than accept life under the mad tyrant Caligula. The plot is a variation on that of *Quo Vadis*, but this time the main character introduces the story himself. While he speaks, we see, first, a brief shot of gladiators in the arena, then a series of images illustrating what he tells us. Main emphasis is on military power, on foreign wealth and slaves pouring into Rome, and, at the end, on the city's slave market. Marcellus Gallio, our hero, is still a pagan, so he does not mention Christianity. Instead, he refers to the evil of slavery. His critical observations prepare us for the fact that he will turn out to be a good Roman by becoming a Christian. The victory of Christianity is again the chief topic since the

12 Cf. Jesuit author Michael Walsh, *The Triumph of the Meek: Why Early Christianity Succeeded* (San Francisco: Harper and Row, 1984), and historian of religion Jaroslav Pelikan, *The Excellent Empire: The Fall of Rome and the Triumph of the Church* (San Francisco: Harper and Row, 1987).
13 Cf. Lev, *Transforming the Screen 1950–1959*, 107–125 and 325–327 (notes), a chapter entitled "Technology and Spectacle."

film's titular garment is the one worn by Jesus at the crucifixion. Marcellus' perspective of Rome and its imperialism will have been familiar to anyone in the theater:

> Rome, master of the earth in the eighteenth year of the Emperor Tiberius. Our legions stand guard on the boundaries of civilization, on the foggy coasts of the northern seas to the ancient rivers of Babylon – the finest fighting machines in history. The people of thirty lands send us tribute: their gold and silk, ivory and frankincense, and their proudest sons to be our slaves. We have reached the point where there are more slaves in Rome than citizens. Some say that we are only looters of what others have created, that we create nothing ourselves. But we have made gods, fine gods and goddesses . . . For the power lies not in *their* hands of marble but in ours of flesh. We, the nobles of Rome, are free to live only for our own pleasure. Could any god offer us more?
>
> Today we traffic in human souls. The slave market is crowded . . .

Militarism and loot, the false freedom to indulge in empty pleasures, the immense exploitation of slaves – the film's wholesale condemnation of Romans who were not Christians is evident. The prologue cleverly manages to increase its indictment by referring to something that ancient authors themselves mentioned on several occasions: more slaves than masters.[14] Americans were ready to apply this circumstance to their own society. Even before the birth of the U.S., future Founding Father George Mason wrote in 1765: "One of the first signs of the decay and perhaps the primary cause of the destruction of the most flourishing government that ever existed was the introduction of great numbers of slaves, an evil very pathetically described by Roman historians."[15]

As was the case with *Quo Vadis*, *The Robe* implies that the pyramid of pagan power is doomed to fall. Slaves are to have a decisive hand in its overthrow. None other than the man at the top, Emperor Tiberius, as much as says so himself. Having been informed about the fate of Jesus, he foresees the end of Rome:

> Miracles – disciples – slaves running away . . . When it comes, this is how it will start. Some obscure martyr in some forgotten province; then

14   Such or related statements for the early empire occur several times in Tacitus (*Annals* 3.53.5, 4.27.3, 14.43.4 and 44.5). The view had regained prominence in the nineteenth century; for a corrective analysis see C. G. Starr, "An Overdose of Slavery," *The Journal of Economic History*, 18 (1958), 17–32. Cf. also Moses I. Finley, *Ancient Slavery and Modern Ideology*, expanded edn.; ed. Brent D. Shaw (Princeton: Wiener, 1998), 147–153. Finley's book first appeared in 1980.

15   Quoted from Richard, *The Founders and the Classics*, 95–96; source reference at 266 note 22.

madness, infecting the legions, rotting the empire; then the finish of Rome
. . . This is more dangerous than any spell . . . It is man's desire to be free.
It is the greatest madness of them all.

Tiberius in this film is a benign and understanding father figure, whose
plot function is to provide a sharp contrast to his successor Caligula. But
the last sentence quoted brands even this kind of Roman ruler as thoroughly un-American. Tiberius cannot be completely good because he is
a pagan and will remain one. In this he contrasts with Marcellus, who
will eventually denounce the tyrannical madman Caligula and thereby
seal his fate. But Marcellus' death is a spiritual victory. He and his
beloved, condemned to martyrdom for their new faith, walk out of
Caligula's palace and, by means of a change in the background image,
appear to go straight up to heaven. Only the sky is visible behind them,
and a disembodied chorus is singing "Hallelujah" on the soundtrack.

The story of *The Robe* continues in Delmer Daves's *Demetrius and the
Gladiators* (1954). Marcellus' slave Demetrius has become a Christian
and is now a gladiator. He defies Caligula and is instrumental in
Caligula's assassination, but he does not have to die. He also achieves his
freedom. The pattern set in these films continues in the most famous
Roman epic of all, William Wyler's *Ben-Hur: A Tale of the Christ* (1959).
It has another omniscient narrator, whom we will later encounter in the
role of Balthazar. He informs us that in the year of Christ's birth "Judaea
for nearly a century had lain under the mastery of Rome." Jerusalem was
"dominated by the fortress of Antonia, the seat of Roman power," and
our early glimpses of the Romans are exclusively of soldiers and legions.
"Even while they obeyed the will of Caesar," the narrator concludes, the
people of Judaea kept hoping for their "redeemer," someone "to bring
them salvation and perfect freedom."

Old Testament stories are liable to exhibit the same perspective. At the
beginning of his last film, *The Ten Commandments* (1956), producer-
director Cecil B. De Mille himself appears on the screen and explains to
the audience the significance, then and now, of Moses, Rameses, and the
Israelites' exodus from Egypt:

we have an unusual subject: the story of the birth of freedom . . . The
theme of this picture is whether men are to be ruled by God's law or
whether they are to be ruled by the whims of a dictator like Rameses. Are
men the property of the state, or are they free souls under God? This same
battle continues throughout the world today. Our intention was not to
create a story but to be worthy of the divinely inspired story created three
thousand years ago.

De Mille's pious attitude, whether genuine or not, tells us how to understand what is to follow on the screen. Despite the modern overtones that characterize his prologue and the way he presents his subject matter – the Cold-War atmosphere of the 1950s is palpable in both – and despite his well-known McCarthyite bias, De Mille's main purpose is uplift rather than politics.[16]

Spartacus is indebted to such films for its perspective on history, even without the facile opposition of evil pagans and good Christians on view in most of Hollywood's Roman films. To faithful filmgoers, the prologue of *Spartacus* contains nothing new, and its reference to Christianity in a story set decades before its appearance is no surprise. But the standard view of the Romans now receives a more specifically American turn. Again an omniscient narrator cues us in, this time not over images of Rome or its environs as in *Quo Vadis* or *The Robe* but over images of slaves working a stone quarry on the farthest frontier. They illustrate the unlimited and inhuman power Rome holds over the entire world. The narrator begins:

> In the last century before the birth of the new faith called Christianity, which was destined to overthrow the pagan tyranny of Rome and bring about a new society, the Roman republic stood at the very center of the civilized world. "Of all things fairest," sang the poet, "first among cities and home of the gods is golden Rome." Yet even at the zenith of her pride and power the republic lay fatally stricken with a disease called human slavery. The age of the dictator was at hand, waiting in the shadows for the event to bring it forth.

The opening sequence of *Spartacus* is one of the most effective in the entire film and presents the best visual exposition to what is to follow. It was filmed by Anthony Mann, the original director of *Spartacus*, in Death Valley. The suffering of the slaves and the shots of Roman guards and slave drivers that we watch belie the narrator's words about civilization, for what, we are to infer, can be civilized in such a world? The closed system of Roman power is a precondition for the film's plot, but in the last century B.C. Rome was still far from its eventual expansion over all or most other countries or civilizations. For the sake of historical accuracy, the narrator calls Rome a republic, but his description of Rome as, again, a kind of pyramid of power and moral corruption – note the imagery of high and low as in the prologue to *Quo Vadis* – fits the Roman

---

16   On the political undertones of this film see Alan Nadel, "God's Law and the Wide Screen: *The Ten Commandments as Cold War 'Epic'*," *Publications of the Modern Language Association of America*, 108 (1993), 415–430.

Empire much better.[17] Marcellus' statement in *The Robe* – "There are more slaves in Rome than citizens" – finds an almost verbatim restatement in *Spartacus*: "There are more slaves in Rome than Romans," a senator will later observe. So the narrator's quotation of ancient praise of the greatness of Rome is meant to ring hollow. More accurately, he should have said "the poets" rather than "the poet" because he combines quotations from two Roman authors. Both wrote after the time of Spartacus; their words are quoted in retrospect. The first part is from Virgil: *rerum . . . pulcherrima Roma*.[18] The second part is from Ausonius, who lived in the fourth century A.D. and began his *Ordo urbium nobilium*, a series of poetic eulogies of twenty ancient cities, with a one-line praise of Rome: *Prima urbes inter, divum domus, aurea Roma*. Ausonius was one of the major Christian authors of late antiquity but seems to have written these poems when he was still a pagan. Virgil, the great poet of Augustan Rome, remained a pagan but eventually had an *anima naturaliter Christiana*, a soul Christian by nature, attributed to him.[19] To the well-educated among the film's audiences, the prologue's combined quotation reinforces the mention of Christianity.[20] Only Christian or naturally Christian Romans are good Romans. From such a point of view, references to destiny and a new birth over images of a valley of death are entirely in order. But spiritual renewal demands the end of the old, which is already carrying a fatal disease. The film's theme of victory in and through death is already evident. In the narrator's apocalyptic words, the end of the Roman republic occurs in the "age of the dictator." Historically, this dictator is Julius Caesar. In *Spartacus*, Caesar learns his political lessons from Crassus, Spartacus' antagonist and the film's villain. The narrator now becomes more explicitly American about all this while continuing the theme of birth and death:

17   The Spartacus novel by Maurice Ghnassia, *Arena* (New York: Viking, 1969), 5, refers to the "Roman Empire" of 87 B.C., that by Jacques Perdue, *Slave and Master* (New York: Macaulay, 1960), 107, has Spartacus envision himself as "Emperor of Imperial Rome." Attentive listeners who are watching *Spartacus* for a second or third time may wonder why the actor whom they will soon see as the foolish and ignoble aristocrat Glabrus is taking the part of an enlightened – i.e., modern and Christian – commentator. This edifying prologue was one of the last additions made to *Spartacus* before its release, but it had been planned from the beginning.

18   Virgil, *Georgics* 2.534.

19   The phrase is adapted from Tertullian, *Apology* 17.6.

20   There is a precedent for this. Lewis Grassic Gibbon (pseudonym of James Leslie Mitchell) began the first chapter of his novel *Spartacus* (1933) with the following epigraph and ended the novel with a repetition of it: "It was Springtime in Italy, a hundred years before the crucifixion of Christ." See the authoritative edition of Gibbon, *Spartacus* (1990; rpt. Edinburgh: Polygon, 2005), 3 and 210.

In that same century, in the conquered Greek province of Thrace, an illiterate slave woman added to her master's wealth by giving birth to a son whom she named Spartacus. A proud, rebellious son, who was sold to living death in the mines of Libya before his thirteenth birthday. There, under whip and chain and sun, he lived out his youth and his young manhood, dreaming the death of slavery two thousand years before it finally *would* die.

Historical sources report that Spartacus had been born free; he may even have been of royal lineage.[21] Here his birth into slavery is analogous to the status of slaves in the ante-bellum American South and helps make his situation and his later rebellion readily understandable to all viewers. It is also meant to reinforce to them Spartacus' extraordinary achievement: his spiritual journey from the lowest of the low to an inspiring model who comes close to achieving freedom for himself and others. In the quarry, Spartacus is utterly removed from anything like liberty and dignity, and the narrator's emphasis on his youth and the abuse we witness him enduring in that hell call forth our sense of compassion. From the very beginning we root for the underdog. Particularly significant is the narrator's last sentence. It contains a quintessential American image, that of the dream as a symbol of noble aspiration, expressed in the familiar term *the American Dream*. The sentence also anticipates the most famous and stirring expression of this idea in connection with slavery and freedom: the speech Martin Luther King, Jr., delivered at the Lincoln Memorial on August 28, 1963, the high point of the March on Washington, D.C.[22] It became famous for King's refrain "I have a dream." Spartacus, we are told, has one, too. That his story is to be understood in American terms becomes even clearer with the narrator's mention of the death of slavery. From 73 B.C., the year in which Spartacus' revolt began, to Lincoln's Emancipation Proclamation it is

21   His name may indicate that Spartacus was a descendant of the dynasty of the Spartocids, founded by Spartocus (Spartokos or Spartakos) I., the ruler of the *Bosporanum regnum* in the late fifth century B.C. Cf. Diodorus of Sicily, *Library of History* 12.31.1 and 12.36.1. Cf. Keith R. Bradley, *Slavery and Rebellion in the Roman World, 140 B.C.–70 B.C.* (Bloomington and Indianapolis: Indiana University Press, 1989; rpt. 1998), on gladiators as "first-generation slaves." In the fourth century A.D., however, the philosopher and orator Themistius states that Spartacus and Crixus were slaves by birth (*Speeches* 7.87a). On Themistius cf. Roberto Orena, *Rivolta e rivoluzione: Il Bellum di Spartaco nella crisi della repubblica e la riflessione storiografica moderna* (Milan: Giuffrè, 1984), 249–259.

22   For a summary account with photographs and the text of King's speech see Juan Williams, *Eyes on the Prize: America's Civil Rights Years, 1954–1965* (1987; rpt. New York: Penguin, 2002), 196–205. The book is a companion to a six-hour documentary film of the same title, directed by Harry Hampton.

1,936 years, close enough to the narrator's "two thousand years" to indicate that America best represents mankind's progress from slavery to freedom. Spartacus' innate qualities of pride in himself as a human being and his rebelliousness, a necessary precondition to shake off the yoke of servitude, are American strengths, embodied from the beginning in the Founding Fathers. And Spartacus' low birth foreshadows the film's later analogies of him with another redeemer, one whose humble birth about a century after Spartacus' led to the death of mankind's spiritual enslavement, at least in the retrospective view of modern America.

Unlike this American Spartacus, the historical Spartacus cannot have been "dreaming the death of slavery," and to impute such a motive to him is anachronistic.[23] No birth, then, of a new society, with or without Christianity. *Spartacus* is not a lesson in Roman history, but it is a lesson in how Americans conceive of history and of themselves. An unsigned essay published in 1823 in *The Christian Spectator* shows how deeply the prologue to *Spartacus* and the plot of the entire film are rooted in American culture. The author's assessment of the state of slaves in America parallels *Spartacus* in its perspective on ancient Rome and in its presentation of Spartacus as a freedom fighter who might have changed history but whose revolt is brutally suppressed. After calculating that the American slave population will rise to millions and millions over the next several decades if nothing is done about slavery, the author concludes:

> Plots! and insurrections! These are words of terror, but their terribleness is no argument against the truth of what we say . . . For notwithstanding all that may be done to keep the slaves in ignorance, they are learning, and will continue to learn something of their own power, and something of the tenure by which they are held in bondage. They are surrounded by the memorials of freedom. The air which they breathe is free; and the soil on which they tread, and which they water with their tears is a land of liberty. Slaves are never slow in learning that they are fettered, and that freedom is the birthright of humanity. Our slaves will not be always ignorant – and when that righteous Providence, which never wants instruments to accomplish its designs, whether of mercy, or of vengeance, shall raise up a Touissaint [sic], or a Spartacus, or an African Tecumseh, his fellow slaves will flock around his standard, and we shall witness scenes – which history describes but from the thought of which the imagination revolts. Not that

---

23 Cf. the views of Erich S. Gruen, *The Last Generation of the Roman Republic* (Berkeley, Los Angeles, and London: University of California Press, 1974), 20 and 406, and Bradley, *Slavery and Rebellion in the Roman World, 140 B.C.–70 B.C.*, 98–101, both quoted in my "Introduction" to the present volume, 11–12.

there is any reason to anticipate such an insurrection as will result in the emancipation of the slaves, and the establishment of a black empire . . . to be finally successful, it must be delayed . . . till the blacks have force enough to resist successfully the energies of the whole American people; for . . . the beacon fires of insurrection would only rally the strength of the nation, and the illfated Africans, if not utterly exterminated, would be so nearly destroyed that they must submit to a bondage more hopeless than ever.[24]

These words almost summarize the plot of *Spartacus*, except for the moral victory that Spartacus achieves in his defeat and death. Less than a decade later, Spartacus came into his own in popular culture. American playwright Robert Montgomery Bird had his greatest success with *The Gladiator* (1831), a drama about Spartacus that ran for more than a thousand performances, with famous actor Edwin Forrest in the title part. Walt Whitman wrote about it in *The Brooklyn Daily Eagle* of December 26, 1846:

This play is as full of 'Abolitionism' as an egg is of meat . . . Running o'er with sentiments of liberty – with eloquent disclaimers of the right of the Romans to hold human beings in bondage – it is a play, this Gladiator, calculated to make the hearts of the masses swell responsively to all those nobler manlier aspirations in behalf of mortal freedom! – The speech of Spartacus, in which he attributes the grandeur and wealth of Rome, to her devastation of other countries, is fine; and Mr. Forrest delivered it passing well.[25]

Spartacus, the inspiring figure of legend or myth far more than the historical Spartacus, is close to Americans' hearts. Howard Fast's novel *Spartacus* (1951) and its screen adaptation continue the tradition.

But the film and its prologue also express the views of one particular modern American. Kirk Douglas, the producer and star of *Spartacus*, was the son of poor and illiterate Russian Jewish immigrants. They exemplified the sentiments of Emma Lazarus' sonnet *The New Colossus* (1883),

24   *The Christian Spectator*, 5 no. 10 (October 1, 1823), 540–551, in a section entitled "Review of New Publications"; quotation at 542. This is the second part of an essay reviewing *The Reports of the American Society for Colonizing the Free People of Colour in the United States* for 1818–1823; its first part appeared in the journal's preceding issue (5 no. 9 [September 1, 1823], 485–494).
25   Walt Whitman, "'The Gladiator' – Mr. Forrest – Acting"; quoted from *The Collected Writings of Walt Whitman: The Journalism*, vol. 2: *1846–1848*, ed. Herbert Bergman (New York: Lang, 2003), 158–159; quotation at 158. Wyke, *Projecting the Past*, 58, provides an illustration of Forrest as Spartacus. For a cinematic anecdote involving Spartacus' speech see Paul F. Boller and Ronald L. Davis, *Hollywood Anecdotes* (New York: Morrow, 1987), 66–67.

in which the Statue of Liberty proclaims: "Give me your tired, your poor, / Your huddled masses yearning to breathe free."[26] Douglas, a self-made man in the classic American mold, had read Fast's novel:

> I was intrigued with the story of Spartacus the slave, dreaming of the death of slavery, driving into the armor of Rome the wedge that would eventually destroy her.
>
> I'm always astounded by the impact, the extent of the Roman Empire . . . How did the Romans get to so many places? . . . It always amazed me *how* they did that, and how *much* they did.
>
> Looking at these [Roman] ruins, and at the Sphinx and the pyramids in Egypt, at the palaces in India, I wince. I see thousands and thousands of slaves carrying rocks, beaten, starved, crushed, dying. I identify with them. As it says in the Torah: "Slaves were we unto Egypt." I come from a race of slaves. That would have been *my* family, *me*.
>
> *Spartacus* would make a terrific picture.[27]

Douglas's view of Spartacus was somewhat at odds with Fast's.[28] As a result, the film lost most of the novel's explicit politics, and for this reason

---

26 Quoted from Emma Lazarus, *Selected Poems*, ed. John Hollander (New York: The Library of America, 2005), 58.

27 Kirk Douglas, *The Ragman's Son: An Autobiography* (New York: Simon and Schuster, 1988), 304. Cf. Douglas, 333–334. Identification with Spartacus is also the case for Maurice Ghnassia, who fought in the French Resistance in World War II: "In the Resistance group to which I belonged, we lived just the same way runaways and guerrilleros have lived throughout the world for thousands of years . . . understood more and more Spartacus' problems at every engagement, in every dangerous situation, during every difficult moment . . . I knew his problems; we were living them." Quoted from "Author's Note" to *Arena*, xiii–xv; quotation at xiv. Although written in French, this book was published in English; Ghnassia had been living in the United States since 1956.

28 Cf. Douglas, *The Ragman's Son*, 306–310 and 314. Cf. also Baxter, *Stanley Kubrick*, 123–125. For Fast's perspective on Spartacus in both novel and film see Howard Fast, *Being Red: A Memoir* (1990; rpt. Armonk and London: Sharpe, 1994), 269, 276–277, and 286–300. Fast summarized his experiences in "*Spartacus* and the Blacklist," an introduction to a reprint of *Spartacus* (Armonk: Sharpe / North Castle Books, 1996), vii–viii. But the dedication page of Fast's novel is fully in the American vein: "The heroes of this story cherished freedom and human dignity, and lived nobly and well. I wrote it so that those who read it . . . may take strength for our own troubled future and that they may struggle against oppression and wrong – so that the dream of Spartacus may come to be in our own time." Cf. also Andrew Macdonald, *Howard Fast: A Critical Companion* (Westport and London: Greenwood Press, 1996), 83–100, and Carl Hoffman, "The Evolution of a Gladiator: History, Representation, and Revision in *Spartacus*," *Journal of American and Contemporary Cultures*, 23 no. 1 (2000), 63–70. Futrell, "Seeing Red," 99, and Marcus Junkelmann, *Hollywoods Traum von Rom: "Gladiator" und die Tradition des Monumentalfilms* (Mainz: von Zabern, 2004), 164, regard the very first image of *Spartacus* – its credit sequence begins with a sculpted hand pointing left – as an indication of the left-wing nature of the film, but this is not convincing. (The body to which a left-pointing hand is attached is on the right.) Rather, the hand, reminiscent of God's hand imparting the spark

right-wing protests like the one by influential columnist Hedda Hopper were largely ineffective: "That story was sold to Universal from a book written by a Commie and the screen script was written by a Commie, so don't go to see it."[29] Instead, *Spartacus* became a mainstream American work.[30] Its prologue has prepared us for an all-American Spartacus, and a number of key scenes make this side of him explicit.

2. Black and White: The Spark of Freedom

In *Spartacus*, new arrivals at the gladiatorial school are branded on their haunches with irons like cattle – a custom unknown in ancient Rome.[31]

of life to Adam in Michelangelo's painting on the ceiling of the Sistine Chapel, is a hint at the film's real theme: the creation of a new man free from the bonds of slavery and inhumanity. A year earlier, the actual image of Michelangelo's painting of the creation of Adam provided the background for the credits of Wyler's *Ben-Hur*, a more apposite, if also more pretentious, model for the hand in *Spartacus*.

29   Quoted from Douglas, *The Ragman's Son*, 332. According to the extremely right-wing John Birch Society, the film was "well-camouflaged" Communist propaganda (Hoberman, *The Dream Life*, 31 note 1). That *Spartacus* was not primarily a political work even to Dalton Trumbo, its blacklisted screenwriter, becomes evident from Jeffrey P. Smith, "'A Good Business Proposition': Dalton Trumbo, *Spartacus*, and the End of the Blacklist," *The Velvet Light Trap*, 23 (Spring, 1989), 75–100. The quotation in Smith's title is from a letter by Trumbo and reports a statement by the lawyer for Douglas's Bryna Productions to hire blacklisted writers as a means to obtain high-quality screenplays at extremely low cost; cf. Smith, 84 and 95. Smith, 92, quotes the following examples of press reactions to *Spartacus*: "There is nothing more subversive in 'Spartacus' than [is] contained in the Bill of Rights and the Fourteenth Amendment" (*The Hollywood Reporter*); "Trumbo has imparted to *Spartacus* a passion for freedom and the men who live and die for it – a passion that transcends all politics" (*Time*). Cf. Smith, 93: "Dalton Trumbo, who had been considered 'un-American' in 1947, emerged in 1960 as an American hero." Smith, 92, quotes a letter by Kirk Douglas describing *Spartacus* as "a courageous and positive statement about mankind's most cherished goal – freedom" months before the film was released. On Trumbo and *Spartacus* see further the brief summary provided s. v. "Trumbo, Dalton," in Gene D. Phillips and Rodney Hill, *The Encyclopedia of Stanley Kubrick* (New York: Facts on File, 2002), 372–376 (with minor misquotations of the film's dialogue).

30   The comment by Derek Elley, *The Epic Film: Myth and History* (London: Routledge and Kegan Paul, 1984), 110, that Douglas "saw *Spartacus* as an opportunity to make a large-scale Zionist statement" is therefore unconvincing. (Similarly Junkelmann, *Hollywoods Traum von Rom*, 158.) Contrast the following comment by Woody Strode: "Kirk Douglas didn't admit he was Jewish until ten years after *Spartacus*." Quoted from Woody Strode and Sam Young, *Goal Dust: An Autobiography* (Lanham, New York, and London: Madison Books, 1990), 248. A Zionist statement by Douglas came six years after Spartacus with Melville Shavelson's *Cast a Giant Shadow*, an epic film about the early history of Israel.

31   On this see C. P. Jones, "Tattooing and Branding in Greco-Roman Antiquity," *Journal of Roman Studies*, 77 (1987), 139–155, and F. Hugh Thompson, *The Archaeology of*

This prepares viewers for the inhuman treatment they will receive. ("I'm not an animal!" Spartacus will soon be driven to exclaim.) Their trainer, a former slave and gladiator, tells them that he wants to be their friend and that both sides have to get along with each other, but nobody believes him. Friendship can exist only between and among the gladiators. By contrast, Draba, the most imposing and the only black gladiator in the school, refuses to be anyone's friend. He tells Spartacus: "Gladiators don't make friends. If we're ever matched in the arena together, I'll have to kill you." This prepares us for the inevitable: Draba and Spartacus will have to fight each other, and the more experienced Draba will defeat Spartacus. But an epic hero cannot die this early in his story, so a plot twist saves him and provides him with the inspiration to revolt when the moment is right. At the end of their duel Draba is holding his trident to Spartacus' throat; the latter, in close-up, braces himself for death. But reverse-angle close-ups on Draba's face reveal to us his innate nobility: he is thinking of the inhumanity of what he has been forced into doing. Repeatedly taunted by the aristocratic Romans for whose pleasure he has been selected to fight ("Kill him! Kill him, you imbecile!"), Draba instead hurls his trident at Crassus and climbs up the balustrade to attack him. He is hit by a guard's spear in the back but manages to get a hold on Crassus' legs. Crassus cuts the sinews between Draba's shoulders, and the dying man falls to the ground. In a close-up his blood had spurted on Crassus' face, a visual sign of the dehumanizing nature of slavery. Spartacus witnesses everything. An intense and lingering close-up on his face immediately following Draba's off-screen death points to the impact of Draba's sacrifice on Spartacus. The man who refused to be anyone's friend has displayed greater nobility of spirit than any other gladiator, including Spartacus. Before the gladiatorial combats had started, Spartacus and his friend Crixus had worried about having to fight each other. Asked by Crixus "Would you try to kill me?" Spartacus replied: "Yes, I'd kill. I'd try to stay alive, and so would you." Draba had expressed a similar view in his first conversation with Spartacus but did not follow through. He lost his life but gained his dignity. The lesson is not lost on Spartacus.

At night the gladiators walk downstairs to their dungeon-like quarters and find Draba's body hanging upside down by the ankles like the carcass of an animal at a butcher's shop – an explicit warning: "He'll

---

Greek and Roman Slavery (London: Duckworth, 2003), 241–242 (section entitled "Marks of Identification"). Romans branded animals, especially horses, with hot irons. Americans brand cattle. The scene in Perdue, *Slave and Master*, 89–90, that refers to the Roman custom of branding slaves shows that this author is chiefly interested in sadism and sex, preferably in conjunction.

hang there till he rots." A number of shots on Spartacus and some other gladiators alone in their cells, looking shocked or pensive, convey to viewers the men's incipient sense of solidarity in their common reaction to Draba's fate. Taunted beyond endurance, Draba had attacked Crassus; taunted and struck across the mouth ("No talking in the kitchen, slave!"), Spartacus begins the revolt. Draba has provided the spark.[32]

The "theme of the black fighter as a savior and moral figure for whites" has a long tradition in American cinema before and after *Spartacus*.[33] Actor Woody Strode, our Draba, was one of the first black athletes to play in the almost all-white National Football League. On the screen he always combined "awesome physical power" with "undaunt[ed] moral presence."[34] A long-time associate of director Kubrick observed him on the set of *Spartacus*:

> Woody Strode was a man of innate dignity. When you just turned the camera on him there was something rather special. Stanley needed a very curious performance out of him. It was the sense of a man turning inward and asking some profound questions of himself.[35]

32   Phillips and Hill, *The Encyclopedia of Stanley Kubrick*, 362–364 s. v. "Strode, Woody (Woodrow)," unpersuasively maintain that "Draba's motivation for sparing Spartacus is not entirely clear" (363). Their discussion of this sequence of the film is superficial.

33   Sam B. Girgus, *America on Film: Modernism, Documentary, and a Changing America* (Cambridge: Cambridge University Press, 2002), 87–112 and 209–212 (notes), gives a detailed account in a chapter entitled "The Black Gladiator and the Spartacus Syndrome." Girgus, 89–95, discusses *Spartacus* and the Draba sequence in some detail; my quotation is from Girgus, 89. A kind of black American Spartacus is Nat Turner, a slave who led a revolt in 1831 for which he claimed divine inspiration; on him and his legend see Kenneth S. Greenberg, *Nat Turner: A Slave Rebellion in History and Memory* (New York: Oxford University Press, 2003). William Styron's novel *The Confessions of Nat Turner* (1967), a kind of companion piece to Fast's *Spartacus*, caused controversy as novel and proposed film; cf. on this Tony Horwitz, "Untrue Confessions," *The New Yorker* (December 13, 1999), 80–86 and 88–89. Styron described his approach to Turner in these terms: "At the time in which it was written, there was a terrific need on the part of the black intellectual community to have a kind of spotless black hero, almost a caricature of Spartacus. Being a novelist, I wouldn't supply that kind of hero. I wanted to give a picture of a man who was tormented by what he was doing, who had doubts about his mission even as he was going to do it." Quoted from Horwitz, 84.

34   Girgus, *America on Film*, 95. Strode is best known for the parts he played in films directed by his mentor John Ford. Immediately after *Spartacus* he played the titular hero of Ford's cavalry Western *Sergeant Rutledge* (1960), a man unjustly accused of murder and rape of whites. He says about blacks: "We been haunted a long time . . . It was all right for Mr. Lincoln to say we were free, but that ain't so – not yet. Maybe some day, but not yet."

35   Writer-director Alexander Singer, quoted in Vincent LoBrutto, *Stanley Kubrick: A Biography* (1997; rpt. New York: Da Capo, 1999), 182. LoBrutto, 182–183, quotes Singer's description of how Kubrick elicited the performance he wanted from Strode.

As a result, Draba acquires a greater importance than many viewers or critics have realized. A recent analysis puts it succinctly:

> In *Spartacus*, the spectacle of the battle between gladiators becomes a meaningful political event. The vision of Strode . . . dramatizes an individual and group demand for freedom. At the dawn of a new era of historic civil rights activism that would be led by figures such as Martin Luther King, Jr., Strode embodies the readiness of African Americans to lead their fight for equality . . . as a living symbol of the drive for freedom. In his actions and presence, he embodies one expression of a new moment in American civil rights history.
>
> Strode's heroic role makes him an example of fighting for freedom, and puts him in the position of a leader and model. He suggests not only the sympathy and support of the film for the situation of blacks in America at the time, his character achieves a form of political authority that derives from the actual condition of inequality of people of color in America . . . Personifying the film's theme of freedom, Strode performs a . . . function that enriches his character's significance by transferring contemporary realities of discrimination and racism onto the back of the black gladiator who fights Spartacus.[36]

That Draba is a prophet of freedom to Spartacus is evident the first moment we see him from the way he is dressed. In several scenes during this sequence, Spartacus and Draba wear simple cloaks, in the latter's case one with a hood. To experienced filmgoers, such a garment is a visual reminder of none other than Jesus. One year after the release of *Spartacus*, the Jesus of Nicholas Ray's *King of Kings* wears just such a cloak, if one of better quality and in a different color. In George Stevens' *The Greatest Story Ever Told* (1965), Jesus wears a simple robe or cloak, if in immaculate white, and frequently appears hooded.[37] At some moments, especially those set in his cell, Spartacus in his cloak is filmed in a manner reminiscent of the way we expect to see Jesus on the screen. The messianic overtones in the visual presentation of Spartacus and Draba are self-evident. Draba's death is somewhat comparable to that of St. Peter, who was crucified upside down, as a memorable moment in *Quo Vadis* had already shown American audiences. Even the fate of Draba's corpse points ahead to the fate of Spartacus' dead body. Although the

36 Girgus, *America on Film*, 94–95. Girgus, 95, next discusses the limitations in the film's portrayal of Draba.

37 So do the apostles, Mary, and assorted other characters in this and comparable films. For their iconography see the numerous illustrations in Roy Kinnard and Tim Davis, *Divine Images: A History of Jesus on the Screen* (New York: Citadel Press, 1992).

rebellious slaves later cut Draba down, Spartacus presumably will hang on the cross till he rots.

Draba prepares the way for Spartacus. Actor Strode was to play a twentieth-century redeemer in Valerio Zurlini's *Seduto alla sua destra* ("Seated at His Right," 1968), a film based on the life of Patrice Lumumba. Its American distributor retitled it *Black Jesus*. Strode wrote about this part in his autobiography:

> I play a Christ-like character who tries to establish peaceful reform with an unnamed African country that's controlled by an overbearing white rule. I travel from village to village preaching to the people. I tell them, "As long as we are united we cannot be defeated, they know this and this is why they will try and infiltrate among you setting brother against brother, and relying on your greed."
>
> The government arrests me for being a revolutionary and orders me to sign papers that would make me forsake my teachings. I refuse. They begin to torture me; I suffer and anguish. They nail my hands to a table. They beat me until I lose my sight. My left side is pierced. The life slowly drains out of me. My face is twisted in pain, and my legs go limp as they drag me from the interrogation room back to my cell. The violence is unbelievable.
>
> Zurlini was trying to show the total devotion to violence of the men who were torturing me, and the horrors of a dictator-style government.[38]

Today, those unfamiliar with Zurlini's small but distinguished body of work may here be reminded of Mel Gibson's *The Passion of the Christ* (2004). Fortunately, Zurlini's film has nothing in common with Gibson's. But it is telling that one and the same actor plays comparable parts of heroic fighters for freedom and dignity within a decade. Both apparently fail and are killed by their ruthless and powerful enemies, but both win spiritual victories and become martyrs. The same is true for Spartacus. Draba is not only a spiritual model who teaches Spartacus about nobility and dignity but also functions as an illustration of how race relations in the U.S. have begun to progress on the verge of the Civil Rights movement. The fight of Spartacus and Draba is the reversal of a similar scene in *Demetrius and the Gladiators*, Hollywood's last gladiatorial epic before *Spartacus*. It featured William Marshall, an imposing black actor, in a prominent role (with screen credit) as a gladiator. (Strode had an uncred-

---

38   Strode and Young, *Goal Dust*, 234. Strode dedicated this book to three people (among them John Ford) "and the proposition that all men are created equal." If Lumumba was a Christ figure in Zurlini's film, he could have been a Spartacus in reality; cf. Hoberman, *The Dream Life*, 23–24, on the civil war in the Congo at the time of *Spartacus*: "It was reported that the nation's beleaguered crypto-Communist leader, Patrice Lumumba, was trying to reach New York – another potential Spartacus defying Rome."

ited bit part, also as a gladiator.) Demetrius, the white gladiator, is forced to fight the black gladiator. As in *Spartacus*, the black fighter is more experienced than the white. They only pretend to fight in the hope that the crowd will spare their lives. But their ruse is discovered, and they have to fight in earnest. As may have been expected in 1954, the white gladiator defeats the black gladiator, who nobly resigns himself to his fate: "Cut clean, friend!" But a hero cannot kill a defenseless man, and Demetrius appeals to Caligula. His request is granted, although at the risk of his own life. "Macro, go down and cut the dog's throat," the evil tyrant commands his Praetorian Prefect. Messalina's interference saves Demetrius from this fate, although he is now forced to fight against tigers. Demetrius kills them and becomes a hero to the crowd. He and the black gladiator live to see the overthrow and death of Caligula.

This scene is not as intense in its effect on audiences as the sequence of Draba's and Spartacus' fight, which much more pointedly expresses the analogy to contemporary American race relations. In a mainstream 1960 film, a black man still cannot kill a white man, and a white cannot simply kill a black, even if they are forced into a deadly confrontation. So the outcome of Spartacus' and Draba's fight is unavoidable. The figure of less importance for the plot wins, spares the hero's life, and sacrifices himself. In this fight sequence, Kubrick pushes his audiences as far into an awareness of contemporary racial tensions as possible. He does so in purely visual terms and without any dialogue. Before the fights, Spartacus, Crixus, Draba, and a fourth gladiator wait outside the arena in the dark entrance passage. The fence of the arena and the surrounding gloom symbolize their status as slaves and their spiritual imprisonment. After Crixus and the fourth gladiator are called in to fight, Draba and Spartacus remain behind in brooding silence. Kubrick now makes excellent use of his film's widescreen format. He first shows Draba and Spartacus waiting, placed far apart from each other at the opposite ends of the frame. Close-ups on their faces then reveal what they must be thinking and feeling. In these shots Kubrick brings them nearer to us to increase our emotional involvement. At the same time he keeps them distant from each other: only one face appears on the screen at a time. During these tense moments the two men briefly look at each other a few times but mainly keep their eyes averted. Through the space between two wooden boards in the door Spartacus watches the fight in the arena. Kubrick then cuts to a shot that shows us what Spartacus sees. Most of the screen is dark, and the duel Spartacus is observing appears in a wide and narrow band in the center. The aspect ratio of this point-of-view shot imitates the screen's format. Experienced cinemagoers will notice Kubrick's triple level of visual presentation: they are watching, from the dark, a screen on which someone with whom they are meant to identify is watching, from the dark, a scene of death. Spartacus' and our spectatorship become inseparable.[39] With Spartacus, emotionally involved viewers feel a strong sense of isolation, helplessness, and impending doom. While Spartacus, in a close-up screen right, is still watching, Kubrick cuts to a medium close-up of Draba screen left. Then both men look at each other. This reinforces our sense of the inhumanity of slavery. Intercutting continues more rapidly. Draba, further away from us than Spartacus, smiles mysteriously. This moment, in which he seems to resolve to fight but not to kill, prepares us for the later moment when he spares Spartacus and makes this surprising plot turn more plausible to us.

Spartacus looks out again, and with him we see the end of the fight that had been in progress. Crixus kills his opponent, and Kubrick immediately cuts back to a medium shot of where Draba and Spartacus are waiting. As Spartacus' back is still toward us, Draba turns and looks at Spartacus, who now also turns around. Both men look at each other again, but only Draba now receives a close-up – the last one. A medium shot shows us both men again, with Draba looking down in a pose of Stoic acceptance. The door is opened, and we see the dead gladiator being dragged from the arena. Crixus returns. Draba and Spartacus exchange a final glance, then enter the arena. After they salute the Romans, they turn to face each other. As enemies, they are standing on opposite ends of the screen. The fight begins.

The scene of Spartacus and Draba awaiting their fight is remarkable for its style, which drives home the contemporary point by bringing its viewers close up to the unspoken racial tension between black and white. In 1960, a white and a black man are face to face, figuratively (as enemies) and literally (through Kubrick's cross-cutting and close-ups). But they and we realize that they are not really enemies. They are victims of an entrenched system that is degrading to both and has to be over-

---

39   This is a fundamental aspect of cinema, important for *Spartacus*. Cf. Ina Rae Hark, "Animals or Romans: Looking at Masculinity in *Spartacus*," in *Screening the Male: Exploring Masculinities in Hollywood Cinema*, ed. Steven Cohan and Ina Rae Hark (London: Routledge, 1993), 151–172, and Leon Hunt, "What Are Big Boys Made Of? *Spartacus*, *El Cid* and the Male Epic," in *You Tarzan: Masculinity, Movies and Men*, ed. Pat Kirkham and Janet Thumim (New York: St. Martin's, 1993), 65–83. (The main title of the latter book is a misquotation.) In general see the classic study by Laura Mulvey, "Visual Pleasure and Narrative Cinema," *Screen*, 16 no. 3 (1975), 6–18; rpt. in Mulvey, *Visual and Other Pleasures* (Bloomington: Indiana University Press, 1989), 14–26, and in *The Sexual Subject: A Screen Reader in Sexuality* (London: Routledge, 1992), 22–34.

come. As ancient slaves and gladiators they are in chains to the power of Rome; as stand-ins for Americans they illustrate the dilemma of modern race relations. This, too, has to be overcome. Spartacus and Draba do not succeed, but they fight the good fight and point the way for others. The Americans have not succeeded in 1960, but the Civil Rights movement is already on the march.[40] What Martin Luther King said in his speech at the Lincoln Memorial fits *Spartacus* at this point in its story: "The whirlwinds of revolt will continue to shake the foundations of our nation until the bright day of justice emerges."

3. United We Stand

After Spartacus and his fellow gladiators have revolted, they ravage the countryside, looting the villas of rich Romans. Two of these we see being dragged to the gladiators' school, in whose arena their captors force them into a mock gladiatorial fight. But Spartacus intervenes. He has just returned from his former quarters. When he went downstairs, the rope from which Draba's body had been hanging is prominently visible. Kubrick uses the same downward-gliding camera movement for Spartacus descending the stairs with which he had first shown us the gladiators seeing Draba's corpse. This stylistic parallel evokes a strong remembrance in us. So it does in Spartacus, who stands near the rope for a pensive moment. We are to understand that he is thinking of Draba's death and of the freedom he never came to be part of. But Draba's example exerts its influence on Spartacus. When he enters the arena through the same door by which he and Draba had entered it for their fight, Spartacus is filmed emerging on the other side, and the image is much brighter, a hint that things are now better. Spartacus reveals his innate qualities as leader and decent human being in a heroic low-angle shot, the arena entrance visible behind him, and ends the mockery of the Romans. When Crixus objects – "I want to see their blood, right over here where Draba died" – Spartacus replies:

---

40   For information on the background of the Civil Rights movement cf. especially Taylor Branch, *Parting the Waters: America in the King Years, 1954–63* (New York: Simon and Schuster, 1988; rpt. 1989), and Williams, *Eyes on the Prize.* Branch's book is the first of three volumes on King; it was followed by *Pillar of Fire: America in the King Years, 1963–65* (New York: Simon and Schuster, 1998; rpt. 1999) and *At Canaan's Edge: America in the King Years, 1965–68* (New York: Simon and Schuster, 2006). The titles indicate that King was an American Moses.

I made myself a promise, Crixus. I swore that if I ever got out of this place
. . . I'd die before I'd watch two men fight to the death again. Draba made
that promise, too. He kept it. So will I. What are we, Crixus? What are we
becoming? Romans? Have *we* learned nothing? What's happening to us?
We looked for wine when we should be hunting bread . . . You can't just
be a gang of drunken raiders.

Referring to Draba's nobility, Spartacus intends to show his fellow slaves
that in order to fight for freedom and dignity they must resist the temp-
tation to pay back their former masters in kind. To someone's question
"What else can we be?" Spartacus replies: "Gladiators. An army of gladiators! There's never *been* an army like that . . . We can beat anything
they send against us if we really want to. Once we're on the march . . .
we'll free every slave in every town and village. Can anybody get a bigger
army than that?" To this, everybody agrees, and we soon see scenes in
which Spartacus' words become reality. "Come join us! All of you, come
join us! Come on and join us!" The brotherhood of slaves is born.

Spartacus' words about an irresistible army of freedom fighters anticipate what Martin Luther King will put into comparable terms in his
speech at the Lincoln Memorial. Spartacus might have expressed his
vision in very similar terms, might even have done so word for word, with
the obvious exception of his and his fellow slaves' need for armed defense:

In the process of gaining our rightful place, we must not be guilty of
wrongful deeds. Let us not seek to satisfy our thirst for freedom by drink-
ing from the cup of bitterness and hatred. We must forever conduct our
struggle on the high plane of dignity and discipline. We must not allow
our creative protest to degenerate into physical violence. Again and
again, we must rise to the majestic heights of meeting physical force with
soul force.

Dignity and discipline Spartacus' army will acquire in due course and so
be able to inflict defeat on superior Roman forces. The ignominious fate
of Glabrus is telling, as his defeat and his account of it in the Roman
Senate will make clear. Glabrus' incomprehension of the humanity of
the oppressed ("They were only slaves!") contrasts with Spartacus' own
words when he spares his life and sends him back to Rome: "Tell them
we want nothing from Rome. Nothing except our freedom!" The divisive
party politics in Rome, especially between Crassus, whose henchman
Glabrus is, and wily Senator Gracchus, further contrasts with the solidarity of Spartacus' people. Martin Luther King expresses Spartacus'
view best if we replace his reference to skin color by one to slave status:

I have a dream that my . . . children will one day live in a nation where
they will not be judged by the color of their skin but by the content of their
character . . .

> With this faith, we will be able to work together, to pray together, to struggle together, to go to jail together, to stand up for freedom together, knowing that we will be free one day.

The unity and solidarity of the slaves appears again and again, most obviously when we watch them carrying out everyday tasks in their camps and when we follow them on their long and arduous journey to the sea in order to leave Italy and find a new home in peace and freedom. This march becomes a virtual exodus patterned on that in the Bible. Spartacus' message to Rome might as well have been: "Let my people go!" But the most compelling instance of the slaves' strong bond of fellowship comes after they have been defeated in a huge battle. Crassus, haunted by the myth of Spartacus, promises to spare the lives of all survivors if they identify Spartacus to him dead or alive. A moment of surprise and hesitation ensues, then Spartacus starts to rise to identify himself. But before he can do so, the other prisoners, first a few, then more, and finally all, stand up and shout: "I'm Spartacus!" Crassus is defeated.

The scene is rightly famous and could be understood as an explicit left-wing moment that reflects the genesis of the film from Howard Fast's novel or the political views of screenwriter Dalton Trumbo. It has been so interpreted, but it is better understood as an American expression of human brotherhood regardless of any specific political convictions. The scene re-enacts one of the most famous and popular patriotic American sayings that goes back to before the American Revolution: *United We Stand, Divided We Fall*. It appeared in slightly different form in a stanza of *The Liberty Song* by future Founding Father John Dickinson that was published in 1768:

> Then join hand in hand, brave Americans all,
> By uniting we stand, by dividing we fall;
> In so righteous a cause let us hope to succeed,
> For heaven approves of each generous deed.

Dickinson once observed that the Americans' disunity against the British had almost cost them their freedom, just as had been the case for the Greeks in the Persian Wars.[41] With Thomas Jefferson, Dickinson wrote a *Declaration of the Causes and Necessity of Taking Up Arms* in 1775, although he was opposed to a separation from Britain and did not sign the Declaration of Independence.[42]

41 Richard, *The Founders and the Classics*, 108; reference at 267 note 47.
42 On Dickinson, who wrote as "Fabius" in the Federalist papers, and classical antiquity see Richard, *The Founders and the Classics*, 31–32, 54, 73, 76, 78, 88, 101, and 111–112.

American poet and journalist George Pope Morris began his patriotic poem *The Flag of Our Union*, collected in his *Poems* of 1853, with the following lines:

> "A song for our banner?" – The watchword recall
> Which gave the Republic her station:
> "United we stand – divided we fall!"
> It made and preserves us a nation!

On June 16, 1858, Abraham Lincoln touched on the same sentiment in his "A House Divided" speech to the Republican State Convention in Illinois after he had been elected the party's candidate for the U.S. Senate:

> We are now far into the *fifth* year, since a policy was initiated, with the *avowed* object, and *confident* promise, of putting an end to slavery agitation.
>
> Under the operation of that policy, that agitation has not only, *not ceased*, but has *constantly augmented*.
>
> In *my* opinion, it *will* not cease, until a *crisis* shall have been reached, and passed.
>
> "A house divided against itself cannot stand."
>
> I believe this government cannot endure, permanently half *slave* and half *free*.
>
> I do not expect the Union to be *dissolved* – I do not expect the house to *fall* – but I *do* expect it will cease to be divided.
>
> It will become *all* one thing, or *all* the other.[43]

Lincoln quotes a famous saying by Jesus: "Every kingdom divided against itself is brought to desolation; and every city or house divided against itself shall not stand."[44] During the Civil War, *United We Stand* was the rallying cry of the North against the secessionist South. The holy cause of freedom is now the holy cause of abolition, just as it later will become the holy cause of Civil Rights. In World War II, *United We Stand* again expressed American patriotism but found wider resonance. Queen Wilhelmina of the Netherlands said in her address to the U.S. Congress on August 5, 1942: "United we stand, and united we will achieve victory." These instances will suffice to indicate that narrower political stances – as when American labor unions adopted *United We Stand* as

---

43   Quoted from Abraham Lincoln, "'A House Divided': Speech at Springfield, Illinois," in *The Collected Works of Abraham Lincoln*, ed. Roy P. Basler, vol. 2 (New Brunswick: Rutgers University Press, 1953; rpt. 1960), 461–469; quotation at 461. On Lincoln as emancipator of slaves cf. now Richard Striner, *Father Abraham: Lincoln's Relentless Struggle to End Slavery* (New York: Oxford University Press, 2006).

44   *Matth.* 12.25.

their slogan in the early twentieth century – are beside the point for *Spartacus*. Solidarity for the cause of freedom is a common American idea.

4. Sermon on the Mount

The slaves as precursors of the modern huddled masses yearning to be free appear in one of the most effective sequences of *Spartacus*. It pits Spartacus and his world against his enemy Crassus and the world of Rome. In Rome, Crassus addresses his legions on the day before they march out to battle the slave army. In the slaves' camp adjacent to a mountainside, Spartacus addresses his people after learning that the pirates hired to transport them out of Italy have betrayed them. Spartacus' speech carries strong American overtones; its setting is patterned on biblical epics. To get the appropriate visual effects, Kubrick filmed Spartacus and the slaves not in a natural location but in the studio. The obvious artifice indicates that Kubrick wanted to be able to control each nuance of presenting Spartacus and his speech. For even greater effect, he intercut the speeches of Spartacus and Crassus although they occur at different times: evening in Spartacus' camp, morning in Rome.

A close-up on Spartacus' face, intense with the weight of his responsibility, dissolves to an extreme long shot of him, standing screen right on the side of the mountain above the assembled crowd, his back to the viewer. This tells us that a decisive moment is at hand. Dedicated filmgoers and devout Christians alike may be reminded of the pictorial and cinematic iconography of the Sermon on the Mount, in particular the version they could have watched a year before in Wyler's *Ben-Hur*. Spartacus gives his people the news that departure from the Roman world is impossible. A closer shot now makes the crowd appear almost identical to that in a biblical film: flowing robes, hoods, and everyone's eyes turned upward in complete attention to the speaker. Then Kubrick cuts to a long shot of the Roman Forum, with some officers and Crassus screen right. The parallel to his set-up for Spartacus is intentional. Unlike Spartacus, Crassus receives a frontal close-up from slightly below eye level. A herald is proclaiming him First Consul and supreme commander of the armies. Crassus' frown expresses his ruthlessness. His title is an anachronism for ancient Rome, but it is appropriate as an indirect reference to another of history's power-hungry leaders: Napoleon, First Consul and later Emperor of France.

Back to Spartacus. Kubrick continues with the same shot, a strong contrast between Crassus and Spartacus because we had seen Crassus alone while we see Spartacus before all his people. He is like a father to them. He tells them: "Rome will not allow us to escape from Italy. We have no choice but to march against Rome herself and end this war the only way it could have ended: by freeing every slave in Italy." This announcement is Spartacus' own emancipation declaration. Like Lincoln's, it serves two purposes: it shows the rightness of the slaves' cause, and it is of practical military value since it may cause major disruptions to the enemy's campaign. Only now, over the last words quoted, does Spartacus receive a close-up, but not a frontal one. He is filmed at a side angle of about forty-five degrees, as if he were standing between *two* crowds: his own people and those in the theater. We also see him from a slightly low angle, which puts the evening sky behind him. In this way Spartacus is elevated above all others and becomes almost godlike. (Compare the ending of *The Robe*.) More importantly, Spartacus' close-up is preceded by one of a young couple looking up at him in reverence, a shot familiar from practically all films about Jesus. The two close-ups express the close ties between Spartacus and his flock and between Spartacus and us. Comparable close-ups will continue throughout this scene.

Kubrick cuts to Rome and to the earlier close-up of Crassus. He contrasts Spartacus' words about universal freedom with Crassus' chilling promise of a universal power structure – his own tyranny, already predicted by Gracchus – and a final victory over the slaves: "I promise you a new Rome, a new Italy, and a new empire. I promise the destruction of the slave army and the restoration of order throughout all our territories." Long shots from different camera positions on soldiers and senators and a medium shot on Gracchus and Caesar listening emphasize Crassus' intimidating power.

Cut to Spartacus' close-up, with heaven behind him as before. His words are the opposite of Crassus' and stress the common humanity of the slaves: "I'd rather be here, a free man among brothers, facing a long march and a hard fight, than to be the richest citizen of Rome, fat with food he didn't work for and surrounded by slaves." These are noble sentiments from which no one in the theater will dissent. We, too, would rather be here with Spartacus than in Rome with Crassus. Unlike Crassus, Spartacus does not look rigidly ahead but moves his head back and forth; as a result, he even looks down from the screen directly at us in the audience. Over his words "a free man among brothers," Kubrick cuts to three medium close-ups of the crowd listening intently. He first shows a young girl embracing her aged mother, then groups of men. After these, he cuts back to Rome. By this time we know that the common people, young and old alike, are the antithesis of inhuman Rome. Whereas the Forum bristles with weapons and soldiers and Crassus is in full military regalia, none of the slaves carries arms or wears a helmet or uniform.

Crassus now briefly appears from a different angle as he continues his speech, but at its climax he is shown again exactly as before: "I promise the living body of Spartacus for whatever punishment you may deem fit. That – or his head. This I vow by the spirits of all my forefathers. This I have sworn in the temple that guards their bones." Classically educated viewers may recognize the reference to Roman ancestry worship, but they and all others will conclude that Crassus' sense of religion is far from making him humane. His words "the living body of Spartacus" are pseudo-biblical and evoke reminiscences of similar expressions about Jesus.

Back to Spartacus. We see him again as at the beginning, in extreme long shot screen right on the mountainside. He now has the last words in this sequence:

> We've traveled a long ways together. We've fought many battles and won great victories. Now, instead of taking ship for our homes across the sea, we must fight again. Maybe there's no peace in this world for us or for anyone else. I don't know. But I do know that, as long as we live, we must stay true to ourselves. I do know that we're brothers, and I know that we're free.

American viewers may be reminded of the patriotic exhortation in *America* (*My Country, 'Tis of Thee*), the secular hymn composed in 1832 by Samuel Francis Smith, from which Martin Luther King quoted at the close of his speech at the Lincoln Monument: "From every mountainside / let freedom ring!" Spartacus' words are again accompanied by close-ups of his people: fathers with young children, old people, young girls, women and children. None of them, these shots imply, could pose the slightest threat to Rome; none of them would ever pose a threat to anybody if only they were treated decently. They are Everyman and Everywoman, and viewers can readily identify themselves with them: There, but for the grace of God, go I! This is reinforced by Kubrick's cut back to the extreme long shot of the crowd we have seen at the beginning. Then, over his familiar close-up, Spartacus calls out: "We march tonight!" Kubrick cuts back to a long shot of the Roman Forum, from which the legions are marching out. The image dissolves to the close-up of Crassus and back to more shots of the legions. For the first time Crassus now moves his head; his gaze follows his soldiers. The visual similarity with the movements of Spartacus' head points to a strong underlying contrast between them. Destructive and dehumanized militarism – there is not one close-up on any of the legionaries, whose individualism is thereby denied them – stands against carefully individualized human decency. The final battle sequence with its clockwork Roman army maneuvers will make the same point with overwhelming power.[45] Now, at the close of the sequence in Rome, military fanfares and the sounds of soldiers in lockstep accompany the image. No music and no sound effects had accompanied the shots of Spartacus and his people. The image of the Romans on the march dissolves to a brief shot of Spartacus' people taking up their exodus again. The contrast of the Romans' gleaming armor and the somber and subdued but warm colors of the slaves' clothing summarizes the meaning of this sequence.

The studio setting for Spartacus' camp appears again during the night before the decisive battle. We are now at a different time and in a different place, but the atmosphere and lighting are almost the same as before, except for a different background. (Another matte seems to be in use.) Spartacus is again on a mountainside, looking down over the slaves' camp in the valley. He then descends and walks among his people. Many of them exchange greetings and smiles with Spartacus, their good shepherd. Several shots of families, an old couple, young children, asleep or awake, and men at a fire indicate harmony, unity, and innate peacefulness. They also reveal everybody's complete trust in Spartacus. Their faces show us the humanity that unites them among themselves and with us viewers. The beatitudes that Jesus pronounces at the beginning of his Sermon on the Mount apply to these slaves: they are the poor in spirit, the meek, the pure in heart, and the ones who hunger and thirst after righteousness. They are the persecuted and reviled, the salt of the earth. In his sermon, Jesus compares such people to the prophets of old,

---

45   Cf. the comment by visual consultant Saul Bass, who designed the movements of the Roman army before the battle, in LoBrutto, *Stanley Kubrick*, 172–173: "I simply took the position that the Roman army was a highly mechanized and disciplined force and I wanted to suggest a certain precision, a mechanization and geometry. I created geometric patterns and had those patterns shift. So what you saw was like a moving painting, where forces would open up from the checkerboard form and would unite as a solid mass. The slaves had a lack of precision. They had no precise uniforms, they lined up but were never straight. We were trying to project the soulless Roman army against the soulful slave army." Not only is this an effective design appropriate, if fanciful, to the situation, but it is also in keeping with Kubrick's own interest in geometry, as with the checkerboard floor in *Paths of Glory* (1957), much of *2001: A Space Odyssey* (1968), the architecture in *Barry Lyndon* (1975), and the maze in *The Shining* (1980). The dehumanization of man is a major theme in *A Clockwork Orange* (1971), *Full Metal Jacket* (1987), *Eyes Wide Shut*, and *Artificial Intelligence: AI* (2001), a Kubrick project eventually directed by Steven Spielberg. Additional details from Kubrick's films illustrating these two interrelated themes could be added.

who suffered similar fates.[46] Spartacus' people are such prophets, har-
bingers of the eventual abolition of slavery. Subdued music, played
mainly on strings, conveys a reverential atmosphere and resembles the
music we associate with film scenes of Jesus. Occasionally, brief brass
fanfares, also played softly, remind us of the decisive trial that awaits
Spartacus and his people. The scene is lit somberly; chiaroscuro effects
and warm brown tones predominate.

5. Crucifixion and Resurrection

Spartacus returns to his tent for his last private moments with Varinia,
his wife and the future mother of his child. Some of their dialogue
restates the film's main theme:

SPARTACUS: I imagine a god for slaves . . . and I pray.
VARINIA: What do you pray for?
SPARTACUS: I pray for a son who'll be born free.
VARINIA: I pray for the same thing.
SPARTACUS: Take care of my son, Varinia. If he never knows me, tell him
                    who I was and what we dreamed of . . .
VARINIA: I can't live without you, Spartacus! . . .
SPARTACUS: Varinia, for you and me there can be no farewells. As long
                    as one of us lives, we all live.

A god for slaves does not yet exist, but Jesus will come to be a god for all.
From the vantage point of believers, Christianity will be the triumph of
the meek, as *Quo Vadis*, *The Robe*, *Demetrius and the Gladiators*, and *Ben-
Hur* have already shown. Like Jesus, who dies on the cross but is eternal
to his followers, Spartacus in his film dies on the cross but is eternal, not
as a god but as a secular Messiah. In the Bible, Jesus was the way, the
truth, and the life.[47] In this film, Spartacus is the way to freedom, the
greatest American truth in life. His crucifixion, an invention that contradicts all historical evidence, is the best visual symbol that ideals and
religion are as good as inseparable in America.[48] According to the Pledge

46   *Matth.* 5.3–13.
47   *John* 14.6.
48   The more astonished the filmmakers may have been had they known that a comparable fate was being propagated for Spartacus on the opposite site of the world: "As late as
the 1960's, Soviet school books portrayed the dying Spartacus as a substitute for Christ
crucified." Quoted from T. E. J. Wiedemann, *Slavery* (Oxford: Clarendon Press, 1987), 47;
see there Plate 8 for an illustration of Spartacus on the cross.

of Allegiance to the Flag in the version current since 1954, the country is "one Nation under God," notwithstanding the separation of church and state that the Founding Fathers had instituted.[49]

Spartacus' words refer primarily to his family, but his last sentence quoted has greater resonance. Death is not the end to this Spartacus. There is a continuation. Spartacus has previously voiced his creed to the emissary of the pirates who will later turn out to be his Judas. Asked if he would fight even if he saw his army destroyed and himself killed, Spartacus replies in the affirmative. He explains:

> All men lose when they die, and all men die, but a slave and a free man lose different things. When a free man dies, he loses the *pleasure* of life. A slave loses his *pain*. Death is the only freedom a slave knows. That's why he's not afraid of it. That's why we'll win.

After death, freedom – a kind of life everlasting and a reminder of Draba's fate. Spartacus and the slaves do not win against Crassus, but their spiritual victory is self-evident. Death, where is thy sting, we might ask. Historically, Spartacus and the slaves only wanted to be free. According to Hollywood, Spartacus, like Jesus, came into the world to end the struggle, as he says on the mountainside, by making all men free. The savior achieves his victory at film's end when he is dying on the cross.[50] He sees

49 Cf. on this now Jon Meacham, *American Gospel: God, the Founding Fathers, and the Making of a Nation* (New York: Random House, 2006) and David L. Holmes, *The Faiths of the Founding Fathers* (New York: Oxford University Press, 2006).

50 The film is not the first re-imagining of Spartacus to associate him directly with Jesus. C. Osborne Ward, *The Ancient Lowly: A History of the Ancient Working People from the Earliest Known Period to the Adoption of Christianity by Constantine*, vol. 1 (1889; rpt. New York: Franklin, 1970), 329, did so and influenced Fast's novel. Gibbon's novel ends with the vision that one of Spartacus' close associates, dying on the cross, has of Spartacus and Jesus (immediately before the recurrence of its epigraph): "And he saw before him, gigantic, filling the sky, a great Cross with a figure that was crowned with thorns; and behind it, sky-towering as well, gladius [= sword] in hand, his hand on the edge of the morning behind that Cross, the figure of a Gladiator. And he saw that these Two were One, and the world yet theirs; and he went into unending night and left them that shining earth" (Gibbon, *Spartacus*, 210). A paragraph before, the dying man's last words ("O Spartacus!") are a cry *de profundis* and could imaginably be followed by "Why hast thou forsaken me?" Theresa Urbainczyk, *Spartacus* (London: Bristol Classical Press, 2004), 107–109, briefly summarizes Gibbon's "Christ-figure" Spartacus. Cf. the death on the cross of the gladiator David, a figure of whom remnants remain in the film, in Fast, *Spartacus*, 246–251. Cf. further Richard G. Lillard, "Through the Disciplines with Spartacus: The Uses of a Hero in History and the Media," *American Studies*, 16 no. 2 (1975), 15–28, at 23, on Arthur Koestler's novel *The Gladiators* (1939): "The book ends with physical defeat but with the suggestion of a Jesus-like resurrection of the faith that Spartacus fought for." Cf. also a

his young son, born in freedom. "He's free, Spartacus, free!" says Varinia, who is also free. "He's free. He'll remember you, Spartacus, because I'll tell him. I'll tell him who his father was and what he dreamed of." We may remember the words of the narrator of *Quo Vadis*: "On a Roman cross in Judaea, a man died to make men free." Here, again on a Roman cross, a man is dying to make men free. Varinia's words may also remind us of "the old Negro spiritual" from which Martin Luther King quoted at the conclusion of his speech at the Lincoln Memorial: "Free at last. Free at last. Thank God Almighty, we are free at last." So it is appropriate that Spartacus on his cross utters only one word in reply to Varinia: "Free." *Consummatum est*: It is finished.[51]

Spartacus does not die in vain; his legacy will live. Earlier in the film we have already received two clear hints at the underlying concept of Spartacus' spiritual immortality, his quasi-resurrection from the dead. The survivors' resounding cry "I'm Spartacus!" tells us that even during his lifetime Spartacus has transcended the limitations of being only one person; he stands for, even has become, all of them. As such, his individual defeat and death are not decisive. In another scene, Spartacus himself expresses the idea of resurrection. After Crassus has forced him to kill his friend Antoninus, Spartacus conquers his conqueror: "Here's your victory!" Referring to Antoninus, he promises Crassus: "He'll come back. He'll come back, and he'll be millions!" His words anticipate the Civil-Rights struggle of the 1960s and especially Martin Luther King's march on Selma, Alabama, on which a recent commentator has written:

> King could have done nothing if poor and excluded blacks had not had the courage to shake off their servitude. The ones who joined the boycotts, the marches, the [voter] registration drives, did it at risk to their jobs, their property, their lives . . . It took great pride in themselves for the blacks to defy generations of repression . . . With this roll of martyrs in mind, it seems almost miraculous to watch . . . the nameless poor, heartbreakingly

recent novel, something of a curiosity, at whose beginning a conversation between God and Spartacus occurs, quoted here in a brief excerpt: "'My name is Spartacus.' . . . 'Spartacus? The gladiator? He of the slaves and the crucifixions? *You?*' 'No more strange than you being God.' 'But Spartacus is dead.' 'Not while one slave remains. Not while one man is subject to another . . .'" Shortly after this, God calls Spartacus "[t]he freedom fighter." Quoted from Christopher Leach, *God, Spartacus and Miss Emily* (London and Melbourne: Dent, 1987), 6. The titular lady is American poet Emily Dickinson. Symbolic survival after death is *de rigueur* for Spartacus; cf. Ghnassia, *Arena*, 295 ("'Spartacus is not dead'"), 298 ("'we would be betraying him now if we didn't carry on his fight, our fight for freedom . . . We're everywhere'" – an echo of "he'll be millions"), and 300 ("'Spartacus is not dead! Spartacus is not dead!'").

51   *John* 19.30.

turned out in their best clothes, marching into danger, being hosed and herded and beaten – and, incredibly, coming back for more.[52]

To this we could add: and coming back in ever greater numbers. Spartacus also will come back.[53] Small wonder that Crassus is afraid of Spartacus dead even more than he had been of him alive: "I knew he could be beaten. But now I fear him." He has every reason to, even if Spartacus is not, as Crassus had surmised earlier, a god. His question to Varinia about the true nature of Spartacus is phrased in a way to evoke comparable questions about Jesus: "What sort of a man was he?"[54] Varinia's answer ("He was a simple man") fits both Jesus and Spartacus. Even the historical Spartacus had an aura of the supernatural and religious about him.[55] Before the final battle, Crassus had told his officers

---

52   Garry Wills, "An American Iliad," *The New York Review of Books* (April 6, 2006), 20, 22, and 24–26; quotation at 26 (in section entitled "Heroism"). This is a review essay on Branch, *At Canaan's Edge*.

53   The play *Les esclaves* (1853) by Edgar Quinet ends with Crassus' belief that Spartacus' son will be "another Spartacus" (*un autre Spartacus*). A comparable perspective appears in Urbain Gohier's *Spartacus* (1905): "This man's breath has passed on the earth . . . and liberty will be reborn" (*Le soufflé de cet homme a passé sur la terre . . . et la liberté renaîtra*). Quoted from André Simon, "Esclaves romains et théâtre français," in *Spectacula*, vol. 1: *Gladiateurs et amphithéâtres*, ed. Claude Domergue, Christian Landes, and Jean-Marie Pailler (Lattes: Imago, 1990), 295–303; quotations at 301 and 302. The cinema, of course, has followed suit. Two films after Kubrick's are noteworthy in this regard: Sergio Corbucci's *Il figlio di Spartacus* (*Son of Spartacus* or *The Slave*, 1963), in which the titular hero is played by muscleman Steve Reeves, and Michele Lupo's *La vendetta di Spartacus* (*The Revenge of Spartacus*, 1965), in which Spartacus is believed to be still alive. At the end of an earlier film, Riccardo Freda's *Spartaco* (*Sins of Rome*, *Sins of Rome: Story of Spartacus*, *Spartacus the Gladiator*; 1953), Spartacus' unborn son embodies hope for a better future as well. Contrast the fate of Spartacus' son in Fast, *Spartacus*, 363, and the comments by Thomas Allen Nelson, *Kubrick: Inside a Film Artist's Maze*, 2nd edn. (Bloomington and Indianapolis: Indiana University Press, 2000), 60, on the film's ending: "Kubrick . . . concludes the film with a composition that recalls the tragic irony of *Paths [of Glory]* . . . In Trumbo's version . . . the audience is encouraged to believe that she [Varinia] and Spartacus's child are traveling into a democratic future that will give value to his sacrifice. In Kubrick's version, one barely visible to this film's audience, they move into an indeterminate landscape where there exists only the certainty of death."

54   Cf. *John* 1.19–22. Such questions are likely to occur in films about mythic-historical heroes. An example from the time of *Spartacus* is Anthony Mann's *El Cid* (1961), in which Christ-like overtones, both visual and verbal ("Who are you?" or "What kind of man is this?"), characterize the protagonist throughout. On this film cf. my "Mythic and Cinematic Traditions in Anthony Mann's *El Cid*," *Mosaic*, 26 no. 3 (1993), 89–111. Mann, it will be remembered, was the original director of *Spartacus*.

55   Cf. the story about Spartacus and the snake prodigy reported in Plutarch, *Crassus* 8.2. Bradley, *Slavery and Rebellion in the Roman World, 140 B.C.–70 B.C.*, 93, comments on this:

that his campaign was "to kill the legend of Spartacus." In this he was anything but victorious. So a modern historian's verdict is apposite: "For us, Spartacus is one of the most powerful of Roman myths."[56] The film itself is proof because it has told the story of Spartacus' passion to millions. It continues to do so.

6. Profiles in Courage

It will by now be evident that the hero of *Spartacus* is equally messianic and American. A speech given by one other famous American less than four months after the film's release shows that *Spartacus* was thoroughly in tune with the spirit of its time. The Inaugural Address by President John F. Kennedy, delivered on January 20, 1961, contains several statements and expressions that, with only minimal adjustments, could have come straight out of the mouth of Spartacus.[57] Kennedy himself called the occasion of his address "a celebration of freedom" in his opening sentence. With Kennedy, Spartacus could have proclaimed:

> Let every nation know . . . that we shall pay any price, bear any burden, meet any hardship, support any friend, oppose any foe, in order to assure the survival and the success of liberty.

As Spartacus exhorted his people to one final struggle for their freedom in his address on the mountainside, so Kennedy summoned his people to heed the call to a similar struggle. Kennedy is referring to the Cold War, a modern fight of freedom against oppression on a worldwide scale:

> Now the trumpet summons us again – not as a call to bear arms, though arms we need; not as a call to battle, though embattled we are – but a call to bear the burden of a long twilight struggle, year in and year out, "rejoicing in hope, patient in tribulation" – a struggle against the common enemies of man: tyranny, poverty, disease, and war itself . . . The energy,

"it indicates that Spartacus was thought to have been a figure who was surrounded by an aura of religiosity, insofar as he is portrayed here as the elect of supernatural forces." Cf. Bradley, 115: "the story in Plutarch suggests . . . the possibility at least that Spartacus saw himself and was seen as a mystical figure."

56   T. P. Wiseman, *The Myths of Rome* (Exeter: University of Exeter Press, 2004), 201.
57   For background information on the address see Theodore Otto Windt, Jr., "President John F. Kennedy's Inaugural Address, 1961," in *The Inaugural Addresses of Twentieth-Century American Presidents*, ed. Halford Ryan (Westport and London: Praeger, 1993), 181–193. Windt, 189, connects the speech to principles of classical oratory.

the faith, the devotion which we bring to this endeavor will light our
country and all who serve it – and the glow from that fire can truly light
the world.

The Spartacus of our film is an Everyman, as we have seen, and what he
says on the screen to his people he says from the screen to all of us: "I do
know that we're brothers, and I know that we're free." Spartacus could
have addressed mankind in Kennedy's own terms: "My fellow citizens of
the world: ask . . . what together we can do for the freedom of man."[58]

Freedom and civil rights were an important part of Kennedy's administration. Noteworthy in our context is his "Radio and Television Report
to the American People on Civil Rights" of June 11, 1963, prompted by
Alabama governor George Wallace's order to block the admission of two
black students to the University of Alabama. Kennedy sent in the
National Guard and gave his address the same evening. Racial equality,
he said, was "primarily . . . a moral issue. It is as old as the scriptures and
is as clear as the American Constitution."[59] That night Medgar Evers was
killed in Mississippi. But even so, the era of the "drivers of negroes," as
Samuel Johnson had called them, was beginning to come to a close.

On February 4, 1961, the second Friday night of Kennedy's presidency, Spartacus' and Kennedy's paths converged. Kennedy crossed the
picket line of the American Legion outside a theater near the White
House to attend a screening of *Spartacus*.[60] The Leader of the Free World
was visiting its – and his – prophet.[61]

Like Spartacus, John F. Kennedy and Martin Luther King were killed
by evil forces. But all three conquered death and became mythical icons
of just causes. Their souls keep marching on.

58   On Kennedy's speech see now Thurston Clarke, *Ask Not: The Inauguration of John F.
Kennedy and the Speech That Changed America* (New York: Holt, 2004; rpt. 2005).

59   Quoted from John F. Kennedy, "Radio and Television Report to the American People
on Civil Rights," available at the John F. Kennedy Library and Museum web site
(http://www.jfklibrary.net/j061163.htm) as text and audio file.

60   Cf. "Kennedy Attends Movie in Capital," *The New York Times* (February 5, 1961), 39.
This short news article also mentions that Kennedy's brother Robert, the Attorney General,
had seen the film and recommended it to him; it further reports: "He . . . picked up a
brochure 'Spartacus, the Rebel Against Rome' [*sic*], and put it in his pocket" and: "'It was
fine,' the President told a reporter on his way out" about the film. Smith, "A Good Business
Proposition'," 93, observes that the American Legion objected not to the content of *Spartacus* but only to "the political association of the person who wrote the film." On Kennedy
and *Spartacus* cf. also Douglas, *The Ragman's Son*, 334. Hoberman, *The Dream Life*, 36, states
that Kennedy's attendance was "the single most important endorsement" of *Spartacus*.

61   Cf. Hoberman, *The Dream Life*, 40–41 note 1, on Kennedy's belief that "history was
the stuff of heroes."

CHAPTER TEN

Spartacus and the Stoic Ideal of Death

Francisco Javier Tovar Paz

Most critics have until now approached Stanley Kubrick's *Spartacus* from one of two perspectives, focusing either on the film's social and political aspects or on its cinematic nature. The former approach deals with the problems of racial discrimination and human rights as a modern sort of slavery in the United States, of Marxism in a capitalist society, and of militarization in the Cold War. The latter approach examines *Spartacus* as an epic film set in ancient Rome, its relationship to other such films, and as a new specimen among such films in which Spartacus the gladiator has become a political or religious figure. That is to say, unlike other spectacle films, *Spartacus* is elevated to the level of political significance.

These interpretations are valid but insufficient. For example, it is difficult to establish a relation of cause and effect between the social and political situation in the United States after World War II and the Rome depicted in the film. After all, Spartacus and his followers refuse to be Romans. They express no demand for Roman citizenship and its attendant rights. Instead, they desire to return to their home countries, which are presumably just as different from Rome as they are from the United States. The idea of freedom embodied by Spartacus does not coincide with the freedom that senator Gracchus, the film's old and wily politician, works for but fails to achieve. Spartacus' idea is of freedom intrinsic to all human beings, Gracchus' idea is of the *libera res publica*, the Roman republic, which is beginning to be usurped by dictatorship.[1] In regard to the tradition of epic cinema, Spartacus is quite a multifaceted figure. He contrasts with standard legendary or mythical heroes and with historical characters whom epic films have usually shown us. He comes closer to the spiritual and religious importance of a Moses or Messiah as a leader of his people living in affliction and oppression.[2] Nevertheless, he differs from the protagonists of films like Fred Niblo's and William Wyler's versions of *Ben-Hur* (1925, 1959) or Mervyn Le Roy's *Quo Vadis* (1951), in which the (fictional) main characters are witnesses of the Christian Messiah and of the victory of his religion. Kubrick's presentation of Spartacus prevents his film from being simply one of a large group of historical spectacles set in antiquity. For instance, Spartacus does not conform to the model of the "strong man" present in numerous historical or quasi-historical films, such as Riccardo Freda's *Spartaco* (1952). Kubrick's Spartacus wins no major gladiatorial fights, and his personal intervention decides no battle. Neither do we see him perform any great, much less superhuman, deeds.

Kubrick's Spartacus is not just a Thracian who has become a slave and gladiator in a Roman world but rather someone who is defined by his contrast to Crassus and Gracchus, Romans of powerful status and political rivals. The more Spartacus appears distanced from Crassus, the closer he comes to Gracchus. What the latter two, radically different as they originally are, come to have in common is the fact that they are the only major characters in the film who die. In the film's general context of gladiatorial games and warfare, their deaths complete, even justify, the plot and confer upon it a kind of unity. This unity becomes evident in their death scenes and in their reflections about death. These derive from a learning process which reveals to the spectator that both of them have come to terms with their deaths.

In *Spartacus*, death is not only related to slavery and gladiatorial or battlefield spectacle but also reflects the production history of the film. Screenwriter Dalton Trumbo's perspective on his subject is not what can

---

1   This is not a historical character, although he takes some features from the Gracchi of Roman republican history. Cf. Gérard Legrand, "La gloire et ses chemins," *Positif*, 45 (1962), 15–21, especially 17.

2   Although it has obvious biblical overtones, most prominently Spartacus' death on the cross but also his ready acceptance of newcomers willing to join him and his people, the slaves' "exodus," and Spartacus' final speech, a kind of "Sermon on the Mount," *Spartacus* makes no religious arguments. At the most, three references to religion occur: Gracchus' declaration of his atheism, Crassus' devotion to his ancestors (more of a political than religious nature), and the wish for a "god of the slaves" expressed by Spartacus and Varinia.

be seen in the final film. One could even argue that here there are two films combined into one. One is the universal story of man's struggle for freedom, an epic in which a rebellious Spartacus, a David to the Roman Goliath, challenges a world empire and its might. The other is a more intimate tragedy of individual heroism, focused on an attempt at rather anarchic rebellion that appears doomed from the start. In Trumbo's script Spartacus was to be crucified only after his death. Like the other rebel slaves who are crucified after the slave rebellion has failed, Spartacus was to be a deterrent to all future potential rebels in the Roman world. But in the film Spartacus is crucified while still alive, with his wife and son at the foot of his cross. This scene especially imparts to him a messianic character.

Kubrick deals with the issue of death from the very beginning of the film. Spartacus has been condemned to a living death in the infernal quarry in which he works. (The opening sequence was filmed, although not by Kubrick, in Death Valley.) Spartacus is saved, but only to become a gladiator. That is to say, he is trained to inflict death on others and, most likely, eventually to be killed by a superior gladiator. In a duel set in the gladiatorial school for the delectation of Crassus and his entourage, Spartacus' fellow gladiator Draba defeats Spartacus and is expected to kill him. But Draba spares Spartacus' life. In a moment of moral outrage and rebelliousness, he attacks Crassus instead and pays with his own life for his noble gesture. Draba's death and the ignoble treatment his dead body receives, hanging upside down like an animal carcass in a butcher shop as a warning to the school's other gladiators, inspires Spartacus to launch a general rebellion at an opportune moment. Draba's sparing of Spartacus' life can be understood as his discovery of Spartacus' rebellious spirit and his potential as a liberator. So he refuses to kill him, dying in his place. From this point of view, the reason for Draba's sacrifice is political. Moreover, we are led to understand that Spartacus, as a slave and gladiator, is already dead as a human being. His rebellion is an attempt to exchange death for a new life, but this life is fated to lead to defeat and further deaths, including his own. Coming to terms with the ubiquity of death will be one of the keys in Spartacus' struggle against Rome. Only someone who is already as good as dead does not fear death. As Spartacus himself will say later, being a slave is akin to being dead.

As is to be expected in a story of gladiators, rebelling slaves, and battles, the importance of death appears in numerous scenes throughout the film. But even a short moment can be significant. For example, the slaves' exodus from Mt. Vesuvius to Brundisium shows us their great numbers, their different ages and origins, and their solidarity. The harshness of the elements to which they are exposed symbolizes their precarious existence in the human world. So the moment when a little child is buried becomes important. It reminds us of the closeness of death that any of the slaves has to reckon with at any moment, and it points us to the birth of another child, Spartacus' own son who, at the end of the film, embodies the triumph of freedom over slavery, of life over death.

Kubrick structures much of *Spartacus* around comparable significant contrasts. The individual and personal moments we observe when the camera takes us among the slaves and shows us their everyday life or the deliberations of Spartacus and his associates contrast with Roman policy, which is made without any participation of the people. The activities of Spartacus and his lieutenants occur in public, as we expect to be the case in ideal modern democracies. Political intrigues behind the scenes impart an anonymous, impersonal, and soulless character to the behavior of those Romans who either are in power or are vying for power. Comparable contrasts also pertain to the film's treatment of death.

This is best seen when Kubrick intercuts speeches by Spartacus and Crassus just before the final battle between slaves and Romans. Spartacus addresses his people, presented as individuals in numerous close-ups; Crassus harangues an anonymous mass of Roman troops. Crassus and Spartacus do not expressly mention death at all, a telling contrast to a number of speeches earlier in the film. Batiatus, the owner of the gladiatorial school, for instance, told his new arrivals that gladiators are defined as men destined to die. In an inspiring speech to the rebel gladiators who are forcing two of their former masters to fight each other, Spartacus told them that, to them, death should not be a spectacle but a route to freedom. When Spartacus and Crixus welcomed new members, they emphasized the importance of each and every one of them, even the elderly. Spartacus told an old woman that her task would be to make shrouds, thus emphasizing the importance of the slave rebels' acceptance of death. Tigranes, the ambassador of the Cilician pirates, pointed out in his first meeting with Spartacus that it would be impossible for the slaves to escape to freedom, but Spartacus responded by explaining the existence of two kinds of death, that of a free man and that of a slave. Slaves are not afraid to die since they are already dead. So fear of death is only possible for those who are free, and to die fighting for freedom is not to die. These words we are meant to remember when we listen to Spartacus' final speech to his people.

As a result, Spartacus' silence about death in this speech becomes an argument about the inevitable acceptance of death in the slaves' utopian attempt to found a new society that will be based on the liberation of all slaves. Moreover, Spartacus does not use any bellicose terms, and his speech acquires the air of an evangelical sermon. (Significantly, Spartacus addresses the slaves from an elevated position, as if he were standing on a mount.) Still, by this silence about death he confirms its fundamental unavoidability. As do Spartacus and his people, viewers come to realize that freedom is more important than death, that the latter is inescapable, and that slavery is a form of living death. The quest for freedom becomes the way to avoid both death and the fear of death; that is to say, Spartacus' words embody a whole doctrine of death. Fundamentally, this doctrine is not merely the filmmakers' invention; rather, it is in keeping with the ancient tradition of Hellenistic and Roman philosophy. Approaches to an avoidance of fear of death were prominent in philosophical schools, especially Epicureanism and Stoicism. The former regarded fear of death as an evil to be overcome by the awareness that death is incidental to all life; its causes and effects encouraged Epicureans to lead their lives in an awareness of physical pleasures, chiefly understood as the absence of pain or affliction, and distanced from political practice. The latter emphasized efforts to understand death rationally: as a process inherent in all forms of life and as a part of life to be accepted with equanimity. As did some other philosophical movements, Stoicism incorporated action into meditation and philosophical contemplation. Action is the practice of philosophy, the exercise of philosophical knowledge; hence the Stoics' call for a politically active life.[3] According to Stoicism, it is not death that is to be feared but rather the fear of death. Interweaving nature and death is the basis of Stoic thought concerning fear of death. This view is expressed, for example, by the Stoic philosopher Epictetus, himself a former slave.[4] With reference to freedom in general, Epictetus believes that no morals are possible without it. But

3   In general cf. Arthur Bodson, *La morale sociale des derniers Stoïciens: Sénèque, Epictète et Marc Aurèle* (Paris: Les Belles Lettres, 1967); the essays collected in *The Stoics*, ed. John M. Rist (Berkeley, Los Angeles, and London: University of California Press, 1978); and Marcia L. Colish, *The Stoic Tradition from Antiquity to the Early Middle Ages*, vol. 1: *Stoicism in Classical Latin Literature* (Leiden: Brill, 1985; rpt. 1990).
4   Epictetus, *Discourses* 2.1.13: "it is not death or hardship that is a fearful thing, but the fear of hardship or death." Quoted from *Epictetus: The Discourses as Reported by Arrian, the Manual, and Fragments*, tr. W. A. Oldfather (Cambridge: Harvard University Press / London: Heinemann, 1925–1928; rpt. 1996), vol. 1, 217. This idea recurs frequently in the Roman Stoicism of Cicero, Seneca, and Marcus Aurelius; cf., e.g., Cicero, *Paradoxes of the Stoics* 34; Seneca, *On Providence* 2.12; and Marcus Aurelius, *Meditations* 4.50. On the Stoic concept of slavery see, e.g., C. E. Manning, "Stoicism and Slavery in the Roman Empire," *Aufstieg und Niedergang der römischen Welt*, 2.36.3 (1989), 1518–1543.

the most important thing about political freedom is inner freedom.[5] The result is the well-known "apathy" of Stoicism, the Stoic sage's freedom from affections: *ataraxia* in Greek, *aequanimitas* in Latin. Thus to avoid slavery is an important imperative of Stoicism, one that encompasses equally one's enslavement to passions and one's submission to other people. *Spartacus* effectively revives and restates the Stoic doctrine of death, if without any explicit reference to it or, perhaps, even without the filmmakers' awareness of it. The film connects the Stoic view of death with the gradual development on Spartacus' part of his commitment to this idea and to the path of action to which it leads him. Regarding death, Spartacus advances from a state of ignorance to a state of knowledge and acceptance.

The height of Spartacus' understanding about life and death comes at the end of the film in the duel with his fellow slave Antoninus that Crassus forces on them. Crassus is sure that Spartacus and Antoninus will fight to the death, not to survive the other but to avoid the more terrible death by crucifixion that he has decreed for the survivor of the fight. Structurally, this duel is a reprise of the fight between Spartacus and Draba – before the same principal spectator at that. Spartacus' learning process had begun when he was defeated but not killed by Draba. Now, when Spartacus kills Antoninus to spare him a worse death, one shortly to be inflicted on himself, he puts into practice his understanding of human existence, of which death is an integral part. Significantly, Spartacus and a dying Antoninus both affirm their mutual love as human beings.

Spartacus' evolution from animal-like slave – the kind who, in the film's opening sequence, had bitten a Roman guard in the leg like a wolf – to profound human being is based on his deepening knowledge about life and death, freedom and slavery. This process reaches an extreme when Kubrick makes us realize that Spartacus understands Crassus much more than Crassus understands Spartacus. It is a telling irony at the end that Crassus does not even recognize Spartacus although he had seen him fight at close range in Batiatus' school. Kubrick gradually turns Spartacus into a more and more philosophical, indeed Stoic, character while de-emphasizing his gladiatorial side, except in the final fight with Antoninus, into which he is forced. Spartacus' acquisition of knowledge in general parallels his increasingly deeper understanding of death.

---

5   Epictetus, *Discourses* 4.1.1: "He is free who lives as he wills, who is subject neither to compulsion, nor hindrance, nor force, whose choices are unhampered, whose desires attain their end, whose aversions do not fall into what they would avoid." Quoted from *Epictetus*, tr. Oldfather, vol. 2, 245.

What does Stoicism add to our understanding of Kubrick's film? Roughly, Stoic philosophy can be divided into three important aspects, all of which are reflected in *Spartacus*. The first postulates that life should be governed by, and death accepted in accordance with, reason, nature, and political action. In Kubrick's film Spartacus is a man who acquires reason: knowledge and understanding. His and his fellow slaves' close relation to nature appears in the scenes that show them as embodying a kind of agrarian ideal, doing simple work and living off the land. More importantly, in an early scene set in the gladiators' school, Spartacus refuses to have sexual intercourse with the slave Varinia so as not to lower himself to the level of an animal. Spartacus is in an underground cell that serves as his quarters; its ceiling has an opening which is barred like a cage and through which others prepare to watch him and Varinia as if they were animals in a modern zoo. "I'm not an animal!" Spartacus shouts up at Batiatus and Marcellus who are posed to watch him with Varinia. Spartacus' sexual ethics contrast with that of the "civilized" Romans, especially of the aristocratic ladies who get their sexual kicks from watching gladiators' fights to the death and of Crassus, whom a key scene ("oysters and snails") reveals to be bisexual. By contrast, Spartacus' development exemplifies and inspires political action destined to free the slaves.

Secondly, slavery and any slavish attitude towards death are morally unacceptable to Stoics. A comparable view is expressed in the film when Spartacus says that death should no more be feared than life. Suicide, however, is understandable if reason, nature, or political circumstances have made a dignified existence impossible. In both Greek and Roman Stoic ethics, suicide represents a major aspect of the fundamental question of how to lead one's life appropriately. The Roman philosopher and statesman Seneca, who committed suicide under Nero, "glorifies it as the road to freedom . . . The thought that death is a refuge from the stresses and pains of life is characteristic of Seneca."[6]

So senator Gracchus commits suicide when it has become evident to him that Crassus intends to have him executed as an enemy of the state

---

6   Quoted from F. H. Sandbach, *The Stoics* (1975; rpt. Indianapolis: Hackett, 1994), 50 (in the context of a section on suicide [48–52]) and 157. Cf. also the chapter on suicide in John M. Rist, *Stoic Philosophy* (1969; rpt. Cambridge: Cambridge University Press, 1990), 233–255, and Adolf Friedrich Bonhöffer, *The Ethics of the Stoic Epictetus: An English Translation*, tr. William O. Stephens (New York: Lang, 1996), 239–244 ("Excursus II: The Stoic Doctrine of Suicide"). For Epictetus on death and suicide see now also A. A. Long, *Epictetus: A Stoic and Socratic Guide to Life* (Oxford: Clarendon Press, 2002), 203–206, 248–250, and passim. All passages contain references to and quotations from Stoic authors.

and that he is powerless to avoid such an ignominious fate unless he pre-empts his ruthless opponent. Rebellion against what appears inevitable, including rebellious suicide as in Gracchus' case, can be an act of polit-ical disobedience, but it can also reflect the nobility of the human spirit and its refusal to bow to the inhuman.[7] So the political character of Gracchus' suicide reflects its underlying Stoic nature, even if Gracchus is characterized by a marked hedonistic – i.e., more Epicurean than Stoic – nature. But then, ancient Romans commonly practiced a mixture of philosophical attitudes that amounts to an eclectic synthesis.[8] Spartacus' rebellion is, first, a rebellion against the idea of slavery and the living death of slaves; then it becomes a rebellion against all of Rome, which exploits the slaves as gladiators for its amusement.

Third, the fatalism characteristic of Stoicism includes the ready acceptance that all life ends in death, irrespective of the type of death that one suffers. So a Stoic's main concern is with life, not death. The way we manage our lives must be focused on our development as spiri-tually free humans and without an excessive concern for death, which is natural and inevitable, anyway. In *Spartacus*, what is important is the fight for freedom and dignity, even if victory is impossible. The final battle thus carries a fundamentally fatalistic tone. The impressive array and maneuvers of the Roman army before the battle make it evident to all, slaves and spectators alike, that Spartacus and his men cannot win. In the character of Spartacus, Kubrick's film expresses philosophical atti-tudes like affirmation of freedom, rebellion against oppression, and fatal-ism in the face of unavoidable death comparable to key Stoic ideals.[9]

So our awareness of the Stoic nature of much of the film, although never expressed or acknowledged in its dialogue or in comments by its principal makers, can deepen our appreciation of the tensions inherent in the film, those between Crassus and Spartacus on the one hand and those within the character of Spartacus as first a human being and then a hero on the other. This then also explains that Spartacus can be both ignorant and wise and that he simultaneously fails and succeeds in a

---

7   Cf. generally Yolande Grisé, *Le suicide dans la Rome antique* (Paris: Les Belles Lettres, 1982).

8   Cf., e.g., Anthony A. Long, *Hellenistic Philosophy: Stoics, Epicureans, Sceptics*, 2nd edn. (Berkeley: University of California Press, 1986).

9   Kubrick's Spartacus, a gladiator and soldier, is reminiscent of Seneca, *On Providence* 4.4, a passage on soldiers' and gladiators' desire for adversity or combat. Cf. Bodson, *La morale sociale des derniers Stoïciens*, 86–90. For Seneca, the gladiator is above all an exem-plar of mankind; cf. on this Pierre Cagniart, "The Philosopher and the Gladiator," *The Clas-sical World*, 93 (2000), 607–618.

kind of impossible synthesis that gives the film an underlying unity. In this regard he is comparable to the protagonist of a particular Roman historical epic on the subject of freedom and tyranny: Lucan's *Pharsalia*, written under Emperor Nero. In the *Pharsalia*, Cato the Younger, faced with the soon-to-be-inevitable monarchy of Julius Caesar, his political and philosophical antagonist, commits suicide to avoid living in an enslaved world. The single most famous line in Lucan's entire epic reveals to its readers Cato's world view and Lucan's own defiant perspective on liberty, tyranny, and suicide: "The victorious cause pleased the gods, but the defeated cause pleased Cato."[10] The defeated are the real victors. With some adjustment to allow for historical and cultural differences between ancient Romans and twentieth-century Americans, Lucan's verdict on Cato is fully applicable to Kubrick's Spartacus.

A brief consideration of a later film directed by Kubrick can be useful here. His *2001: A Space Odyssey* (1968) shows a related perspective on life and death. The human race reaches the limit of its knowledge, and man is confronted with his own death, which he faces in dignity and without fear. Human life is no more than the process by which such knowledge is acquired. This knowledge, or philosophical awareness, in turn makes a humane existence and a humane death possible. And just as Spartacus does not vanish without a trace after his physical existence has ended – he leaves a legacy embodied in his son, who survives and who will live in freedom – so the protagonist of *2001*, representative of the human race at large, does not reach the end of his existence when he dies an old man but is reborn as the Star Child.[11]

The end of *Spartacus*, with the protagonist's son who will be a free man, and the end of *2001*, with the image of a new man yet to be born, are an exhortation to overcome the fear of death. *2001* and *Spartacus* are comparable in the Stoic elements they contain. Both films show us a search for a new man and a better understanding of life and death, in the past as well as in the future.

---

10   *Pharsalia* 1.128. On Lucan's Cato see especially Frederick M. Ahl, *Lucan: An Introduction* (Ithaca and London: Cornell University Press, 1976), 231–279.

11   This perspective on death can be extended to Kubrick's last film, *Eyes Wide Shut* (1999), on which cf. my comments in "Las puertas de los sueños auténticos y de los sueños falaces en la película *Eyes Wide Shut* (1999), de Stanley Kubrick," in *Homenaje a la Profesora Carmen Pérez Romero* (Cáceres: Universidad de Extremadura, 2000), 365–372.

CHAPTER ELEVEN

"Culturally Significant and Not Just Simple Entertainment": History and the Marketing of *Spartacus*

Martin M. Winkler

Ancient history has always played an important part in the American cinema, which produced films set in classical antiquity as early as 1897 and 1898. The first of them was Walter W. Freeman's *The Passion Play*, "almost certainly . . . America's first feature film with a storyline."[1] It was followed by *The Passion Play of Oberammergau*, directed by Rich G. Hollaman and made as a rival of the earlier film.[2] Both derived respectability from their subject matter, even if religious topics on the screen were liable to raise the concerns of clergymen and educators.[3]

1   On this film, which does not survive, see Kemp R. Niver, *Klaw and Erlanger Present Famous Plays in Pictures*, ed. Bebe Bergsten (Los Angeles: Locare Research Group, 1976), 1–12. My quotation is from page 4. The film was a record of the passion play performed that year in Höritz, Austria. Its producers were Marc Klaw and Abraham Lincoln Erlanger, the theatrical impresarios who two years later were to bring *Ben-Hur* to the stage.

2   Niver, *Klaw and Erlanger Present Famous Plays in Pictures*, 13–27, provides background information on this film. Despite its title, it was not an adaptation of the Austrian passion play but an American recreation filmed on a rooftop in New York City.

3   On passion plays and their influence on early cinema see Terry Ramsaye, *A Million and One Nights: A History of the Motion Picture through 1925* (1926; rpt. New York: Simon and Schuster, 1986), 366–378 (chapter entitled "The Saga of Calvary"), and Charles Musser, *The Emergence of Cinema: The American Screen to 1907* (New York: Scribner, 1990), 208–221. On the cultural contexts of early biblical films see William Uricchio and Roberta E. Pearson, *Reframing Culture: The Case of the Vitagraph Quality Films* (Princeton: Princeton University Press, 1993), 160–194 and 240–244 (notes), in a chapter entitled "Biblical Qualities: Moses."

1. From Cheap Origins to Cultural Respectability

Geared toward mass consumption, the cinema had first become popular at fairs and in nickelodeons: "cheap places for cheap people."[4] But cinematic spectacle, born with Freeman's film, found wide acceptance. Films like his and Hollaman's could demonstrate their makers' artistic, educational, and moral seriousness and draw attention away from their commercial interests. As has rightly been observed: "Religious subjects in general were an important genre for the early film industry."[5] Besides Old and New Testament topics, literary masterpieces and subjects taken from history could lend status to the cinema and deflect criticism of the new medium from respectable citizens and spiritual or civic institutions. As film and cultural historian Siegfried Kracauer observed, the theater furnished a model for early cinema:

> The trend in favor of the theatrical story was initiated as early as 1908 by *Film d'Art*, a new French film company whose first production . . . represented a deliberate attempt to transform the cinema into an art medium on a par with the traditional literary media. The idea was to demonstrate that films were quite able to tell, in terms of their own, meaningful stories after the manner of the theater or the novel . . . From the lower depths the cinema thus rose to the regions of literature and theatrical art. Cultured people could no longer look down on a medium engaged in such noble pursuits . . . Producers, distributors, and exhibitors were quick to realize that Art meant big business.[6]

Especially in the United States, the Bible and the plays of Shakespeare supplied respectable stories. The early cinematic history of Shakespeare's

4   Benjamin B. Hampton, *A History of the Movies* (1931; rpt. New York: Arno, 1970), 61.
5   Musser, *The Emergence of Cinema*, 219.
6   Siegfried Kracauer, *Theory of Film: The Redemption of Physical Reality* (1960; rpt. Princeton: Princeton University Press, 1997), 216–217. The 1908 French film is *L'assassinat du Duc de Guise*, directed by André Calmettes and Charles Le Bargy. The subject had first been made into a film in 1897. The screenplay of the new version was written by a member of the Académie Française, the music score was by Camille Saint-Saëns, and the principal cast came from the Comédie Française. Calmettes directed a considerable number of films on ancient history and on various literary subjects (including Shakespeare). For a detailed outline of the representative process of cinema's cultural elevation and social acceptability, achieved primarily through epic films on ancient topics and adaptations of literary masterpieces, cf. Richard Abel, *The Ciné Goes to Town: French Cinema 1896–1914*, 2nd edn. (Berkeley, Los Angeles, and London: University of California Press, 1999), 246–277. For a general overview of European cinema and society in this regard see, e.g., Gian Piero Brunetta, "Identità e radici culturali," in *Storia del cinema mondiale*, ed. Gian Piero Brunetta, vol. 1: *L'Europa*, pt. 1: *Miti, luoghi, divi* (Turin: Einaudi, 1999), 3–50.

Julius Caesar is an instructive case.[7] Films based on this play could make a double claim: their subject is a famous turning point in Roman history, itself a venerable period of the past, and it derives from a revered author. Consequently the first version, *Julius Caesar: An Historical Tragedy* (1908), directed by J. Stuart Blackton and William V. Ranous, restages Caesar's assassination by imitating Jean-Léon Gérôme's painting *The Death of Caesar* (1869). The film depicts the senate hall just after Caesar's assassination in an almost exact copy of Gérôme's painting, if in black and white rather than in color. The point is clear: the educated filmmakers want the educated among their viewers to recognize their source and to appreciate the cultured representation of this decisive moment. This one image in this one film exemplifies what many other films on historical subjects have demonstrated as well: when done right, the cinema is artistic, uplifting, educating, and inspiring. It always remains a commercial product, but it is good for you. Fred Niblo's *Ben-Hur: A Tale of the Christ* (1925) is a case in point. Its souvenir program makes the cultural significance of the story's progress from novel to stage to screen explicit and emphasizes its public appeal and its edifying and instructive qualities – not without the requisite advertising hyperbole. The souvenir book begins with a "Foreword: 1880–1925" that links novel and film:

> SINCE GENERAL LEW WALLACE wrote the last words of BEN-HUR forty-five years ago . . . that immortal story . . . has been the greatest of fictional themes. Eagerly read in every English-speaking community and translated into many foreign languages, millions of copies have been sold and the circulation during the period has been as great as that of the Bible itself. This tale of Bible times was blessed by His Holiness Leo XIII . . .
> MR. A. L. ERLANGER . . . realized the deep desire for a stage play based on the book . . . The success was instantaneous . . . The vogue of BEN-HUR

---

7   On this see especially Roberta E. Pearson and William Uricchio, "How Many Times Shall Caesar Bleed in Sport: Shakespeare and the Cultural Debate About Moving Pictures," *Screen*, 31 (1990), 243–262; rpt. in Uricchio and Pearson, *Reframing Culture*, 87–95 (on the 1908 American film of *Julius Caesar*), and, with abridgments, in *The Silent Cinema Reader*, ed. Lee Grieveson and Peter Krämer (London and New York: Routledge, 2004), 155–168. An amusing instance of the cultural pretentiousness that Shakespeare met with in Hollywood is the program for Warner Brothers' *A Midsummer Nights Dream* (1935), directed by William Dieterle and Max Reinhardt: "For the premiere in Beverly Hills, an elaborate program had been presented to each member of the audience, embossed on the cover of which were four golden plaques, each containing a well-known profile: the three Warner brothers and William Shakespeare." Quoted from David Niven, *Bring on the Empty Horses* (New York: Putnam, 1975), 30.

was due not only to the theme, the spectacle and the admirable acting but equally to Mr. Erlanger's foresight and wisdom in maintaining the fine and reverential treatment of its grand subject by the author.

A FEW YEARS SINCE – in the newer art of the motion picture – Mr. Marcus Loew undertook the tremendous enterprise of visualizing BEN-HUR . . . and now presents it as a Metro-Goldwyn-Mayer picture. The direction of the work was entrusted to Mr. Fred Niblo, with the aid of the most distinguished players of the screen and Metro-Goldwyn-Mayer's unrivaled art and technical resources.

MR. NIBLO has handled the story of BEN-HUR in motion pictures with all the tenderness and delicacy and dramatic power that the subject matter calls for. The most casual reader of the book or former patron of the spectacle knows the richness of the material and the splendor and poignancy of the romance for picturization. It is now offered with the happy confidence that this immortal story has been filmed to the continual delight of millions of theatergoers in every part of the world where the newer art holds sway.

These points were thought to be so important that they could be made again. The next text section of the program book ("The Production of 'Ben-Hur'") is equally emphatic about the transition of respectability from stage to screen:

TRADITION clusters around "Ben-Hur" as the most remarkable stage achievement of America. It is fitting that this well-grounded tradition is upheld by the Picture Spectacle, in its turn the capstone of the picturizing art.

"Ben-Hur" [on the stage] effected epochal changes . . . the nature of its action and the fineness of its handling called to the patronage of the Better Drama millions of persons whose training hitherto had been sharply opposed to the theatre.

. . . the causes of its vogue are not hard to seek, for it was great drama and great Spectacle in the historical setting of the birth of Christianity in the eastern half of the Roman Empire . . . Throughout its stage career "Ben-Hur" was wisely maintained at the level of its original excellence, elaboration, and reverent spirit . . .

The Greater Ben-Hur exceeds the stage play, even as the Newer Art that has the whole world for its picturizing, exceeds the older one.[8]

So the cinema demonstrated its seriousness as a new art form and in the process killed two birds with one stone. It presented well-established

8   The quotations are from the inside front cover and pages 5–6 of the souvenir booklet for *Ben-Hur* (New York: Metro-Goldwyn-Mayer, 1926).

topics that were educational and elevating but that did not neglect audiences' demands for thrills or spectacle. What better way to achieve such a goal than by putting classical Greeks and Romans and their biblical "relatives" on the screen – people whose status as the very founders of western civilization was known to all?[9]

2. Classical Educators and the Cinema

Educators quickly realized how important for their teaching and how attractive to their students the new "photo plays" could be. Teachers and scholars of classical antiquity became aware of the educational potential of film early on. In 1915, B. L. Ullman, professor of Latin at the University of Pittsburgh and editor of the widely read *Classical Weekly*, made the point emphatically:

> Moving pictures are an excellent means of showing that the Classics are not dead. The classical teacher not only makes Latin and Greek alive, but makes the Greeks and Romans seem like living beings (if he does not do so, he should). He contributes matters of lively interest to the life of to-day and he draws on the same life to make his subject alive. The circle is perfect. Here is where the cinematograph plays its part . . . An institution which seems to some only an evil may be turned into useful channels. I have heard several teachers complaining that their students do no work because they are at the 'Movies' much of the time after School hours. This is undoubtedly true and will remain true. There is no question that the cinematograph is to become an even more important factor in our civilization than it is . . . As classical teachers, let us seize an opportunity . . . the cause of the Classics will be greatly benefited, for the people as a whole will become familiar with classical life and history. It is to the advantage of the Classics that these [photo-]plays be seen by the greatest possible number of persons, and that more and more plays of this sort be produced.[10]

---

9   Eileen Bowser, *The Transformation of Cinema 1907–1915* (New York: Scribner, 1990), 128 and 255–256, respectively, mentions the 1910 version of *Elektra*, based on Richard Strauss's recent opera, and the Italian *Quo Vadis?* (1912), directed by Enrico Guazzoni, as examples of films that appealed to a better clientele, even though the production company of *Elektra* had advised distributors to "bill it like a circus."

10   B. L. Ullman, *The Classical Weekly*, 8 no. 26 (May 8, 1915), 201–202 (editor's letter). Ullman quotes a contemporary newspaper: "The classicists have a new ally. They have labored in vain to get the public to listen to them . . . , but now people are flocking by the thousand to the theater to see what they would not read or hear about in the classroom. Teachers may now be seen on a Saturday afternoon leading schoolboys who have refused to be driven" (202).

Ullman (1882–1965) was "one of the leading classical scholars in the world when he died" and had long been "preeminent as a teacher of teachers." Many of his numerous publications were intended to be "of practical application to those involved in classical pedagogy."[11] Ullman was an early champion of the cinema's engagement with antiquity, which he treated as a modern phenomenon worthy of serious attention from educators and scholars. In this way he lent considerable respectability to the new medium. Ullman's confidence in the cinema was restated in the same journal five years later, if from a more alarmist perspective, by another scholar of comparable authority. This was George Hadzsits (1873–1954), professor of Latin at the University of Pennsylvania and soon to become editor-in-chief of *Our Debt to Greece and Rome*, a book series of forty-four volumes published from 1922 to 1948. In the course of his professional life, Hadzsits made "substantial contributions to the development of classics in America," not least "through his energetic advocacy of classics as an important and enriching field of study."[12] In 1920, Hadzsits wrote about the state of classical education:

> The present status of our High School and College curricula but mildly reflects the menace of an ignorance almost incredible and indescribable . . . the comparatively brief time with difficulty snatched from other innumerable obligations for the joy of research is ill-spent, if there be no appreciation of such work in a world turning away from the totality of those things, of which each piece of research represents but a small fraction. The pathos of research work that does not gain a hearing will soon become bathos.

For classical education to continue successfully, Hadzsits called for "enlightenment on the subject of the value of the Classics, after which the will may assert itself to return to the Classics." One of the most effective ways to achieve this goal, he believed, was screenings of films on ancient topics:

> If these great films were exhibited in every High School, there would be a revival of interest which no other means would accomplish. After all, our work suffers from its fragmentary nature, and mere glimpses of reality

11   My quotations are from R. L. Den Adel, "Ullman, Berthold Louis," in *Biographical Dictionary of North American Classicists*, ed. Ward W. Briggs, Jr. (Westport: Greenwood Press, 1994), 659–661, at 659 and 660.
12   Quoted from Judith P. Hallett, "Hadzsits, George Depue," in *Biographical Dictionary of North American Classicists*, 246–247; quotation at 246.

through individual pages of Latin do not, in the nature of things, satisfy any normal or natural human craving. Great film spectacles, even though it may be said that their educational value is ephemeral, ought at least to arouse the slumbering synthetic process which alone can energize knowledge. Whatever historical inaccuracies may mar one or another of these great moving pictures, their value, on the whole, is incalculable in stimulating enthusiasm. In place of the mosaic representations of human life and its problems, extracted from one page, one paragraph, and even one sentence, a brilliant revelation is brought to mind and to eye of the totality of ancient life in all its vitality.[13]

It is a measure of his concern about the state of education that Hadzsits should have used a word with religious connotations in the title of his article ("Media of Salvation") in order to characterize a mass medium that not too long ago had suffered from the stigma of being low-class entertainment. At a time when classical studies and a classical education carried great prestige and had great influence on society, Ullman and Hadzsits were in the vanguard of elevating cinema culturally and of making film acceptable in the classroom.

3. The Cinema Profits from the Prestige of History and Scholarship

Film producers and advertising managers or directors of publicity campaigns like to call on scholars for the making or marketing of historical films. Recent examples are the involvement of a classical scholar from Harvard University as historical consultant for Ridley Scott's *Gladiator* (2000) and the exhibition *Troy Retold*, organized by a curator in the Department of Greek and Roman Antiquities at the British Museum in connection with Wolfgang Petersen's *Troy* (2004).[14] The prestige of scholars, producers hope, only enhances the prestige of their films, which often appear with hyperbolic claims to be correct in every detail

13   George Depue Hadzsits, "Media of Salvation," *The Classical Weekly*, 14 no. 9 (December 13, 1920), 70–71.
14   On these see Kathleen M. Coleman, "The Pedant Goes to Hollywood: The Role of the Academic Consultant," in *Gladiator: Film and History*, ed. Martin M. Winkler (Oxford: Blackwell, 2004), 45–52, and J. Lesley Fitton, "*Troy* and the Role of the Historical Advisor," in *Troy: From Homer's Iliad to Hollywood Epic*, ed. Martin M. Winkler (Oxford: Blackwell, 2006), 99–106. For another recent example cf. Paul Cartledge, "The Greeks for All? The Media and the Masses," in *Greek Art in View: Essays in Honour of Brian Sparkes*, ed. Simon Keay and Stephanie Moser (Oxford: Oxbow Books, 2004), 159–167.

or to be no less than history come alive. But historical or archaeological authenticity is usually absent from the screen for obvious reasons.[15] Nevertheless it is important for marketing strategies to claim that a film is accurate in its portrayal of the past and to let it be known that such accuracy was achieved with the guidance of acknowledged experts. Such claims may take a variety of forms.

The manual for a re-release of C. B. De Mille's *Cleopatra* (1934) advises theater owners to act by "following through full-force on the tried-and-proven exploitation stunts described on this page." "Arouse the kind of avid interest that sells tickets," the exhibitors are exhorted; the first strategy suggested to them is this:

> ANTIQUE DISPLAY: With the cooperation of a local museum or library, set up a lobby display of historic paraphernalia used by the ancient Egyptians and Romans. Exhibited material could include coins, figurines, scarabs and other crowd-stopping curios and antiques . . . surround the entire project with [film] stills and prominently placed credit cards.

The same page recommends to exhibitors to obtain "sponsorship of a men's fraternal organization or a group of society women" and to secure "the cooperation of a highly esteemed civic or society group," the latter for a fancy-dress ball "in the dazzling costumes of Cleopatra's Egypt and Caesar's Rome." Its proceeds are to be donated to charity.[16]

In 1951 MGM advertised Mervyn LeRoy's *Quo Vadis* with becoming modesty ("THIS IS THE BIG ONE!") and piety: "MGM feel privileged to add something of permanent value to the cultural treasure house of mankind."[17] These boasts drew attention to the film's giant size and to the significance of its story, which depicted the victory of Christianity over the "Antichrist" Nero. The studio's claims were bolstered by the extensive historical research done for the film by Hugh Gray, its historical advisor. A native of England, Gray had been educated at the universities of Louvain and Oxford. His notebooks for *Quo Vadis*, MGM

15 I have addressed, and provide further references to, this aspect of historical film in *"Gladiator* and the Traditions of Historical Cinema," in *Gladiator: Film and History*, 16–30, especially 16–24 (section entitled "Film and Historical Authenticity"). For pseudo-historical, i.e., mainly myth-based, films cf. my "Neo-Mythologism: Apollo and the Muses on the Screen," *International Journal of the Classical Tradition*, 11 (2005), 383–423, and my "Editor's Introduction" to *Troy: From Homer's Iliad to Hollywood Epic*, 1–19.

16 The quotations are from page 11 of the 1952 *Paramount Showmanship Manual* for *Cleopatra*.

17 The quotation is from Leslie Halliwell, *Halliwell's Filmgoer's and Video Viewer's Companion*, ed. John Walker, 11th edn. (New York: HarperCollins, 1995), 491.

announced, were to be donated to the University of Rome or the University of California at Los Angeles, presumably for the benefit of future scholars and researchers, academic or cinematic, in America or Europe.[18] But as has been plausibly observed: "Most of Gray's fact-filled notebooks went unread, for MGM had a film to shoot, not a lecture to give."[19]

The Big One deserved a big campaign. The studio suggested, among many other things, that theater owners turn to libraries, distributing "BOOK MARKS" in schools and public libraries (but also at beauty salons), to children for a coloring contest of drawings taken from scenes of the film ("You can run them off yourself for throw-aways to be distributed in elementary schools"), and to parents:

> EXPLOIT PARENTS' MAGAZINE MEDAL
> "Quo Vadis" won Parents' Magazine medal for extraordinary achievement. This award carries a lot of weight with parents, educators, P.T.A.'s, the clergy and the general public . . .
> MENTION the award or reproduce it in . . . all promotion intended to influence teachers, parents and the clergy . . .

A remarkable strategy, at least from today's perspective, is a "LATIN SAYINGS CONTEST":

> "Quo Vadis," which means "whither thou goest" [well, not exactly], is one of the many Latin expressions which have become part of the English language. Interest high school and local newspapers in a contest in which the reader translates the Latin expression. The first correct answers will win complimentary passes or promoted prizes.[20]

---

18   On this cf. Maria Wyke, *Projecting the Past: Ancient Rome, Cinema and History* (New York and London: Routledge, 1997), 139.

19   Quoted from Jon Solomon, *The Ancient World in the Cinema*, 2nd edn. (New Haven: Yale University Press, 2001), 217. Cf. Gray's own perspective as expressed in "When in Rome . . . ," *Hollywood Quarterly*, 10 no. 3 (1956), easily accessible now in *Hollywood Quarterly: Film Culture in Postwar America, 1945–1957*, ed. Eric Smoodin and Ann Martin (Berkeley, Los Angeles, and London: University of California Press, 2002), 345–353. *Hollywood Quarterly* was founded in 1945 and sponsored by the University of California and the Hollywood Writers Mobilization. An editorial note to Gray's article stated: "Mr. Gray was recently appointed an assistant professor in the Motion Picture Division of the Department of Theater Arts, University of California, Los Angeles." Gray (1900–1981) later became Professor of Film, Theater, Aesthetics, and Humanities at the same university and also taught at Loyola Marymount University in Los Angeles, whose Center for Modern Greek Studies he co-founded.

20   The quotations are from pages 10–11 of the MGM press book for a 1964 re-release of *Quo Vadis*.

To help out the probably Latin-less exhibitor, a list of twelve phrases and their translations or equivalents are given next, beginning with Caesar's *veni, vidi, vici* and ending with *non sequitur*. It does not follow from this and other such ingenious concoctions that they significantly advanced actual awareness of the past and its continuing influence on the present, but, at least while the film was playing in town, bad pagans and good Christians were on people's minds. The combination of history and religion is good for society and good for business, and studios were ready to rise to each occasion. The souvenir program of King Vidor's *Solomon and Sheba* (1959) informs its readers:

> Construction of Solomon's Temple posed many problems for Vidor's research staff, since many weeks had to be spent searching not only The Bible but also the works of all other authorities on the period to establish the exact dimensions mentioned. Translation of Biblical cubits and spans into modern terms . . . became a major project which had to be resolved before the architectural designers could begin their sketches. The Temple was built according to the description in the sixth chapter of I Kings in The Bible, King James Version. A very similar problem confronted the costume designers, who had to make certain that the hundreds of costumes, vehicles, weapons . . . and jeweled ornaments were absolutely authentic and would bring the picture full approval from Biblical scholars and historical experts.[21]

The capitals of certain key words or phrases, especially in the two occurrences of "The Bible" (not "the Bible," as most readers would expect), are revealing. They are meant to express reverence before sacred scripture and to signal exactitude in each detail.[22] The problems mentioned were,

---

21 Quoted from page 5 of the *Solomon and Sheba* souvenir program. On page 15 we are assured that the film is "A SCRUPULOUSLY FAITHFUL RE-ENACTMENT" and that "the producers . . . adhered to the original Biblical text . . . with scrupulous fidelity to the Biblical version." Cf. the similar assertion in the unpaginated program book of the MGM-Samuel Bronston production of Nicholas Ray's *King of Kings* (1961): "Bronston drew upon the learning of outstanding religious scholars, seeking authoritative counsel of all faiths in the preparation of the screenplay." This booklet next claims that Bronston discussed the film prior to production with Pope John XXIII. In this, however, he had been outclassed by LeRoy, who had his copy of the script for *Quo Vadis* blessed by Pope Pius XII; cf. Mervyn LeRoy with Dick Kleiner, *Take One* (New York: Hawthorn, 1974), 174. (LeRoy does not neglect to mention that the papal blessing was in Latin.) Bronston, however, later received the order of the Holy Sepulchre from the Vatican. The Polish remake of *Quo Vadis* (2001) by Jerzy Kawalerowicz had its premiere in the Vatican before Pope John Paul II.
22 The title of MGM's *Quo Vadis*, both on the screen and on posters, goes even further than this. The novel by Henryk Sienkiewicz and all earlier film versions had been *Quo Vadis?*

the text implies, solved splendidly. With such noble efforts, who could criticize the film and its picture of the past for one of the most amazing production credits ever given ("Orgy-Sequence Adviser: Granville Heathway") or for some unintentionally hilarious dialogue? (The latter includes a sensible warning against Sodomite patrols.) Still, viewers, and not only the scholars and experts, were more likely to give their full approval to the architectural design of Gina Lollobrigida's amazing brassiere than to any other absolutely authentic construction in the established exact dimensions.

Old Testament history and archaeology are difficult to reconstruct. Similar problems and, consequently, incentives to claim to have done the virtually impossible face filmmakers who turn to another subject of proven cultural respectability: Homer's *Iliad* and *Odyssey*, the founding texts of Western civilization. Films based on the myth of the Trojan War and the return of Odysseus have been a staple of cinema since the silent days. The steady progress of our archaeological knowledge about Bronze-Age Greece has inspired filmmakers to follow suit in their re-creations of pre-classical cities such as Troy, especially when they could show off their sets in color and on the wide screen: "In Olympian scope and vastness," as the trailer for Robert Wise's *Helen of Troy* (1956) proclaims. Warner Bros. promoted this epic by taking recourse to another powerful mass medium. In connection with some of the studio-produced television series, popular contract-actor Gig Young hosted *Behind the Cameras*, short but elaborate and carefully structured promotions of upcoming feature films. In three such segments – "The Look of Troy," "Interviewing Helen," and "Sounds of Homeric Troy" – Young points out the extensive research done for this not-to-be-missed film. Standing behind a model of the set of Troy, he informs his viewers:

> Here is a model of the city of Troy. Later on, you're going with our team of research workers and see how the ruins on the site of Troy were used to rebuild that city, the city of Helen and Paris, the city that Homer wrote about.

But the Bronze-Age city that Homer wrote about, if indeed there ever was a Homer who wrote down the *Iliad*, did not look anything like the city Young and the studio's researchers show their viewers. (These researchers presumably included Hugh Gray, one of the film's two credited screenwriters and one of its two credited story adaptors.) Rather,

(The Latin phrase is a question.) But the question mark is now missing because Romans did not use it. And the words themselves appeared capitalized as QVO VADIS (not QUO VADIS) in imitation of Roman inscriptions.

Warner Bros. rebuilt a city that was modeled on a completely different and historically and architecturally unrelated culture, that of Minoan Crete. Except for its walls, the studio's Troy could almost be a rather faithful reconstruction of Knossos, the largest and best-known Minoan site. Young also promises: "Later on we'll explore the ruins of ancient Troy," and documentary footage of archaeologists working on a major ancient site appears in the third installment. But this site is not Troy; it is not even in Asia Minor. Over the images of temples that had been built after the Bronze Age and of archaeologists discovering in the ground a statue too recent by centuries to date from the appropriate period, Young tells us: "Like the study of Troy itself, here is where preparation for the picture *Helen of Troy* had to begin, not in Hollywood but at the feet of ancient temples."

This statement is revealing, for it lays claim to the serious research demanded by dedication to authenticity and simultaneously informs us of the reverence with which such stringent demands were met. This is "a great moment in history, a great moment on the motion-picture screen," Young will soon tell us. But the images we see discredit every word we hear. And the same goes for the sounds we hear. Demonstrations of how studio technicians re-created the whistle of flying arrows, the clang of helmets and armor being struck by them, and the reverberations of bronze gates being battered all sound thoroughly convincing, but they are nevertheless inauthentic. Still, Young claims that *Helen of Troy* is making it possible for us to hear what has not been heard for "three thousand years." And when, at the very end, he holds up a modern translation of the *Iliad* ("This book was our challenge"), experts on the Bronze Age or Homer may be skeptical about the grandiose claims that Young has been making, but all other viewers will most likely have been as impressed as they were meant to be. Watching *Helen of Troy* is good for you. And cannot even the experts be thrilled by the spectacular looks of a Minoan Troy in WarnerColor and CinemaScope?[23]

---

23   Minoan architecture, especially its characteristic columns, came to be *de rigeur* for the "right" look of Troy on the screen. Examples are Mario Camerini's *Ulisse* (*Ulysses*, 1954) and Giorgio Ferroni's *La guerra di Troia* (*The Trojan Horse, The Trojan War*, or *The Wooden Horse of Troy*; 1961), Marino Girolami's *L'ira di Achille* (*Fury of Achilles*, 1962), and, most recently, John Kent Harrison's *Helen of Troy* (2003) and Petersen's *Troy* (2004). The columns in Harrison's television film are even fluted. But if Troy can look attractive in Minoan guise, so can other cities or buildings. The palaces of Phaeacian king Alcinous in Camerini's film, of King Eurytus at Oechalia in Vittorio Cottafavi's *La vendetta di Ercole* (*Vengeance of Hercules* or *Goliath and the Dragon*, 1960), and of Odysseus on Ithaca, Menelaus in Sparta, and Alcinous on Scheria in Andrey Konchalovsky's television film *The Odyssey* (1997) sport Minoan columns as well. Even the Moabite temple in Henry Koster's *The Story of Ruth* (1960) and the palaces of King Saul and the king of the Philistines in Ferdinando Baldi and Richad Poirier's *David e Golia* (*David and Goliath*, 1960) have Minoan-inspired columns. Examples could be added.

The final big-screen Roman epic before *Gladiator* was Anthony Mann's *The Fall of the Roman Empire* (1964). Its credit sequence prominently names highly respected historian Will Durant as its historical consultant, although Durant had originally declined to be involved in a production whose historical inaccuracies he considered excessive. But director Mann succeeded in changing Durant's mind. The film's souvenir program opened with "A Prologue by Will Durant" that is spread over no fewer than four pages. It was accompanied by a color photograph of a distinguished-looking Durant in coat and tie, standing on the gigantic set of the Roman Forum and holding open a copy of *Caesar and Christ* (1945), the volume on Roman history in his series *The Story of Civilization*. The last page of the souvenir book features an epilogue that is unsigned but worded in such a way that it could have come straight from Durant's pen. Durant also wrote the brief voice-over prologue that announces to viewers the significance of the film's subject. With this film and the story it tells we have reached the apex of classical antiquity in epic cinema: a momentous historical topic, the fall of Rome, that is comparable in its long-term impact on Western history and culture to the story of Jesus. Like films about the latter, the fall of Rome is presented as important to audiences' own days. Mann's film is meant to be seen as thrilling and appealing, edifying and instructive.[24]

4. *Spartacus*: Educators Selling History for Hollywood

During the silent era, Italy and the United States were the chief producers of cinematic "spectaculars," as they were then called. The early Italian spectacles about ancient Rome became popular hits in the U.S. and influenced American producers and directors.[25] Italian films about Spartacus exemplify this influence.[26]

The most famous of all films to tell the story of Spartacus, however, and the one to eclipse all others in popular memory, is the version produced by Kirk Douglas and directed by Stanley Kubrick. It conforms to

---

24 I provide a first assessment of its qualities in "Cinema and the Fall of Rome," *Transactions of the American Philological Association*, 125 (1995), 135–154.

25 Examples are Guazzoni's *Quo Vadis?*, Mario Caserini's *Gli ultimi giorni di Pompeii* (*The Last Days of Pompeii*, 1913), and Giovanni Pastrone's mammoth *Cabiria* (1914). On these see, e.g., Bowser, *The Transformation of Cinema 1907–1915*, 210–212 and 258. Bowser, 266–272, examines the emergence of the perception of film as an art form immediately after her discussion of film as spectacle.

26 These are listed in note 15 of my "Introduction" to the present book.

the basic narrative and stylistic patterns of historical cinema that were by then firmly in place, notwithstanding the complicated circumstances of its production and its social and political place in American culture. Made at gigantic expense, *Spartacus* had to reach the largest audiences possible. Its marketing campaign had to ensure the film's wide accept-ance, especially in the face of such controversial features as censorship and the blacklist. What better way to obtain such acceptance than to fall back on the tried and true?

It is not my intention here to trace the marketing of *Spartacus* in all its ramifications. Instead, I will turn to two examples which exemplify the selling strategies outlined above. Both were in the form of written contributions by respected scholars approached to raise the public's awareness of the film's educational and historical significance. One text, a study guide, was intended for high-school teachers. The other, a short historical essay for the film's souvenir program, addressed a smaller segment of the film's audiences, in particular professionals in positions to influence large numbers of people. Both texts were commissioned because of their authors' prestige.

4.1. *The Study Guide to* Spartacus

The idea of a guide for teachers to discuss with their students a film set in antiquity is something that Professor Hadzsits could have approved of. The author of the *Spartacus* guide was Joseph E. Mersand (1907–1981), chairman of the English Department at Jamaica High School in the state of New York and a well-known teacher of English, with bachelor's, master's and doctoral degrees from New York University. His academic specialty was modern drama, an area in which he published several anthologies and studies. His other areas of expertise were the teaching of English and general education. Mersand was a long-standing member of the National Council of Teachers of English and received its Distin-guished Service Award in 1979. In 1938 he had published the short article "Radio Makes Readers" in the *English Journal,* the NCTE's publi-cation for teachers in junior and senior high schools and middle schools. Mersand followed this with "Radio and Reading," a contribution to an essay collection called *Radio and English Teaching: Experiences, Problems, and Procedures,* published by the NCTE in 1941. These are only two of several of his essays on radio. Also in 1941, Mersand published a pamphlet entitled *What Do Our Students Think? Four Studies in Pupils' Reactions to Radio, Moving Pictures, Newspapers and Plays.* Three years before, he had written but not published an essay on "Facts and Fiction

About the Educational Value of the Moving Pictures," presumably using it for his later publications.

Mersand's guide to *Spartacus* appeared in a series of guides that had been published by the NCTE since 1935.[27] Co-founder and general editor of this series was William Lewin. The last page of the *Spartacus* guide ("EXTRAORDINARY ANNOUNCEMENT," 31) reminds readers that the NCTE had published Lewin's "pioneer monograph" *Photoplay Appreciation In American High Schools* in 1934. The NCTE now advertises its new monthly, *Mass Media Studies*, that will include *Photoplay*, *Drama*, *Television*, *Magazine*, and *Newspaper Studies* and "other mass media studies from time to time." The general editor of this new series will be Mersand. The rationale for his editorship and for the entire series is given as well (31):

> Dr. Mersand is a leader in the movement to include in the teaching of English a critical appreciation of America's mass media. The aim of this movement is to build "natural censorship" by developing independent critical judgment. It seeks to teach students to do better those worthwhile things they will do anyway.

The preceding pages of the *Spartacus* guide contained "Lewin's Unit in Photoplay Appreciation" (28–29), prepared under NCTE auspices, and a template of "Lewin's Photoplay Rating-Scale for Building a Critical Vocabulary of About 60 Words" (30). "Primary Objectives" of the former are (28):

1. Enjoyment of literature experiences through the medium of the theatrical motion picture.
2. Establishment of standards of taste in judging photoplays, as a phase of training in the right use of leisure.
3. Development of desirable ideals and attitudes.

The *Spartacus* guide exemplifies this approach and aids teachers in how to use the film in their classrooms.

With his impressive credentials and well-documented interest in modern media, Mersand had just the right background to promote the

---

27 *A Guide to the Study and Enjoyment of the Motion Picture SPARTACUS* (so page 3), *Photoplay Studies*, 25, no. 4 (August, 1960). The cover displays the film's title in its distinctive design and includes this information about the guide's author: "Prepared by Joseph Mersand, Ph.D. / Chairman, English Department, Jamaica High School, NY / Past President, National Council of Teachers of English." Below, numbers in parentheses identify the pages from which quotations of the guide are taken.

educational value of *Spartacus*. And he had been honored with the presidency of the NCTE the year before the film was released, as the guide's front cover does not neglect to inform readers.

Before we turn to the guide itself, it is instructive to examine the comments that Mersand's submission to the studio received from executives before it was revised for publication. Mersand described his approach to writing the guide in a memorandum of March 24, 1960, to Jeff Livingston of the "Office of Executive Co-ordinator of Sales & Advertising" for *Spartacus* at Universal's headquarters in New York City:

> I have spent a great deal of time (more than I usually spend) on the historical background, and on my essay on the significance of the Spartacus Rebellion. I kept in mind that when the film was shown in Washington at the N E A [National Education Association] meeting, you would be giving copies of the guide to each member, and they would all be teachers. I tried to impress them with the authenticity of the film and the guide.[28]

Livingston forwarded Mersand's memo the next day to Stan Margulies, the publicity director of the film's production company and a production assistant at Universal Studios. Margulies later became a well-known film and television producer. Livingston reported in a cover letter that the guide as submitted to him contained some "unnecessarily political" aspects. Margulies summarized his impression of Mersand's text in a memo to Livingston of April 5:

> Overall, I think it is a commendable effort. It sounds like all the other study guides, but I guess that's good. I felt it accomplished reasonably well the identification of Spartacus as a man worth all this attention. I am not an expert in the study guide field, but I assume that Mersand and Lewin are, so I will only comment on items relating directly to the film SPARTACUS, on which I am an expert.

Margulies' first such comment addresses the history of Spartacus from a rather anachronistic understanding of Roman historiography that has resurfaced repeatedly in modern times: "It has always been interesting to me that no contemporary historians ever wrote about Spartacus – possibly because they wanted to erase the memory of his rebellion?"

---

28 This and subsequent quotations from Mersand's guide and from Universal executives' reactions and comments are taken from materials on *Spartacus* collected in Boxes 33–39 of the Kirk Douglas Papers, deposited at the Wisconsin Center for Film and Theater Research, part of the Wisconsin Historical Society Archives in Madison, Wisconsin. The background materials on the film's souvenir program that will be quoted below come from this collection as well.

But the memory of his rebellion was *not* erased, not even by the Romans. (Cf. on this below.) More revealing is Margulies' reaction to another observation by Mersand because it addresses the fundamental dilemma that confronts all creative artists who deal with an insufficiently documented past:

> Mersand states . . . that the film modifies historical fact. I do not know if he is referring to the overall Crassus strategy or to the statement that Spartacus died in battle. It has always been assumed that he was killed in battle, but he was never identified and we felt perfectly justified in keeping him alive for the crucifixion outside the gates of Rome. When no accurate historical facts exist, it is difficult to say how or if they have been modified.

This is an important observation. Even the committed scholarly historians are often hard pressed to give an accurate portrayal of the past – to show, in the famous phrase of Leopold von Ranke, "how it essentially was" (*wie es eigentlich gewesen*) – in the absence of complete or consistent historical documentation.[29] We can only sympathize with the dilemma of filmmakers and other creative artists who must build a complete and consistent image of history on a combination of fact and fiction, of limited knowledge and imaginative reconstruction. So we understand Margulies' complaint about Mersand's characterization of Crassus and Gracchus:

> I would like Mersand to define better Crassus' feeling of "an awesome emptiness in life." He certainly does not feel this at the start of the picture, but rather is consumed by desire to restore Rome to the Patricians, with himself in command. Gracchus also does not feel "the same elusive emptiness." All our characters have positive motivations, and I think we should spell them out rather than relying on elusive, empty phrases.

We may grant Margulies that the film's Gracchus has positive motivations, but does Crassus, its villain? Margulies' own words about Crassus' desire for power seem to tell us otherwise. His assertion that all characters have only the best intentions is negated by the finished film. It is also evident that Margulies' characterization of Crassus and Gracchus is based solely on the dramatic underpinnings of the film's plot and has

---

29   For a thorough examination of Ranke's famous phrase from 1824, which became a kind of mythical dictum in its own right, see Stephen Bann, *The Clothing of Clio: A Study of the Representation of History in Nineteenth-Century Britain and France* (Cambridge: Cambridge University Press, 1984), 8–14. Bann, 10, quotes Ranke in the original.

nothing to do with history. The same is true when Margulies turns to Spartacus himself, but he reveals passion and commercial astuteness in his comments on Mersand's view of Spartacus:

> Mersand says, "Spartacus was just one more exponent of freedom and dignity." We don't want our leader denigrated. He was much more than *just another* exponent. He was perhaps the first leader of an organized rebellion, etc. etc. – a semantic difference but important in the total effect.

Historical evidence takes a back seat to a film that is being made because of its legendary or symbolic, not its historical, importance for the present. Margulies' "perhaps" is telling: Spartacus *may* have been important in history, but, whether he was or not, he *is* important now. When Margulies immediately turns to the political aspects of Mersand's text, Spartacus' importance as Margulies sees it becomes evident:

> I think we must be careful to relate our picture to the wide-spread, unassailable and noble human longing for freedom – and not be too specific in connecting it with African nationalism, subjugated peoples behind the Iron Curtain, etc. That is an inference I certainly hope many writers and reviewers will make, but I think they should say it, not us.

With this we can fully agree. Spelling out the modern overtones is an act of condescension, even in a study guide meant for teachers of those who need help with approaching a historical film. Margulies' criticisms of Mersand are shrewd and to the point. Almost half a century after they were made they still appear sensible. Margulies was not an expert in Roman history, but he *was* an expert in how to present it effectively to large audiences.

As a scholar and teacher of English, Mersand may have been an expert in the study-guide field, but he was not an expert in the Roman-history field. Nevertheless he delivered a substantial guide to a particularly complex historical episode – or better: to its modern popular retelling. The published version of the guide provides introductions to ancient Rome, Spartacus, and the film. Its first section ("The Rome of the Gladiators," 3–6) is representative of its overall approach (3):

> ROME, the glorious republic that it was, and the empire that it was to become, has been remembered through the ages for its almost indescribable splendor . . .
> The people of Rome – the ruling, noble patricians, and the richest of the plebeians – were people of high sentiments and great refinement. Their

tastes in dress, in food, in manners, were such as to dwarf most of what was to come after. Indeed, their love of luxury, the exquisiteness of their tastes, were to degenerate into decadence which led to the end of their civilization.

Mersand's mention of the eventual fall of Rome in connection with a story set at a time in history even before the establishment of the empire and more than half a millennium before the end of the Western Empire reveals the standard modern perception of the course of Roman history: high sentiments and excessive refinement lead to luxury, luxury leads to decadence, decadence leads to political ruin. These are easily understood simplifications of complex processes. Widely read novels like Edward Bulwer-Lytton's *The Last Days of Pompeii* (1834), Lew Wallace's *Ben-Hur: A Tale of the Christ* (1880), and Henryk Sienkiewicz's *Quo Vadis?* (1895, Nobel Prize 1905), and theatrical "toga plays" and "pyro dramas" ensured that these historical clichés remained in the popular imagination. Spectacular stage adaptations of *The Last Days of Pompeii* and *Ben-Hur* but also of works directly written for the theater like Robert Montgomery Bird's Spartacus play *The Gladiator* (1831) and Wilson Barrett's *The Sign of the Cross* (1895) also propagated this simplistic view of the Romans. Their clichéd plotlines found even wider audiences in screen epics.[30] Such films pit pagan decadence against Christian nobility of spirit. *Spartacus* belongs to this tradition, and it is not surprising that its prologue should refer to the triumph of Christianity or that Spartacus himself should have become Christ-like.

Simplified and distorted as such a perspective on Roman history is, it has some ancient authority to bolster it. In particular, the Roman historian Sallust dealt in his surviving monographs with crises that exemplify aspects of the moral, social, and political decline of the previously exemplary republic. Sallust, whom Mersand does not quote or name, points to refinement, riches, luxury, and avarice as decisive factors in its decline.[31] Nevertheless, to deduce from such moralizing a straight and inevitable historical path all the way to the end of Rome, and over the course of centuries to boot, is to take simplification too far.[32]

30 The anthology *Playing Out the Empire:* Ben-Hur *and Other Toga Plays and Films, 1883–1908: A Critical Anthology*, ed. David Mayer (Oxford: Clarendon Press, 1994), is a useful introduction to the topic.

31 Especially instructive is Sallust's overview of Roman history in *The Conspiracy of Catiline*, 6–13.

32 Alexander Demandt, *Der Fall Roms* (Munich: Beck, 1984), 695, lists no fewer than 210 reasons that scholars have adduced for the fall of Rome, many of them contradictory or mutually exclusive.

After mentioning, in good Sallustian fashion, the import of luxury goods, military conquests, and banquets, Mersand reaches a conclusion appropriate for the film to be studied (4–5):

> we know that we are concerned with a people who had carried the exquisiteness of living to a high point indeed – perhaps the highest in recorded history.
>
> Yet, as the people . . . developed their republic . . . and as the republic in turn fell to consuls who became dictators, and ultimately emperors, we know that there was at the core of the Roman civilization something rotten which in the end had to bring about its doom.
>
> We have not far to look for what that rottenness was. Historians and social scientists agree that it was slavery – the extreme luxury of the few depending for its existence on the labor extracted from the abject misery of the many – and the disdain of human dignity, which were the underlying causes of the fall of Rome.

The images of the credit sequence of *Spartacus* give us a powerful parallel to Mersand's point of view. Designer Saul Bass used imitations of Roman sculptures and Latin texts for a highly atmospheric opening. He ends on an aristocratic head reminiscent of the colossal statue of Emperor Constantine that is now in the Vatican Museums. It survives only in fragments. The head of Bass's statue crumbles into several pieces at the sequence's fade-out. The implication is obvious: Spartacus and his revolt eventually bring down the power of Rome.

We know that we are concerned here with a perspective that is a serious, if handy, distortion of historical truth. Historians and social scientists are the modern authorities whom Mersand invokes collectively to back up his assertions. But historians and social scientists do *not* agree that slavery was decisive for Rome's fall. Had this been the case – i.e., had slavery been such a powerful social and political force that it brought about the end of slave-holding societies or, in the case of the Romans, the end of an entire civilization – then slavery would have been one of the principal factors of historical causation, for all ancient and many later and modern societies had slaves.[33] But only the Romans are

---

33 Cf. the summary of Moses I. Finley, "Slavery and the Historian" (1979), in the corrected reprint in Finley, *Ancient Slavery and Modern Ideology*, expanded edn.; ed. Brent D. Shaw (Princeton: Wiener, 1998), 285–309, at 299: "In the context of universal history, free labour, wage labour, not slavery is *the* peculiar institution. For most of the millennia of human history in most parts of the world, labour power was not a commodity which could be bought and sold apart from, abstracted from, the person of the labourer." Finley alludes to Kenneth M. Stampp, *The Peculiar Institution: Slavery in the Ante-Bellum South* (1956; rpt. New York: Vintage, 1989).

popularly seen as evil slave drivers and exploiters who come to exactly the end they deserve. Mersand mentions the Roman custom of freeing slaves, but he refers to freedmen only in passing and only to add that many of them "were not free, in our modern sense" (5). No word about another aspect of ancient slavery: Christian Romans, the supposedly good and noble kind, owned slaves just as the evil pagans did. The Bible states so unequivocally, but many modern Christians do not wish to know.[34] If the triumph of one slave-holding religion, Christianity, over another slave-holding religion, Roman paganism, was unavoidable, then slavery cannot have been a factor. Nor can slavery alone make a society evil, for then the American Founding Fathers, great and revered figures all, would have been immoral as slave holders and hypocrites in their assertion that all men are created equal. The American republic, modeled chiefly on that of the Romans, could hold slaves and still consider itself righteous. So Mersand's perspective on Roman slavery is seriously flawed, even beyond the simplifications that a brief overview such as this one necessitates. But his view is entirely in keeping with that promoted in *Spartacus*, whose prologue reveals to us that "the [Roman] republic lay fatally stricken by the disease called human slavery." The decisive point for our understanding of the Rome which both film and guide show us is that what counts is not history but Hollywood. The proposition that the fall of Rome was a direct, if long delayed, consequence of the revolt of Spartacus is historically untenable.

After slavery, slave-gladiators. Mersand's description of gladiatorial games – "Gladiatorial fights to the death . . . the more inhumanly onesided the contests the better" (6) – are pithy, clichéd, and wrong.

---

34   Biblical references to Christians and their slaves are in the letters of St. Paul: *1 Cor.* 7.21 and 12.13, *Gal.* 3.28, *Eph.* 6.5–8; *Col.* 3.11 and 22, *1 Tim.* 6.1–2, *Tit.* 2.9–10, *1 Petr.* 2.18–25, and the entire letter to Philemon. On Paul see S. Scott Bartchy, *First-Century Slavery and the Interpretation of 1 Corinthians 7:21* (1973; rpt. Atlanta: Scholars Press, 1985), and Peter Garnsey, *Ideas of Slavery from Aristotle to Augustine* (Cambridge: Cambridge University Press, 1996), 173–190. Garnsey's immediately following two chapters are on the church fathers Ambrose and Augustine. Cf. also the old but still useful work by Paul Allard, *Les esclaves chrétiens: Depuis les premiers temps de l'Église jusqu'à la fin de la domination romaine en Occident*, 5th edn. (1914; rpt. Hildesheim and New York: Olms, 1974). See further Finley, *Ancient Slavery and Modern Ideology* (expanded edn.), 82–86 (adducing numerous works of scholarship), and the assessment by Shaw in his "Introduction" to Finley's work (44): "There is no longer much serious argument made in support of the amelioration of the conditions and status of individual slaves because of Christian ideas and beliefs, and, least of all, any fundamental change in the slave system itself . . . with the exception of scholars writing from a Christian viewpoint or, more recently, from a 'Religious Studies' perspective."

There is no mention that not all gladiators were slaves, that they did not always fight to the death, that many survived for years, some for decades, or that referees were usually present in the arena during fights.[35] No film shows us this, and neither does *Spartacus*. Mersand next turns to "Spartacus as a Theme in Literature" (7–8); this is followed by a plot summary of the film (9–10). Margulies' suspicion about Roman historians duly appears in the former: "Could it be that Rome wanted to erase the memory of this rebellion against its power and its way of life?" (7) But Crassus' and Gracchus' spiritual emptiness has vanished from the latter.[36] Mersand's next and final essay ("The Historical and Human Significance of Spartacus," 11–12) is fully in line with Margulies' wishes about the greatness of Spartacus: "The path of human freedom has been a long one and a hard one, but Spartacus stands forth as one of the giants in the fight for freedom and dignity" (11). This is why, according to Mersand, *Spartacus* neatly fits in the elevating tradition that has already "inspired countless artists and writers" to turn to Spartacus: "The film SPARTACUS is another such expression on a grand scale told in modern terms" (11). In keeping with Margulies' perspective, modern political analogies now appear only in understated terms. They do not obtrude on those who prefer to ignore current nationalism or Communism and only nudge those who wish to pick up on them (11–12):

> Today, people all over the world are throwing off the bonds of colonialism and proclaiming their freedom. A dozen new nations have arisen since

35   David S. Potter, "Gladiators and Blood Sport," in *Gladiator: Film and History*, 73–86, is a convenient introduction to this subject. For detailed information on all aspects of Roman gladiators see Marcus Junkelmann, "*Familia Gladiatoria*: The Heroes of the Amphitheatre," in *Gladiators and Caesars: The Power of Spectacle in Ancient Rome*, ed. Eckart Köhne and Cornelia Ewigleben; English edn. by Ralph Jackson (Berkeley and Los Angeles: University of California Press, 2000), 31–74, and *Das Spiel mit dem Tod: So kämpften Roms Gladiatoren* (Mainz: von Zabern, 2000). Cf. further Alison Futrell, *The Roman Games* (Oxford: Blackwell, 2006), 120–159 and 239–241 (notes), a chapter entitled "The Life of the Gladiator," with brief discussion of Spartacus at 125–129.

36   Only Crassus' victory over Spartacus was "an empty one" (13, in a section introducing the film's main characters). It may be due to an editorial oversight that Margulies' emphasis on the positive motivation of all characters in the film is contradicted on the same page by this statement about Batiatus, the owner of the gladiatorial school: his "major thought is how to enhance his fortune regardless of the price in human life." – On this page, as earlier on page 2, the aristocratic Roman ladies who appear at Batiatus' school are identified as "Helena Glabrus" and "Claudia Marius," an absurdity in regard to both Roman culture and Latin grammar. But Hollywood had already given us a foretaste with the tomb inscription "Marcellus + Diana Gallio" at the beginning of Delmer Daves' *Demetrius and the Gladiators* (1954).

World War II, and several independent nations will be formed in Africa this year or soon thereafter. Yet great as the progress toward human freedom has been, there are still hundreds of millions today who serve masters not of their choosing, but the whole story of human history informs us that eventually human subjection will reach the limit and the cry for human freedom will not be denied.

The story of Spartacus as retold in the film, we can deduce, exemplifies all this. Spartacus' moral and spiritual victory over Crassus foreshadows the great progress toward human freedom, while, by analogy, his defeat in battle and his death explain why human subjection will not reach the limit at which it can be overcome for a long time. For this, history has to await the arrival of Americans. In this way Mersand achieves a kind of chiaroscuro image of Rome. A strange mixed metaphor in the passage to be quoted next betrays Mersand's equivocation about Roman culture and history. Predictably, however, in the end he comes down on the expected side (13):

> Roman life, which we saw as through a page darkly, now assumes in SPARTACUS some of the grandeur of which so many poets and historians have written. But some of its cruelty and contempt for human life, and values other than our own, are equally clear. One comes away from SPARTACUS understanding why the slave revolt was so ruthlessly suppressed, and with the knowledge that the seeds of liberty, once sown on such fertile soil, would inevitably ripen into the destruction of the Roman Empire.

Spartacus as an exemplary history lesson: Mersand the educator echoes the perspective that Kracauer summarized in regard to the early French art films: Mersand's guide, too, is a "deliberate attempt to transform the cinema into an art medium on a par with the traditional literary media," as Kracauer put it. So we need not wonder that Mersand's praise of *Spartacus*, required as it is in such a commission, is on the same level as Gig Young's praise of *Helen of Troy*. *Spartacus* presents history and its meaning "in vivid scenes and colors" (12) and "with all the resources of the newest film techniques in sound, scenery and superb action" (11). Soon after, the guide reveals to us "Some Interesting Facts About the Production" (14–15), presumably supplied by the film's publicity staff. This section reveals the involvement of experts: "Professor Vittorio Novarese of Rome, one of the foremost authorities on ancient military history, was invited to supervise the authenticity of the production" (14), specifically of the final battle.[37] The battle sequence is described in logistical terms, both historically ("the classic full-scale tactical deployment of troops," 15) and cinematically ("Kubrick trained his movie army for six weeks prior to filming," 15). Where Young had boasted that viewers of *Helen of Troy* could for the first time in three millennia hear the authentic sounds of Homeric Troy, the guide emphasizes a comparable visual experience: "For the first time since Roman fighting formations actually terrorized the civilized world, audiences will view first-hand the unique formation which military experts call history's most efficient and deadliest" (15). The negative slant on the Romans as militarists trampling civilized countries under their boots again exhibits the standard inauthentic and illogical perspective on their history.

The next text sections in the guide present twenty "Questions for Discussion" (18) and suggest twenty "Activities and Projects" (20–23). Some of the questions restate the view of Roman history found on earlier pages, some others reinforce the idea that the screen brings history to new life:

> 2. Why do you think the Roman and Greek historians gave such a one-sided view of Spartacus?
> 12. Some historians have stated that Rome was destroyed by its own wealth. What evidence does the film show of its impending [!] doom?
> 20. What aspects of film technique make you feel that you are actually reliving the time of 73–71 B.C.?

The activities include readings (Howard Fast's novel, the film's source; Bird's play, Roman and modern historians), projects on Latin (as for *Quo Vadis*: "17. Words from the Latin language or Roman history frequently

---

37   On this sequence of *Spartacus* cf. "Training + Tactics = Roman Battle Success" and the contribution by Allen Ward, both elsewhere in this book. Novarese (1907–1983) had a long career in Italy and Hollywood as screenwriter, art director, second-unit director, assistant director, and costume designer on a wide variety of films with historical and contemporary settings and in various genres. Besides *Spartacus*, he worked on the following films set in antiquity: *Messalina* (*The Affairs of Messalina*, 1951), *La regina di Saba* (*The Queen of Sheba*, 1952), *L'amante di Paride* (*Loves of Three Queens* or *The Face That Launched a Thousand Ships*, 1954; a film for which Hugh Gray received story credit), *Nel segno di Roma* (*Sign of Rome* or *Sign of the Gladiator*, 1959), *La regina delle Amazoni* (*Colossus and the Amazon Queen*, 1960), *The Story of Ruth* (1960), *Cleopatra* (1963), *The Greatest Story Ever Told* (1965), *Masada* (1981; television film), and *Peter and Paul* (1981; television film). The titles reveal that imagination must have played at least as large a part as history in his reconstructions of the past. The study guide is silent on this side of Novarese's qualifications.

appear in our daily lives," 23), on the Roman army, and on Roman "organizing ability" as the basis of its rule over "the western world" (22). The last suggestion is once again the expected one (23):

> 20. Despite all her power, for several hundred years, Rome was finally beaten by people whom she called "barbarians." Study the causes of Rome's downfall in some standard history text, and report to the class.

A brief bibliography (25) and additional information on some of the filmmakers (26) round out the guide. Illustrations, which appear throughout, are mainly film stills, a few publicity photographs, and paintings of the stars (16–17) as "depicted by REYNOLDS BROWN, distinguished American artist, now working in Hollywood" (16).

My description of Mersand's guide will lead those familiar with Roman culture and history to a verdict not quite as positive as Margulies' had been. Specifically, Mersand's emphasis on the historical background of Spartacus is disappointing, although we should keep in mind that Mersand was not a historian or classical scholar and did not write for historians or classical scholars – just as *Spartacus* was not made for them. But Margulies' other point about the guide – that it is like all other such guides – might give us pause. Is the *Spartacus* guide representative of the level of media education in or around 1960? Is this all there was? Or are we demanding more than any educator could deliver, then and now, within the constraints of limited space and under a studio's or production company's pressure? Should we be grateful to Lewin and Mersand, dedicated educators as they clearly were, for their pioneering work in integrating new media, especially film, into their classrooms – even if these are media of salvation neither for history nor for the teaching of history? Regardless of how we approach or answer such questions, the *Spartacus* guide remains instructive today. It is a revealing example of how and how not to present the distant past in the age of mass media, of the marketing of history as cultural commodity, and of what we could call, with Walter Benjamin, the "aura" of a work of popular art.[38]

4.2. *The Ivy League Meets* Spartacus

A different segment of the audience was to be reached with program or souvenir books, a long-established part of the marketing of classy, expen-

---

38   Cf. Walter Benjamin, "The Work of Art in the Age of Mechanical Reproduction," in *Illuminations*, ed. Hannah Arendt, tr. Harry Zohn (1968; new edn. New York: Schocken, 1969; rpt. 1986), 217–251.

sive, and otherwise memorable films, as we have seen. The one for *Spartacus* is an exceptionally handsome specimen. Unlike others, this one names its editor: none other than Margulies.[39] It is in hardcover and contains numerous lavish illustrations: color photos, drawings, diagrams, a large fold-out, and essays on various aspects of the film and its theme. Among them is a two-page outline of gladiatorial games: "We Who Are About To Die . . . ," with the sub-headings "Ancient Gladiators" and "Modern Gladiators." The book emphasizes the contributions of the film's historical and technical advisor among profiles of the filmmakers, production heads, technicians, and cast. The essays are short, and there are only a few. A four-page illustrated "Portrait of a Production" opens the book; it is immediately followed by a three-page essay on the film's historical background. The essay's title and author are given as follows:

SPARTACUS, REBEL AGAINST ROME by C. A. Robinson, Jr., *David Benedict Professor of Classics, Brown University*

Charles Alexander Robinson, Jr. (1900–1965) was the son of a professor of classics at Princeton University and held B.A. and M.A. degrees from Princeton. At Princeton, he had won fellowships to the American School of Classical Studies in Athens and the American Academy in Rome. Robinson taught at Brown University for over thirty-five years. His scholarship was chiefly on Alexander the Great, ancient history, and Hellenistic Greece. The year he died, the Classics Department inaugurated the annual Charles Alexander Robinson, Jr., Memorial Lecture, "delivered by a distinguished, senior scholar on a topic of broad interest to scholars, students, and community members at Brown," as the department's website describes it. By all accounts, Robinson was a dedicated, successful, and inspiring teacher and a distinguished scholar.[40] Where Mersand was the right man for the study guide, Robinson was the right choice for the souvenir book, lending the weight of his academic authority to a part of the marketing campaign that was to reach especially important people. Robinson "was very pleased to be involved in this opportunity to spread the word about ancient history."[41] His participa-

---

39 *Spartacus: The Illustrated Story of the Motion Picture Production,* ed. Stan Margulies (Bryna Productions and Universal Pictures, 1960).

40 Cf. John Rowe Workman, "Robinson, Charles Alexander, Jr.," in *Biographical Dictionary of North American Classicists,* 527–528. The immediately preceding entry is on Robinson's father.

41 E-mail communication of March 7, 2006, to me from his son Frank Robinson, Cornell University.

tion in the promotion campaign for *Spartacus* is a telling example of an American academic's involvement with an epic film and an equally revealing example of what may happen in the process.

A letter of February 15, 1960, written by Livingston from Universal's office in New York to Robinson in nearby Providence and copied to Margulies and other executives, describes the studio's intent:

> The purpose of the article is to establish the historical importance of the story unfolded in the film, SPARTACUS, so that the readers of your article will be convinced that the film is culturally significant and not just simple entertainment.

Livingston next reminds Robinson that in exchange for his compensation Universal will be sole owner and copyright holder of the article "for use in any manner the Company desires toward the advertising and publicizing of the film." Livingston adds: "With your approval the article may be edited and used in shorter forms." Its intended readers are "newspaper editorial writers, columnists and magazine writers, film reviewers, educators and high level opinion-makers – whatever they are." Then Livingston comes to the most important point:

> The article should establish that the story of Spartacus is one of the great and heroic stories of the pre-Christian era, little known perhaps, because the rulers of those days wanted to and almost succeeded in blotting out this outstanding episode in the story of man's continual struggle for freedom. You might want to write about the classes of society existing in Spartacus' world, previous and subsequent slave revolts, etc. If you feel that Spartacus' revolt contributed to the downfall of the great Roman Empire, please emphasize this; if it can be said that this revolt was the first *organized* fight for freedom, that would be good; if Spartacus as an individual can be properly compared to other great, noble and well-known figures in history, that would also be good.

Understandably, Livingston, like Margulies, wants to give the slave revolt and its leader as much historical importance as possible, and so the specter of the fall of Rome appears again. Livingston and Margulies favor the view that Spartacus came close to altering the course of history forever. Livingston continues: "It might be amusing to speculate on what changes there might have been in world history if Spartacus had defeated Crassus." Robinson is unlikely to have found such speculation amusing, for he does not ask any *What if . . . ?* question in his essay. But then, Livingston only offers a suggestion. Before requesting a preliminary outline from Robinson, Livingston adds: "More than anything else, it is important that the article convey the fact that the story of Spartacus is essentially true and historically important."

The last sentence quoted presents us with the heart of the matter in regard to the cinema's portrayal of history, not least in the telling words *fact* and *story* and the way Livingston used them. Was he aware that both appear as if in opposition to each other? Does not the phrase *essentially true* indicate that the film's story is and must be partly fictional, even if only in minor aspects or details? But where, in any portrayal of the past, does the fictional remain inessential or become separable from the factual? Where, if at all, does the factual remain unaffected by the fictional? Such truth as *Spartacus* or any film contains is not so much essentially true as only approximately true.

It is difficult to believe that Livingston or Margulies did not realize that historical films cannot keep fiction out of their plots. But their chief duty was not to history but to Hollywood. The best strategy they could adopt was to pretend that fact and fiction could be successfully fused. In this, Hollywood marketers are not completely wrong and could point to a weighty ancient authority if they knew of it. None other than Aristotle had broken a lance for the truth of fiction, for the superiority of myth over history. In a well-known passage of his *Poetics*, Aristotle contrasts historiography and poetry, as he calls fiction:

> The poet and the historian differ [in that] one relates what has happened, the other what may happen. Poetry, therefore, is a more philosophical and a higher thing than history: for poetry tends to express the universal, history the particular.[42]

To Aristotle, myth or fiction as it was presented on the classical Greek stage reveals the essential, while the underlying significance of history has to be abstracted from the individual event to make it, in Livingston's words, "historically important." Both fact and fiction profit from being important. As marketers might argue and as Aristotle might understand, if facts or historical characters lack significance, it is necessary and defensible to impart it to them.

Academic authors usually look with skepticism on anyone editing or shortening their work, even if such editors are their fellow scholars. But Robinson agreed, and his text was indeed revised and condensed.[43] He obliged Livingston with the outline requested in a letter he wrote on

---

42   Aristotle, *Poetics* 9.2–3 (=1451b1–7); quoted from S. H. Butcher, *Aristotle's Theory of Poetry and Fine Arts*, 4th, corrected, edn. (1911; rpt. New York: Dover, 1951 and later), 35.
43   Compare the composite of Robinson's original essay and the published version elsewhere in this book.

March 12. The most important part of his outline was its last paragraph, for it elicited vehement disagreement from Margulies, to whom Livingston forwarded it. After summarizing what aspects of Roman history and historiography he would address in his article on Spartacus, Robinson wrote:

> Conclusion. The terrible war for freedom did result in the improvement of the condition of slaves. And ultimately the Roman Empire settled down to a long era of peace and prosperity.

Margulies reacted to this in a memo to Livingston of April 6. In general, Margulies found Robinson's outline "comprehensive and slanted from the proper point of view" – a revealing characterization not so much of Robinson as of himself. But Robinson's conclusion was enough to alert Margulies that not all was well:

> With one exception! His conclusion is all wrong for us, I believe! His state-ment that Rome settle[d] down to a long period of peace and prosperity and that the slaves had better working conditions sounds like a dismissal of the Spartacus uprising. The rebellion is then merely a disease which was cured and the patient was only bothered temporarily. Our conclusion, if it does not distort history too much and if Robinson will go along, is that Spartacus set in motion a chain of events that led to the fall of Rome and that is why he is remembered – an early important figure in the never-ending fight, etc.
>   Okay?

Margulies' outburst at the beginning of this passage reveals his and the studio's own slant on history, and his phrase *wrong for us* (not: *wrong about history*) gives this slant away. Spartacus is less a historical figure than a culturally significant one and must be presented from the correct point of view. Margulies shrewdly picks up on Robinson's opinion of Spartacus from just two short sentences, and he is fully justified in his worry about Robinson's view of the historical importance of Spartacus. Something has to change. As editor of the book in which Robinson's essay is to appear, Margulies will see to it that Spartacus is shown in a different light, whether it distorts history too much or not.

Robinson did not see Margulies' objection. He adhered to his outline and revealed his view of the significance of Spartacus' revolt in the con-cluding paragraphs of his essay:

> The war was over, but the memory of the terrible fear it had instilled lasted on. Steadily the Romans improved the living conditions and treat-

ment of their slaves. More free men were required by law to be hired on the great plantations to lessen the danger of large slave concentrations and revolts. Six short years after Spartacus' death, there was born in southern Italy a son of a freedman who was destined to be one of Rome's greatest and most wonderful poets. This was Horace, an ornament of the Augustan Age together with Virgil and Livy. The freeing of slaves became a common custom at Rome, until finally the clever and able freedmen filled up the Roman imperial bureaucracy. With the establishment of the Emperors, however, foreign conquests came pretty much to an end, and with them the capture of prisoners of war and their enslavement. Slavery thenceforth counted for less and less in the imperial economy, for housebred slaves are notoriously expensive. Still, the institution continued and was not vigorously attacked in antiquity until the triumph of Christianity.

Spartacus lost his bid for freedom, his army of oppressed malcontents, which he so skillfully organized, was utterly destroyed, and everyone tried to forget. A terrible episode in history had come to an end. But further generations of slaves could be grateful for the heroic sacrifice which made their own lot better. And the generality of mankind, forty years after Spartacus, was able to settle down with the Emperor Augustus to a period of prosperity never before equaled and to an era of peace that is thus far the longest on record.[44]

Robinson did not hesitate to refer to the organizational skills of Spartacus, for which the historical record provides sufficient evidence. But he did not see Spartacus' revolt to have "contributed to the downfall of the great Roman Empire," as Livingston had put it. Nor does Robinson compare Spartacus to any "other great, noble and well-known figures in history." Instead, the only effect that Spartacus' revolt appears to have had is that the fate of slaves improved – not so much because "everybody wanted to forget" (a dubious generalization that Robinson might have omitted) but because the Romans remembered, as Robinson correctly states in the first sentence of his conclusion. Ancient sources show that Spartacus was anything but forgotten.[45] A modern historian concludes:

---

44   For an almost contemporary parallel to Robinson's statement about the improvements in the slaves' conditions after Spartacus cf. the conclusion of Jean-Paul Brisson, *Spartacus* (Paris: Le club français de livre, 1959), 243–252 ("Le déclin de l'esclavage antique et l'héritage de Spartacus").

45   Cicero, *On the Response of the Haruspices* 26 and *Philippics* 4.15; Horace, *Odes* 3.14.19 and *Epodes* 16.5; Lucan, *Pharsalia* 1.43 and 2.554, the latter following mention of Crassus; Claudian, *Against Rufinus* 1.255. While gladiators were being subdued after an unsuccessful attempt to escape from Praeneste (Palestrina) in 64 A.D., the common people were immediately reminding each other of Spartacus (Tacitus, *Annals* 15.46.1). As late as 393 A.D., a Roman senator thought of Spartacus when twenty-nine Saxons committed

it is undeniable that the memory of the slave leaders, kept alive for generation after generation, long reminded slave-owners of events which were
not to be repeated . . . But it was Spartacus who became the most powerful symbol of the dangers slaves posed to free society and of the need therefore for constant vigilance . . . By the time of Horace, Spartacus had
become one of Rome's canonical enemies of the past, . . . assuming mythical proportions.[46]

So the presentation of Spartacus as promoted in the film is historically
untenable, although it still persists. Producer and star Kirk Douglas
restated it himself decades later: "Rome was ashamed; this man had
almost destroyed them. They wanted to bury him."[47] Remembrance of
Spartacus does not fit a story in which the Romans systematically denied
him a place in history. Nor is the Roman Empire in any danger of falling,
for the only chain of events that, according to Robinson, Spartacus set
in motion was to have made the slaves' lot somewhat better rather than
to have made the Romans' lot decidedly worse. On the contrary, the
Romans came to enjoy unprecedented "peace and prosperity" instead of
being punished for their inhumanity.

Apparently, to Margulies (and Livingston) the general Roman prosperity that Robinson emphasizes in his references to two famous good
Romans, Horace and Augustus, unduly overshadowed the achievement
of Spartacus. After carefully going over Robinson's text, Margulies sent
another memo to Livingston on April 28, in which he presents his "con-
structive criticism." He is correct in his main point: "I still feel the major
lack in the piece is a unifying point-of-view." Margulies was to address
this lack with considerable efficiency. Robinson dealt with history,
Margulies is concerned with the present: "Seriously, I do feel very

collective suicide rather than fight in the gladiatorial games he was putting on (Symmachus, *Letters* 2.46). See further sources in Keith R. Bradley, *Slavery and Rebellion in the
Roman World, 140 B.C.–70 B.C.* (Bloomington and Indianapolis: Indiana University Press,
1989; rpt. 1998), 169 note 8, and Zvi Yavetz, *Slaves and Slavery in Ancient Rome* (New
Brunswick and Oxford: Transaction Books, 1988; rpt. 1990), 106–110.

46   Bradley, *Slavery and Rebellion in the Roman World, 140 B.C.–70 B.C.*, 131.

47   Kirk Douglas, *The Ragman's Son: An Autobiography* (New York: Simon and Schuster,
1988), 304. For a far older and different assessment, although one reached from a general
view of Spartacus that Douglas could easily share, see Charles Creighton Hazewell, "Spartacus," *The Atlantic Monthly*, 1 no. 3 (January, 1858), 288–300, at 293 (note): "These
ravages [of Spartacus' men in Southern Italy] seem to have made a great impression on
the Romans, and were by them long remembered." This text is a historical survey and
virtual hagiography of Spartacus as noble leader and military genius by a well-known and
popular American journalist and editor.

strongly that in the first page there must be some relation between Spartacus and today" as a "spring-board to bridge the gap between a 20th century reader and the years before Christ."[48] This link could be forged in several ways, of which Margulies lists three. One of them puts Spartacus firmly into the course of American history:

> This is not a natural connection, but I think it might be handled – to relate the upcoming centennial of the Civil War to Spartacus. This approach might concentrate on the historic American drive for freedom, including the Boston Tea Party, Paul Revere, Valley Forge, Lincoln, etc.

History, this implies, is best understood from one's own perspective, not from that of the people whose history is being told. In this particular case the connection is indeed not natural, but it fits Margulies' general strategy.[49] More importantly, it echoes, if unwittingly and not in every respect, the famous thesis of historian Benedetto Croce that all true history is contemporary history. Croce's analysis is worth remembering in our context, and I quote those of its parts that most directly shed light on historical cinema:

> 'non-contemporary' or 'past' history, if it really is history, that is to say, if it means something and is not an empty echo, is also *contemporary* . . . the condition of its existence is that the deed of which the history is told must vibrate in the soul of the historian . . . Thus if contemporary history springs straight from life, so too does that history which is called non-contemporary, for it is evident that only an interest in the life of the present can move one to investigate past fact. Therefore this past fact does not answer to a past interest, in so far as it is unified with an interest of the present life . . .

---

48   Robinson actually made such a connection at the beginning of his essay. Either Margulies erred, or there was another (unpreserved?) version of Robinson's text.

49   And not only his. To show the past by emphasizing its meaning for the present is a virtually necessary narrative and artistic strategy. In the case of *Spartacus*, the following words by composer Alex North express it directly: "The story . . . has something to say about the world which existed then and which still exists." And: "I decided . . . to conjure up the atmosphere of pre-Christian Rome . . . in terms of my own contemporary, modern style – simply because the theme of *Spartacus*, the struggle for freedom and human dignity, is every bit as relevant in today's world as it was then. I wanted to write music that would interpret the past in terms of the present." Quoted from Sanya Shoilevska Henderson, *Alex North: Film Composer: A Biography* (Jefferson and London: McFarland, 2003), 131; source references at 246 notes 5–6. Henderson, 129–158 and 245–246 (notes), examines the score of *Spartacus* in detail.

I have recalled these forms of historical technique in order to remove the aspect of paradox from the proposition that 'every true history is contemporary history.'[50]

Related to this point is Margulies' criticism of Robinson's overview of the history of slave revolts before Spartacus. Livingston suggested to Robinson to include such an overview, and Robinson did. But Margulies does not want to have it divert attention from Spartacus:

I think we have to be careful not to give too many details or too much attention to the rebellions of Eunus and Salvius. I don't want to ignore or distort history (heaven forbid) and I note that Robinson in several places says that Spartacus' rebellion was the best organized and the best led – but I think I would like to go past these earlier uprisings a little quicker and thus give the impression that Spartacus was really the key man.

Margulies' parenthetical exclamation and its immediate context are apt to appear amusing today, but they merit attention. We can agree that a short essay like Robinson's should not lose itself in "too many details" like those about Eunus and Salvius, of whom most readers and filmgoers will never have heard. Nor will they have cared to learn about them. So Margulies is right after all, and we may believe him when he says that he cares about history, if perhaps not as much as he cares about *Spartacus* and his obligation to promote the film in the best way he can. But what about his juxtaposition of *impression* and *really?* Do not these terms imply an incompatibility, or can impression and reality be reconciled? The dilemma that we may glimpse behind these words actually surfaces when Margulies follows the quotation above with this suggestion: "I'd like a more dispassionate observer than I [*sic*] to evaluate this."

Neither Eunus nor Salvius nor Athenion and not even Spartacus' own fellow leader Crixus, all of whom Robinson mentions in his essay, made it into the published version, which kept a closer focus on Spartacus. Robinson's title ("Spartacus – Rebel or Hero?") was changed to "Spartacus, Rebel Against Rome," an improvement because Robinson never sufficiently addressed his own question. The new title is pithy, to the point, and historically accurate. But more important is what happened to Robinson's conclusion. In the published version it appears significantly condensed:

50   Benedetto Croce, *History: Its Theory and Practice*, tr. Douglas Ainslie (1921; rpt. New York: Russell and Russell, 1960), 12.

The war was over, but the memory of the terrible fear it had instilled lasted on. Steadily, the Romans improved the treatment of their slaves, and the freeing of slaves became a common custom.

Spartacus lost his bid for freedom, his army of oppressed malcontents was utterly destroyed, and everyone tried to forget. A terrible episode in history had come to an end. But further generations of slaves could be grateful for the heroic sacrifice which made their own lot better.

And the generality of mankind, forty years after Spartacus, was able to settle down to a period of prosperity never before equaled, and to an era of peace that is thus far the longest on record.

Gone are the good Romans Horace and Augustus and most of the details on Roman history. Gone also is Christianity. But is the new conclusion "slanted from the proper point of view"? Not quite, for we read only that Spartacus and the slaves lost and that their main legacy was the improvement in the lot of future slaves. The Roman Empire does not fall. On the other hand, the statement that freeing slaves became a common custom *is* a slant, an overstatement in its hint that slavery came to be seriously diminished. The Augustan peace and prosperity in Robinson's earlier version, from which primarily the ruling Romans profited, have now been extended to all – thanks to Spartacus. Spartacus, it is implied, may not have been a cause for the fall of Rome, but he and his Christ-like death for dignity and freedom represent the first link in a chain of improvements in mankind's lot that extends from ancient Rome to modern America. This chain could not have been forged if *Spartacus* had not acquired, in tried and true Hollywood fashion and sanctioned by the prominent support of prestigious figures like Mersand and Robinson, the seal of quality: "culturally significant and not just simple entertainment." Partly because of their contributions, the film is not merely an epic spectacle but has become an uplifting and educational lesson in history and morality. *Spartacus* is good for you. We may be reminded of the souvenir book of the silent *Ben-Hur*, part of whose text fits *Spartacus* like a glove. With only a few minor adjustments, it could read like this:

A FEW YEARS AGO Mr. Kirk Douglas undertook the tremendous enterprise of visualizing SPARTACUS and now presents it as a Bryna–Universal picture. The direction of the work was entrusted to Mr. Stanley Kubrick, with the aid of the most distinguished players of the screen and Universal's unrivaled art and technical resources.

MR. KUBRICK has handled the story of SPARTACUS with all the tenderness and delicacy and dramatic power that the subject matter calls for. The most casual patron knows the richness of the material and the splendor and poignancy of the romance. It is now offered with the happy confidence that this immortal story has been filmed to the continual delight of millions of theatergoers in every part of the world where the new art holds sway.

The Principal Ancient Sources
on Spartacus

EDITOR'S NOTE: The Greek historians Plutarch and Appian provide us with the longest and best-known accounts of the rebellion of Spartacus (73–71 B.C.). They appear as the first of the translations included here. Roman historians follow according to their authors' chronology; only the most important passages are included. The ancient sources on the Roman slave wars and on Spartacus are available in translation in the following works: Thomas Wiedemann, *Greek and Roman Slavery* (1981; rpt. New York and London: Routledge, 2004); Zvi Yavetz, *Slaves and Slavery in Ancient Rome* (New Brunswick and Oxford: Transaction Books, 1988; rpt. 1990); *Spartacus and the Slave Wars: A Brief History with Documents*, ed. Brent D. Shaw (Boston and New York: Bedford / St. Martin's, 2001). Patrick McGushin, *Sallust: The Histories*, vol. 2 (Oxford: Clarendon Press, 1994), provides the fragments on Spartacus from Book 3 of Sallust's lost *Histories* (translations: pages 34–37 and 39; detailed notes: pages 133–136). His and Shaw's translations incorporate "major reconstruction" (McGushin, 119) of some fragments. These reconstructions and other words or phrases surviving in the fragments without immediate context are not included here.

All translations are my own except those of passages by Plutarch, Appian, and Florus. These are taken, respectively, from *Plutarch's Lives*, tr. Bernadotte Perrin, vols. 3 and 5 (Cambridge: Harvard University Press / London: Heinemann, 1916 and 1917); *Appian's Roman History*, tr. Horace White, rev. E. Iliff Robson, vol. 3 (Cambridge: Harvard University Press / London: Heinemann, 1913); and *Lucius Annaeus Florus: Epitome of Roman History*, tr. Edward Seymour Forster (Cambridge: Harvard University Press / London: Heinemann, 1929). Translators' notes have been omitted. My editorial additions appear in square brackets.

1. Plutarch (Early Second Century A.D.)

Crassus 8–11

8. The insurrection of the gladiators and their devastation of Italy, which is generally called the war of Spartacus, had its origin as follows. A certain Lentulus Batiatus had a school of gladiators at Capua, most of whom were Gauls and Thracians. Through no misconduct of theirs, but owing to the injustice of their owner, they were kept in close confinement and reserved for gladiatorial combats. Two hundred of these planned to make their escape, and when information was laid against them, those who got wind of it and succeeded in getting away, seventy-eight in number, seized cleavers and spits from some kitchen and sallied out. On the road they fell in with waggons conveying gladiators' weapons to another city; these they plundered and armed themselves. Then they took up a strong position and elected three leaders. The first of these was Spartacus, a Thracian of Nomadic stock, possessed not only of great courage and strength, but also in sagacity and culture superior to his fortune, and more Hellenic than Thracian. It is said that when he was first brought to Rome to be sold, a serpent was seen coiled about his face as he slept, and his wife, who was of the same tribe as Spartacus, a prophetess, and subject to visitations of the Dionysiac frenzy, declared it the sign of a great and formidable power which would attend him to a fortunate issue. This woman shared in his escape and was then living with him.

9. To begin with, the gladiators repulsed the soldiers who came against them from Capua, and getting hold of many arms of real warfare, they gladly took these in exchange for their own, casting away their gladiatorial weapons as dishonourable and barbarous. Then Clodius the praetor was sent out from Rome against them with three thousand soldiers, and laid siege to them on a hill which had but one ascent, and that a narrow and difficult one, which Clodius closely watched; everywhere else there were smooth and precipitous cliffs. But the top of the hill was covered with a wild vine of abundant growth, from which the besieged cut off the serviceable branches, and wove these into strong ladders of such strength and length that when they were fastened at the top they reached along the face of the cliff to the plain below. On these they descended safely, all but one man, who remained above to attend to the arms. When the rest had got down, he began to drop the arms, and after he had thrown them all down, got away himself also last of all in safety. Of all this the Romans were ignorant, and therefore their

enemy surrounded them, threw them into consternation by the suddenness of the attack, put them to flight, and took their camp. They were also joined by many of the herdsmen and shepherds of the region, sturdy men and swift of foot, some of whom they armed fully, and employed others as scouts and light infantry.

In the second place, Publius Varinus [i.e., Varinius], the praetor, was sent out against them, whose lieutenant, a certain Furius, with two thousand soldiers, they first engaged and routed; then Spartacus narrowly watched the movements of Cossinius, who had been sent out with a large force to advise and assist Varinus in the command, and came near seizing him as he was bathing near Salinae. Cossinius barely escaped with much difficulty, and Spartacus at once seized his baggage, pressed hard upon him in pursuit, and took his camp with great slaughter. Cossinius also fell. By defeating the praetor himself in many battles, and finally capturing his lictors and the very horse he rode, Spartacus was soon great and formidable; but he took a proper view of the situation, and since he could not expect to overcome the Roman power, began to lead his army toward the Alps, thinking it necessary for them to cross the mountains and go to their respective homes, some to Thrace, and some to Gaul. But his men were now strong in numbers and full of confidence, and would not listen to him, but went ravaging over Italy.

It was now no longer the indignity and disgrace of the revolt that harassed the senate, but they were constrained by their fear and peril to send both consuls into the field, as they would to a war of the utmost difficulty and magnitude. Gellius, one of the consuls, fell suddenly upon the Germans, who were so insolent and bold as to separate themselves from the main body of Spartacus, and cut them all to pieces; but when Lentulus, the other consul, had surrounded the enemy with large forces, Spartacus rushed upon them, joined battle, defeated the legates of Lentulus, and seized all their baggage. Then, as he was forcing his way towards the Alps, he was met by Cassius, the governor of Cisalpine Gaul, with an army of ten thousand men, and in the battle that ensued, Cassius was defeated, lost many men, and escaped himself with difficulty.

10. On learning of this, the senate angrily ordered the consuls to keep quiet, and chose Crassus to conduct the war, and many of the nobles were induced by his reputation and their friendship for him to serve under him. Crassus himself, accordingly, took position on the borders of Picenum, expecting to receive the attack of Spartacus, who was hastening thither; and he sent Mummius, his legate, with two legions, by a circuitous route, with orders to follow the enemy, but not to

join battle nor even skirmish with them. Mummius, however, at the first promising opportunity, gave battle and was defeated; many of his men were slain, and many of them threw away their arms and fled for their lives. Crassus gave Mummius himself a rough reception, and when he armed his soldiers anew, made them give pledges that they would keep their arms. Five hundred of them, moreover, who had shown the greatest cowardice and been first to fly, he divided into fifty decades, and put to death one from each decade, on whom the lot fell, thus reviving, after the lapse of many years, an ancient mode of punishing the soldiers. For disgrace also attaches to this manner of death, and many horrible and repulsive features attend the punishment, which the whole army witnesses.

When he had thus disciplined his men, he led them against the enemy. But Spartacus avoided him, and retired through Lucania to the sea. At the Straits, he chanced upon some Cilician pirate craft, and determined to seize Sicily. By throwing two thousand men into the island, he thought to kindle anew the servile war there, which had not long been extinguished, and needed only a little additional fuel. But the Cilicians, after coming to terms with him and receiving his gifts, deceived him and sailed away. So Spartacus marched back again from the sea and established his army in the peninsula of Rhegium. Crassus now came up, and observing that the nature of the place suggested what must be done, he determined to build a wall across the isthmus, thereby at once keeping his soldiers from idleness, and his enemies from provisions. Now the task was a huge one and difficult, but he accomplished and finished it, contrary to all expectation, in a short time, running a ditch from sea to sea through the neck of land three hundred furlongs in length and fifteen feet in width and depth alike. Above the ditch he also built a wall of astonishing height and strength. All this work Spartacus neglected and despised at first; but soon his provisions began to fail, and when he wanted to sally forth from the peninsula, he saw that he was walled in, and that there was nothing more to be had there. He therefore waited for a snowy night and a wintry storm, when he filled up a small portion of the ditch with earth and timber and the boughs of trees, and so threw a third part of his force across.

11. Crassus was now in fear lest some impulse to march upon Rome should seize Spartacus, but took heart when he saw that many of the gladiator's men had seceded after a quarrel with him, and were encamped by themselves on a Lucanian lake. This lake, they say, changes from time to time in the character of its water, becoming sweet, and then again bitter and undrinkable. Upon this detachment Crassus fell, and

drove them away from the lake, but he was robbed of the slaughter and pursuit of the fugitives by the sudden appearance of Spartacus, who checked their flight.

Before this Crassus had written to the senate that they must summon Lucullus from Thrace and Pompey from Spain, but he was sorry now that he had done so, and was eager to bring the war to an end before those generals came. He knew that the success would be ascribed to the one who came up with assistance, and not to himself. Accordingly, in the first place, he determined to attack those of the enemy who had seceded from the rest and were campaigning on their own account (they were commanded by Caius Canicius and Castus), and with this in view, sent out six thousand men to preoccupy a certain eminence, bidding them keep their attempt a secret. And they did try to elude observation by covering up their helmets, but they were seen by two women who were sacrificing for the enemy, and would have been in peril of their lives had not Crassus quickly made his appearance and given battle, the most stubbornly contested of all; for although he slew twelve thousand three hundred men in it, he found only two who were wounded in the back. The rest all died standing in the ranks and fighting the Romans.

After the defeat of this detachment, Spartacus retired to the mountains of Petelia, followed closely by Quintus, one of the officers of Crassus, and by Scrophas, the quaestor, who hung upon the enemy's rear. But when Spartacus faced about, there was a great rout of the Romans, and they barely managed to drag the quaestor, who had been wounded, away into safety. This success was the ruin of Spartacus, for it filled his slaves with over-confidence. They would no longer consent to avoid battle, and would not even obey their leaders, but surrounded them as soon as they began to march, with arms in their hands, and forced them to lead back through Lucania against the Romans, the very thing which Crassus also most desired. For Pompey's approach was already announced, and there were not a few who publicly proclaimed that the victory in this war belonged to him; he had only to come and fight and put an end to the war. Crassus, therefore, pressed on to finish the struggle himself, and having encamped near the enemy, began to dig a trench. Into this the slaves leaped and began to fight with those who were working there, and since fresh men from both sides kept coming up to help their comrades, Spartacus saw the necessity that was upon him, and drew up his whole army in order of battle. In the first place, when his horse was brought to him, he drew his sword, and saying that if he won the day he would have many fine horses of the enemy's, but if he lost it he did not want any, he slew his horse. Then pushing his way towards Crassus himself through many flying weapons and wounded men, he did not indeed reach him, but slew two centurions who fell upon him together. Finally, after his companions had taken to flight, he stood alone, surrounded by a multitude of foes, and was still defending himself when he was cut down. But although Crassus had been fortunate, had shown most excellent generalship, and had exposed his person to danger, nevertheless, his success did not fail to enhance the reputation of Pompey. For the fugitives from the battle encountered that general and were cut to pieces, so he could write to the senate that in open battle, indeed, Crassus had conquered the slaves, but that he himself had extirpated the war. Pompey, accordingly, for his victories over Sertorius and in Spain, celebrated a splendid triumph; but Crassus, for all his self-approval, did not venture to ask for the major triumph, and it was thought ignoble and mean in him to celebrate even the minor triumph on foot, called the ovation, for a servile war.

Pompey 21.1–2

After this, he [Pompey] remained in Spain long enough to quell the greatest disorders and compose and settle such affairs as were in the most inflammatory state; then he led his army back to Italy, where, as chance would have it, he found the servile war at its height. For this reason, too, Crassus, who had the command in that war, precipitated the [final] battle [against Spartacus] at great hazard, and was successful, killing twelve thousand three hundred of the enemy. Even in this success, however, fortune somehow or other included Pompey, since five thousand fugitives from the battle fell in his way, all of whom he slew, and then stole a march on Crassus by writing to the senate that Crassus had conquered the gladiators in a pitched battle, but that he himself had extirpated the war entirely. And it was agreeable to the Romans to hear this said and to repeat it, so kindly did they feel towards him.

2. Appian, *The Civil Wars* 1.14.111 and 116–121.1 (early to mid-second century A.D.)

111. The following year [73 B.C.] ... the gladiatorial war in Italy ... started suddenly and became very serious.

116. At the same time Spartacus, a Thracian by birth, who had once served as a soldier with the Romans, but had since been a prisoner and

sold for a gladiator, and was in the gladiatorial training-school at Capua, persuaded about seventy of his comrades to strike for their own freedom rather than for the amusement of spectators. They overcame the guards and ran away, arming themselves with clubs and daggers that they took from people on the roads, and took refuge on Mount Vesuvius. There many fugitive slaves and even some freemen from the fields joined Spartacus, and he plundered the neighbouring country, having for subordinate officers two gladiators named Oenomaus and Crixus. As he divided the plunder impartially he soon had plenty of men. Varinius Glaber was first sent against him and afterwards Publius Valerius, not with regular armies, but with forces picked up in haste and at random, for the Romans did not consider this a war as yet, but a raid, something like an outbreak of robbery. They attacked Spartacus and were beaten. Spartacus even captured the horse of Varinius; so narrowly did the very general of the Romans escape being captured by a gladiator.

After this still greater numbers flocked to Spartacus till his army numbered 70,000 men. For these he manufactured weapons and collected equipment, whereas Rome now sent out the consuls with two legions. 117. One of them overcame Crixus with 30,000 men near Mount Garganus, two-thirds of whom perished together with himself. Spartacus endeavoured to make his way through the Apennines to the Alps and the Gallic country, but one of the consuls anticipated him and hindered his flight while the other hung upon his rear. He turned upon them one after the other and beat them in detail. They retreated in confusion in different directions. Spartacus sacrificed 300 Roman prisoners to the shade of Crixus, and marched on Rome with 120,000 foot, having burned all his useless material, killed all his prisoners, and butchered his pack-animals in order to expedite his movement. Many deserters offered themselves to him, but he would not accept them. The consuls again met him in the country of Picenum. Here there was fought another great battle and there was, too, another great defeat for the Romans.

Spartacus changed his intention of marching on Rome. He did not consider himself ready as yet for that kind of a fight, as his whole force was not suitably armed, for no city had joined him, but only slaves, deserters, and riff-raff. However, he occupied the mountains around Thurii and took the city itself. He prohibited the bringing in of gold or silver by merchants, and would not allow his own men to acquire any, but he bought largely of iron and brass and did not interfere with those who dealt in these articles. Supplied with abundant material from this source his men provided themselves with plenty of arms and made frequent forays for the time being. When they next came to an engagement with the Romans they were again victorious, and returned laden with spoils.

118. This war, so formidable to the Romans (although ridiculed and despised in the beginning, as being merely the work of gladiators), had now lasted three years. When the election of new praetors came on, fear fell upon all, and nobody offered himself as a candidate until Licinius Crassus, a man distinguished among the Romans for birth and wealth, assumed the praetorship and marched against Spartacus with six new legions. When he arrived at his destination he received also the two legions of the consuls, whom he decimated by lot for their bad conduct in several battles. Some say that Crassus, too, having engaged in battle with his whole army, and having been defeated, decimated the whole army and was not deterred by their numbers, but destroyed about 4000 of them. Whichever way it was, when he had once demonstrated to them that he was more dangerous to them than the enemy, he overcame immediately 10,000 of the Spartacans, who were encamped somewhere in a detached position, and killed two-thirds of them. He then marched boldly against Spartacus himself, vanquished him in a brilliant engagement, and pursued his fleeing forces to the sea, where they tried to pass over to Sicily. He overtook them and enclosed them with a line of circumvallation consisting of ditch, wall, and paling.

119. Spartacus tried to break through and make an incursion into the Samnite country, but Crassus slew about 6000 of his men in the morning and as many more towards evening. Only three of the Roman army were killed and seven wounded, so great was the improvement in their *moral* inspired by the recent punishment. Spartacus, who was expecting a reinforcement of horse from somewhere, no longer went into battle with his whole army, but harassed the besiegers by frequent sallies here and there. He fell upon them unexpectedly and continually, threw bundles of fagots into the ditch and set them on fire and made their labour difficult. He also crucified a Roman prisoner in the space between the two armies to show his own men what fate awaited them if they did not conquer. But when the Romans in the city heard of the siege they thought it would be disgraceful if this war against gladiators should be prolonged. Believing also that the work still to be done against Spartacus was great and severe they ordered up the army of Pompey, which had just arrived from Spain, as a reinforcement.

120. On account of this vote Crassus tried in every way to come to an engagement with Spartacus so that Pompey might not reap the glory of the war. Spartacus himself, thinking to anticipate Pompey, invited

Crassus to come to terms with him. When his proposals were rejected with scorn he resolved to risk a battle, and as his cavalry had arrived he made a dash with his whole army through the lines of the besieging force and pushed on to Brundusium with Crassus in pursuit. When Spartacus learned that Lucullus had just arrived in Brundusium from his victory over Mithridates he despaired of everything and brought his forces, which were even then very numerous, to close quarters with Crassus. The battle was long and bloody, as might have been expected with so many thousands of desperate men. Spartacus was wounded in the thigh with a spear and sank upon his knee, holding his shield in front of him and contending in this way against his assailants until he and the great mass of those with him were surrounded and slain. The Roman loss was about 1000. The body of Spartacus was not found. A large number of his men fled from the battle-field to the mountains and Crassus followed them thither. They divided themselves in four parts, and continued to fight until they all perished except 6000, who were captured and crucified along the whole road from Capua to Rome.

121. Crassus accomplished his task within six months, whence arose a contention for honours between himself and Pompey.

3. SALLUST, Fragments from Book 3 of *The Histories* (ca. 44–35 B.C.)

3.96 (Maurenbrecher) = 3.64 (McGushin) . . . over the fire they heated . . . their stakes, which gave them the appearance needed for war and with which it was possible to inflict wounds almost as if they had been of iron. But as the fugitive slaves were busy with this, Varinius had sent his quaestor Gaius Thoranius [i.e., Toranius] to Rome so that the true situation could easily be assessed in the presence of someone who had been there. For a part of Varinius' soldiers was sick from the oppressive autumn weather, none were returning to their legionary standards from their last defeat and flight although a strict command ordered them to, and – this was the worst disgrace – the rest were shirking their military duties. Nevertheless, with the help of four thousand soldiers still willing to serve . . . [Varinius] meanwhile fortified [his camp] under great exertions. Then the runaways, who had used up their supplies and to avoid an attack from the nearby enemy while they were out looting, all left in utter silence during the second night watch, leaving only a trumpeter in their camp. For they were used to the soldierly practice of posting watchmen and guards and carrying out other military tasks. They had propped up fresh corpses, secured to firm stakes, to look like guards to everybody who saw them from far away, and they had built numerous fires . . . When it was broad daylight, Varinius wondered what had happened to the insults and the showers of rocks that the fugitive slaves were used to hurling and also noticed the absence of noise, commotion, and general sounds of those who were usually besetting him all around. So he sent his cavalry to reconnoiter up a hill that overlooked all the surroundings . . . to [follow] quickly their tracks, believing them, however, far away . . . A few days later, contrary to custom, our troops' confidence returned, and their tongues were ready for action, so Varinius, spurred on but disregarding what he himself had seen happen, led his soldiers, raw and untried recruits and those shocked by the defeats of others, at a brisk pace against the fugitive slaves' camp. But now they were quiet and did not approach a battle with as much swagger as they had demanded one before. But the other side had argued among themselves in council and were now close to splitting apart. Crixus and his tribes, Gauls and Germans, wanted to meet the enemy head on and voluntarily offer battle; on the other hand, Spartacus . . .

3.98 B-C (Maurenbrecher) = 3.66 B-C (McGushin). [. . . Spartacus' (?) plan] seemed best. Then he advised them to move out into wider plains which were richer in herds of cattle and where chosen men would increase their number before Varinius could arrive with a fresh army. He quickly found a suitable man from among the Picentines as a guide, then, hidden by the Eburine mountains, he came to [the narrow mountain pass of] Nares in Lucania and from there at daybreak to [the town of] Forum Annii without being noticed by the farmers. At once the runaway slaves started to rape young girls and married women, against the express command of their leader. Others . . . Now those who resisted . . . and they tried to get away, at the same time [mistreating their enemy] in an inexpressibly horrible manner by twisting the blade in the wound, and sometimes left the mangled bodies of half-dead people behind; others threw firebrands onto roofs. And many local slaves, whom their natural disposition prompted to be [Spartacus'] allies, dragged what their masters had hidden or their masters themselves out of their hiding places: to the wrath of barbarians and to the nature of slaves nothing is sacred or too unspeakable [to commit]. These things Spartacus was powerless to prevent although he begged them with frequent entreaties quickly to anticipate . . . messengers . . .

4. LIVY, *Periochae* 95–97 (ca. Early First Century A.D.)

95 (excerpt). Seventy-four gladiators in Capua escaped from the school of Lentulus, and when a crowd of slaves and prisoners had gathered, war broke out under the leadership of Crixus and Spartacus. They defeated Claudius Pulcher [= Gaius Claudius Glaber], a legate [really, praetor], and the praetor Publius Varenus [Varinius] in battle.

96. Quintus Arrius, the praetor [really, propraetor], defeated Crixus, the leader of the escaped slaves, with 20,000 men. The consul Gnaeus Lentulus fought a battle against Spartacus and was defeated. The same man defeated the consul Lucius Gellius and the praetor Quintus Arrius in battle . . . Proconsul Gaius Cassius and praetor Gnaeus Manlius fought against Spartacus and were defeated, and the conduct of this war was handed over to Marcus Crassus, the praetor.

97 (excerpt). Praetor Marcus Crassus first fought successfully with the part of the runaway slaves that consisted of Gauls and Germans, killing 35,000 of the enemy and their leaders Castus and Gannicus. Then he fought a decisive battle with Spartacus. 60,000 men and Spartacus himself were killed.

5. Velleius Paterculus, *Compendium of Roman History* 2.30.5–6 (ca. 30 A.D.)

As war against Sertorius was being waged in Spain, sixty-four runaway slaves led by Spartacus escaped from a gladiatorial school in Capua. In that city they got hold of swords and at first made for Mt. Vesuvius; soon, when their crowd increased daily, they inflicted serious ruin on Italy on various occasions. Their number grew to such an extent that in the final battle in which they fought they faced the Roman army with 90,000 men. Marcus Crassus had the glory of finishing off this war; soon, everybody was in agreement that he was the leading citizen in the republic.

6. Lucius Annaeus Florus, *Epitome of Roman History* 2.8 (3.20) (ca. 125–135 A.D.)

One can tolerate, indeed, even the disgrace of a war against slaves; for although, by force of circumstances, they are liable to any kind of treatment, yet they form as it were a class (although an inferior class) and can be admitted to the blessings of liberty which we enjoy. But I know not which name to give to the war which was stirred up at the instigation of Spartacus; for the common soldiers being slaves and their leaders being gladiators – the former men of the humblest, the latter men of the worse, class – added insult to the injury which they inflicted upon Rome.

Spartacus, Crixus and Oenomaus, breaking out of the gladiatorial school of Lentulus with thirty or rather more men of the same occupation, escaped from Capua. When, by summoning the slaves to their standard, they had quickly collected more than 10,000 adherents, these men, who had been originally content merely to have escaped, soon began to wish to take their revenge also. The first position which attracted them (a suitable one for such ravening monsters) was Mt. Vesuvius. Being besieged here by Clodius Glabrus [Glaber], they slid by means of ropes made of vine-twigs through a passage in the hollow of the mountain down into its very depths, and issuing forth by a hidden exit, seized the camp of the general by a sudden attack which he never expected. They then attacked other camps, that of Varenius [Varinius] and afterwards that of Thoranus; and they ranged over the whole of Campania. Not content with the plundering of country houses and villages, they laid waste Nola, Nuceria, Thurii and Metapontum with terrible destruction. Becoming a regular army by the daily arrival of fresh forces, they made themselves rude shields of wicker-work and the skins of animals, and swords and other weapons by melting down the iron in the slave-prisons. That nothing might be lacking which was proper to a regular army, cavalry was procured by breaking in herds of horses which they encountered, and his men brought to their leader the insignia and fasces captured from the praetors, nor were they refused by the man who, from being a Thracian mercenary, had become a soldier, and from a soldier a deserter, then a highwayman, and finally, thanks to his strength, a gladiator. He also celebrated the obsequies of his officers who had fallen in battle with funerals like those of Roman generals, and ordered his captives to fight at their pyres, just as though he wished to wipe out all his past dishonour by having become, instead of a gladiator, a giver of gladiatorial shows. Next, actually attacking generals of consular rank, he inflicted defeat on the army of Lentulus in the Apennines and destroyed the camp of Publius [i.e., Gaius] Cassius at Mutina. Elated by these victories he entertained the project – in itself a sufficient disgrace to us – of attacking the city of Rome. At last a combined effort was made, supported by all the resources of the empire, against this gladiator, and Licinius Crassus vindicated the honour of Rome. Routed and put to flight by him, our enemies – I am ashamed to give them this title – took refuge in the furthest extremities of Italy. Here, being cut off in the angle of Bruttium and preparing to escape to Sicily, but being unable to obtain ships, they tried to launch rafts of beams and casks bound together with withies on the swift waters of the straits. Failing in this attempt, they finally made a sally and met a death worthy of men, fighting to the death as became those who were commanded by a gladiator. Spartacus himself fell, as became a general, fighting most bravely in the front rank.

7. Sextus Julius Frontinus, *Strategies* (late first century A.D.)

1.5.20. Spartacus filled the ditch with which Marcus Crassus had surrounded him at night with the bodies of slaughtered captives and cattle and marched across it.

1.5.21. The same man, besieged on Mt. Vesuvius where it was roughest [i.e., steepest] and therefore unguarded, twined together ropes of osiers collected from the woods. Letting himself down on them, not only did he escape but also, appearing from another direction, scared Clodius so much that several cohorts gave way to only seventy-four gladiators.

1.5.22. The same man, when he had been encircled by the proconsul Publius Varinius, put stakes at short distances before the gate of his own camp. He propped up and bound dead bodies to them, dressed in clothes and equipped with weapons, so that to anybody seeing them from far away they appeared to be sentries. He also lit fires all over his camp. With this empty spectacle he deceived his enemy, and in the silence of the night he led his troops away.

1.7.6. Spartacus and his troops had shields made from osiers that were covered with hides.

2.4.7. In the war against the escaped slaves, Licinius Crassus was going to lead his soldiers against Castus and Cannicus [Gannicus], the leaders of the Gauls, at Camalatrum. He sent twelve cohorts with Gaius Pomptinius and Quintus Marcius Rufus, his legionary commanders, around from behind the mountain. When the battle had already begun, these cohorts raised a shout and came running down the mountain from the rear. They put the enemy to flight so thoroughly that they ran off everywhere and no battle was joined anywhere.

2.5.34. In the war against the escaped slaves, Crassus fortified his two camps with palisades very close to the enemy camp near Mt. Cantenna. Then, at night, he moved his troops but left his headquarters in the larger camp to deceive the enemy. He led all his troops out himself and stationed them at the foot of the mountain just mentioned. He divided his cavalry and ordered Lucius Quintius to put up one half against Spartacus and deceive him with a feigned battle, with the other half to lure the Gauls and Germans from Castus and Cannicus' [Gannicus'] group out to battle and, by pretending to flee, draw them over to where he himself had set up his own battle line. When the barbarians had followed them [as planned], the cavalry retreated to the flanks, and suddenly the Roman battle front lay open and swiftly advanced with a battle cry. 35,000 armed men were killed in that battle with their leaders, as Livy reports; five Roman eagles and twenty-six standards were recaptured, and a lot of other spoils was taken, among them five bundles of rods with their axes.

8. Paulus Orosius, *History against the Pagans* 5.24 (fifth century A.D.)

1–8. In the 679th year from the foundation of the city of Rome [= 73 B.C.], when Lucullus and Cassius were consuls, seventy-four gladiators in Capua ran away from the school of Gnaeus Lentulus. At once, under their leaders Crixus and Oenomaus, both Gauls, and the Thracian Spartacus they occupied Mt. Vesuvius. Making a sortie from there, they seized the camp of Clodius the praetor, who had surrounded them and was placing them under siege. Clodius himself was driven to flight, and they hauled off everything as their spoils. Then, led around [the towns of] Consentia and Metapontum, in a short time they collected a gigantic army, for reports state that Crixus had a crowd of 10,000 men, Spartacus, however, three times that number at that time. (Oenomaus had been killed in an earlier battle.) And so they combined acts of killing, arson, robbery, and rape indiscriminately. Once, at the funeral of a married woman whom they had taken prisoner and who had killed herself in agony because her honor had been violated, they put on a gladiatorial show of 400 of their captives – that is to say, those who had once been the objects of spectators were going to be spectators themselves, inasmuch as they now functioned as trainers of gladiators rather than as leaders of soldiers. Then the consuls [of 72 B.C.], Gellius and Lentulus, were sent against them with an army; Gellius defeated Crixus, who fought back most vigorously, in a battle, while Lentulus was defeated by Spartacus and fled. Afterwards both consuls were dealt a serious defeat and fled, even though their forces had been combined, but in vain. Then that same Spartacus defeated Gaius Cassius the proconsul in battle and killed him. As a result, the City of Rome was struck by terror almost as much as it had trembled with fear when Hannibal had been howling at the gates. The senate sent out Crassus with the consuls' legions and with new recruits. He soon initiated a battle with the fugitives and killed 6,000 but took 900 of them prisoner. Then, before he attacked Spartacus himself, who was setting up his camp at the head of the River Silarus, Crassus defeated Spartacus' Gallic and German auxiliaries, killing 30,000 of their men and their leaders. At the very last he struck out at Spartacus himself, who was coming against him in a well-ordered battle line, and at his forces. (The largest troops of fugitive slaves were with Spartacus.) 60,000 of them are reported to have been killed and 6,000 captured; 3,000 Roman citizens were freed. The others who had escaped this battle and were wandering around here and there were hunted down by several [Roman] commanders and rubbed out.

18–19. . . . this war against runaway slaves – or, to put it more truthfully, against gladiators – caused a general fright since it was no longer a show for just a few but a cause of fear everywhere. Because it is called a slave war, nobody should mistake it for something insignificant according to its name. Often in its course individual consuls and sometimes both, with their forces joined, although to no avail, were defeated and large numbers of the nobility were slaughtered. The runaway slaves, on the other hand, who were killed numbered more than 100,000.

Bibliography

Abel, Richard. *The Ciné Goes to Town: French Cinema 1896–1914.* 2nd edn. Berkeley, Los Angeles, and London: University of California Press, 1999.

Additional Dialogue: Letters of Dalton Trumbo, 1942–1962. Ed. Helen Manfull. 1970. Rpt. New York: Bantam, 1972.

The Age of McCarthyism: A Brief History with Documents. Ed. Ellen Schrecker. 2nd edn. Boston: Bedford / St. Martin's, 2002.

Ahl, Frederick M. *Lucan: An Introduction.* Ithaca and London: Cornell University Press, 1976.

Allard, Paul. *Les esclaves chrétiens: Depuis les premiers temps de l'Église jusqu'à la fin de la domination romaine en Occident.* 5th edn. 1914. Rpt. Hildesheim and New York: Olms, 1974.

Antike in der Moderne. Ed. Wolfgang Schuller. Konstanz: Universitätsverlag Konstanz, 1985.

Appian's Roman History. Tr. Horace White, rev. E. Iliff Robson. Vol. 3. Cambridge: Harvard University Press / London: Heinemann, 1913.

Auguet, Roland. *Cruelty and Civilization: The Roman Games.* 1972. Rpt. New York: Barnes and Noble, 1998.

Badian, E. "The Clever and the Wise." *Bulletin of the Institute of Classical Studies.* Supplement 51 (1988), 1–11.

——. *Publicans and Sinners: Private Enterprise in the Service of the Roman Republic.* Ithaca and London: Cornell University Press, 1972; rpt. 1983.

Bann, Stephen. *The Clothing of Clio: A Study of the Representation of History in Nineteenth-Century Britain and France.* Cambridge: Cambridge University Press, 1984.

Bartchy, S. Scott. *First-Century Slavery and the Interpretation of 1 Corinthians 7:21.* 1973. Rpt. Atlanta: Scholars Press, 1985.

Bartoli, Alfonso. *Curia Senatus: Lo Scavo e il Restauro.* Roma: Istituto di Studi Romani, 1963.

Baxter, John. *Hollywood in the Sixties.* New York: Barnes, 1972.

———. *Stanley Kubrick: A Biography.* New York: Carroll and Graf, 1997.

Ben-Hur (souvenir program). New York: Metro-Goldwyn-Mayer, 1926.

Benjamin, Walter. *Illuminations.* Ed. Hannah Arendt; tr. Harry Zohn. 1968. New edn. New York: Schocken, 1969; rpt. 1986.

Bibliographie zur antiken Sklaverei. Ed. Heinz Bellen and Heinz Heinen; rev. Dorothea Schäfer and Johannes Deissler. 2 vols. Stuttgart: Steiner, 2003.

Biographical Dictionary of North American Classicists. Ed. Ward W. Briggs, Jr. Westport: Greenwood Press, 1994.

Bodson, Arthur. *La morale sociale des derniers Stoïciens: Sénèque, Epictète et Marc Aurèle.* Paris: Les Belles Lettres, 1967.

Boller, Paul F., and Ronald L. Davis. *Hollywood Anecdotes.* New York: Morrow, 1987.

Bonhöffer, Adolf Friedrich. *The Ethics of the Stoic Epictetus: An English Translation.* Tr. William O. Stephens. New York: Lang, 1996.

Bowser, Eileen. *The Transformation of Cinema 1907–1915.* New York: Scribner, 1990.

Bradley, Keith R. *Slavery and Rebellion in the Roman World, 140 B.C.–70 B.C.* Bloomington and Indianapolis: Indiana University Press, 1989; rpt. 1998.

Branch, Taylor. *At Canaan's Edge: America in the King Years, 1965–68.* New York: Simon and Schuster, 2006.

———. *Parting the Waters: America in the King Years, 1954–63.* New York: Simon and Schuster, 1988; rpt. 1989.

———. *Pillar of Fire: America in the King Years, 1963–65.* New York: Simon and Schuster, 1998; rpt. 1999.

Brennan, T. Corey. *The Praetorship of the Roman Republic.* Oxford and New York: Oxford University Press, 2000.

Brisson, Jean-Paul. *Spartacus.* Paris: Le club français de livre, 1959.

Broughton, T. R. S. *The Magistrates of the Roman Republic.* 3 vols. 1951–1952. Rpt. Chico: Scholars Press, 1985–1986.

Butcher, S. H. *Aristotle's Theory of Poetry and Fine Arts.* 4th, corrected, edn. 1911. Rpt. New York: Dover, 1951 and later.

Cagniart, Pierre. "The Philosopher and the Gladiator." *The Classical World,* 93 (2000), 607–618.

Canutt, Yakima, and Oliver Drake. *Stuntman: The Autobiography of Yakima Canutt.* 1979. Rpt. Norman: University of Oklahoma Press, 1997.

Casson, Lionel. *Everyday Life in Ancient Rome.* Rev. edn. Baltimore and London: Johns Hopkins University Press, 1998.

Ceplair, Larry, and Steven Englund. *The Inquisition in Hollywood: Politics in the Film Community, 1930–1960.* 1980. Rpt. Urbana: University of Illinois Press, 2003.

Ciment, Michel. *Kubrick: The Definitive Edition*. Tr. Gilbert Adair and Robert Bononno. New York: Faber and Faber, 2001; rpt. 2003.

Clarke, Thurston. *Ask Not: The Inauguration of John F. Kennedy and the Speech That Changed America*. New York: Holt, 2004; rpt. 2005.

Classical Myth and Culture in the Cinema. Ed. Martin M. Winkler. New York: Oxford University Press, 2001.

Cleopatra (1934). Paramount Showmanship Manual, 1952.

Colish, Marcia L. *The Stoic Tradition from Antiquity to the Early Middle Ages*. Vol. 1: *Stoicism in Classical Latin Literature*. Leiden: Brill, 1985; rpt. 1990.

A Companion to Latin Literature. Ed. Stephen Harrison. Oxford: Blackwell, 2005.

Cook, Bruce. *Dalton Trumbo*. New York: Scribner, 1977.

Croce, Benedetto. *History: Its Theory and Practice*. Tr. Douglas Ainslie. 1921. Rpt. New York: Russell and Russell, 1960.

Crouch, Barry A. " 'Booty Capitalism' and Capitalism's Booty: Slaves and Slavery in Ancient Rome and the American South." *Slavery and Abolition*, 6 (1985), 3–24.

Crowther, Bosley. "Spartacus Enters The Arena." *The New York Times* (October 7, 1960), Entertainment section, 28.

Curtis, Tony, and Barry Paris. *Tony Curtis: The Autobiography*. New York: Morrow, 1993.

Cyrino, Monica S. *Big-Screen Rome*. Oxford: Blackwell, 2005.

Davis, David Brion. *Inhuman Bondage: The Rise and Fall of Slavery in the New World*. New York: Oxford University Press, 2006.

——. *The Problem of Slavery in the Age of Revolution, 1770–1823*. 1975. Rpt. New York: Oxford University Press, 1999.

——. *The Problem of Slavery in Western Culture*. 1966. Rpt. New York: Oxford University Press, 1988.

Davis, Natalie Zemon. *Slaves on Screen: Film and Historical Vision*. Cambridge: Harvard University Press, 2000; rpt. 2002.

——. "Trumbo and Kubrick Argue History." *Raritan*, 22 (2002), 173–190.

Demandt, Alexander. *Der Fall Roms*. Munich: Beck, 1984.

Doherty, Thomas. *Cold War, Cool Medium: Television, McCarthyism, and American Culture*. New York: Columbia University Press, 2003; rpt. 2005.

Douglas, Kirk. *The Ragman's Son*. New York: Simon and Schuster, 1988.

Duncan, Paul. *Stanley Kubrick: Visual Poet 1928–1999*. Cologne: Taschen, 2003.

Dyck, Andrew R. *A Commentary on Cicero, De Officiis*. Ann Arbor: University of Michigan Press, 1996.

Elley, Derek. *The Epic Film: Myth and History*. London: Routledge and Kegan Paul, 1984.

Epictetus: The Discourses as Reported by Arrian, the Manual, and Fragments. 2 vols. Tr. W. A. Oldfather. Cambridge: Harvard University Press / London: Heinemann, 1925–1928; rpt. 1996.

Fast, Howard. *Being Red: A Memoir*. 1990. Rpt. Armonk and London: Sharpe, 1994.

———. *Spartacus*. 1951. Rpt. Armonk and London: Sharpe, 1996.

Finley, Moses I. *Ancient Slavery and Modern Ideology*. Ed. Brent D. Shaw. Expanded edn. Princeton: Wiener, 1998.

Fox-Genovese, Elizabeth, and Eugene D. Genovese. *The Mind of the Master Class: History and Faith in the Southern Slaveholders' Worldview*. Cambridge: Cambridge University Press, 2005.

Futrell, Alison. *Blood in the Arena: The Spectacle of Roman Power*. Austin: University of Texas Press, 1997; rpt. 2000.

———. *The Roman Games*. Oxford: Blackwell, 2006.

Garnsey, Peter. *Ideas of Slavery from Aristotle to Augustine*. Cambridge: Cambridge University Press, 1996.

Gelmis, Joseph. *The Film Director as Superstar*. New York: Doubleday, 1970.

Genovese, Eugene N. *The Slaveholders' Dilemma: Freedom and Progress in Southern Conservative Thought*. Columbia: University of South Carolina Press, 1992; rpt. 1995.

Ghnassia, Maurice. *Arena: A Novel*. New York: Viking, 1969.

Gibbon, Lewis Grassic. *Spartacus*. 1990; rpt. Edinburgh: Polygon, 2005. Originally published 1933.

Girgus, Sam B. *America on Film: Modernism, Documentary, and a Changing America*. Cambridge: Cambridge University Press, 2002.

Gladiator: Film and History. Ed. Martin M. Winkler. Oxford: Blackwell, 2004.

Gladiators and Caesars: The Power of Spectacle in Ancient Rome. Ed. Eckart Köhne and Cornelia Ewigleben; tr. Anthea Bell. Berkeley and Los Angeles: University of California Press, 2000.

The Goebbels Diaries: 1942–1943. Ed. and tr. Louis P. Lochner. Westport: Greenwood Press, 1970. First published 1948.

Greek Art in View: Essays in Honour of Brian Sparkes. Ed. Simon Keay and Stephanie Moser. Oxford: Oxbow Books, 2004.

Greenberg, Kenneth S. *Nat Turner: A Slave Rebellion in History and Memory*. New York: Oxford University Press, 2003.

Grisé, Yolanda. *Le suicide dans la Rome antique*. Paris: Les Belles Lettres, 1982.

Gruen, Erich S. *The Last Generation of the Roman Republic*. Berkeley, Los Angeles, and London: University of California Press, 1974.

Guarino, Antonio. *Spartaco: Analisi di un mito*. Naples: Liguori, 1979.

Hadzsits, George Depue. "Media of Salvation." *The Classical Weekly*, 14 no. 9 (December 13, 1920), 70–71.

Halliwell, Leslie. *Halliwell's Filmgoer's and Video Viewer's Companion*. Ed. John Walker. 11th edn. New York: HarperCollins, 1995.

Hampton, Benjamin B. *A History of the Movies*. 1931. Rpt. New York: Arno, 1970.

Hanson, Peter. *Dalton Trumbo, Hollywood Rebel: A Critical Survey and Filmography*. Jefferson and London: McFarland, 2001.

Harmetz, Aljean. *Round Up The Usual Suspects: The Making of Casablanca: Bogart, Bergman, and World War II*. New York: Hyperion, 1992.

Hazewell, Charles Creighton. "Spartacus." *The Atlantic Monthly*, 1 no. 3 (January, 1858), 288–300.

Hellman, Lillian. *Scoundrel Time*. Boston: Little, Brown, 1976; rpt. 2000.

Henderson, Sanya Shoilevska. *Alex North: Film Composer: A Biography*. Jefferson and London: McFarland, 2003.

Hoberman, J. *The Dream Life: Movies, Media and the Mythology of the Sixties*. New York and London: The Free Press, 2003; rpt. 2005.

Hoffman, Carl. "The Evolution of a Gladiator: History, Representation, and Revision in *Spartacus*." *Journal of American and Contemporary Cultures*, 23 no. 1 (2000), 63–70.

Hollywood Directors 1941–1976. Ed. Richard Koszarski. New York: Oxford University Press, 1977.

Hollywood Quarterly: Film Culture in Postwar America, 1945–1957. Ed. Eric Smoodin and Ann Martin. Berkeley, Los Angeles, and London: University of California Press, 2002.

Holmes, David L. *The Faiths of the Founding Fathers*. New York: Oxford University Press, 2006.

Homenaje a la Profesora Carmen Pérez Romero. Cáceres: Universidad de Extremadura, 2000.

Horton, James Oliver, and Lois E. Horton. *Slavery and the Making of America*. New York: Oxford University Press, 2005; rpt. 2006.

Horwitz, Tony. "Untrue Confessions." *The New Yorker* (December 13, 1999), 80–86 and 88–89.

Howard, James. *Stanley Kubrick Companion*. London: Batsford, 1999.

Hughes, David. *The Complete Kubrick*. London: Virgin, 2000; rpt. 2001.

The Ideology of Slavery: Proslavery Thought in the Antebellum South, 1830–1860. Ed. Drew Gilpin Faust. Baton Rouge: Louisiana State University Press, 1981; rpt. 1985.

Imperial Projections: Ancient Rome in Modern Popular Culture. Ed. Sandra R. Joshel, Margaret Malamud, and Donald T. McGuire, Jr. Baltimore and London: Johns Hopkins University Press, 2001; rpt. 2005.

The Inaugural Addresses of Twentieth-Century American Presidents. Ed. Halford Ryan. Westport and London: Praeger, 1993.

Irving, David. *Goebbels: Mastermind of the Third Reich*. London: Focal Point Publications, 1996.

Jefferson, Thomas. *Writings*. Ed. Merrill D. Peterson. New York: Library of America / Viking, 1984.

Johnson, Samuel. *The Yale Edition of the Works of Samuel Johnson*. Vol. 10: *Political Writings*. Ed. Donald J. Greene. New Haven and London: Yale University Press, 1977.

Jones, C. P. "Tattooing and Branding in Greco-Roman Antiquity." *Journal of Roman Studies*, 77 (1987), 139–155.

Junkelmann, Marcus. *Hollywoods Traum von Rom: "Gladiator" und die Tradition des Monumentalfilms*. Mainz: von Zabern, 2004.

——. *Das Spiel mit dem Tod: So kämpften Roms Gladiatoren*. Mainz: von Zabern, 2000.

Kaiser Augustus und die verlorene Republik (exhibition catalogue). Ed. Mathias René Hofter. Mainz: von Zabern, 1988.

Kanfer, Stefan. *A Journal of the Plague Years*. New York: Atheneum, 1973.

Karl Marx–Friedrich Engels: Werke. Vol. 30. Berlin: Dietz, 1974.

"Kennedy Attends Movie in Capital." *The New York Times* (February 5, 1961), 39.

Kennedy, John F. "Radio and Television Report to the American People on Civil Rights." June 11, 1963. At http://www.jfklibrary.net/j061163.htm.

Keppie, Lawrence. *The Making of the Roman Army: From Republic to Empire*. New edn. Norman: University of Oklahoma Press, 1998.

King of Kings (souvenir program). Metro-Goldwyn-Mayer and Samuel Bronston Productions, 1961.

Kinnard, Roy, and Tim Davis. *Divine Images: A History of Jesus on the Screen*. New York: Citadel Press, 1992.

Koestler, Arthur. *Darkness at Noon*. Tr. Daphne Hardy. New York: Macmillan, 1941.

——. *The Gladiators*. Tr. Edith Simon. 1939. Rpt. New York: Macmillan, 1967.

——. *The Invisible Writing: The Second Volume of an Autobiography: 1932–40*. 1954. Rpt. New York: Macmillan, 1969.

Kohler, Charlie. "Stanley Kubrick Raps" (interview). *The East Village Eye* (August, 1968).

Kracauer, Siegfried. *Theory of Film: The Redemption of Physical Reality*. 1960. Rpt. Princeton: Princeton University Press, 1997.

Kyle, Donald G. *Spectacles of Death in Ancient Rome*. London and New York: Routledge, 1998.

Lattimore, Richmond. *The Odyssey of Homer*. New York: Harper and Row, 1965; several rpts.

Lazarus, Emma. *Selected Poems*. Ed. John Hollander. New York: The Library of America, 2005.

Leach, Christopher. *God, Spartacus and Miss Emily*. London and Melbourne: Dent, 1987.

Legrand, Gérard. "La gloire et ses chemins." *Positif*, 45 (1962), 15–21.

LeRoy, Mervyn, with Dick Kleiner. *Take One*. New York: Hawthorn, 1974.

Lev, Peter. *Transforming the Screen 1950–1959*. New York: Scribner, 2003.

Lillard, Richard G. "Through the Disciplines with Spartacus: The Uses of a Hero in History and the Media." *American Studies*, 16 no. 2 (1975), 15–28.

Lincoln, Abraham. *The Collected Works of Abraham Lincoln*. Ed. Roy P. Basler. Vol. 2. New Brunswick: Rutgers University Press, 1953; rpt. 1960.

LoBrutto, Vincent. *Stanley Kubrick: A Biography*. 1997. Rpt. New York: Da Capo, 1999.

Long, Anthony A. *Epictetus: A Stoic and Socratic Guide to Life*. Oxford: Clarendon Press, 2002.

——. *Hellenistic Philosophy: Stoics, Epicureans, Sceptics*. 2nd edn. Berkeley: University of California Press, 1986.

Lucius Annaeus Florus: Epitome of Roman History. Tr. Edward Seymour Forster. Cambridge: Harvard University Press / London: Heinemann, 1929.

Macdonald, Andrew. *Howard Fast: A Critical Companion*. Westport and London: Greenwood Press, 1996.

Macgowan, Kenneth. *Behind the Screen: The History and Techniques of the Motion Picture*. New York: Dell, 1965; rpt. 1967.

The Making of 2001: A Space Odyssey. Ed. Stephanie Schwam. New York: Modern Library, 2000.

Mann, Anthony. "Empire Demolition." *Films and Filming*, 10 no. 6 (March, 1964), 7–8.

Manning, C. E. "Stoicism and Slavery in the Roman Empire." *Aufstieg und Niedergang der römischen Welt*, 2.36.3 (1989), 1518–1543.

Marshall, Bruce A. *Crassus: A Political Biography*. Amsterdam: Hakkert, 1976.

McCarthyism: The Great American Red Scare: A Documentary History. Ed. Albert Fried. New York: Oxford University Press, 1997.

McGushin, Patrick. *Sallust: The Histories*. Vol. 2. Oxford: Clarendon Press, 1994.

McPherson, James M. *Battle Cry of Freedom: The Civil War Era*. New York: Oxford University Press, 1988; rpt. 2003.

——. "Was It a Just War?" *The New York Review of Books* (March 23, 2006), 16 and 18–19. Review of Stout, *Upon the Altar of the Nation*.

Meacham, Jon. *American Gospel: God, the Founding Fathers, and the Making of a Nation*. New York: Random House, 2006.

Mersand, Joseph. *A Guide to the Study and Enjoyment of the Motion Picture SPARTACUS*. *Photoplay Studies*, 25, no. 4 (August, 1960).

Missiaen, Jean-Claude. "Conversation with Anthony Mann." Tr. Martyn Auty. *Framework*, 15–17 (1981), 17–20.

Monaco, James. *How to Read a Film: The World of Movies, Media, and Multimedia: Language, History, Theory*. New York and Oxford: Oxford University Press, 2000.

Morgan, Ted. *Reds: McCarthyism in Twentieth-Century America*. New York: Random House, 2003; rpt. 2004.

Morgenthau, Henry. *Germany Is Our Problem*. New York: Harper, 1945.

Mulvey, Laura. *Visual and Other Pleasures*. Bloomington: Indiana University Press, 1989.

——. "Visual Pleasure and Narrative Cinema." *Screen*, 16 no. 3 (1975), 6–18.

Munn, Michael. *Kirk Douglas*. Rev. edn. New York: St. Martin's, 1989.

Musser, Charles. *The Emergence of Cinema: The American Screen to 1907*. New York: Scribner, 1990.

Nadel, Alan. "God's Law and the Wide Screen: *The Ten Commandments* as Cold War 'Epic'." *Publications of the Modern Language Association of America*, 108 (1993), 415–430.

Nash, Gary B. *The Forgotten Fifth: African Americans in the Age of Revolution.* Cambridge: Harvard University Press, 2006.

Navasky, Victor. *Naming Names.* 1980. Rpt. New York: Hill and Wang, 2003.

Nelson, Thomas Allen. *Kubrick: Inside a Film Artist's Maze.* 2nd edn. Bloomington and Indianapolis: Indiana University Press, 2000.

Niven, David. *Bring on the Empty Horses.* New York: Putnam, 1975.

Niver, Kemp R. *Klaw and Erlanger Present Famous Plays in Pictures.* Ed. Bebe Bergsten. Los Angeles: Locare Research Group, 1976.

Orena, Roberto. *Rivolta e rivoluzione: Il Bellum di Spartaco nella crisi della repubblica e la riflessione storiografica moderna.* Milan: Giuffrè, 1984.

Otto, A. *Die Sprichwörter und sprichwörtlichen Redensarten der Römer.* Hildesheim and New York: Olms, 1988. First published 1890.

Palmer, Tim. "Side of the Angels: Dalton Trumbo, the Hollywood Trade Press, and the Blacklist." *Cinema Journal,* 44 no. 4 (2005), 57–74.

Parenti, Michael. *The Assassination of Julius Caesar: A People's History of Ancient Rome.* New York and London: The New Press, 2004.

Past Imperfect: History According to the Movies. Ed. Mark C. Carnes et al. New York: Holt, 1995.

Patronage in Ancient Society. Ed. Andrew Wallace-Hadrill. London and New York: Routledge, 1989; rpt. 1990.

Pearson, Roberta E., and William Uricchio. "How Many Times Shall Caesar Bleed in Sport: Shakespeare and the Cultural Debate About Moving Pictures." *Screen,* 31 (1990), 243–262.

Pelikan, Jaroslav. *The Excellent Empire: The Fall of Rome and the Triumph of the Church.* San Francisco: Harper and Row, 1987.

Perdue, Jacques. *Slave and Master.* New York: Macaulay, 1960.

Peterson, Merrill D. *Lincoln in American Memory.* New York and Oxford: Oxford University Press, 1994; rpt. 1995.

Phillips, Gene D. *Stanley Kubrick: A Film Odyssey.* New York: Popular Library, 1975.

——, and Rodney Hill. *The Encyclopedia of Stanley Kubrick.* New York: Facts on File, 2002.

Phillips, Patrick. *Understanding Film Texts.* London: BFI [British Film Institute], 2000.

Playing Out the Empire: Ben-Hur and Other Toga Plays and Films, 1883–1908: A Critical Anthology. Ed. David Mayer. Oxford: Clarendon Press, 1994.

Plutarch's Lives. Tr. Bernadotte Perrin. Vols. 3 and 5. Cambridge: Harvard University Press / London: Heinemann, 1916 and 1917.

Quo Vadis (1951). Metro-Goldwyn-Mayer press book. 1964 (re-release).

Ramsaye, Terry. *A Million and One Nights: A History of the Motion Picture through 1925.* 1926. Rpt. New York: Simon and Schuster, 1986.

Raphael, Frederic. *Eyes Wide Open: A Memoir of Stanley Kubrick.* New York: Ballantine, 1999.

Reeves, Thomas C. *The Life and Times of Joe McCarthy: A Biography*. Lanham: Madison Books, 1997. First published 1982.

Reinhold, Meyer. *Classica Americana: The Greek and Roman Heritage in the United States*. Detroit: Wayne State University Press, 1984.

"Review of New Publications." *The Christian Spectator*, 5 no. 10 (October 1, 1823), 540–551.

Richard, Carl J. *The Founders and the Classics: Greece, Rome, and the American Enlightenment*. Cambridge and London: Harvard University Press, 1994.

Richardson, Lawrence, Jr. *A New Topographical Dictionary of Ancient Rome*. Baltimore and London: Johns Hopkins University Press, 1992.

Rist, John M. *Stoic Philosophy*. 1969. Rpt. Cambridge: Cambridge University Press, 1990.

Rubinsohn, Wolfgang Zeev. *Die großen Sklavenaufstände der Antike: 500 Jahre Forschung*. Darmstadt: Wissenschaftliche Buchgesellschaft, 1993.

——. *Spartacus' Uprising and Soviet Historical Writing*. Tr. John G. Griffith. Oxford: Oxbow Books, 1983.

Saller, Richard P. *Personal Patronage under the Early Empire*. Cambridge: Cambridge University Press, 1982; rpt. 2002.

Sandbach, F. H. *The Stoics*. 1975. Rpt. Indianapolis: Hackett, 1994.

Schrecker, Ellen. *Many Are the Crimes: McCarthyism in America*. 1998. Rpt. Princeton: Princeton University Press, 1999.

Schama, Simon. *Rough Crossings: Britain, the Slaves and the American Revolution*. 2005. Rpt. New York: Ecco, 2006.

Schwartz, Nancy Lynn, and Sheila Schwartz. *The Hollywood Writers' War*. 1982. Rpt. New York: McGraw-Hill, 1983.

Screening the Male: Exploring Masculinities in Hollywood Cinema. Ed. Steven Cohan and Ina Rae Hark. London: Routledge, 1993.

Selected Satires of Lucian. Ed. and tr. Lionel Casson. New York: Norton, 1968. First published 1962.

The Sexual Subject: A Screen *Reader in Sexuality*. London: Routledge, 1992.

Sheehan, Henry. "The Fall and Rise of *Spartacus*." *Film Comment*, 27 no. 2 (March–April, 1991), 57–58, 60, and 63.

The Silent Cinema Reader. Ed. Lee Grieveson and Peter Krämer. London and New York: Routledge, 2004.

Slavery and the Law. Ed. Paul Finkelman. Madison: Madison House, 1997.

Slavery Defended: The Views of the Old South. Ed. Eric L. McKitrick. Englewood Cliffs: Prentice-Hall, 1963.

Smith, Jeffrey P. " 'A Good Business Proposition': Dalton Trumbo, *Spartacus*, and the End of the Blacklist." *The Velvet Light Trap*, 23 (1989), 75–100.

Smith, R. R. R. Review of *Kaiser Augustus und die verlorene Republik*. *Journal of Roman Studies*, 79 (1989), 214.

Sodrowski, Andrew. " 'Something Like a Rich Widow': Spartacus and the Protestant Work Ethic." *Latent Image* (2003). http://pages.emerson.edu/organizations/fas/latent_image/issues/2003-01/printed_version/Spartacus.htm.

Solomon, Jon. *The Ancient World in the Cinema*. 2nd edn. New Haven and London: Yale University Press, 2001.

Solomon and Sheba (souvenir program). United Artists, 1959.

"Spartacus: An Interview with Howard Fast." June 28, 2000. http://www.trussel.com/hf/ancient.htm.

Spartacus: The Illustrated Story of the Motion Picture Production. Ed. Stan Margulies. Bryna Productions and Universal Pictures Studios, 1960.

Spartacus and the Slave Wars: A Brief History with Documents. Ed. Brent D. Shaw. Boston and New York: Bedford / St. Martin's, 2001.

Spectacula. Vol. 1: *Gladiateurs et amphithéatres*. Ed. Claude Domergue, Christian Landes, and Jean-Marie Pailler. Lattes: Imago, 1990.

Spottiswoode, Raymond. *A Grammar of the Film: An Analysis of Film Technique*. Berkeley: University of California Press, 1950; rpt. 1973.

Stampp, Kenneth M. *The Peculiar Institution: Slavery in the Ante-Bellum South*. 1956. Rpt. New York: Vintage, 1989.

"Stanley Kubrick: A Cinematic Odyssey." *Premiere* (August, 1999), 85–93 and 98–100.

Stanley Kubrick: Interviews. Ed. Gene D. Phillips. Jackson: University Press of Mississippi, 2001.

Starr, C. G. "An Overdose of Slavery." *The Journal of Economic History*, 18 (1958), 17–32.

Stierlin, Henri. *The Roman Empire: From the Etruscans to the Decline of the Roman Empire*. Tr. Suzanne Bosman. Cologne and New York: Taschen, 2002.

The Stoics. Ed. John M. Rist. Berkeley, Los Angeles, and London: University of California Press, 1978.

Storia del cinema mondiale. Vol. 1: *L'Europa*, pt. 1: *Miti, luoghi, divi*. Ed. Gian Piero Brunetta. Turin: Einaudi, 1999.

Stout, Harry S. *Upon the Altar of the Nation: A Moral History of the American Civil War*. New York: Viking, 2006.

Striner, Richard. *Father Abraham: Lincoln's Relentless Struggle to End Slavery*. New York: Oxford University Press, 2006.

Strode, Woody, and Sam Young. *Goal Dust: An Autobiography*. Lanham, New York, and London: Madison Books, 1990.

Swain, Joseph Ward. *The Ancient World*. Vol. 2: *The World Empires: Alexander and the Romans After 334 B.C.* 1950. Rpt. New York: Harper and Row, 1962.

Thompson, F. Hugh. *The Archaeology of Greek and Roman Slavery*. London: Duckworth, 2003.

Thompson, Kristin. *Storytelling in the New Hollywood: Understanding Classical Narrative Technique*. Cambridge: Harvard University Press, 1999.

Tise, Larry E. *Proslavery: A History of the Defense of Slavery in America, 1701–1840*. Athens and London: University of Georgia Press, 1987.

Troy: From Homer's Iliad to Hollywood Epic. Ed Martin M. Winkler. Oxford: Blackwell, 2006.

Trumbo, Dalton. *Johnny Got His Gun*. New York: Bantam, 1970. First published 1939.

Ullman, B. L. *The Classical Weekly*, 8 no. 26 (May 8, 1915), 201–202 (editor's letter).

Urbainczyk, Theresa. *Spartacus*. London: Bristol Classical Press, 2004.

Uricchio, William, and Roberta E. Pearson. *Reframing Culture: The Case of the Vitagraph Quality Films*. Princeton: Princeton University Press, 1993.

Ustinov, Peter. *Dear Me*. Boston and Toronto: Little, Brown / Atlantic Monthly Press, 1977.

van Hooff, Anton J. *Spartacus: De vonk van Spartacus: Het voortleven van een antieke rebel*. Nijmegen: SUN, 1992.

Velleius Paterculus: Compendium of Roman History and *Res gestae divi Augusti*. Tr. Frederick W. Shipley. Cambridge: Harvard University Press / London: Heinemann, 1924; several rpts.

Verboven, Koenraad. *The Economy of Friends: Economic Aspects of* amicitia *and Patronage in the Late Republic*. Brussels: Latomus, 2002.

Vidal, Gore. *Screening History*. Cambridge: Harvard University Press, 1992.

Wallinga, H. T. "Bellum Spartacium: Florus' Text and Spartacus' Objective." *Athenaeum*, 80 (1992), 25–43.

——. *Der famoseste Kerl: Over Spartacus en zijn opstand*. Utrecht: Faculteit der Letteren, Rijksuniversiteit Utrecht, 1990.

Walsh, Michael. *The Triumph of the Meek: Why Early Christianity Succeeded*. San Francisco: Harper and Row, 1984.

Ward, Allen M. *Marcus Crassus and the Late Roman Republic*. Columbia and London: University of Missouri Press, 1977.

Ward, C. Osborne. *The Ancient Lowly: A History of the Ancient Working People from the Earliest Known Period to the Adoption of Christianity by Constantine*. Vol. 1. 1889. Rpt. New York: Franklin, 1970.

Warry, John. *Warfare in the Classical World: An Illustrated Encyclopedia of Weapons, Warriors and Warfare in the Ancient Civilisations of Greece and Rome*. 1980. Rpt. Norman: University of Oklahoma Press, 1995.

Watson, Alan. *Roman Slave Law*. Baltimore and London: Johns Hopkins University Press, 1987.

——. *Slave Law in the Americas*. Athens and London: University of Georgia Press, 1989; rpt. 1990.

Weber, Max. *The Agrarian Sociology of Ancient Civilizations*. Tr. R. I. Frank. 1976. Rpt. London and New York: Verso, 1998.

Whitfield, Stephen J. *The Culture of the Cold War*. 2nd edn. Baltimore and London: Johns Hopkins University Press, 1996.

Whitman, Walt. *The Collected Writings of Walt Whitman: The Journalism*. Vol. 2: *1846–1848*. Ed. Herbert Bergman. New York: Lang, 2003.

Wicker, Tom. *Shooting Star: The Brief Arc of Joe McCarthy*. Orlando: Harcourt, 2006.

Wicking, Christopher, and Barrie Pattison. "Interviews with Anthony Mann." *Screen*, 10 no. 4 (1969), 32–54.

Wiedemann, T. [Thomas] E. J. *Slavery*. Oxford: Clarendon Press, 1987.

——. *Greek and Roman Slavery*. 1981. Rpt. New York and London: Routledge, 2004.

Wilentz, Sean. *The Rise of American Democracy: Jefferson to Lincoln*. New York: Norton, 2005.

Williams, Juan. *Eyes on the Prize: America's Civil Rights Years, 1954–1965*. 1987. Rpt. New York: Penguin, 2002.

Wills, Garry. "An American Iliad." *The New York Review of Books* (April 6, 2006), 20, 22, and 24–26. Review of Branch, *At Canaan's Edge*.

——. *Lincoln at Gettysburg: The Words That Remade America*. New York: Simon and Schuster, 1992; rpt. 1993.

Wiltshire, Susan Ford. *Greece, Rome, and the Bill of Rights*. Norman: University of Oklahoma Press, 1992.

Winkler, Martin M. "Altertumswissenschaftler im Kino, oder: *Quo vadis, philologia?*" *International Journal of the Classical Tradition*, 11 (2004), 95–110.

——. "Cinema and the Fall of Rome." *Transactions of the American Philological Association*, 125 (1995), 135–154.

——. "Mythic and Cinematic Traditions in Anthony Mann's *El Cid*." *Mosaic*, 26 no. 3 (1993), 89–111.

——. "Neo-Mythologism: Apollo and the Muses on the Screen." *International Journal of the Classical Tradition*, 11 (2005), 383–423.

——. "Quomodo stemma *Gladiatoris* pelliculae more philologico sit constituendum." *American Journal of Philology*, 124 (2003), 137–141.

——. "The Roman Empire in American Cinema After 1945." *The Classical Journal*, 93 (1998), 167–196.

Wiseman, T. P. *The Myths of Rome*. Exeter: University of Exeter Press, 2004.

——. *New Men in the Roman Senate 139 B.C.–A.D. 14*. London: Oxford University Press, 1971.

Wollen, Peter. *Signs and Meaning in the Cinema*. 4th edn. London: BFI [British Film Institute], 1998.

Wood, Michael. *America in the Movies; or, "Santa Maria, It Had Slipped My Mind."* 1975. Rpt. New York: Columbia University Press, 1989.

Wood, Robin. *Hitchcock's Films Revisited*. Rev. edn. New York: Columbia University Press, 2002.

Wyke, Maria. *Projecting the Past: Ancient Rome, Cinema and History*. New York and London: Routledge, 1997.

Yavetz, Zvi. *Slaves and Slavery in Ancient Rome*. New Brunswick and Oxford: Transaction Books, 1988; rpt. 1990.

You Tarzan: Masculinity, Movies and Men. Ed. Pat Kirkham and Janet Thumim. New York: St. Martin's, 1993.

Index

This index covers the Introduction and Chapters 1–11. Entries for the titles of Howard Fast's novel and Stanley Kubrick's film and for Spartacus as fictional character in literature and on the screen have been excluded because of their ubiquitous occurrences throughout this book. Names of characters from Kubrick's film, whether fictional – e.g., Gracchus, Varinia – or based on historical models – e.g., Crassus, Caesar – have also been omitted. Historical figures are included, however, when they are mentioned in historical contexts.